HISTORIC PHOTOS OF
ARIZONA

TEXT AND CAPTIONS BY
LINDA AND DR. DICK BUSCHER

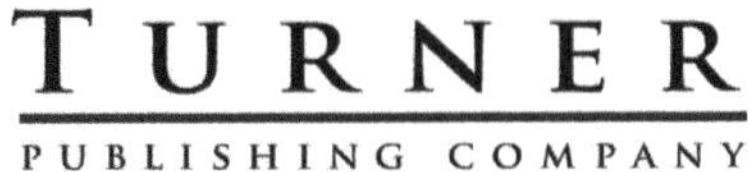

No frontier town in America has more legends and historic lore than Tombstone, Arizona. The mythic "town too tough to die" has fed America's hunger for stories of the Wild West for over 100 years. At least a dozen television shows and movies have been produced concerning the famous Gunfight at the OK Corral, which took place in Tombstone on October 26, 1881. Some of the most famous outlaws and lawmen of the Old West walked the streets of Tombstone during the 1880s.

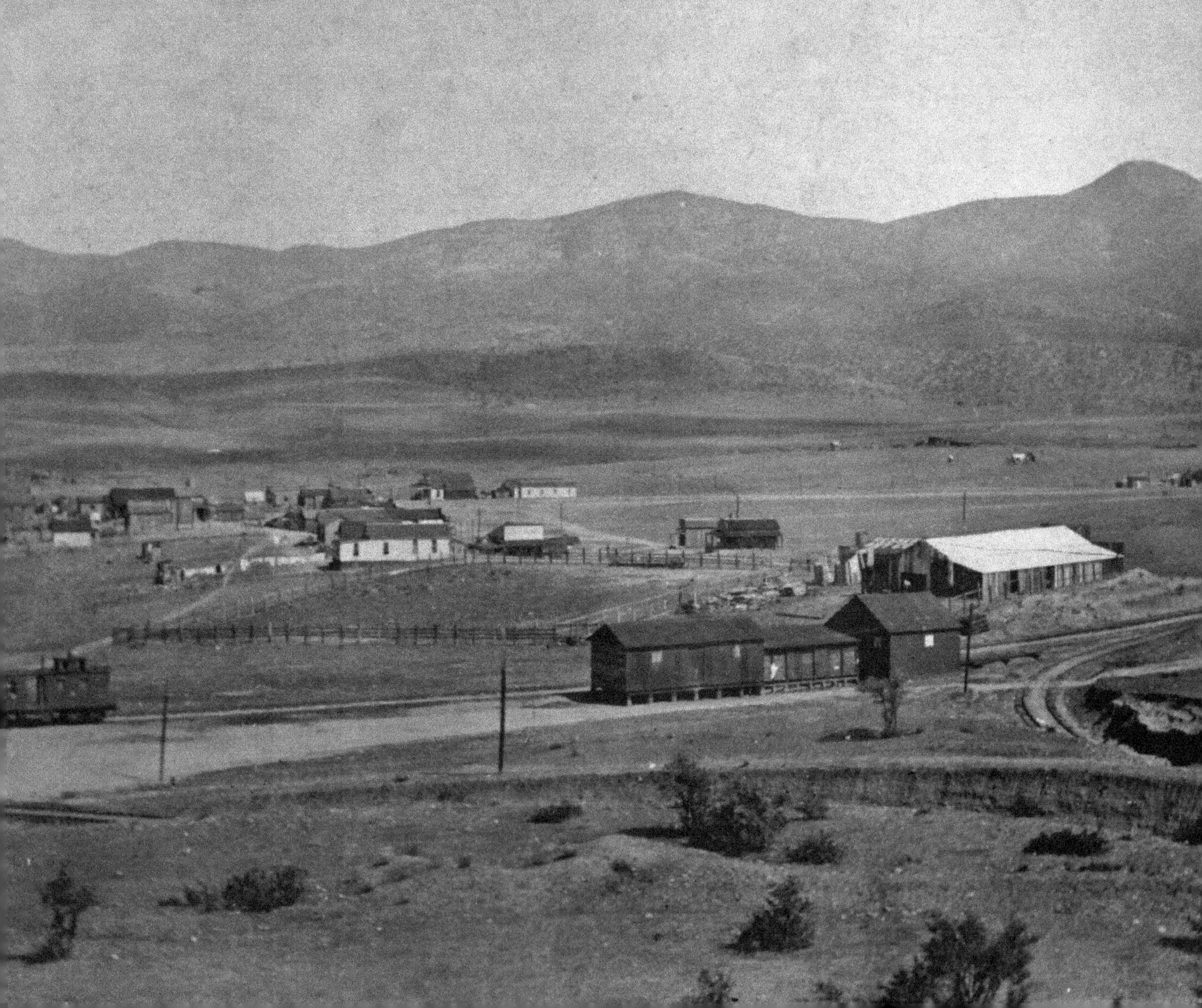

HISTORIC PHOTOS OF
ARIZONA

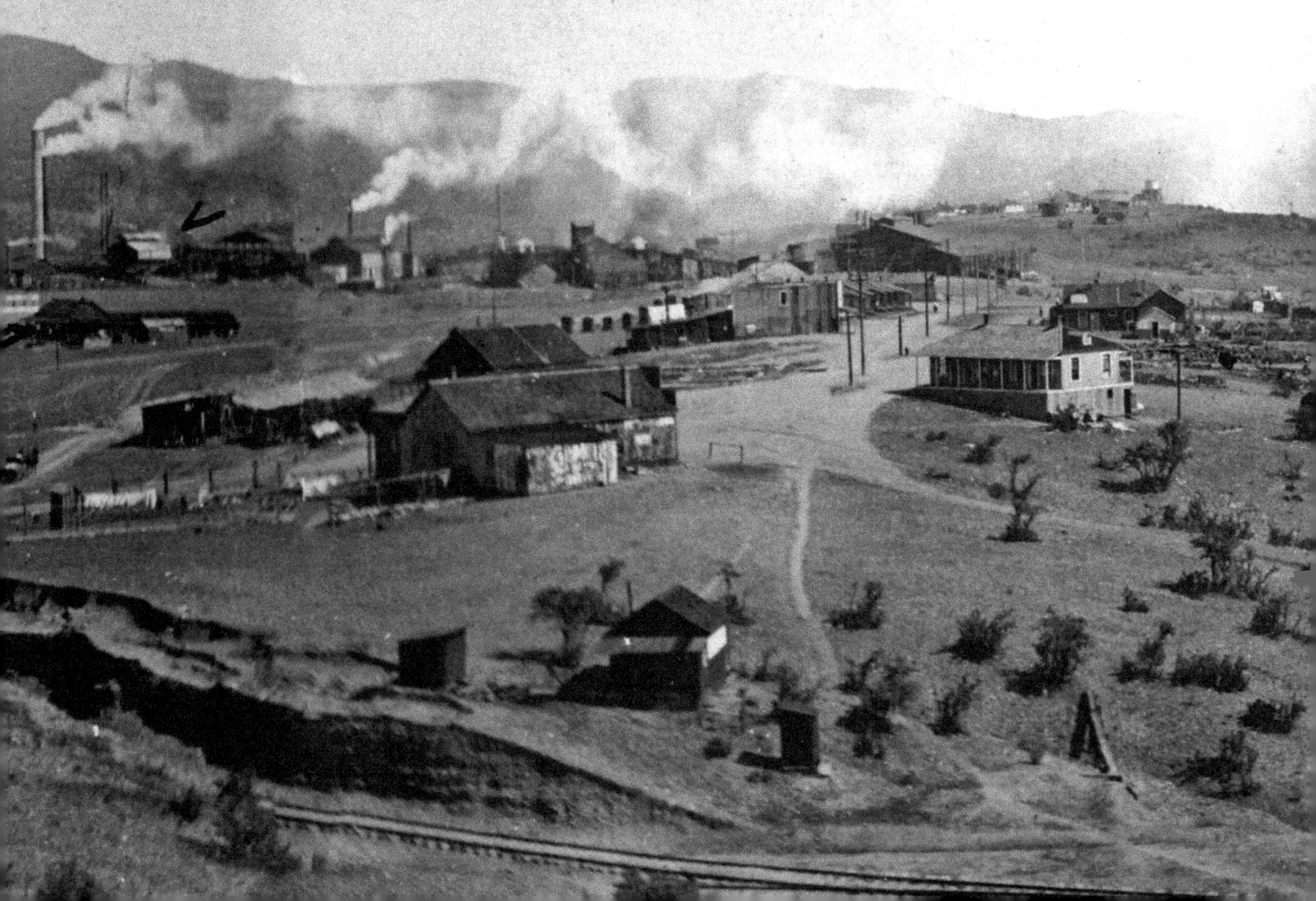

Turner Publishing Company
www.turnerpublishing.com

Historic Photos of Arizona

Library of Congress Control Number: 2008941039

ISBN-13: 978-1-59652-518-4

ISBN 978-1-68442-075-9 (hc)

Contents

Acknowledgments VII

Preface VIII

Wild West Territory
(1850–1899) 1

Statehood and Change
(1900–1919) 43

Modern Arizona Takes Shape
(1920–1939) 101

Desert Airfields and Postwar Growth
(1940–1970) 153

Notes on the Photographs 200

The first Southern Pacific Railroad steam locomotive to cross this bridge at Yuma, Arizona, did so on September 30, 1877. The bridge contained a "swinging span" that would open to allow the many Colorado River steamboats to pass underneath safely. Fort Yuma is visible on the California side of the river.

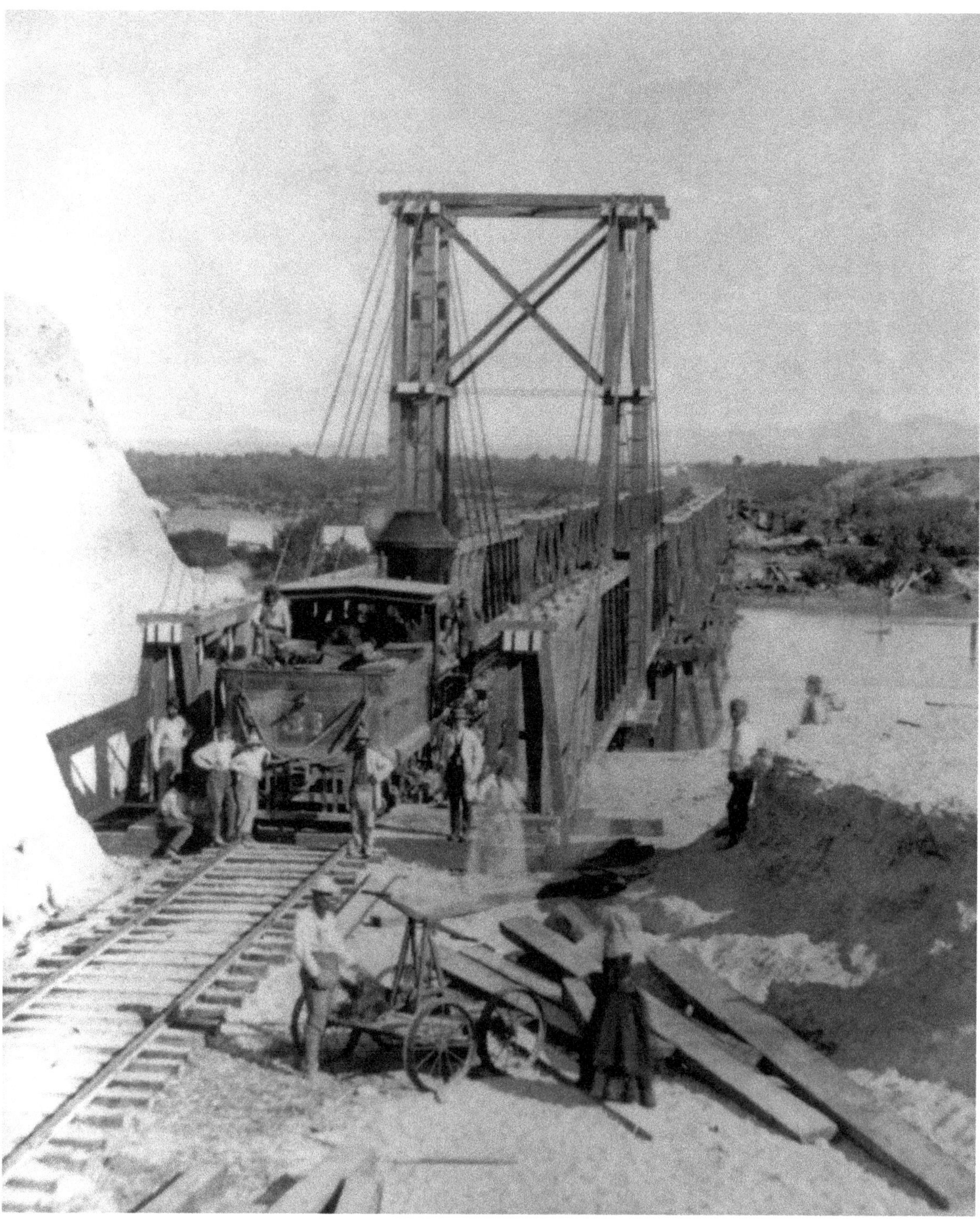

ACKNOWLEDGMENTS

This volume, *Historic Photos of Arizona,* is the result of the cooperation and efforts of many individuals, organizations, and corporations. It is with great thanks that we acknowledge the valuable contribution of the following for their generous support:

Library of Congress
Arizona State Library, Archives and Public Records, History and Archives Division, Phoenix

---

We would like to thank our lifelong Arizona traveling companions and friends Teresa and Ken Jackway. Without their support and thirst for adventure, our knowledge and love of Arizona would be incomplete, and so our lives less blessed.

In special memory of our beloved cat, Valentino, who we lost while completing this book. We sure did love that cat!

PREFACE

Arizona has thousands of historic photographs that reside in archives, both locally and nationally. This book began with the observation that, while those photographs are of great interest to many, they are not easily accessible. During a time when Arizona is looking ahead and evaluating its future course, many people are asking, How do we treat the past? These decisions affect every aspect of the city—architecture, public spaces, commerce, infrastructure—and these, in turn, affect the way that people live their lives. This book seeks to provide easy access to a valuable, objective look into the history of Arizona.

The power of photographs is that they are less subjective than words in their treatment of history. Although the photographer can make decisions regarding subject matter and how to capture and present it, photographs do not provide the breadth of interpretation that text does. For this reason, they offer an original, untainted perspective that allows the viewer to interpret and observe.

This project represents countless hours of review and research. The researchers and writers have reviewed thousands of photographs in numerous archives. We greatly appreciate the generous assistance of the organizations listed in the acknowledgments of this work, without whom this project could not have been completed.

The goal in publishing this work is to provide broader access to this set of extraordinary photographs that seek to inspire, provide perspective, and evoke insight that might assist people who are responsible for determining Arizona's future. In addition, the book seeks to preserve the past with adequate respect and reverence.

With the exception of touching up imperfections that have accrued with the passage of time and cropping where necessary, no other changes have been made. The focus and clarity of many images is limited to the technology and the ability of the photographer at the time they were taken.

The work is divided into eras. Beginning with some of the earliest known photographs of Arizona, the first section records photographs through the end of the nineteenth century. The second section spans the beginning of the twentieth century through World War I. Section Three moves from the 1920s through the 1930s. The last section covers the World War II era to recent times.

In each of these sections we have made an effort to capture various aspects of life through our selection of photographs. People, commerce, transportation, infrastructure, religious institutions, and educational institutions have been included to provide a broad perspective.

We encourage readers to reflect as they go walking in Arizona, strolling through its parks, its countryside, and the neighborhoods of its cities. It is the publisher's hope that in utilizing this work, longtime residents will learn something new and that new residents will gain a perspective on where Arizona has been, so that each can contribute to its future.

—Todd Bottorff, Publisher

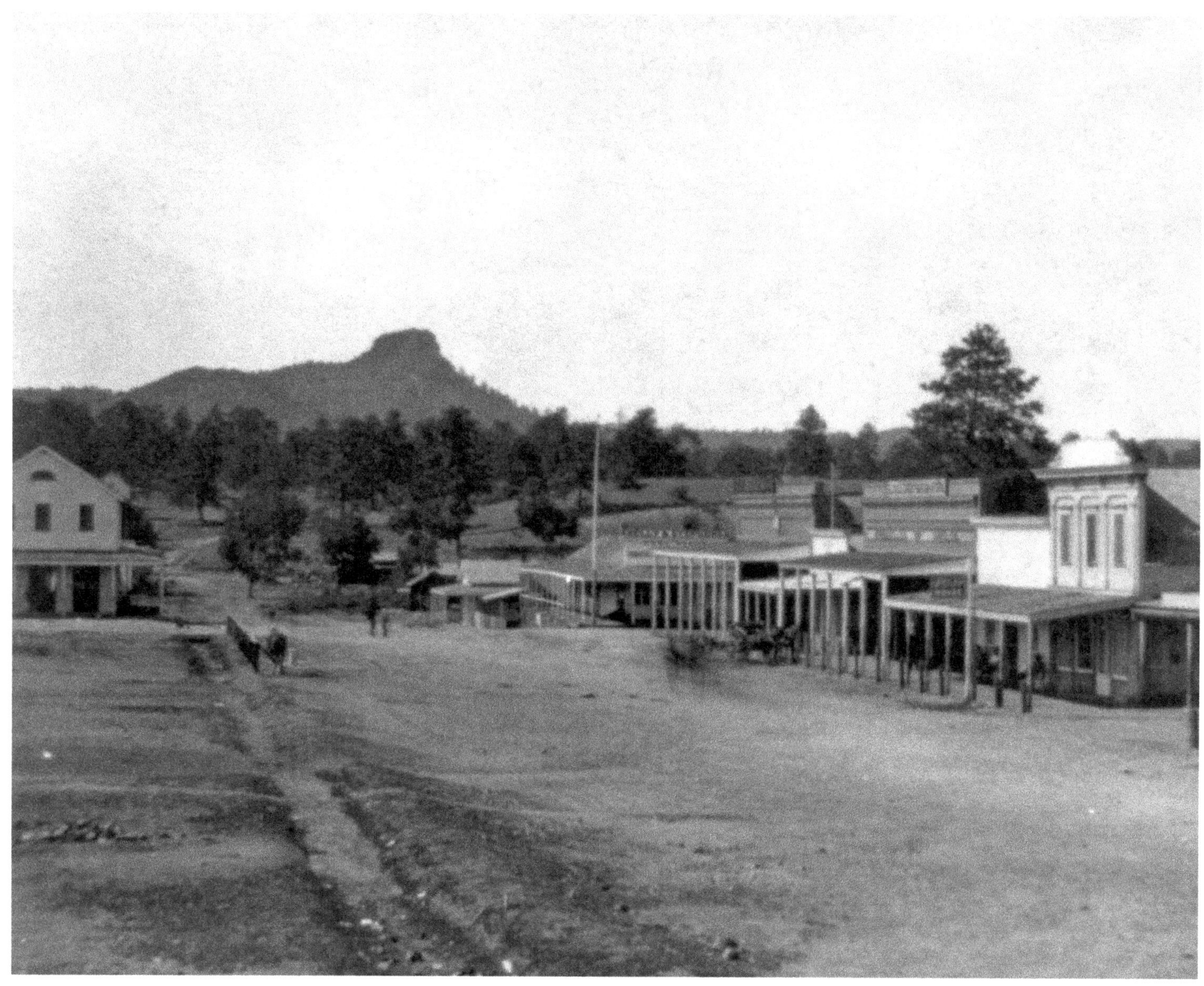

This view is facing west on Gurley Street in Prescott in 1877 when Prescott was the capital of the Territory of Arizona. Prescott citizens believed their town would remain the territorial capital and someday become a state capital. Little did they know that the legislators of Tucson and Phoenix would band together and move the territorial capital to Phoenix in 1889. The mountain in the background is Thumb Butte, a favorite hiking destination then and now.

Wild West Territory

(1850–1899)

Most of present-day Arizona became part of the United States in 1848 with the ending of the Mexican War and the signing of the Treaty of Guadalupe Hidalgo. The section south of the Gila River would join the rest of Arizona (still part of the Territory of New Mexico at the time) with ratification of the Gadsden Purchase in 1854. On February 24, 1863, Arizona became a separate territory.

American Indian cultures had been present in the Arizona region since prehistory. Arriving around 300 B.C., the Hohokam people would farm the area by means of hundreds of miles of irrigation canals. In the years just before European contact, 17 distinct tribes called the region home.

Europeans had been fascinated by this harsh yet beautiful land with its lure of mineral wealth since Spanish conquistador Francisco Vasquez de Coronado led an expedition in search of the Seven Cities of Cibola in 1540. Coronado failed to find those minerals, which lay underground, because he thought they would be adorning the streets of fabulous cities, as Hernán Cortés had found in 1519 at Tenochtitlán. The Jesuit priest Father Eusebio Francisco Kino arrived in 1687, but he was in search of souls more than gold. When Spain's control crumbled in 1821, the region became the northern frontier of Mexico until ceded to the United States in 1848.

After gold was discovered at Sutter's Mill in 1848, thousands rushed across the Southwest to reach the California gold fields. A Civil War battle was fought in Arizona at Picacho Peak, between present-day Phoenix and Tucson, in 1862. Both events prepared Arizona for its most famous role—as an archetypal Wild West territory.

The Territory of Arizona grew up right in the middle of the Wild West era—roughly the 20 years from 1865 to 1885. The names of Arizona cowboys became known around the world. Good guys and bad guys roamed the streets in town after town, creating stories that are still told today. At the same time, a great Apache medicine man, Geronimo, led his people in resistance against overwhelming military odds, then negotiated a peace that saved his people from extermination.

Developed in the late 1870s and 1880s, the territory's first large copper mines connected both worlds—the Wild West and modern industry—and pointed Arizona to a fast-approaching new century.

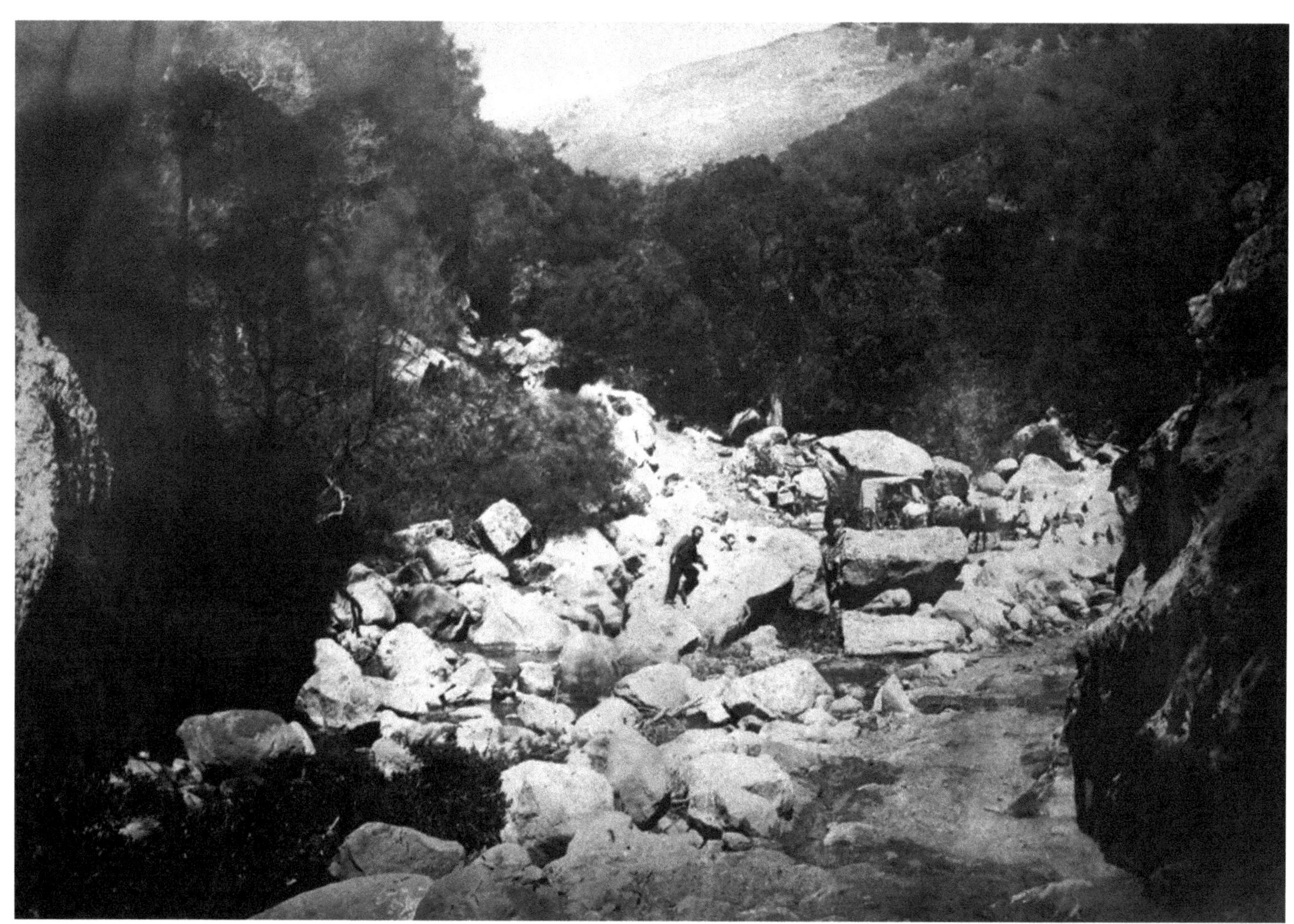

The dream of striking it rich has been a part of Arizona's story since the first Spanish conquistadors arrived. For the vast majority of treasure seekers, prospecting in the rugged wilderness of Arizona ended in failure. Some, like this explorer photographed on his way to Arizona's "diamond fields," sought riches that existed only in the made-up stories of other men. The diamond fields of Arizona were a hoax of the early 1870s.

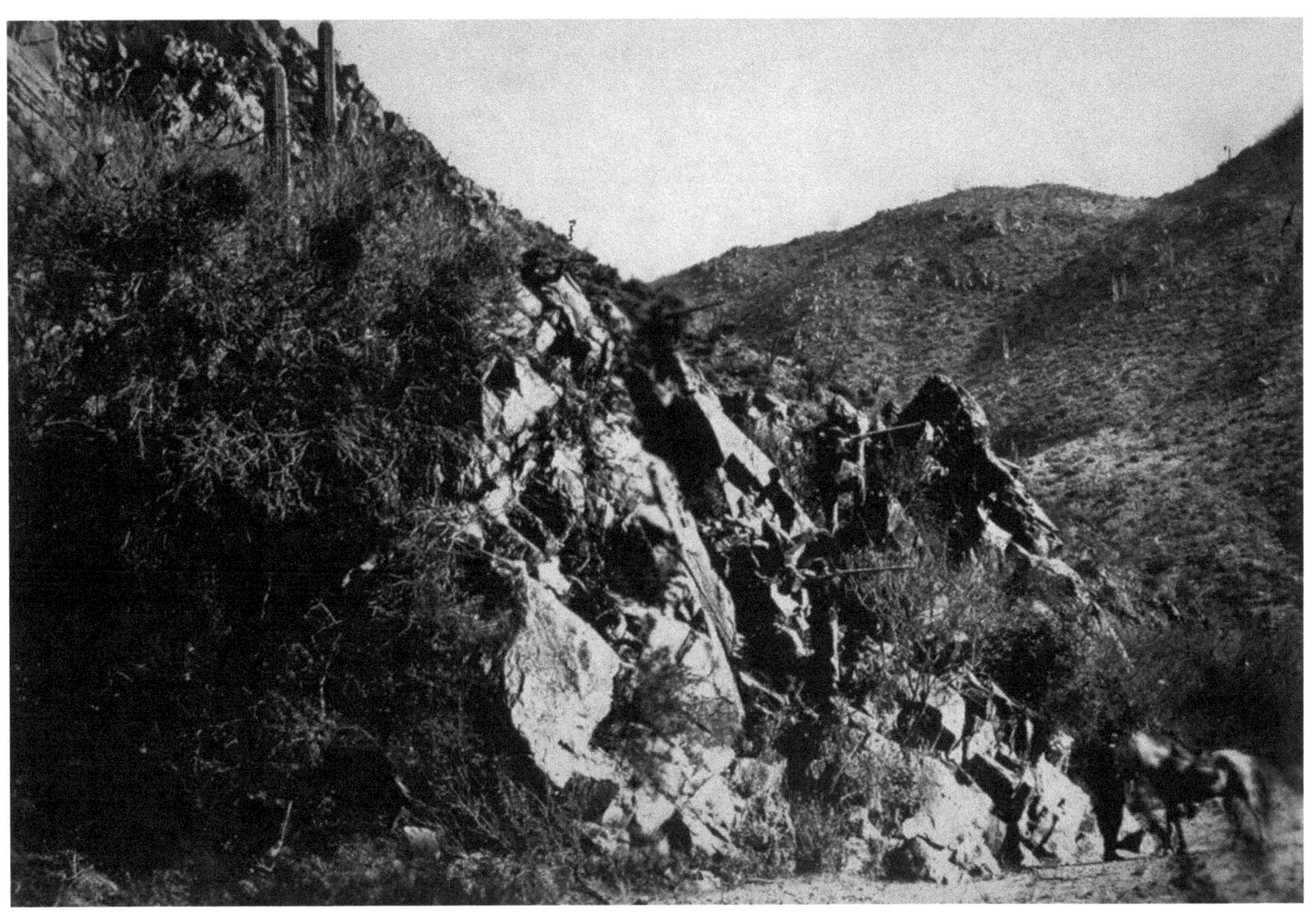

Conflict between settlers and the many bands of Southwest Apache Indians escalated with the Camp Grant Massacre of April 30, 1871, in which an estimated 144 Aravaipa and Pinal Apaches were slaughtered in a raid at dawn by a vigilante group of Anglos, Mexicans, and Tohono O'odham Indians. All but 8 of the Apaches killed were women and children. More than a hundred men were tried for murder, but none were convicted. For another 15 years, the Apache Wars raged throughout southeastern Arizona. They ended with the surrender of Geronimo on September 4, 1886. Here a group of United States Cavalry takes part in one of the many battles between soldiers and Apaches during this tragic time in Arizona's history.

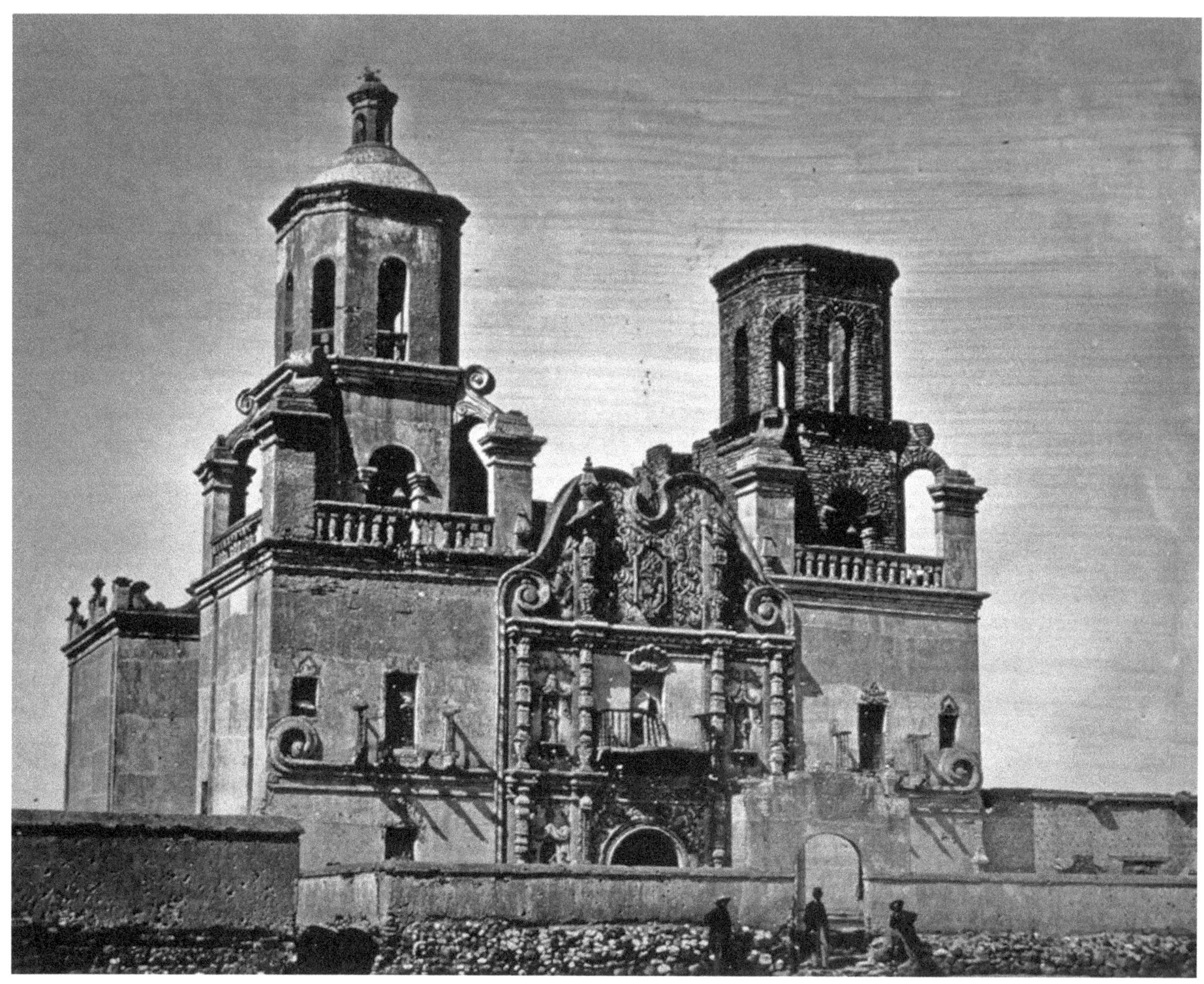

San Xavier del Bac is located on the Tohono O'odham Reservation some 10 miles south of downtown Tucson. The great Jesuit priest Eusebio Francisco Kino first visited the native people of Bac in 1692, hoping to move his missionary headquarters there. Photographed around 1870, this church was constructed by Franciscan priests between 1783 and 1797 and is still a living church today, serving the people of the Tohono O'odham Nation and thousands of visitors.

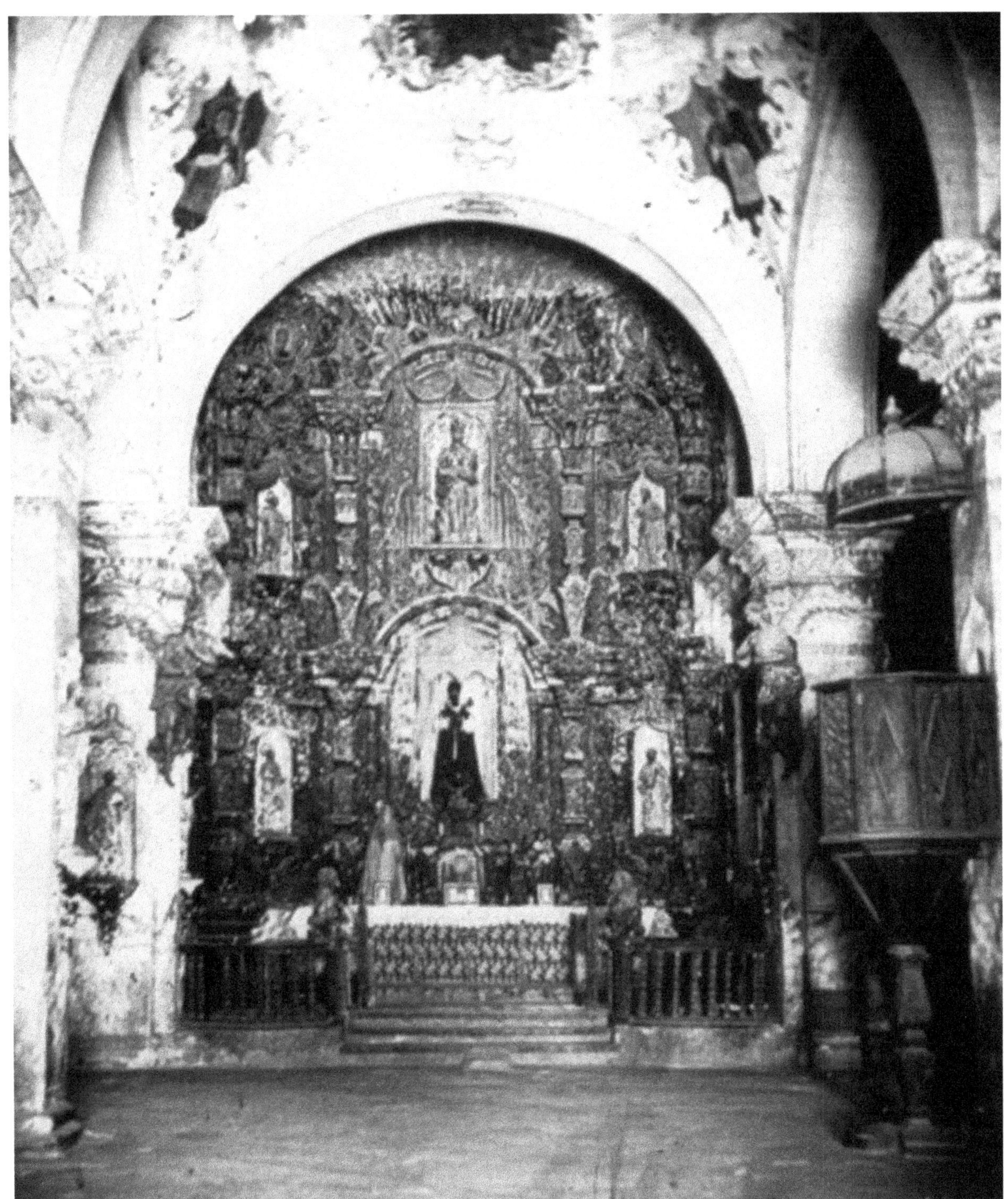

The interior of San Xavier del Bac is a living museum of some of the best examples of mission architecture found in the United States. The interior is a blend of Moorish, Byzantine, and late Mexican Renaissance architecture and is open daily for the public to tour. An extensive, ongoing renovation project has cleaned the interior and brought it back to its original eighteenth-century colors.

From 1869 to 1879, a U.S. Army Corps of Engineers unit under the supervision of Lieutenant George M. Wheeler completed geographical surveys of the United States west of the 100th meridian. Their object was to record the region's people, flora, fauna, geological wealth, and rail and road routes, and to identify possible sites for future military forts. Survey party photographer William Bell took this picture of a wind-weathered rock found in 1872 in northwestern Arizona.

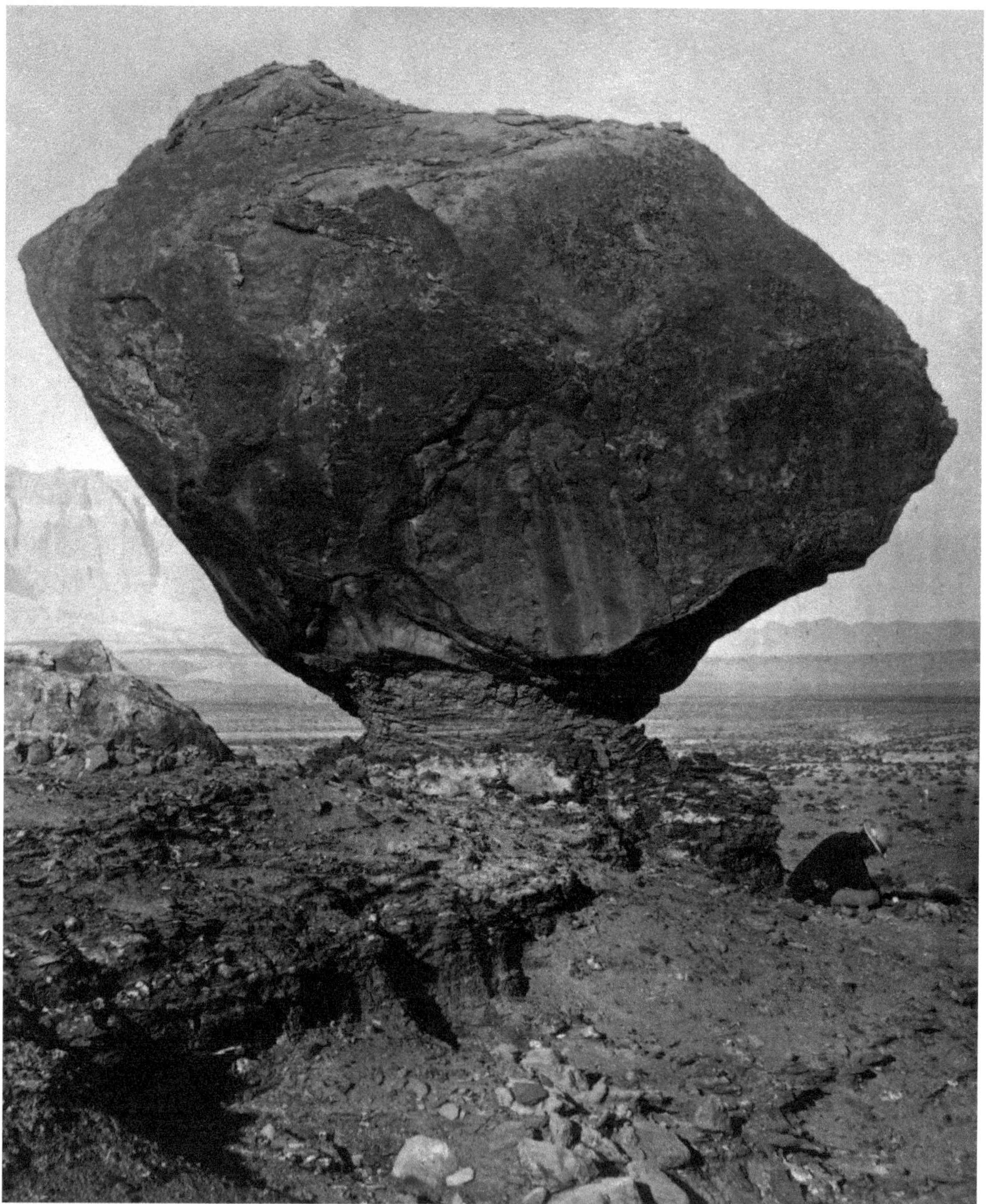

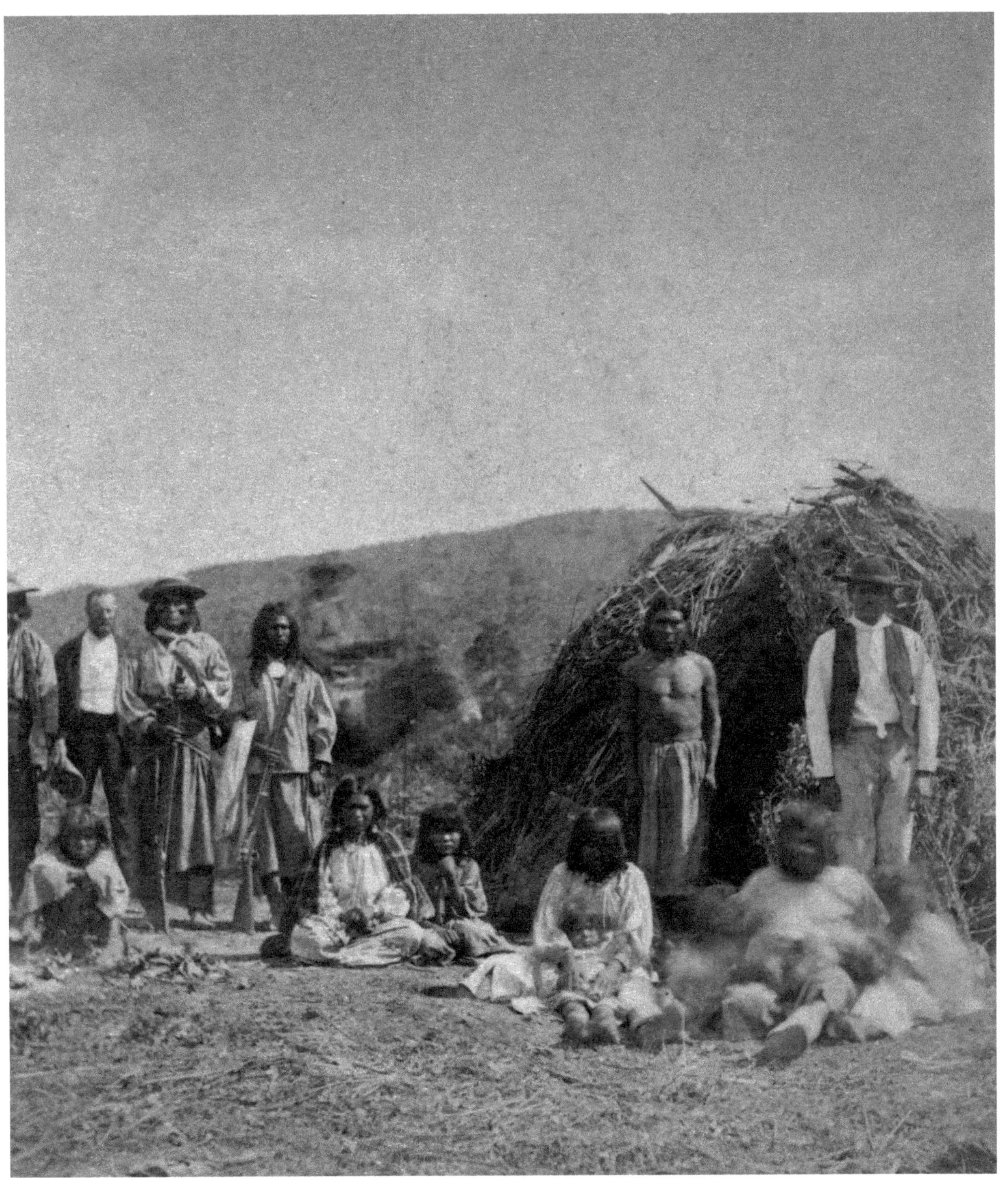

A family group of Apaches stand in front of their wickiup shelter to be photographed by Timothy O'Sullivan somewhere in southeastern Arizona in 1873. Being a nomadic people, Apache families could quickly build their wickiup shelters from local flora and then simply abandon them when moving to the next home site. O'Sullivan, a famous Civil War photographer, participated in Wheeler's survey of the regions west of the 100th meridian from 1871 to 1874.

An 1871 surveying party in Prescott is frozen in time by photographer Timothy O'Sullivan.

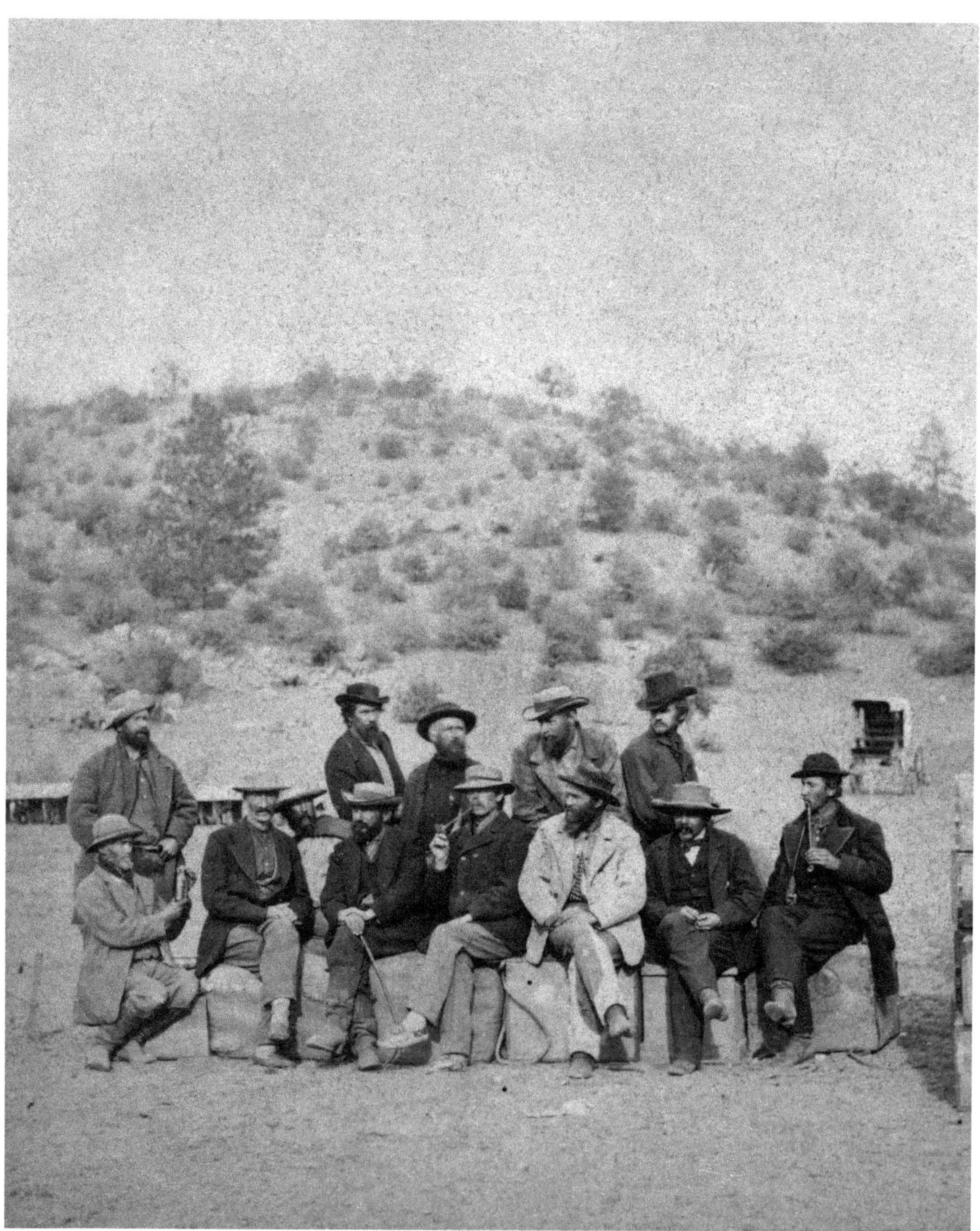

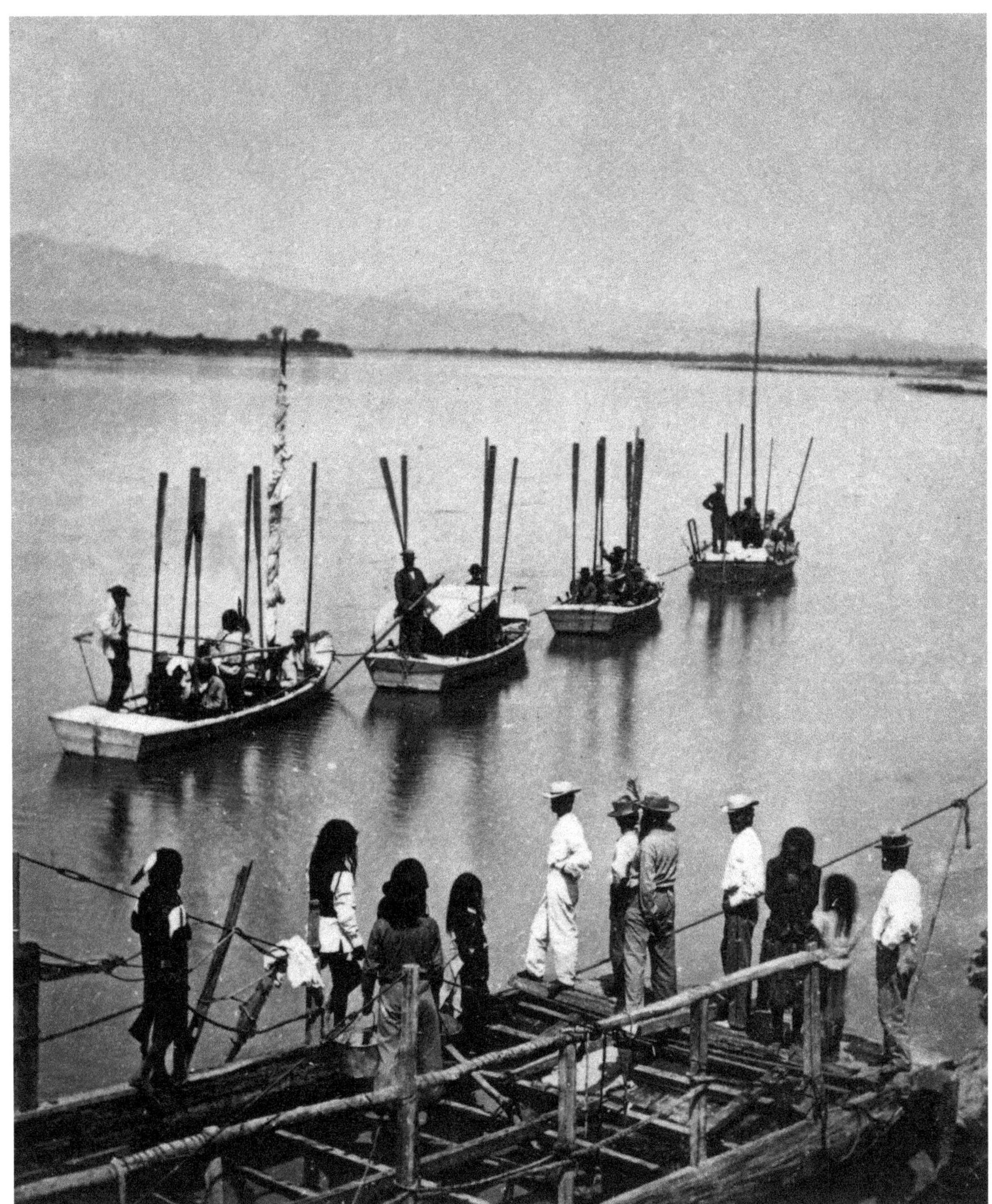

In 1858 Camp Colorado, later to be known as Camp Mojave, and later still as Fort Mojave, was founded by the United States Army to keep watch over Beale's Road while miners and settlers crossed the Colorado River on their way to California. Here an exploration party from the Army Corps of Engineers leaves Camp Mojave and crosses the river in 1871.

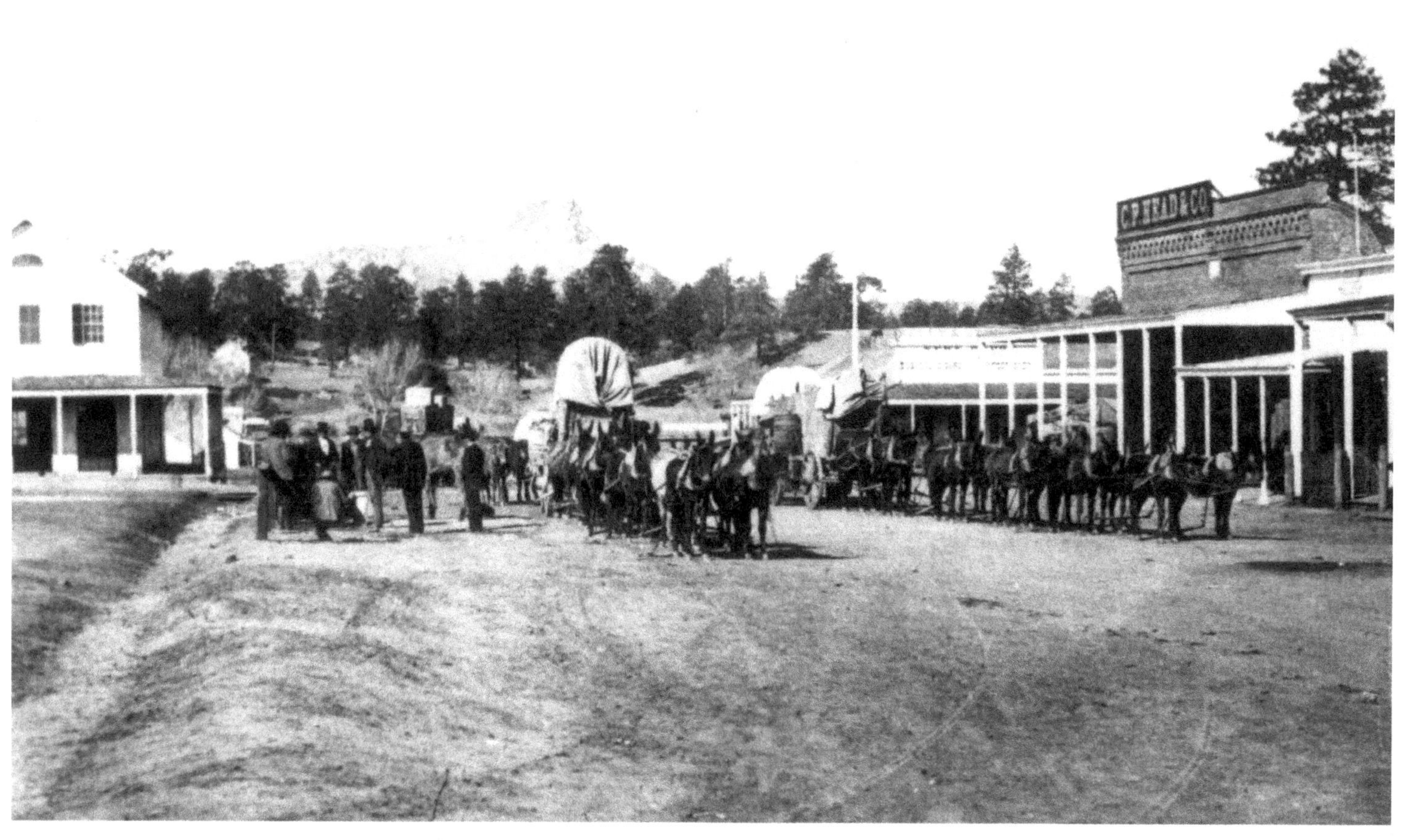

The town of Prescott was named in 1864 to honor the great American historian William Hickling Prescott. Prescott's book *History of the Conquest of Mexico* had been hugely popular with American readers since the 1846-48 Mexican War. This photo of Prescott shows local wagons traveling west past several Gurley Street saloons.

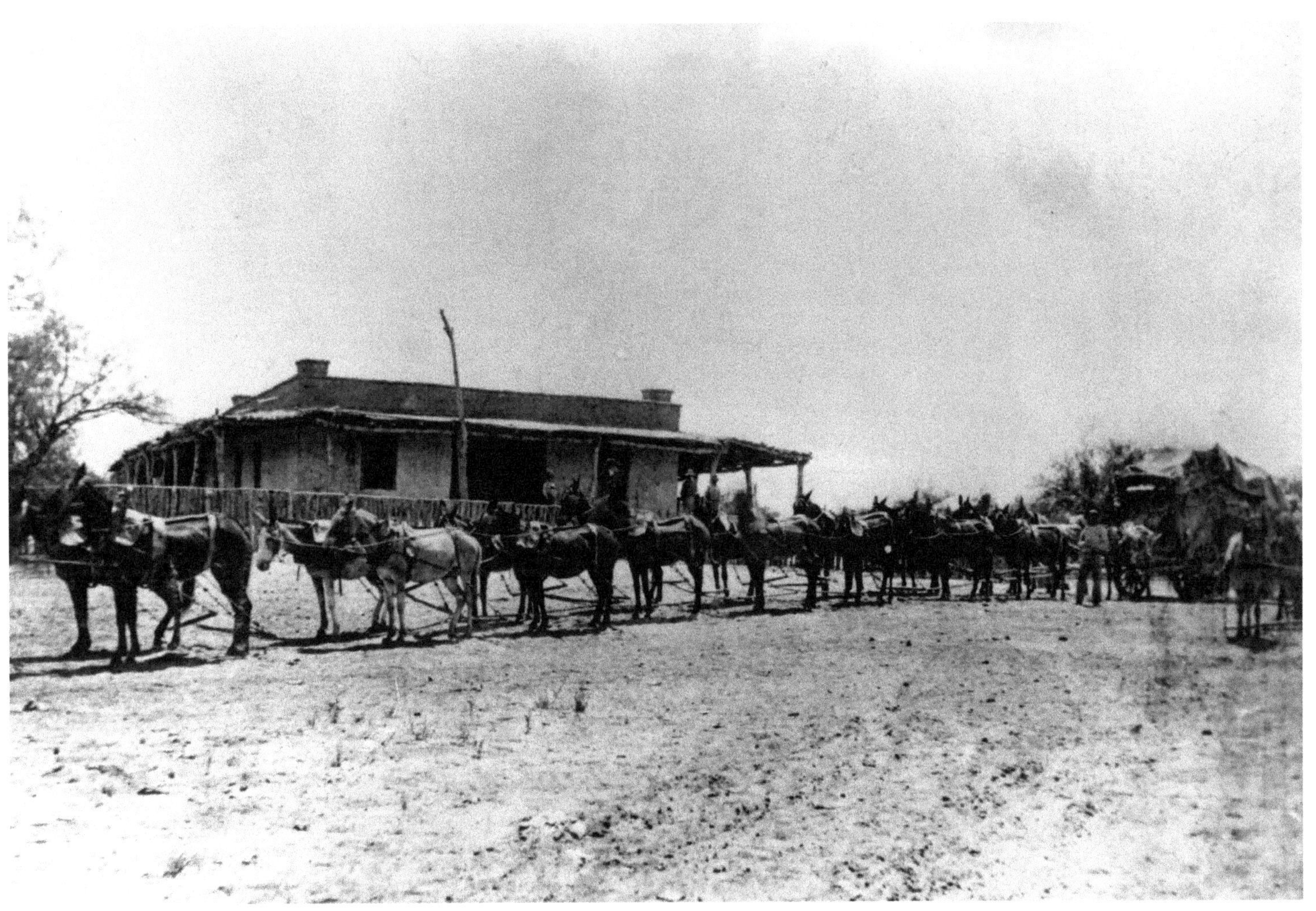

Freight wagons were used to move goods and supplies between the few small settlements of the Arizona Territory. Loading their supplies at Fort Yuma, these freighters could successfully cross the many desolate miles of the Sonoran Desert. Here a territorial freighter passes in front of the freight and mail station at Gila Ranch about 1878. By 1880 the settlement would move to be near the railroad and would be renamed Gila Bend.

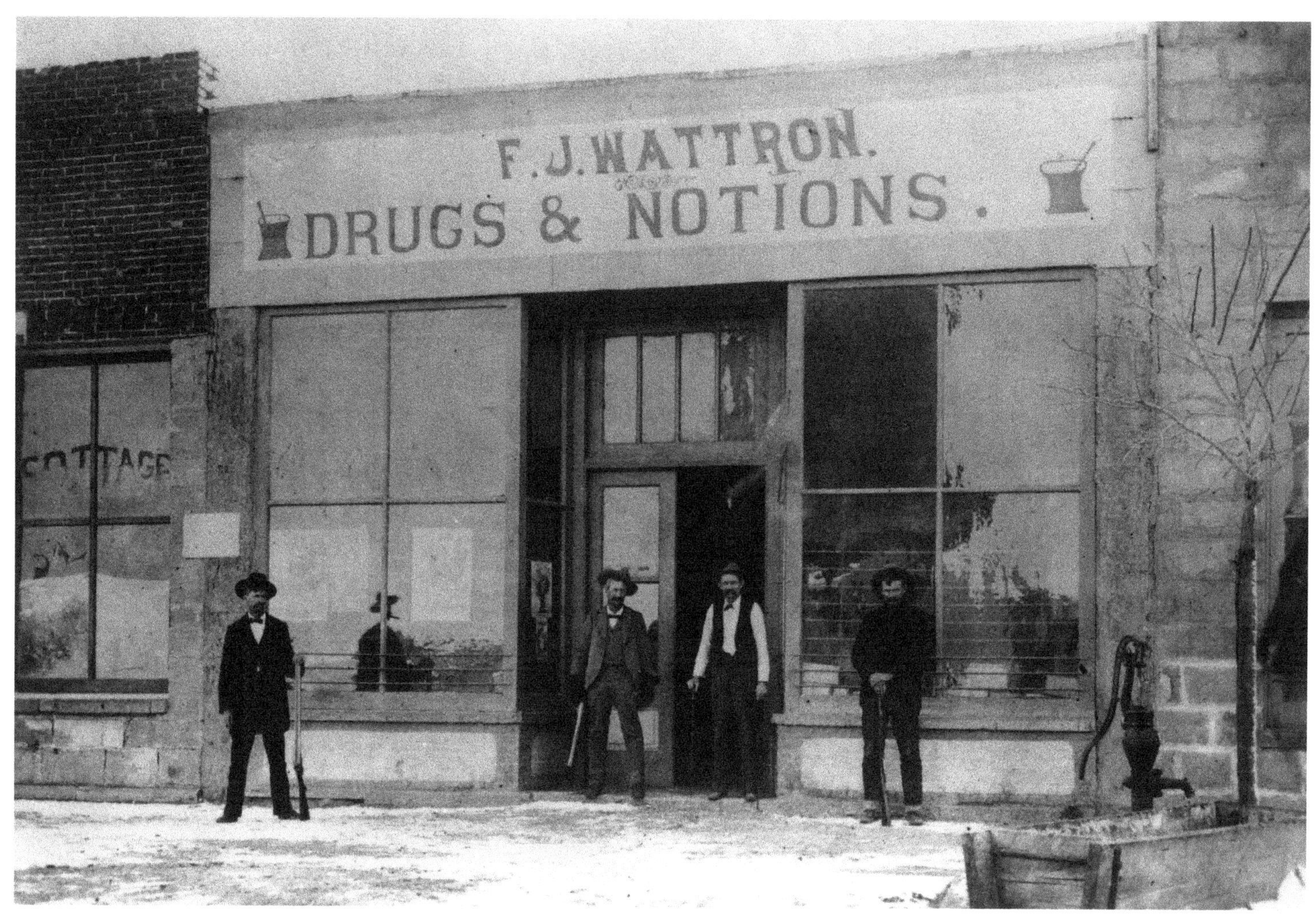

Holbrook sheriff (and perhaps druggist) Frank Wattron watches over his town while standing in front of F. J. Wattron Drugs & Notions around 1880. Holbrook in the 1880s was the headquarters of the Aztec Land and Cattle Company and its infamous "Hashknife" cowboys, described as the "thievinist, fightinest bunch of cowboys" in the West. The company once kept 33,000 head of cattle on a range that extended from just east of Flagstaff to the Arizona–New Mexico border.

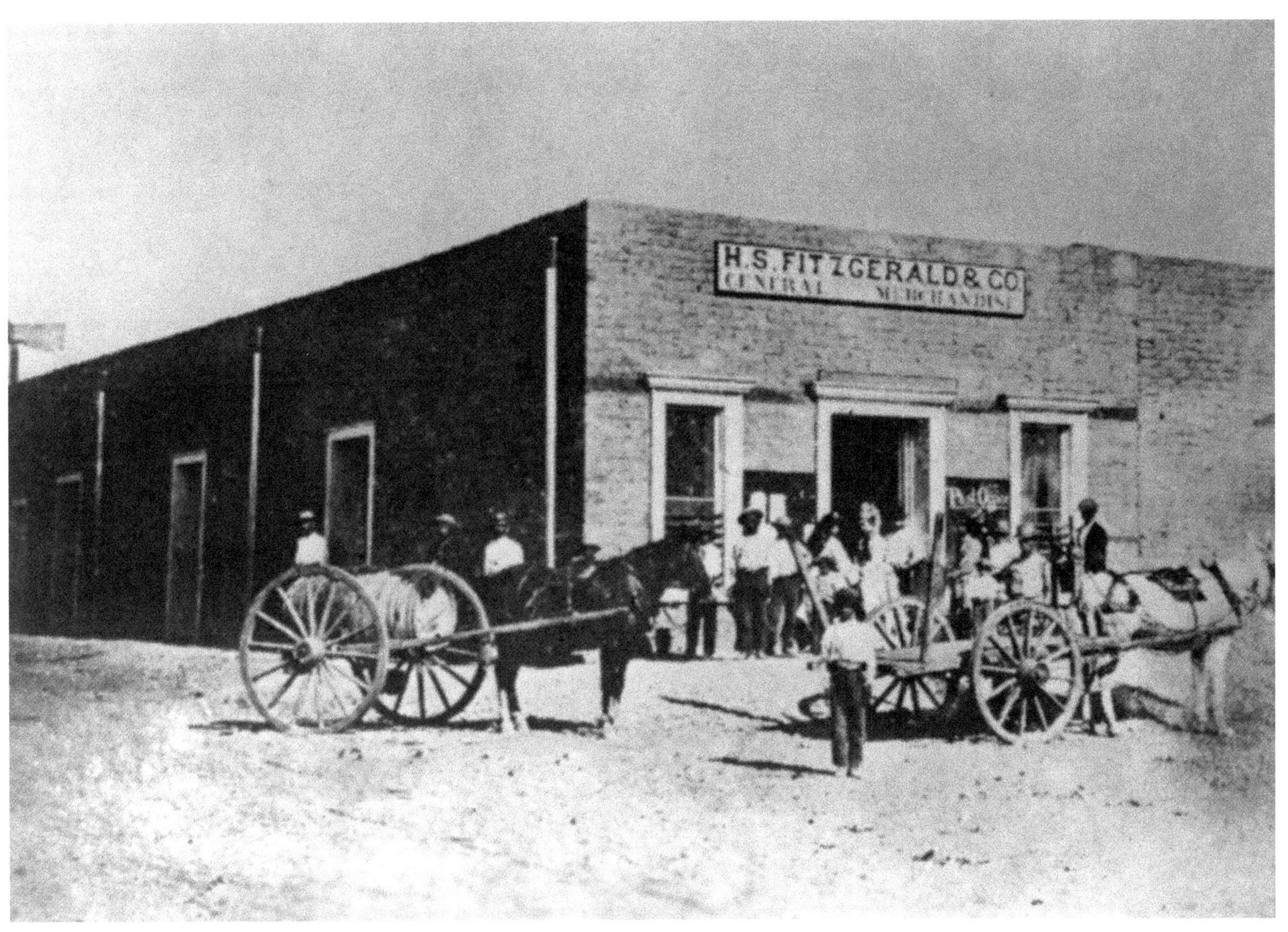

In 1854 this Colorado River crossing site was called Colorado City. In 1858 the citizens of the town decided to change the name to Arizona, then decided to change the name again, to Yuma, in 1866. However, in 1869 the town was renamed Arizona City, only for it to be changed back to Yuma in 1873. This photo shows a few of the citizens of Yuma—formerly Arizona City, formerly Colorado City—in the early 1880s.

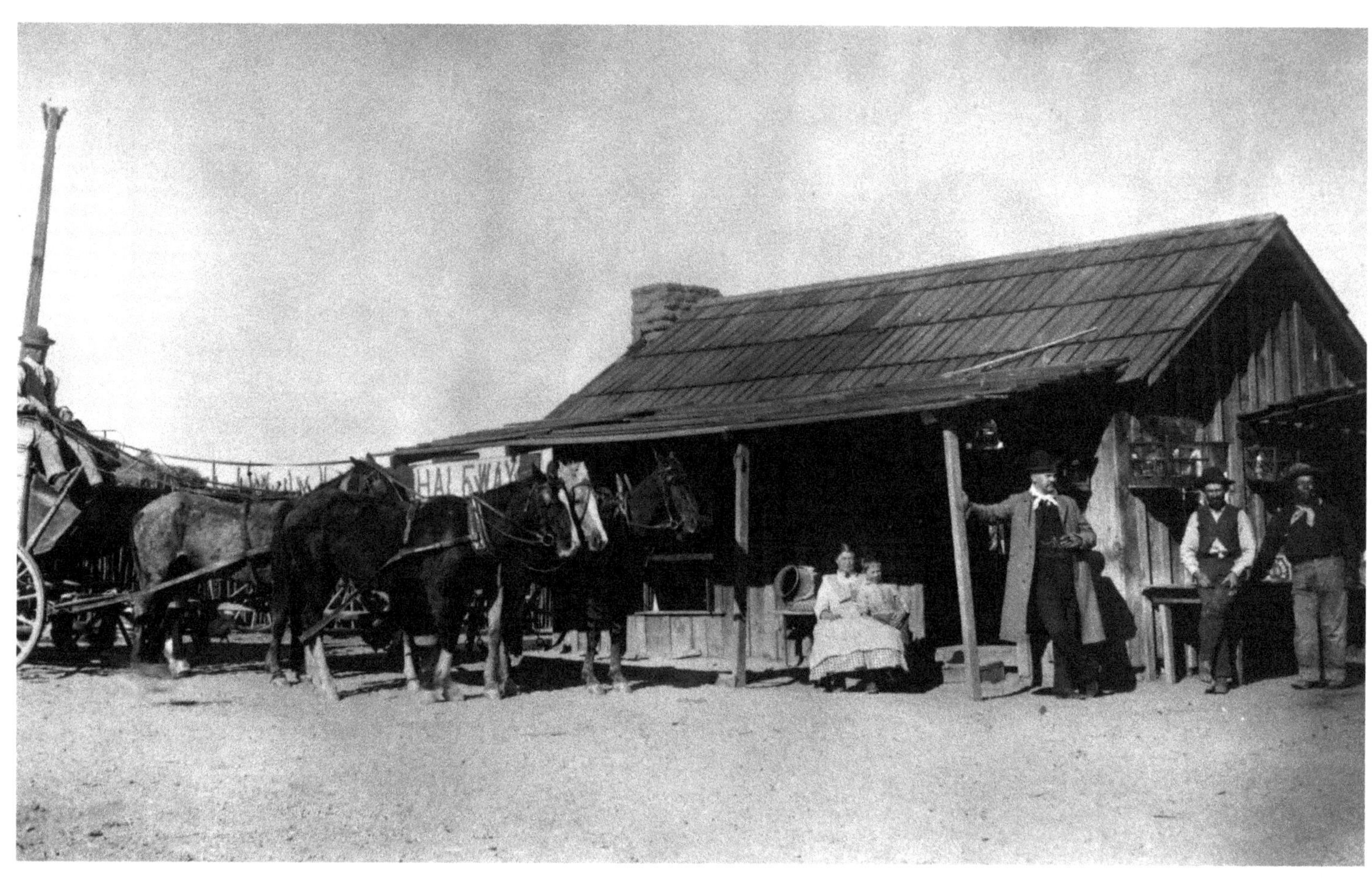

The Concord Stagecoach was built in Concord, New Hampshire, and was an important means of transportation for Arizona Territory citizens in the 1880s. Each 2,500-pound coach was 8 ½ feet long, 8 ½ feet tall, and 5 feet wide. If someone agreed to ride on the roof, the Concord could carry 12 passengers. Stage stations like this one in Pima County were built 20 miles apart so that horses and passengers could rest and refresh.

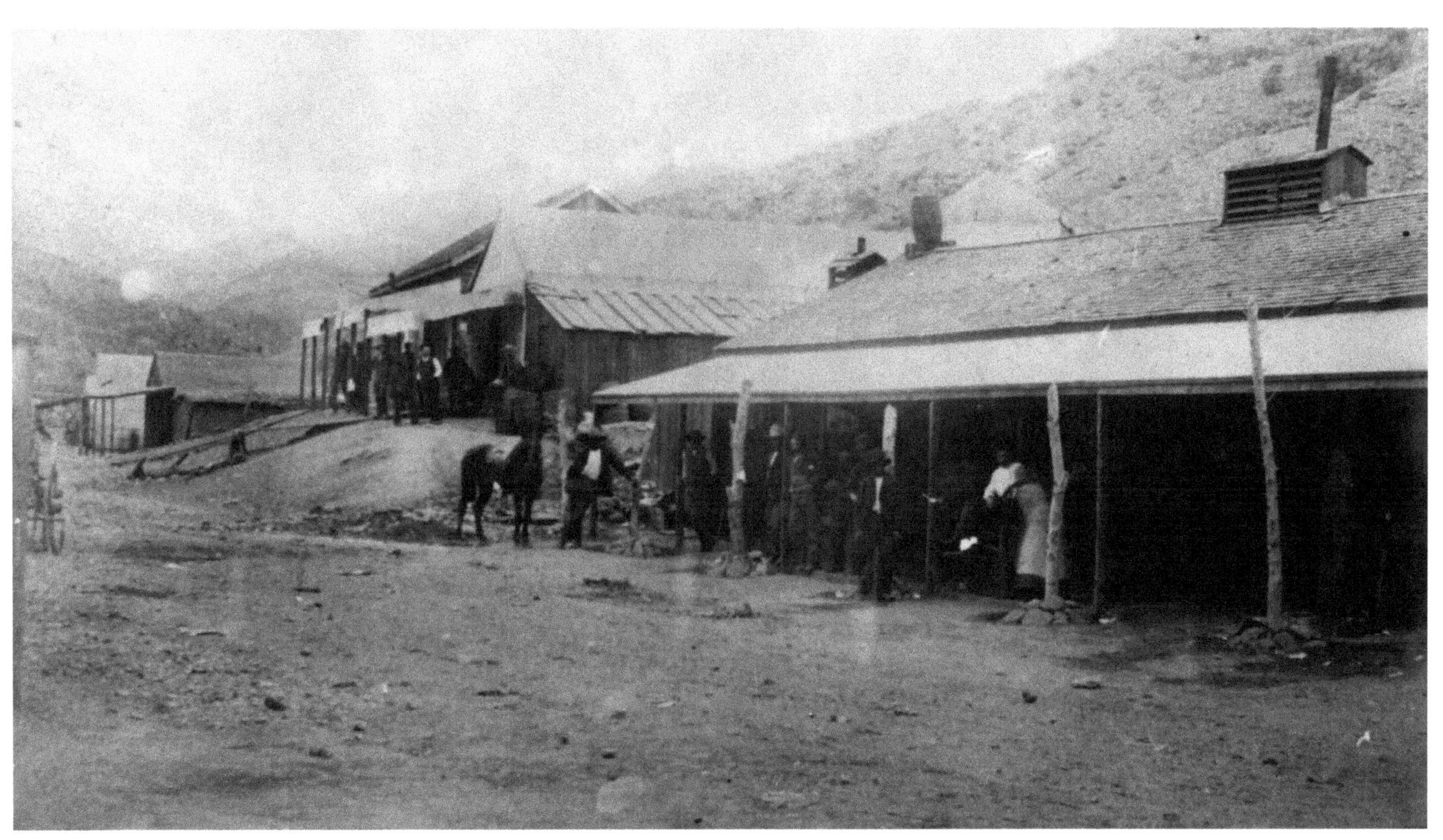

Clifton is a copper mining town in the far southeast corner of Arizona. The town is located along the San Francisco River, with high, mountain cliffs rising from the canyon floor. The name Clifton probably originated as a shortening of "cliff town." A U.S. post office opened at Clifton in 1875. This photo shows a few stores along the town's main street in 1884.

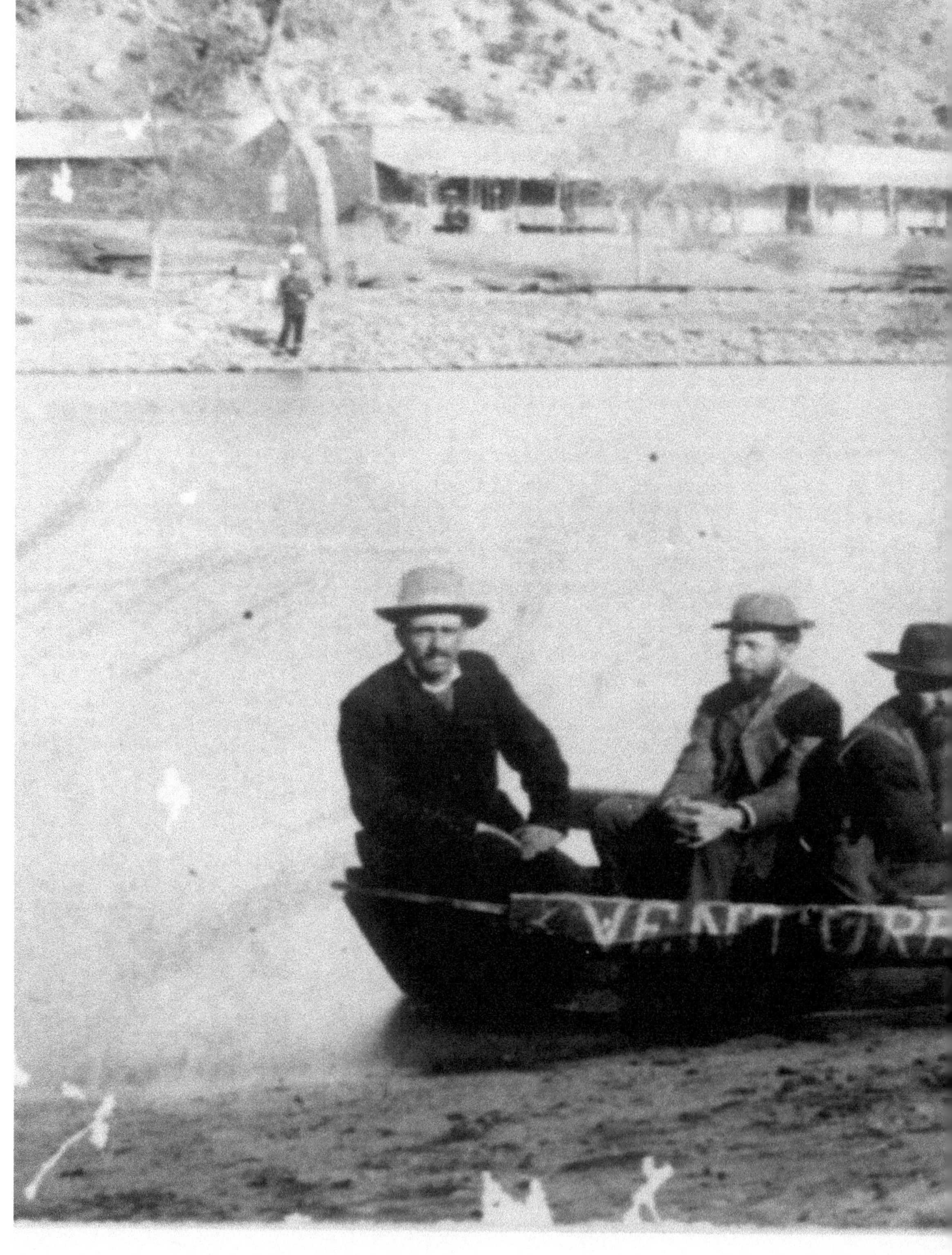

Though famous for its desert terrain, Arizona can receive much rainfall in a short period. When the heavy rains do come, flooding is a common result. This 1884 photo shows citizens of Clifton helping to rescue fellow townsfolk from the flood-swollen San Francisco River, which runs through the center of the copper mining town. Most of the year, this desert river would be referred to as a creek.

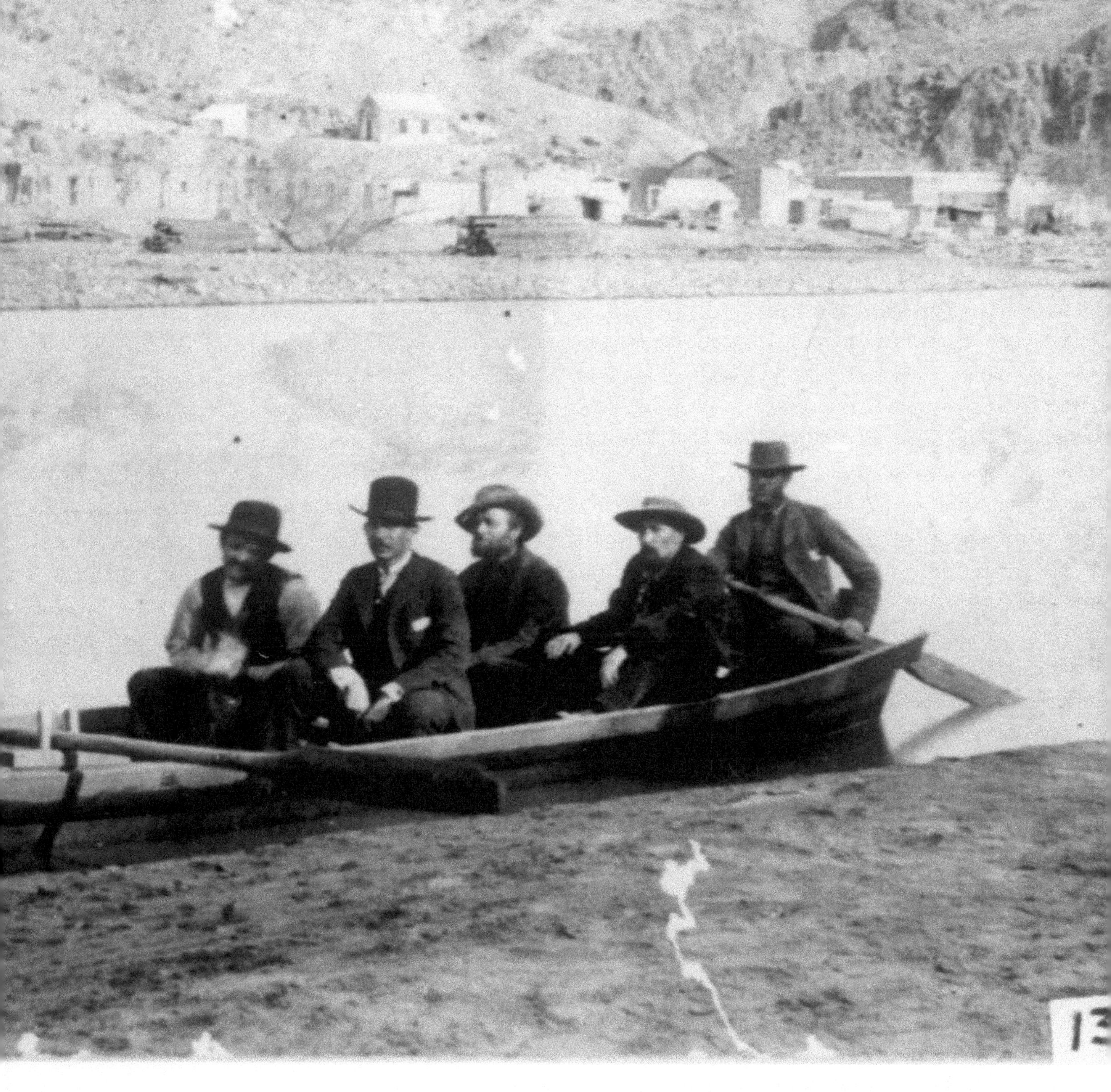
13

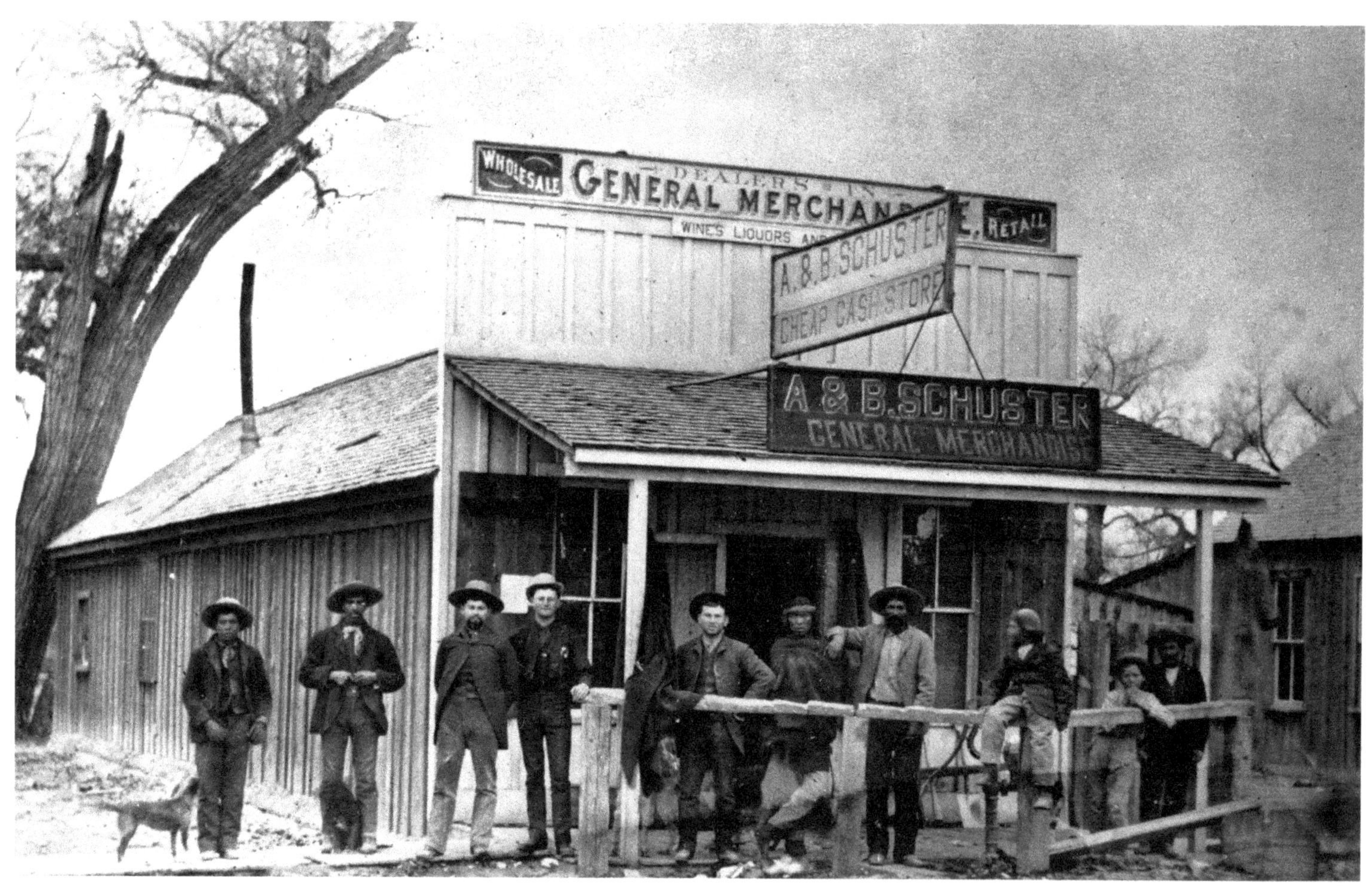

The town of Holbrook received its name in 1882 to honor H. R. Holbrook, a local railroad executive. It was a rough-and-tumble cowboy town said to be "too tough for women and churches!" All the vices typical of a territorial town were found there in places such as a saloon named the Bucket of Blood. This photo shows the A. & B. Schuster General Store, located just down the street from the famous Bucket of Blood.

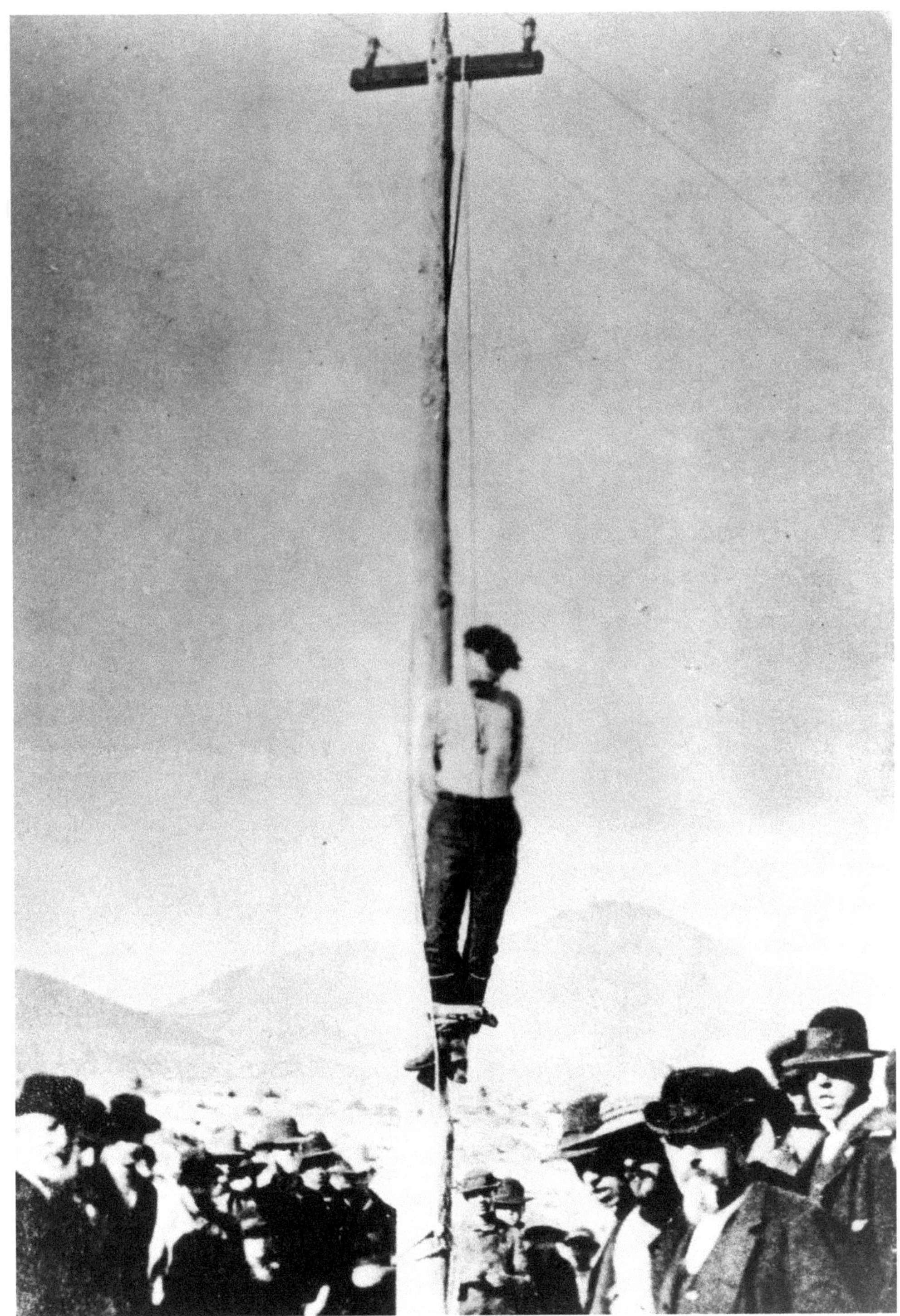

Lynchings are perpetrated by mobs acting outside the rule of law. In 1884 John Heath was taken from the Tombstone jail and lynched by a mob from the town of Bisbee. Heath was the leader of a gang whose robbery of a Bisbee store resulted in the deaths of four people. A sign placed at the bottom of the telegraph pole where he was lynched stated the mob did this deed to "advance Arizona" in becoming more civilized.

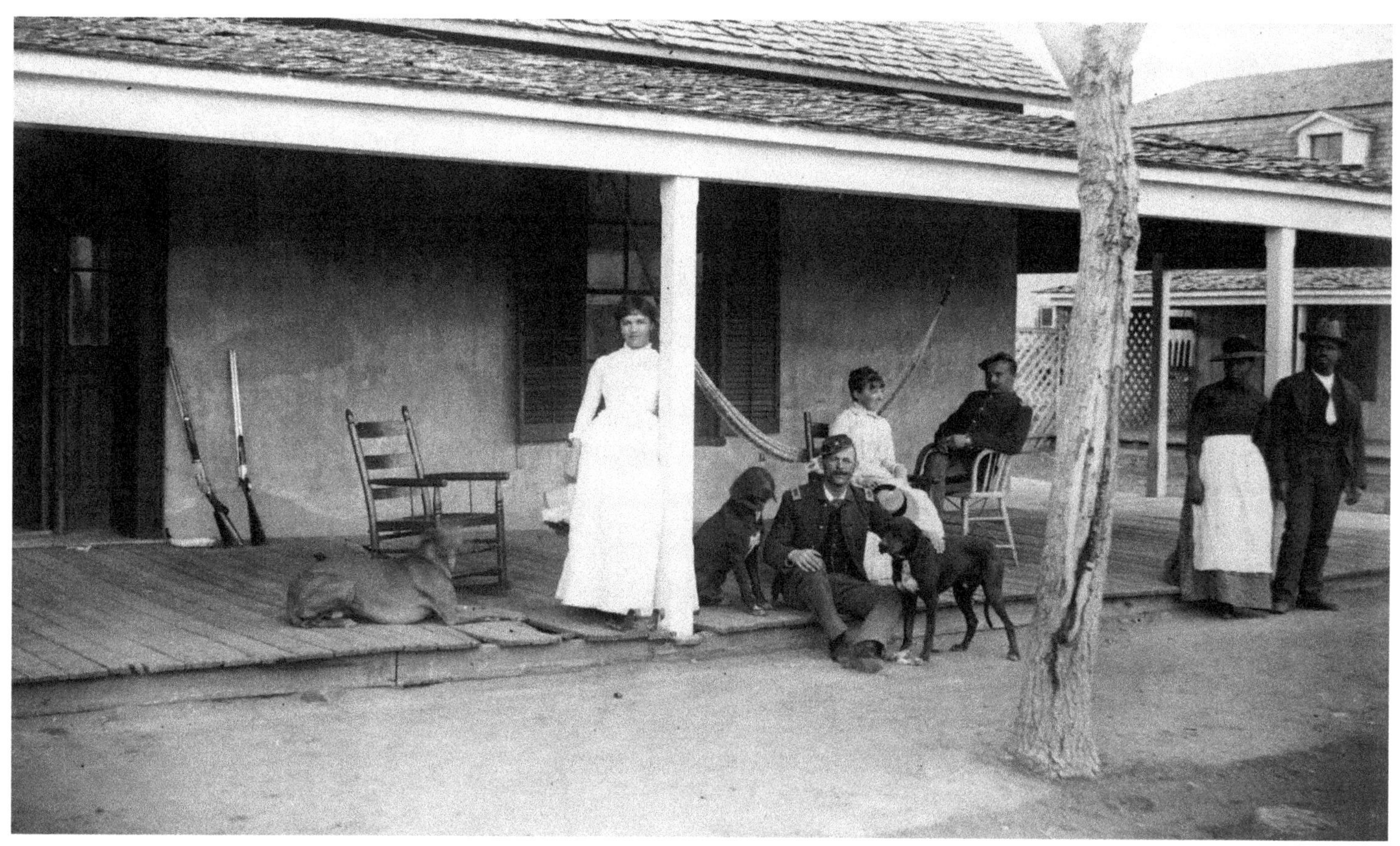

In 1866 settlers in the Verde River Valley created their own private fort at the junction of the Verde River and Clear Creek and named it Camp Lincoln. Army regulars soon occupied the fort, and in 1868 they renamed it Camp Verde. Disease was common near the river, so the camp was moved a mile south in 1871, and in 1879 it was renamed Fort Verde. This photograph shows soldiers and civilians at Fort Verde in 1886.

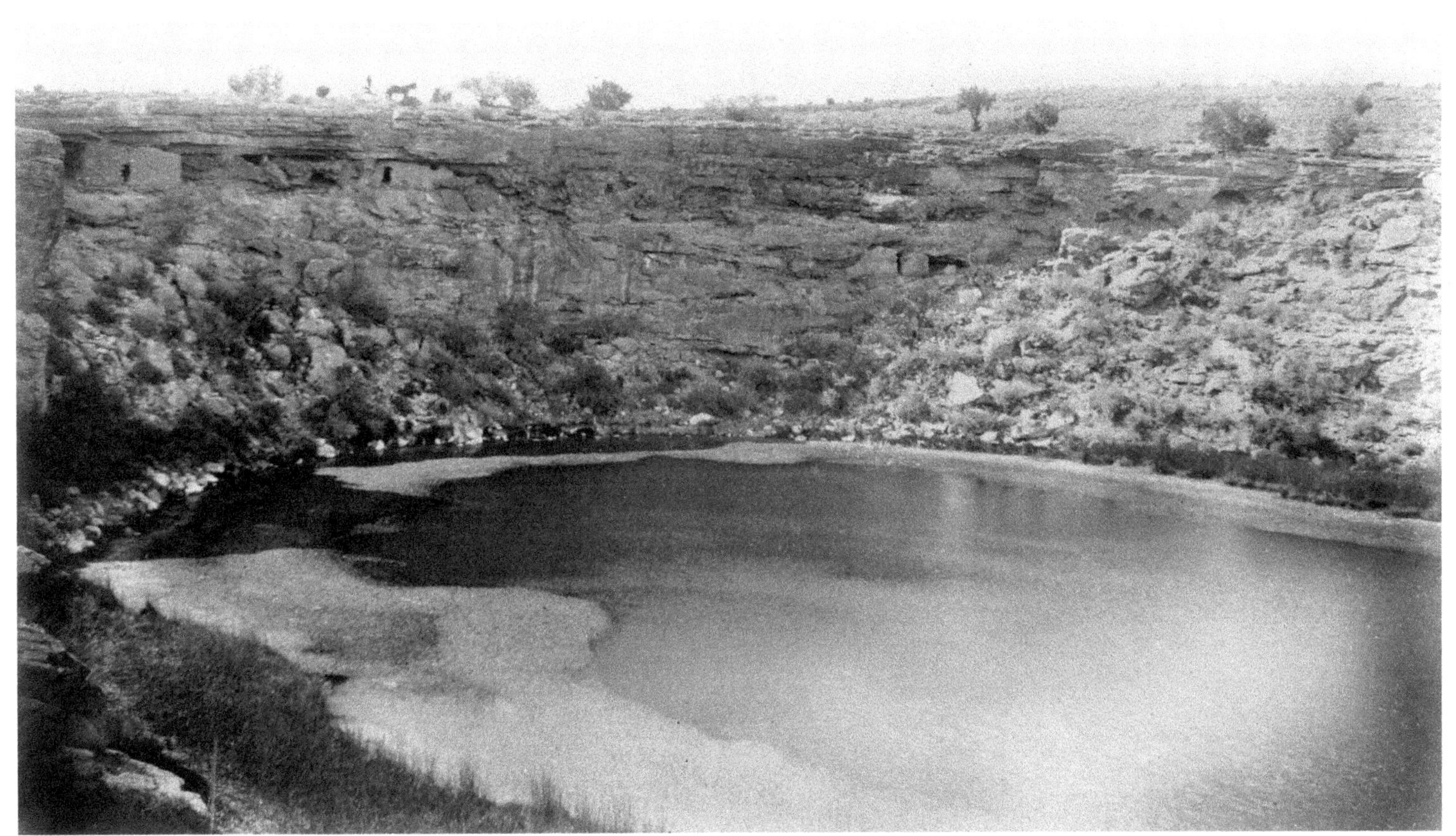

Montezuma Well is a collapsed underground limestone cavern located some 15 miles north of Fort Verde. Each day more than a million gallons of water pass through this high desert sinkhole, which is 368 feet across, 55 feet deep, and home to several unique plant and animal species. Photographed in 1887, the cliff dwellings seen above the water date to the time of the Sinagua people, seven centuries ago.

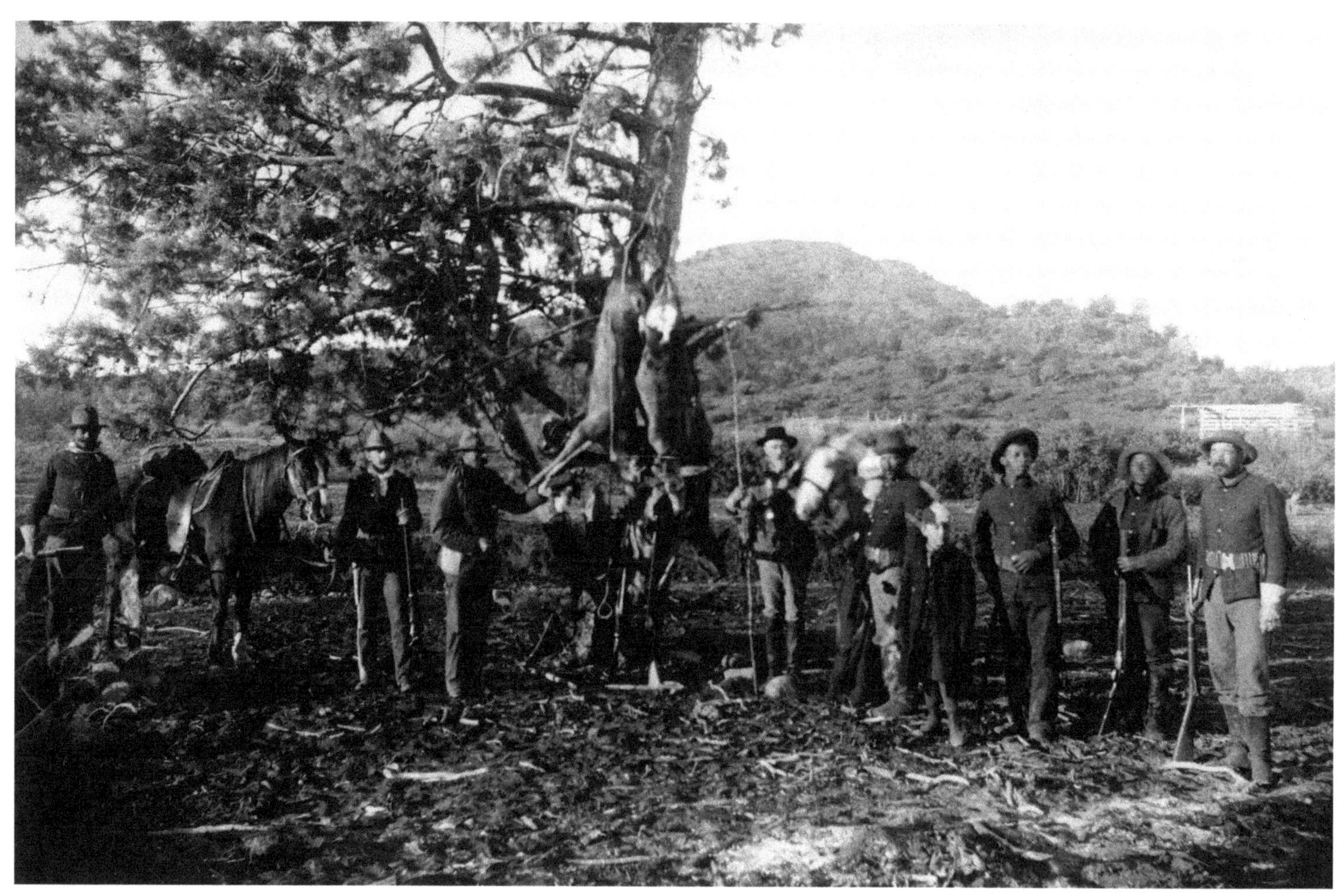

Dr. Edgar Alexander Mearns served his country as a surgeon in the United States Army from 1882 to 1889. Assigned to Fort Verde in 1883, he was also an avid ornithologist, field naturalist, and photographer. In 1887 he photographed this group of Fort Verde soldiers showing off their hunting skills along Oak Creek in central Arizona.

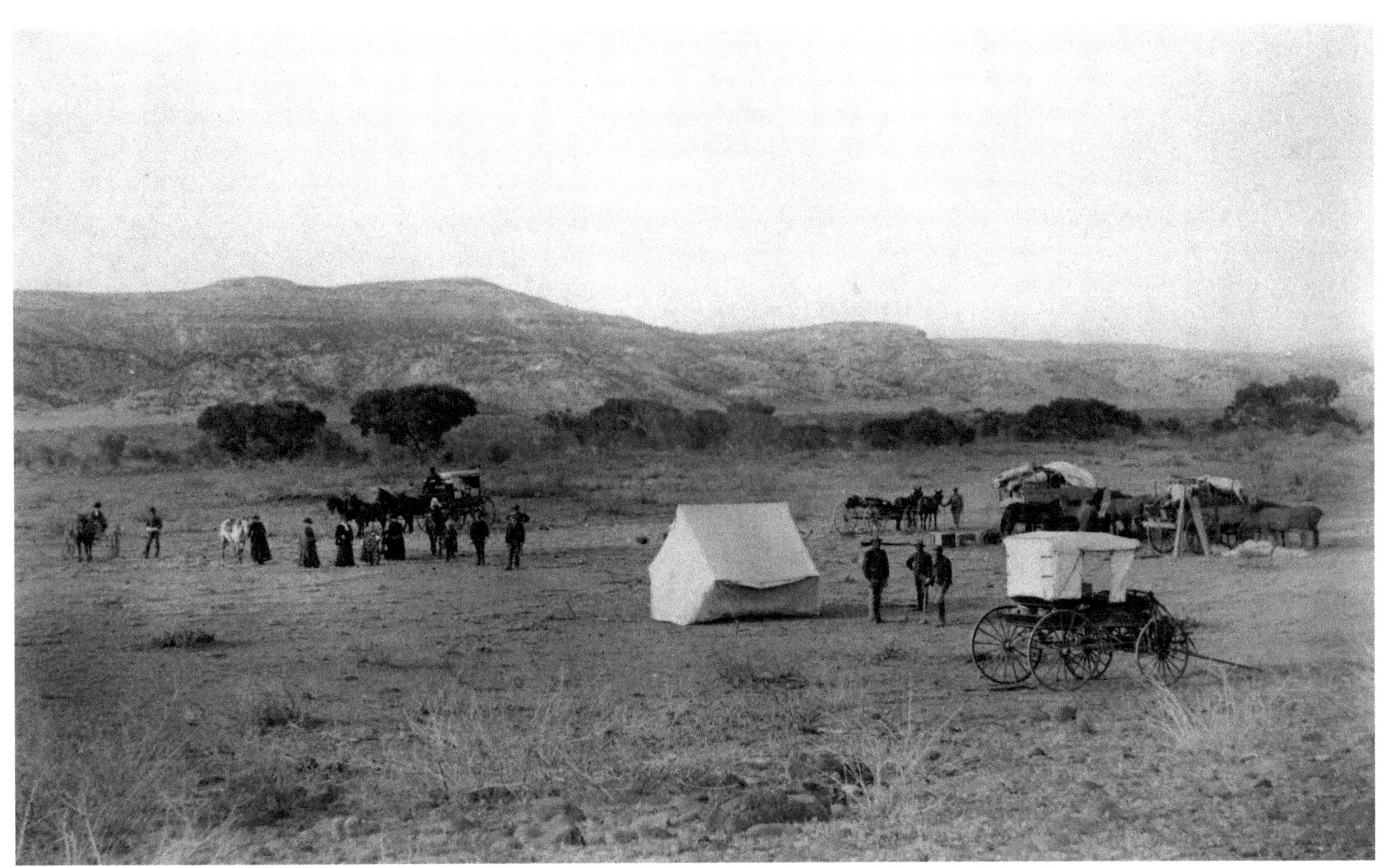

This 1887 photograph taken by Dr. Edgar Mearns shows an overnight bivouac at Clear Creek for a detachment of Fort Verde soldiers traveling the 150 miles to Fort Thomas, which was located in the Gila River Valley in southern Arizona. The commanding officer was Major C. B. McLellan, whose tent is shown here at center.

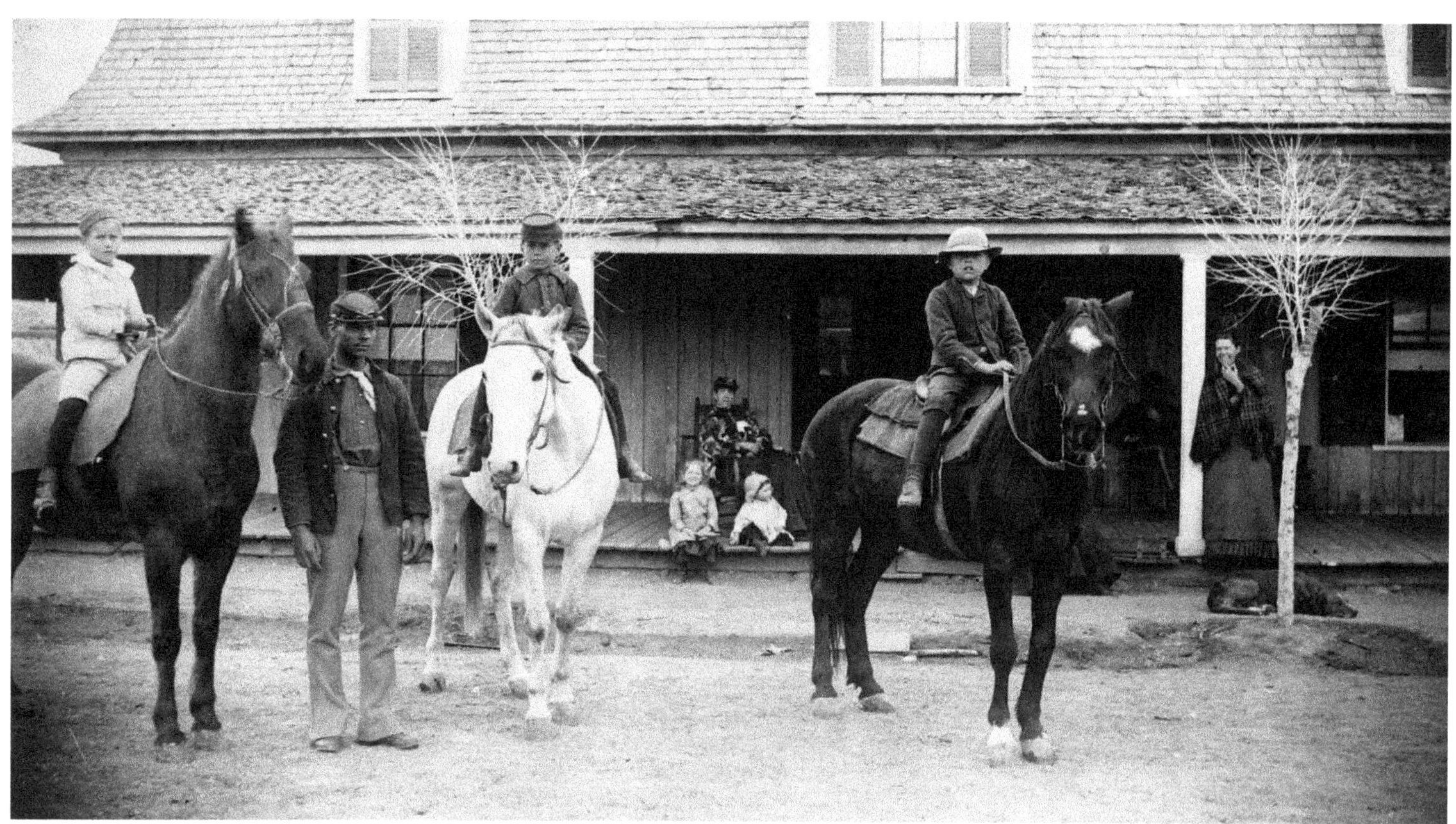

Fort Verde became the headquarters of General George Crook when he took command of the Department of Arizona in 1871 and began a military campaign known as the Indian Wars. Like all nineteenth-century army posts in Arizona, Fort Verde was never enclosed by walls or stockades. In addition, Fort Verde never came under attack by hostiles. In 1887 Dr. Edgar Mearns photographed these three officers' children under the watchful eye of a Buffalo Soldier—the name given by the Indians to the African American troops who served out west after the Civil War.

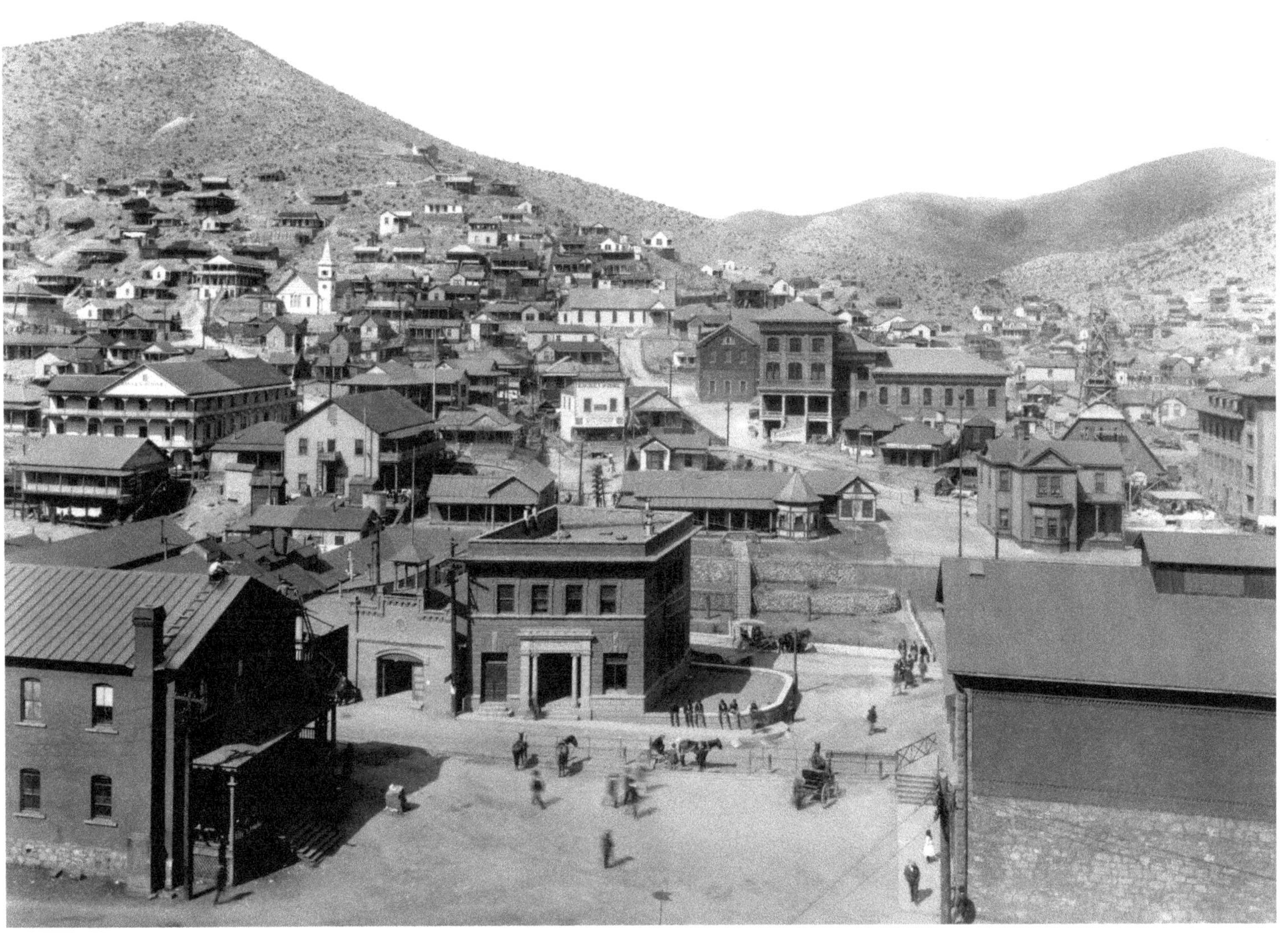

This 1890s photograph shows Bisbee, the "Queen of Arizona's Copper Camps." In 1877, while tracking Apache Indians in the Mule Mountains, army scout John Dunn came upon an outcropping of ore. Because of his army duties, he could not work the claim, so he grubstaked local miner George Warren to work the ore. They named their mine at Bisbee the Copper Queen, and by the early 1900s it was the most productive copper mine in Arizona.

Holbrook readers picked up the first issue of the *Holbrook Times* newspaper on May 17, 1884. Henry Reed, editor of the *Times,* sat for this portrait around 1890.

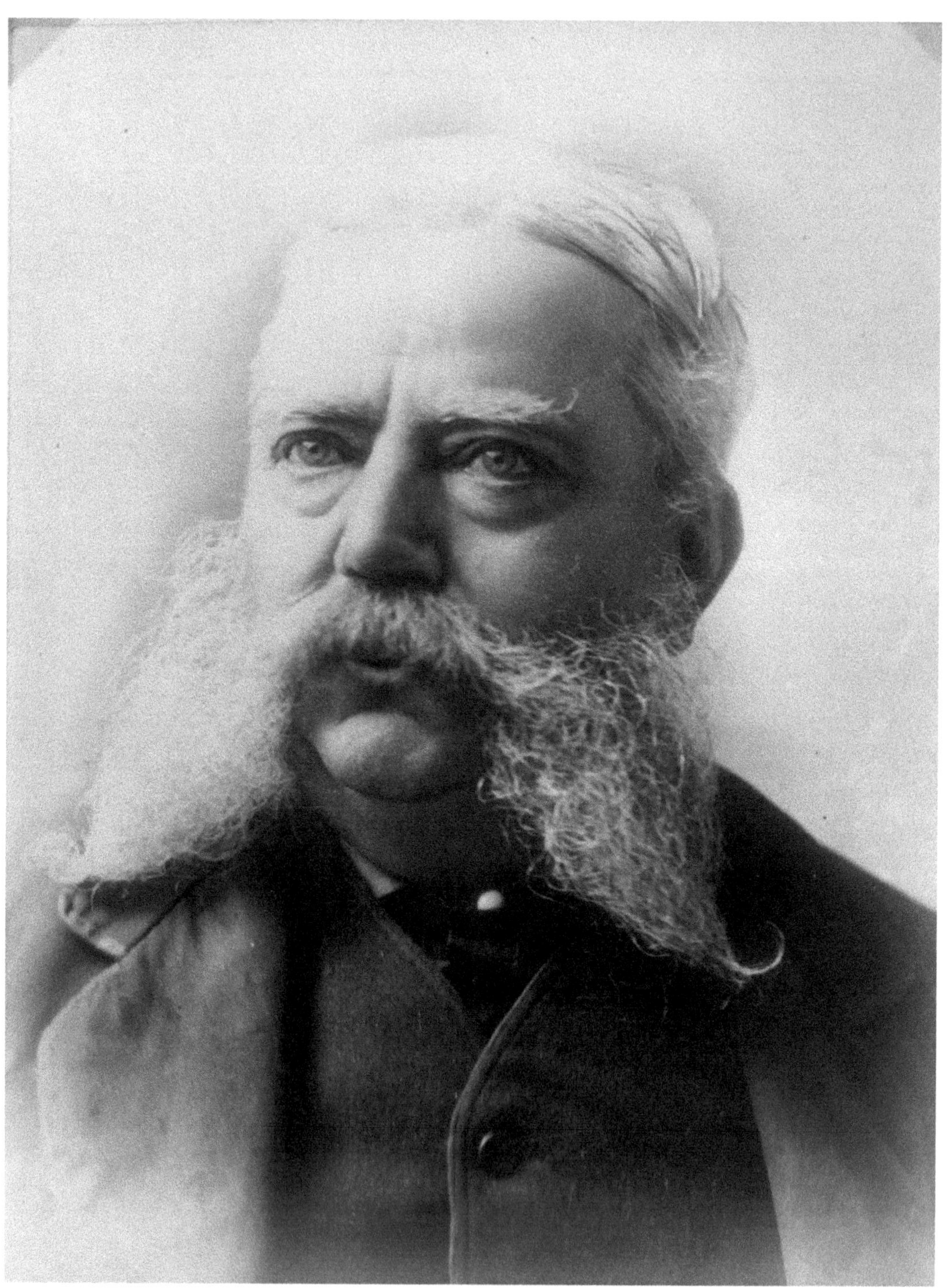

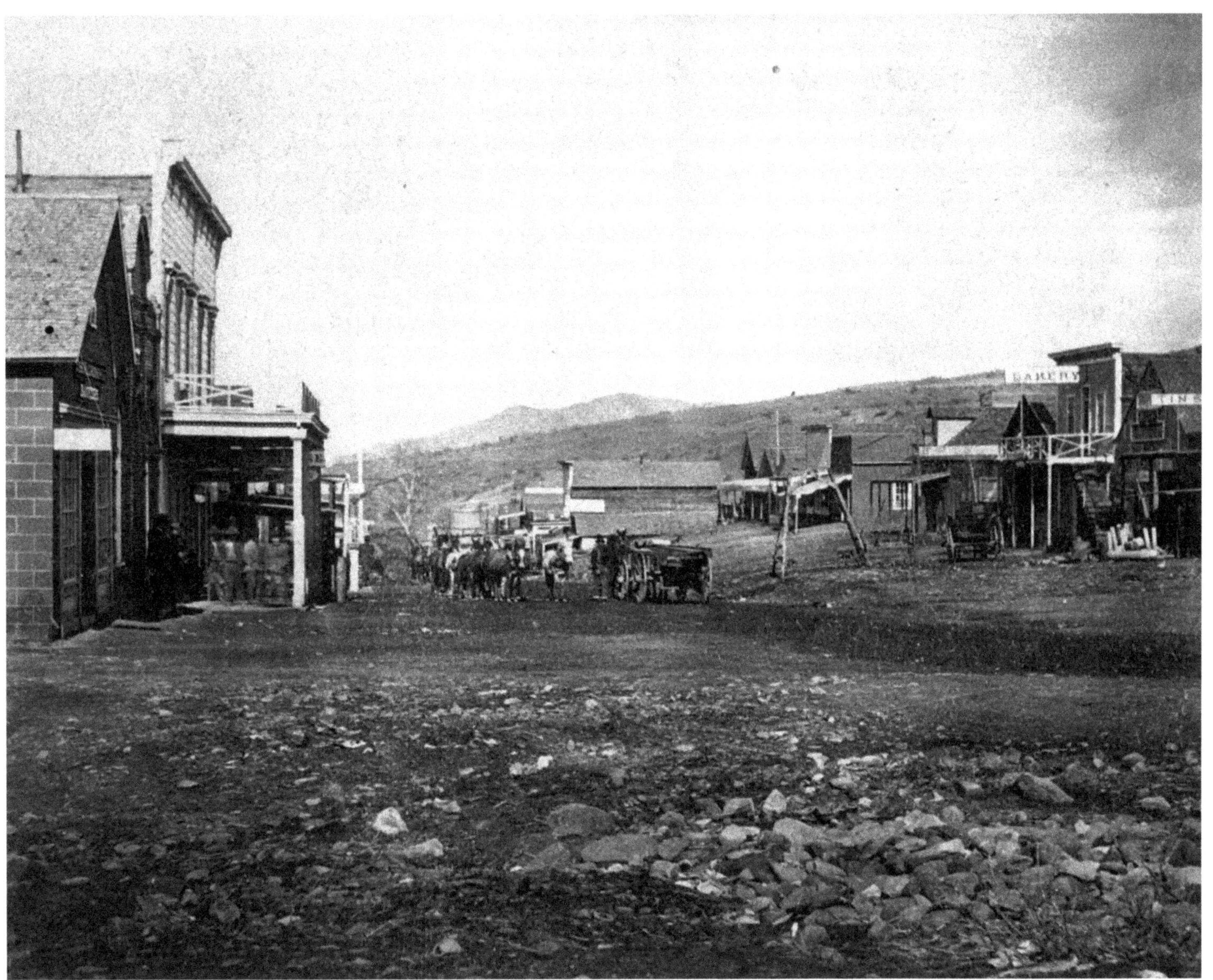

Globe is one of many Arizona towns founded as a result of early prospectors' lust for silver and gold. Legend tells that in the early 1870s two men came upon a boulder of silver so large they announced to the world it "was as big as the globe." By the time of this 1890s view of the town's principal street, Broad Street, copper ore had become king of Globe.

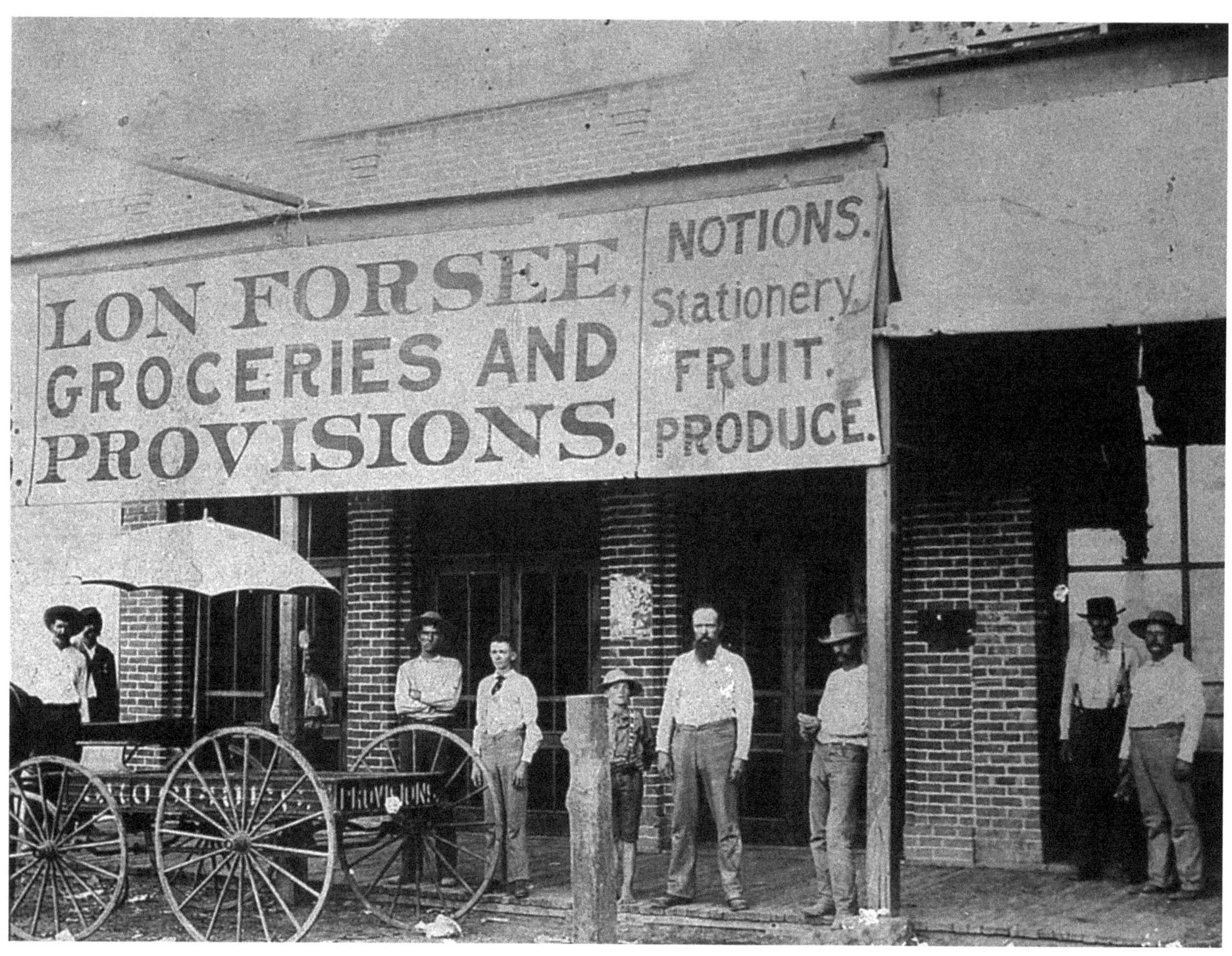

Tempe is located on the south side of the Salt River and in the 1890s was some nine miles east of Phoenix. Tempe received its name because the frontiersman "Lord" Darrell Duppa said its beautiful, riverside location reminded him of the lovely Vale Tempe Thessaly of ancient Greece. Here Tempe residents stand in front of the Lon Forsee Groceries and Provisions store, considered the leading grocery house in the Salt River Valley.

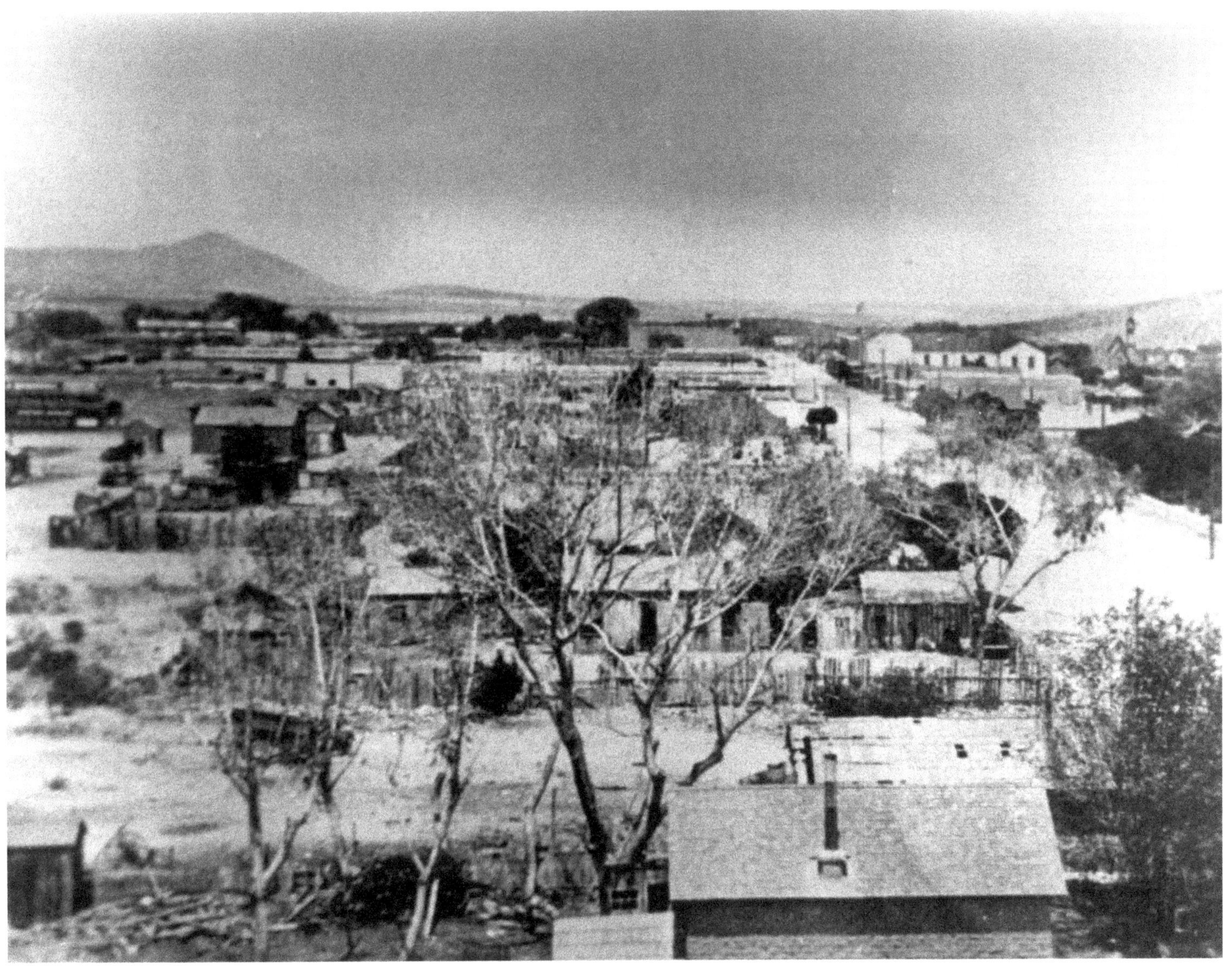

By the late 1880s the mines of Tombstone were reaching a depth of 500 feet. Groundwater began to seep into the mining shafts, completely filling many of them by 1887. As the mines filled with water, the citizens of Tombstone began to leave. This view shows Tombstone in the 1890s, by which time the town's 1881 population of 15,000 had shriveled to less than 1,000.

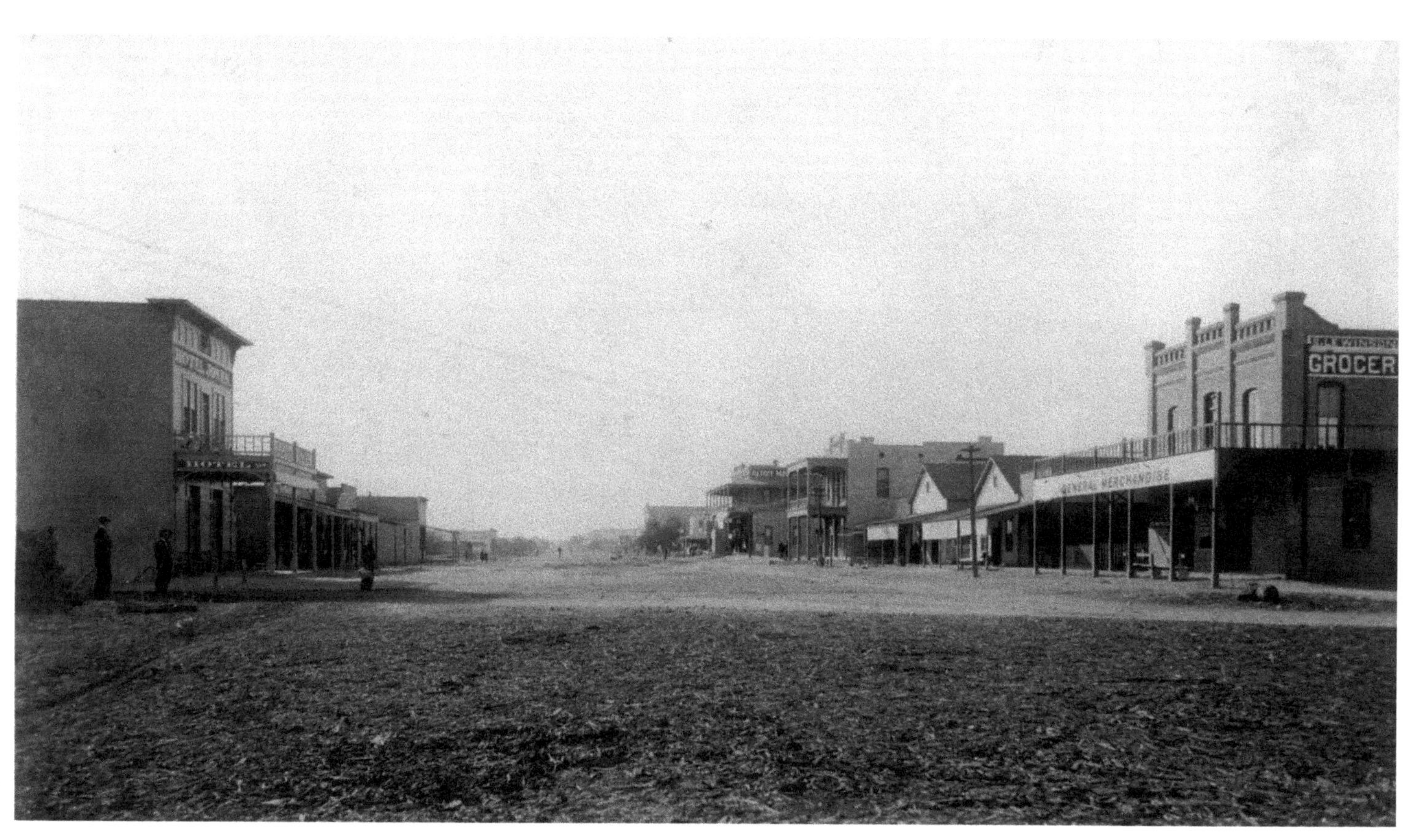

This 1890s view of Main Street in Yuma shows the Hotel Jones and the Lewinson General Merchandise store. Luckily it seldom rained in Yuma—when it did, this 1890s dirt street turned into a quagmire of mud and manure.

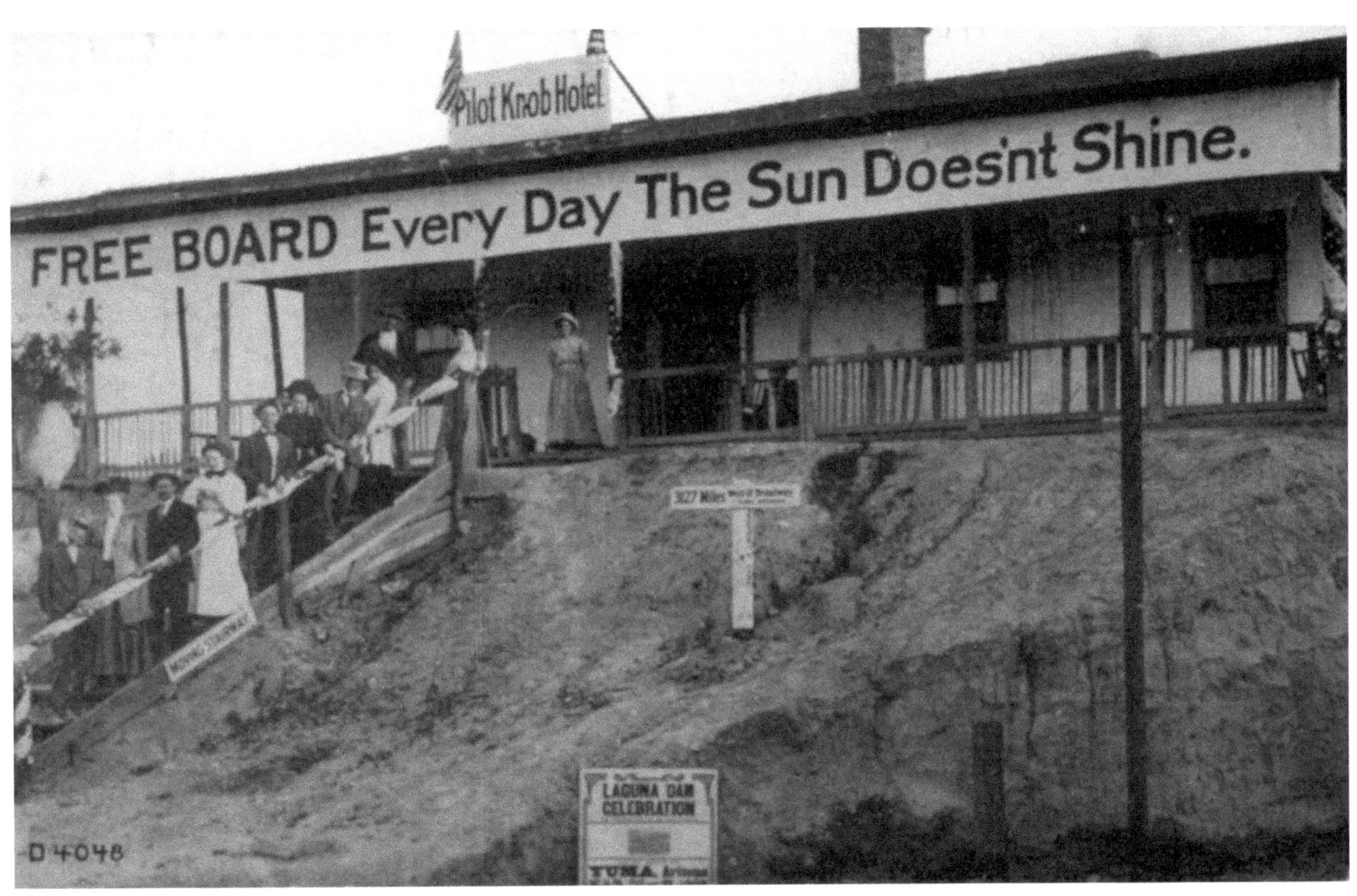

Yuma receives 93 percent of each year's possible 4,400 hours of sunshine, meaning 4,133 hours of solar energy fall upon this Sonoran Desert town annually. This fact was not lost on the owners of Yuma's Pilot Knob Hotel, whose advertising scheme, aimed at visiting easterners, offered free meals to hotel guests any day the sun didn't shine.

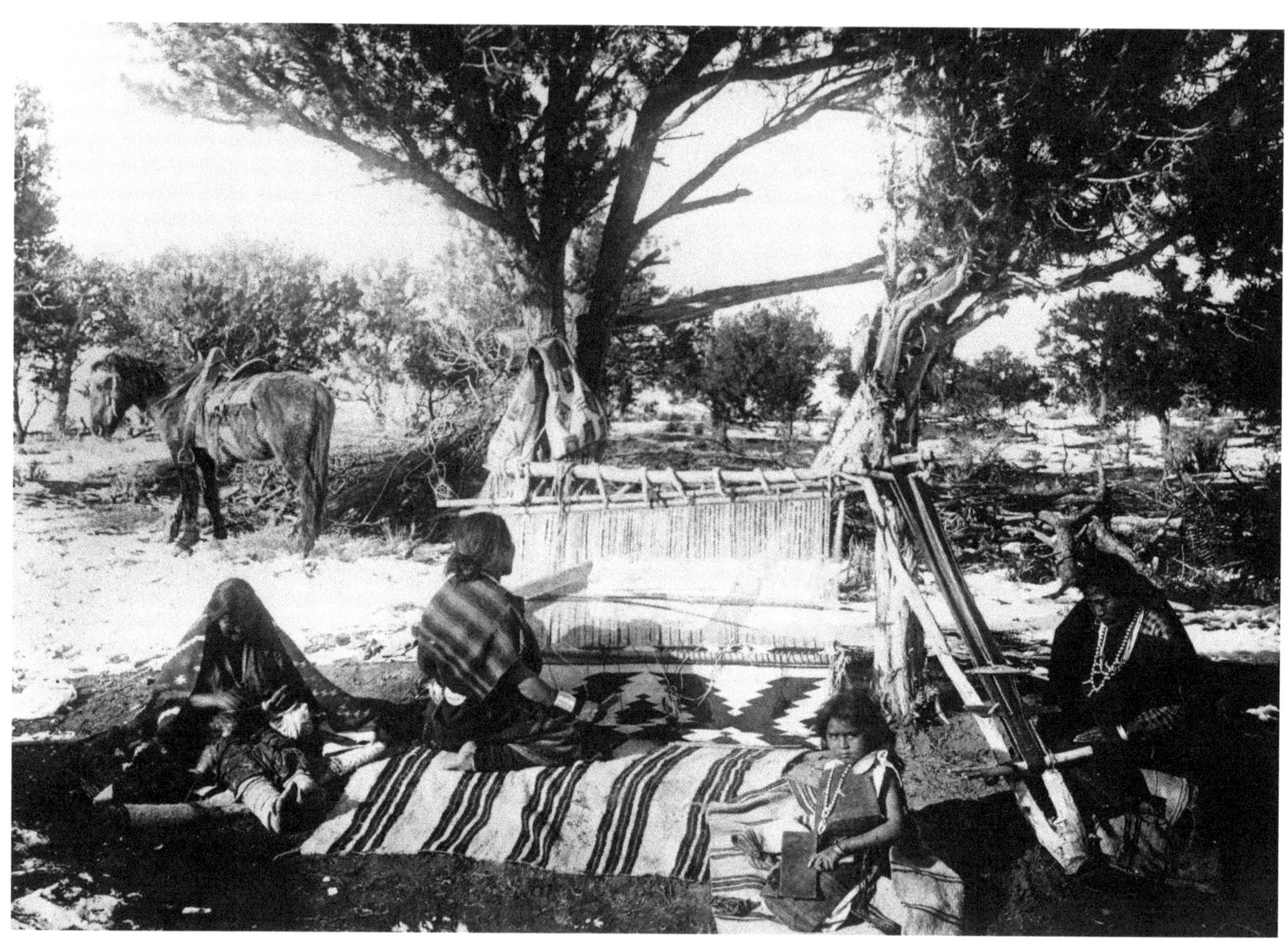

Photographer James Mooney took this picture of Navajo women weaving on a horizontal loom in a camp at Keams Canyon in northeastern Arizona, about 1893. The Navajo, known even then for their beautiful woven wool rugs, were just one of many American Indian tribes that Mooney photographed. He was a self-taught ethnologist who worked for the Smithsonian's Bureau of American Ethnology from 1885 until his death in 1921.

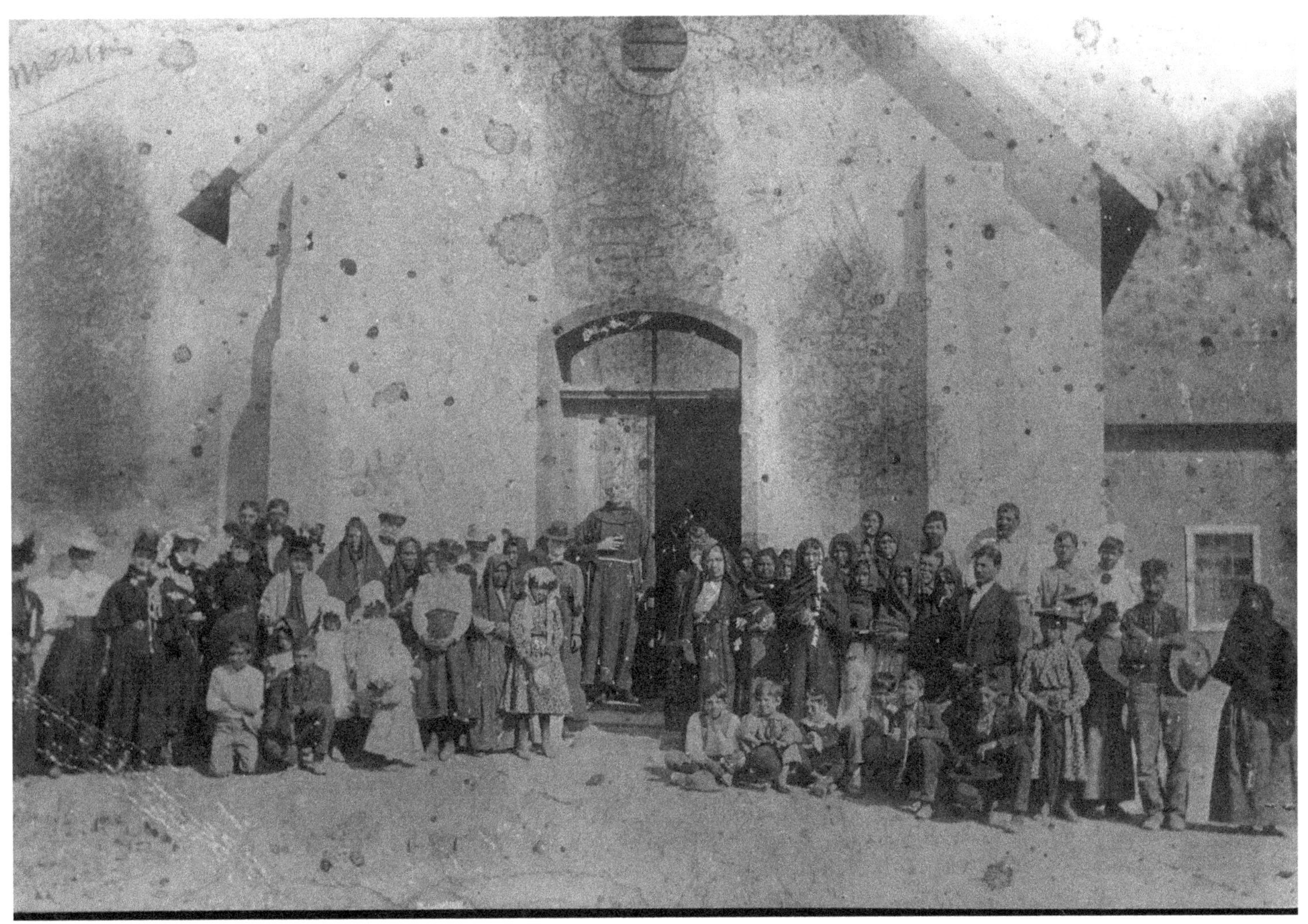

Our Lady of Mount Carmel Catholic Church was an adobe structure built in the 1880s by the Hispanic community of San Pablo in what today would be a part of Tempe. Father Severinus Westhoff, a German priest who had come to serve the people in 1895, stands at center in this view. The little adobe chapel sat by a small mountain that today is the location of Arizona State University's Sun Devil Stadium.

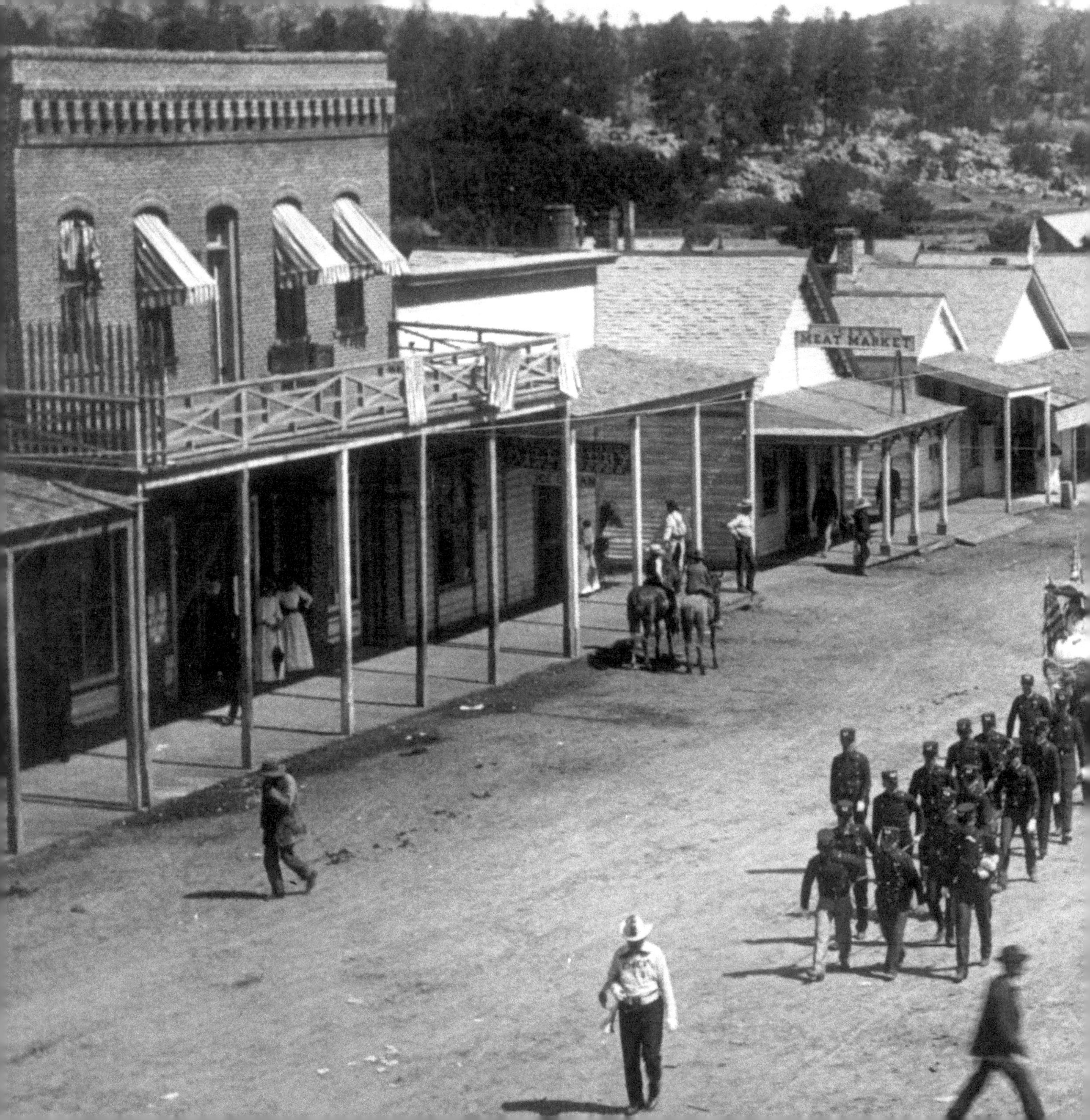
MEAT MARKET

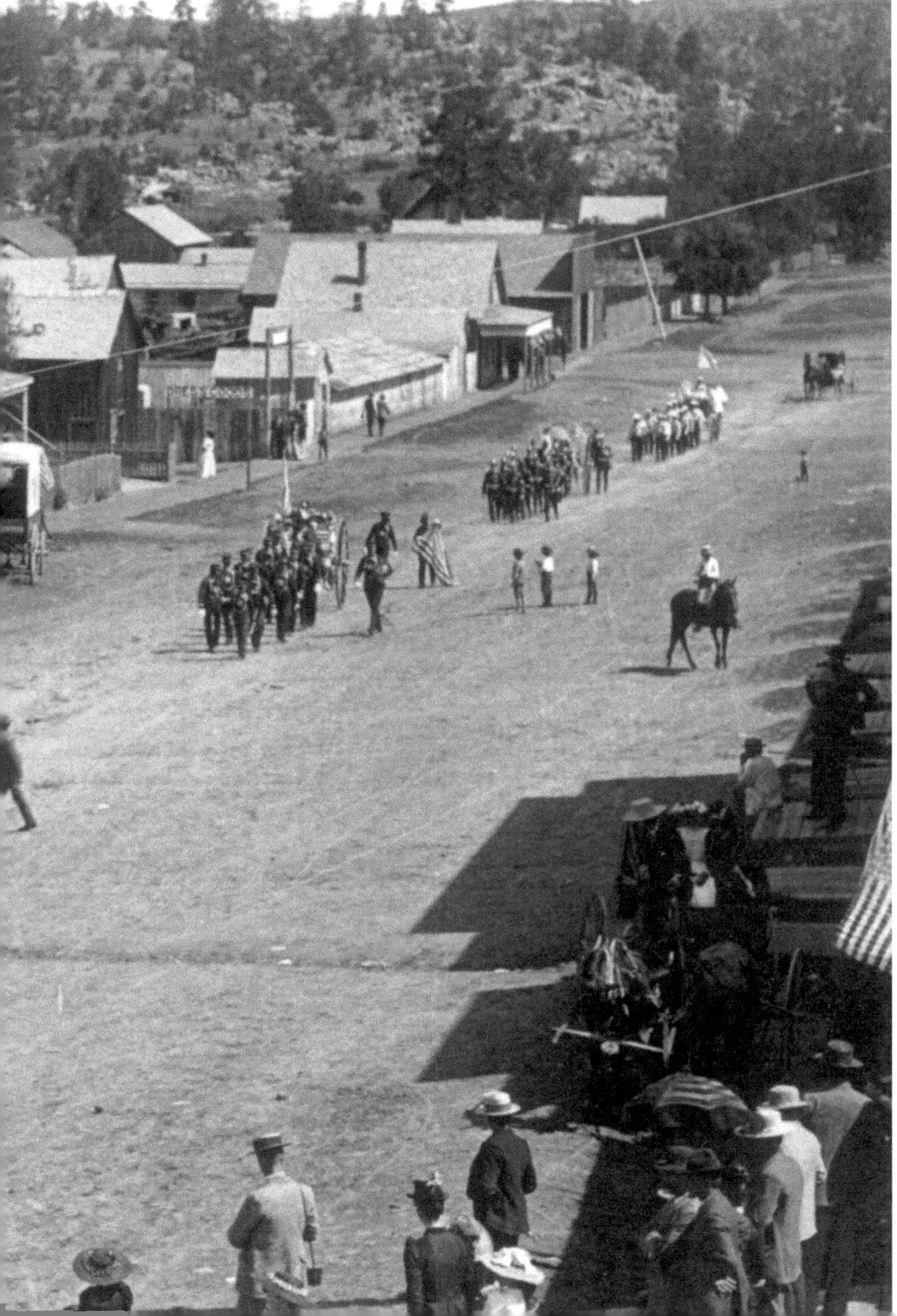

Prescott photographer E. M. Jennings captured this image of a company of Prescott fire fighters marching down Montezuma Street on Independence Day of 1891. Just three years earlier, on July 4, 1888, the birth of professional rodeo in America took place during this annual Prescott celebration. Today, the Prescott Frontier Days Rodeo claims to be the "World's Oldest Rodeo."

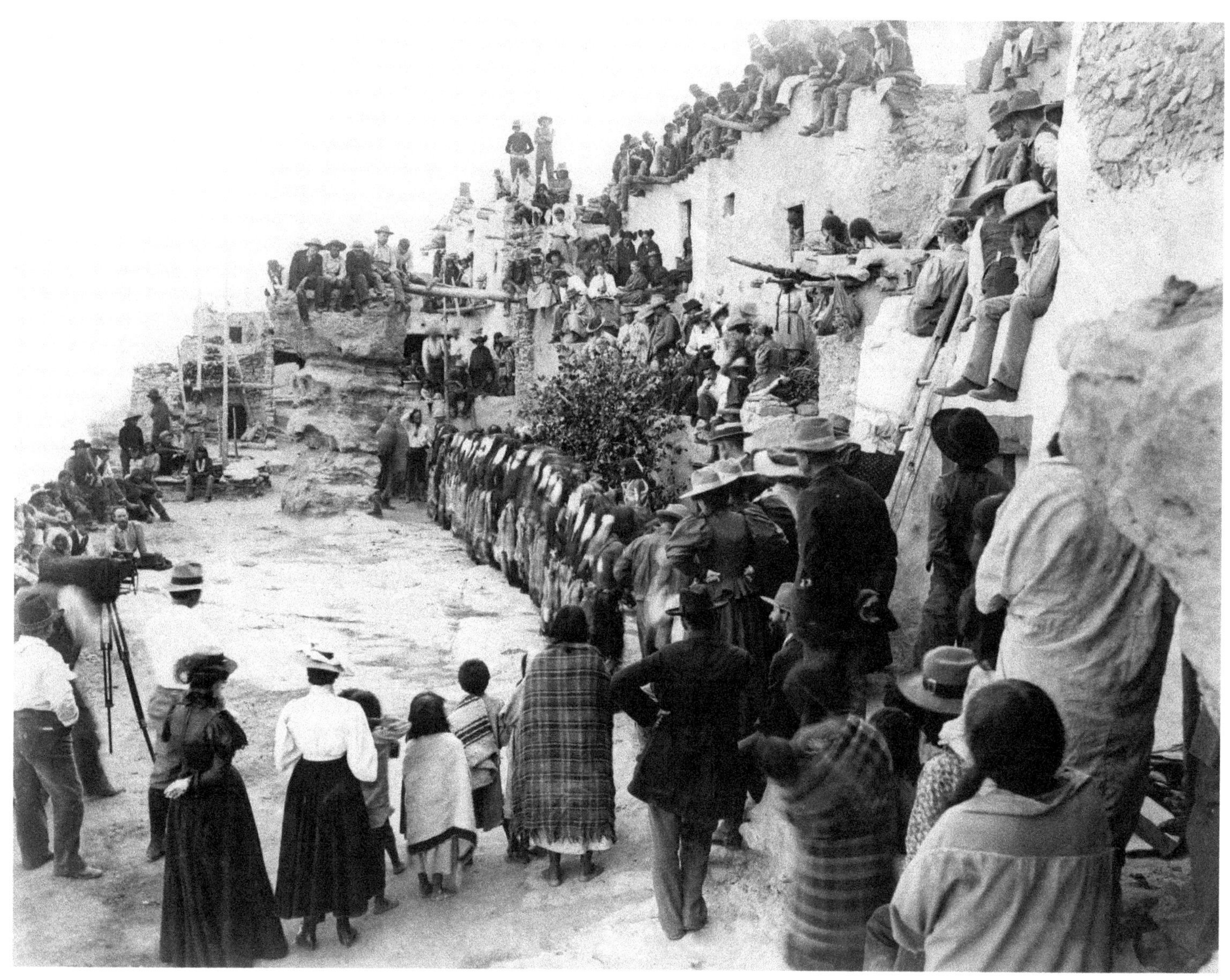

Ben Wittick photographed this snake dance at the Hopi village of Walpi, located on First Mesa, in 1897. Wittick brought his camera to the Wild West in 1878 as an employee of the Atlantic and Pacific Railroad. He traveled tirelessly throughout the Southwest, photographing the land, the railroad, and the American Indian people. Wittick died in 1903 after being bitten by a rattlesnake.

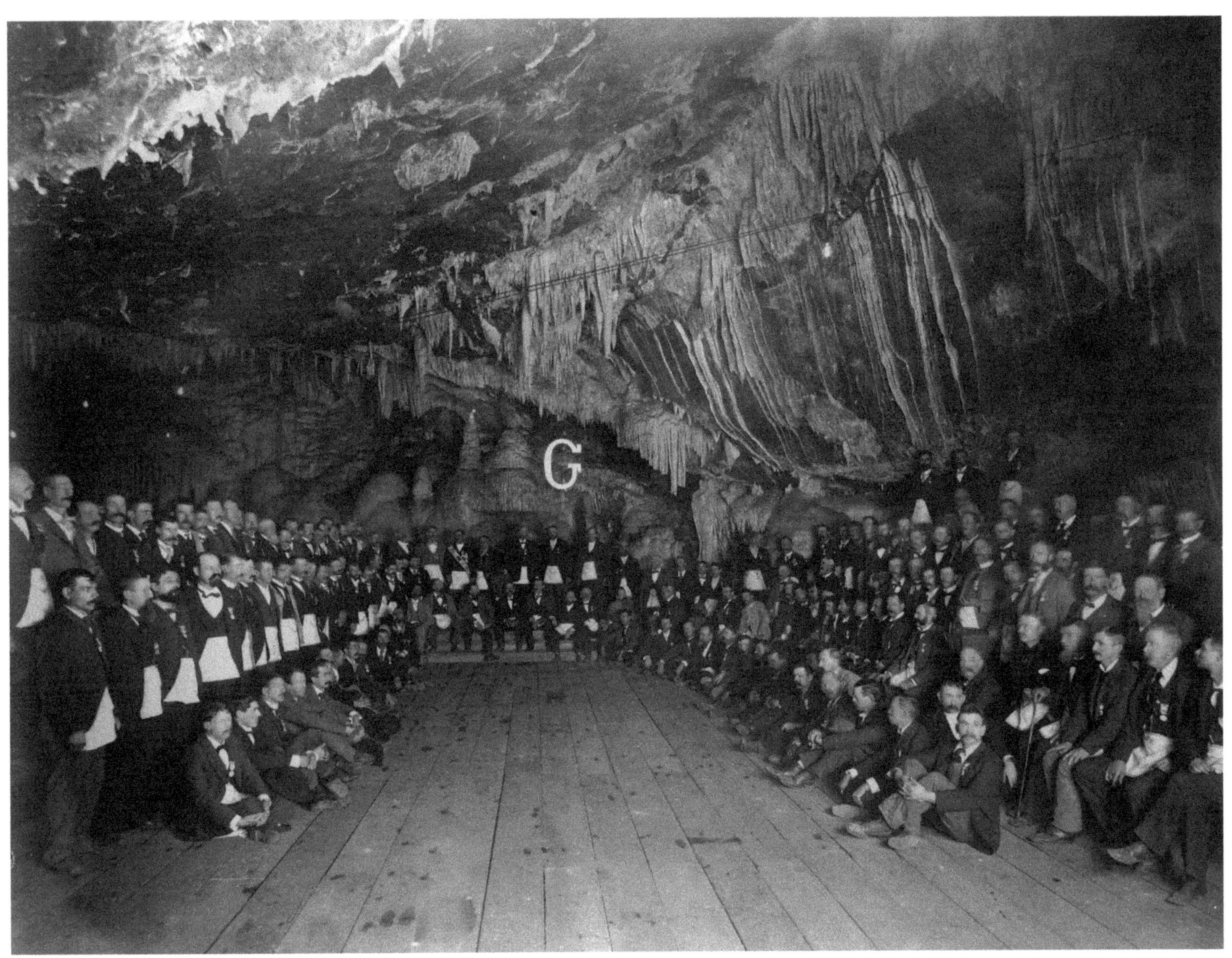

Freemasons played important roles in the settlement and development of most Arizona frontier towns. Here the men of the Grand Lodge of Arizona meet in a cave of the Copper Queen Mine of Bisbee on November 12, 1897. A wooden plank floor has been laid inside the cave, and the Masonic symbol G appears to be suspended from the cave's ceiling.

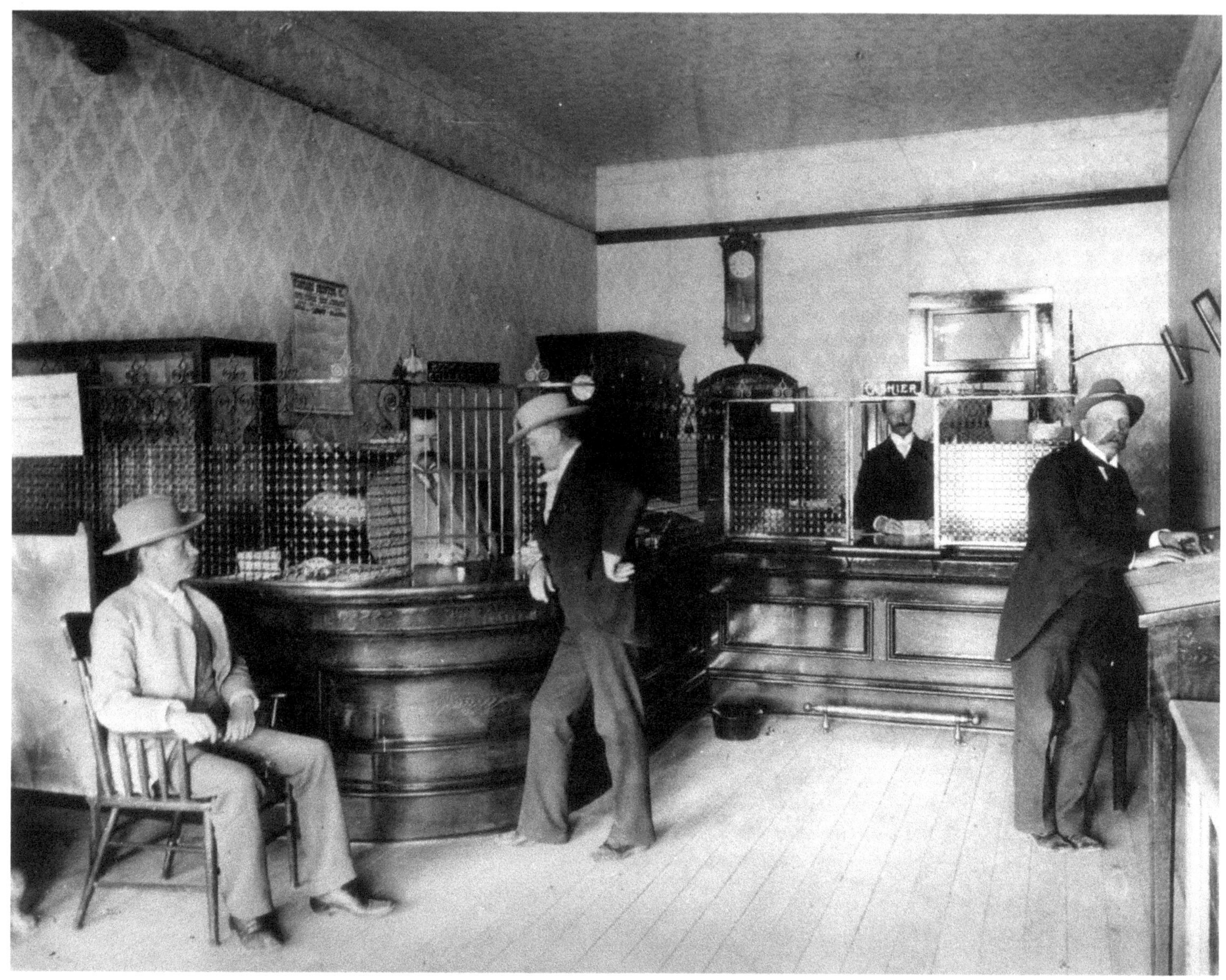

William "Buckey" O'Neill (center) and two friends pose inside the Prescott Bank of Arizona in 1897. O'Neill was a larger-than-life politician, lawman, miner, and writer. When the Spanish-American War began, he became the first man from Prescott to volunteer as one of Teddy Roosevelt's Rough Riders. O'Neill was killed at the Battle of Kettle Hill, Cuba, on July 1, 1898.

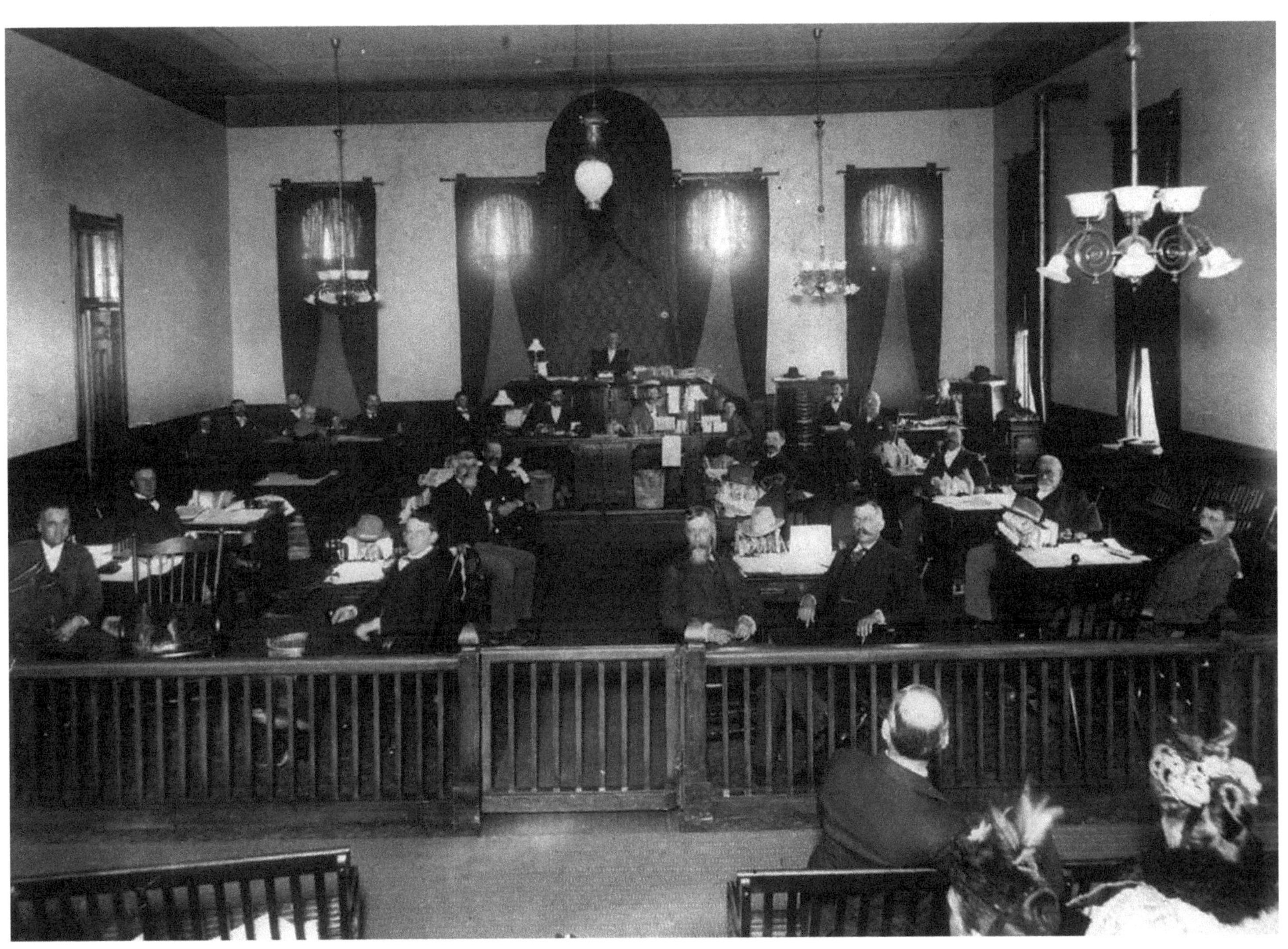

When most of present-day Arizona became a part of the United States in 1848, it did so as a segment of the Territory of New Mexico. It wasn't until February 24, 1863, that President Abraham Lincoln signed the bill creating the Territory of Arizona. This photograph shows Arizona's 19th territorial legislature in session in Phoenix in 1897.

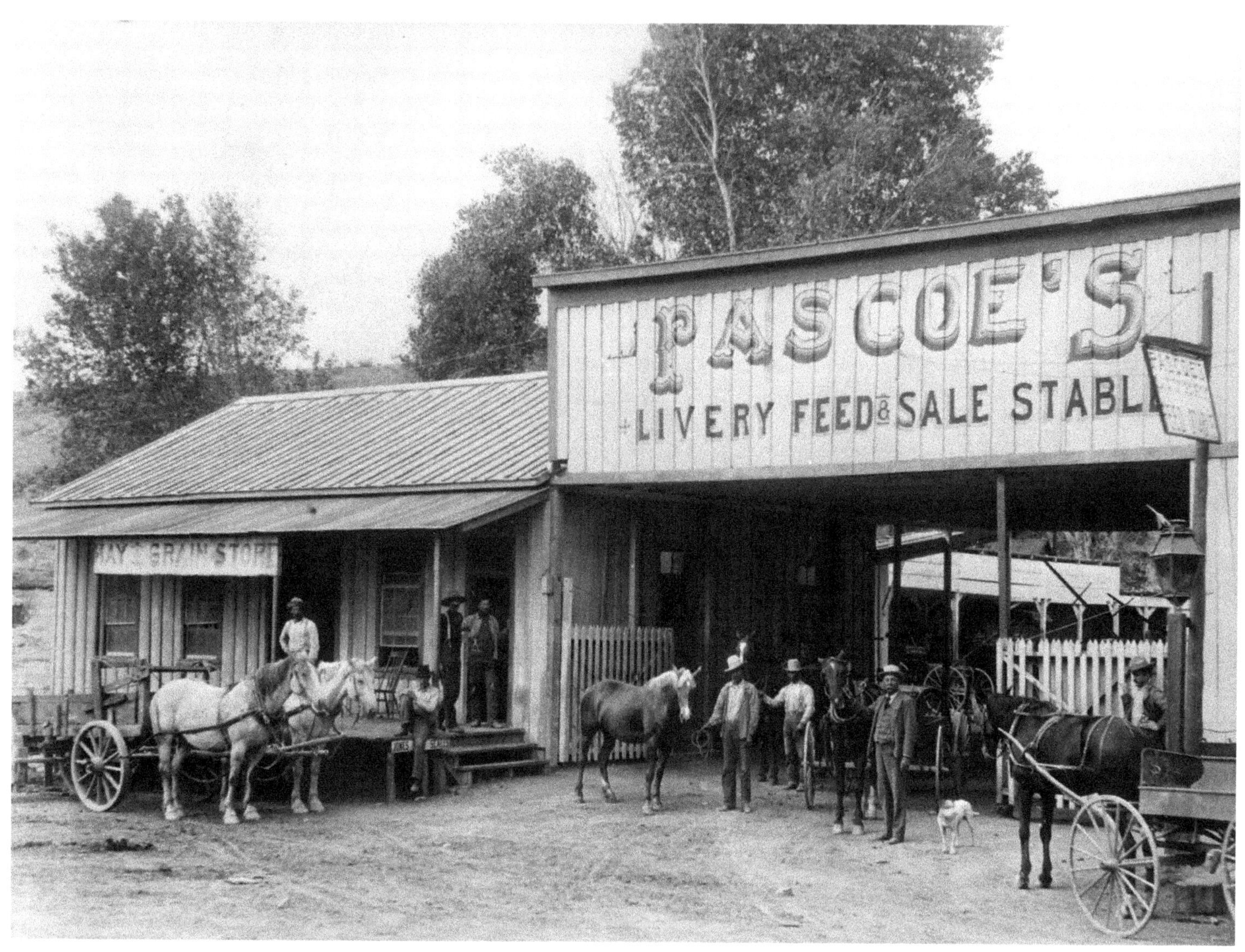

Thomas A. Pascoe came to Globe in 1886 and began a hay and grain business. His enterprise thrived, as suggested by this 1898 photo, but he sold the store in 1899 to his brother. With two other men from Globe, Thomas also developed the town's first water reservoir, which held 140,000 gallons of spring-feed water.

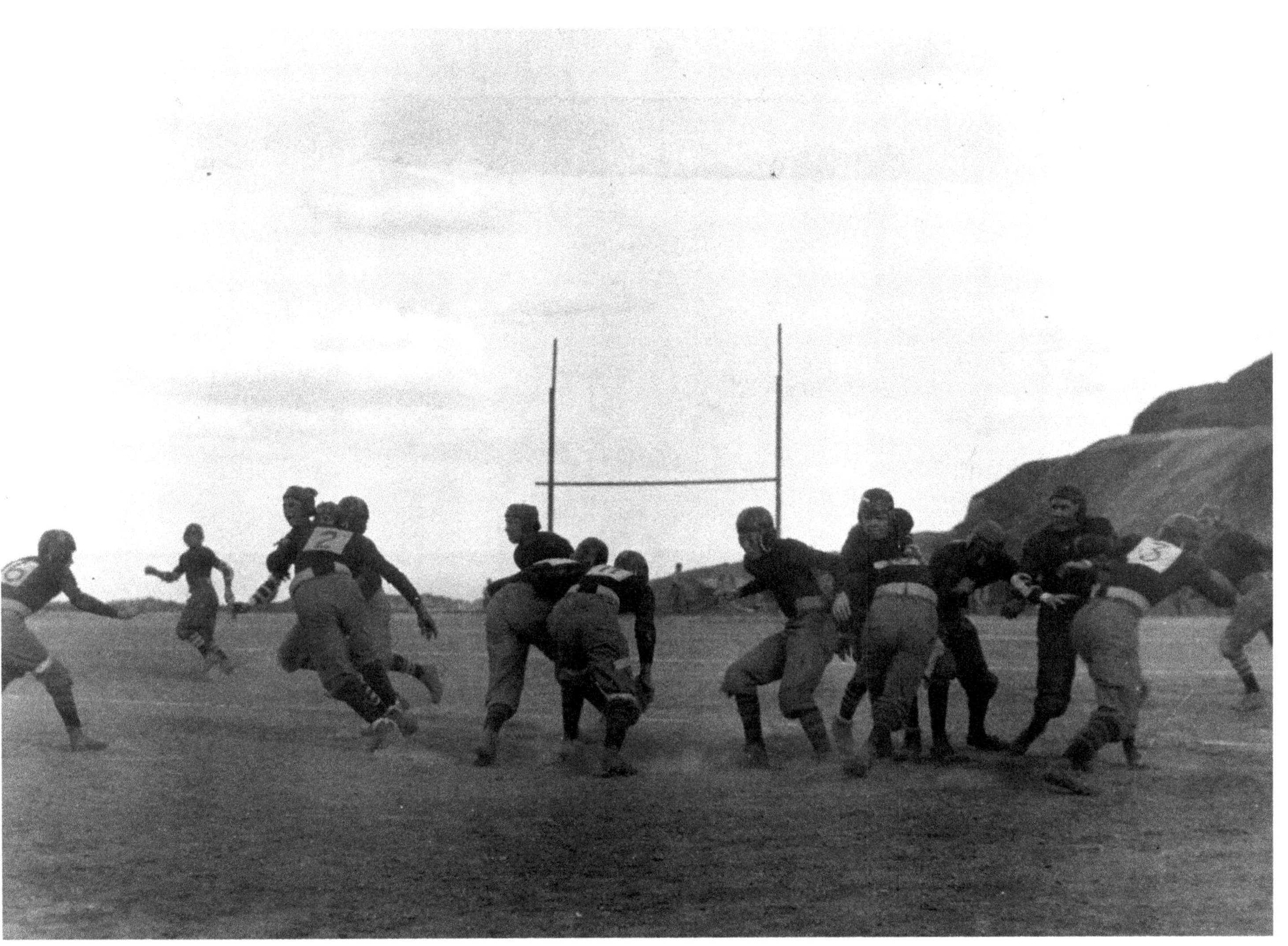

The Jerome High School football team takes on an opponent in 1899. The town of Jerome was established on the side of Cleopatra Hill in 1883 when copper was discovered. All the characters of the Wild West rushed to this Arizona boomtown. In 1903 Jerome was nicknamed the "wickedest town in the West."

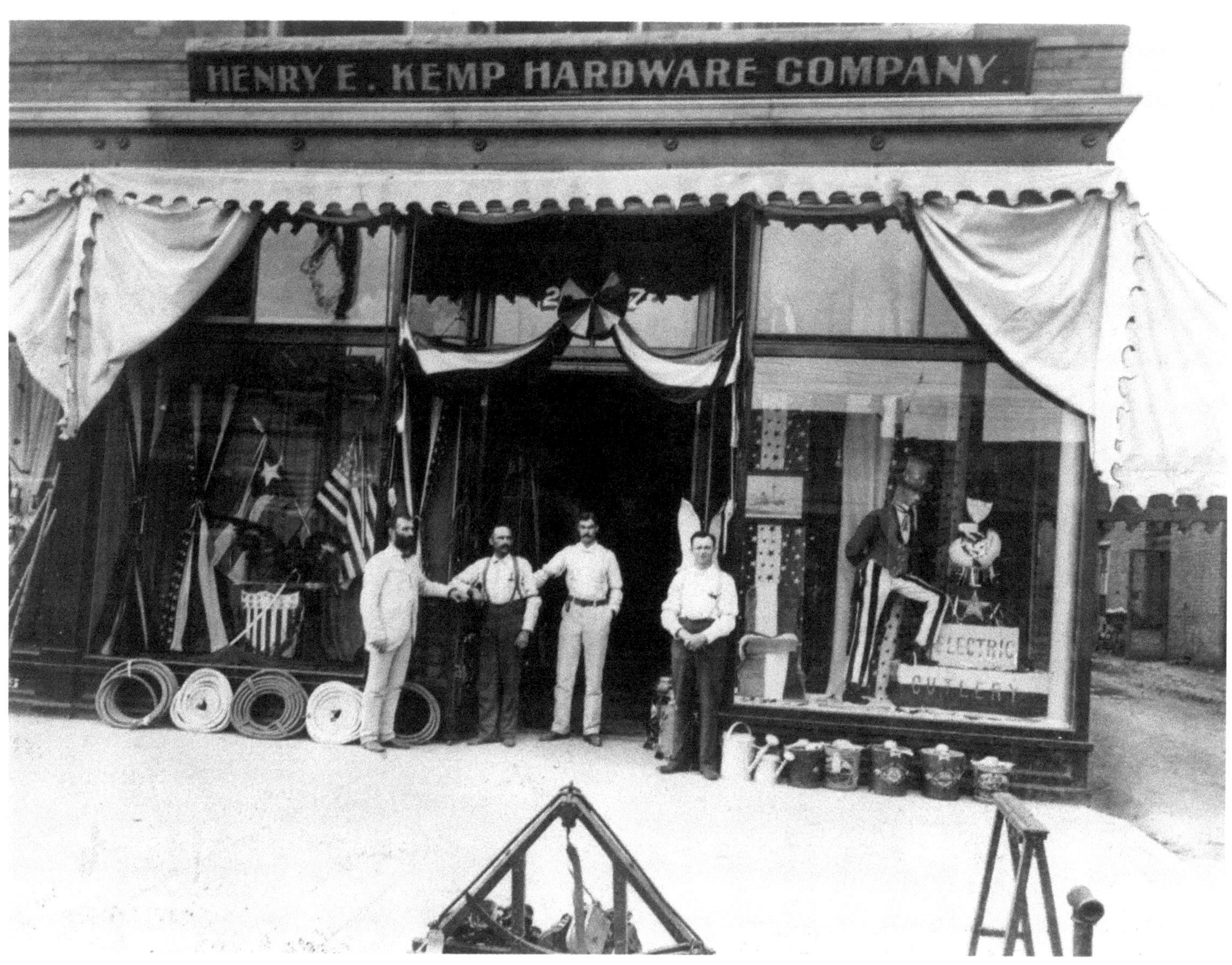

In 1899 Phoenix was a rapidly growing farming community on the banks of the Salt River, a new territorial capitol was being constructed 12 blocks west of downtown, and the Henry E. Kemp Hardware Company was stocked with the latest merchandise. The Kemp store awning would be opened to help provide welcome shade during the hot Arizona summers.

Statehood and Change

(1900–1919)

Arizonans in 1900 had one dominant topic on their minds: statehood. When the territory was authorized to hold a constitutional convention in 1910, a two-year struggle to become the 48th state of the United States of America began.

Water, either too much or too little, was also a major topic of conversation, especially for citizens living in the Salt River Valley. The Newlands Reclamation Act of 1902 opened the door for federal money to be provided to construct great dams on the rivers of the West, and Arizonans jumped at the chance. They pooled their land as collateral, secured a loan, and built Roosevelt Dam, completed in 1911.

It is said that Arizona was born of copper, and copper was surely king during this time. Great copper mines like the United Verde, Copper Queen, and Old Dominion produced 24 hours a day, 365 days a year in Arizona to meet demand as the electricity industry expanded worldwide.

This was also a time when well-known towns and people were just getting started in Arizona. A young woman named Sedona Miller Schnebly lent her first name to a settlement in the beautiful red-rock country north of Phoenix. Two brothers named Riordan married two sisters and built them identical houses so there would be no family conflicts. Two miles up the road from them, Percival Lowell gazed into the universe through his telescope atop Mars Hill. The brothers, their wives, and the astronomer all lived in a place called Flagstaff.

In partnership with the Atchison, Topeka and Santa Fe Railroad since 1876, Fred Harvey continued to build his Harvey House eating and rooming establishments along the rails of northern Arizona. Many of the Harvey Girls who came west to work in those Harvey Houses became the wives and mothers in northern Arizona families. During this time, a Mexican revolutionary named Pancho Villa had the whole state upset that he might raid the border towns or even blow up the new Roosevelt Dam.

This was Arizona at the beginning of the twentieth century, a time of growth and change.

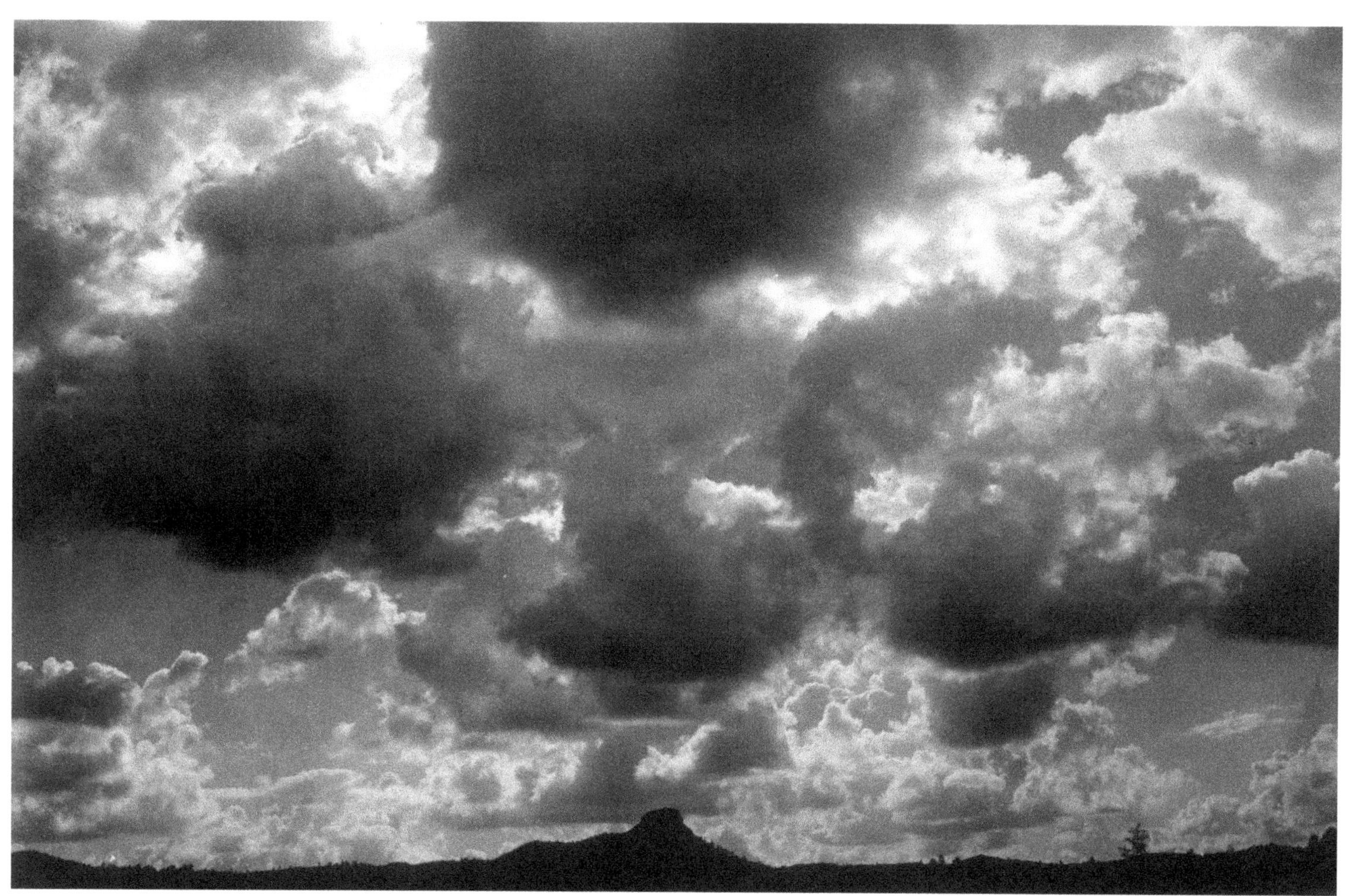

Arizona's rugged, varied landscape has always been a photographer's paradise. From the beautiful Sonoran Desert of the south, to the large ponderosa pine forest of the Mogollon Rim, to the stark beauty of the Colorado Plateau, Arizona has all manner of views to attract the camera's lens. This turn-of-the-century photo shows a cloudy sky above Thumb Butte, just west of downtown Prescott.

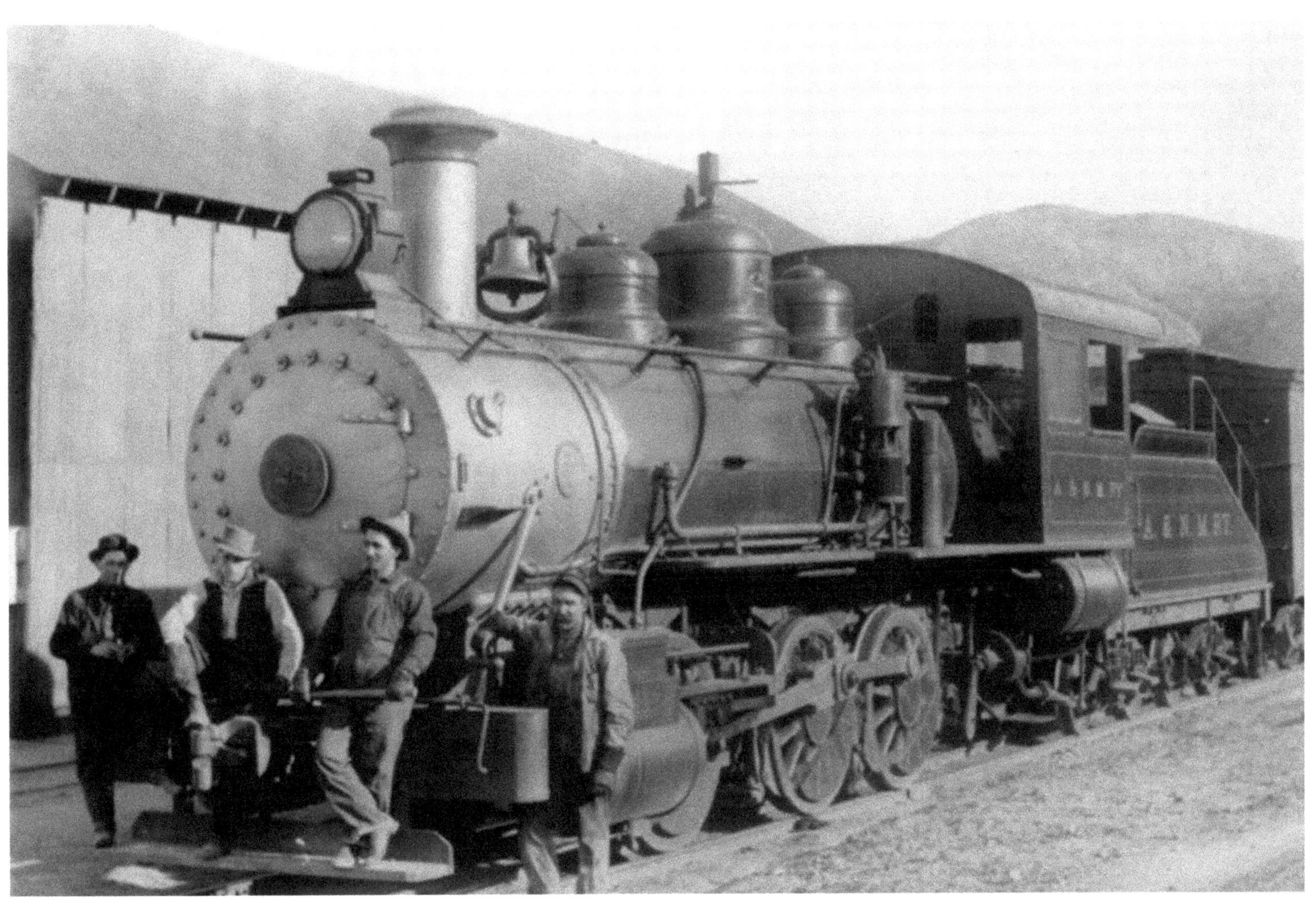

The railroad played a key role in the copper mining industry of Arizona. Railroad spurs were built to the mining camps to bring copper ore from the mines to the main, east-west railroad lines. This steam locomotive was used to transport copper ore from the mines in Clifton.

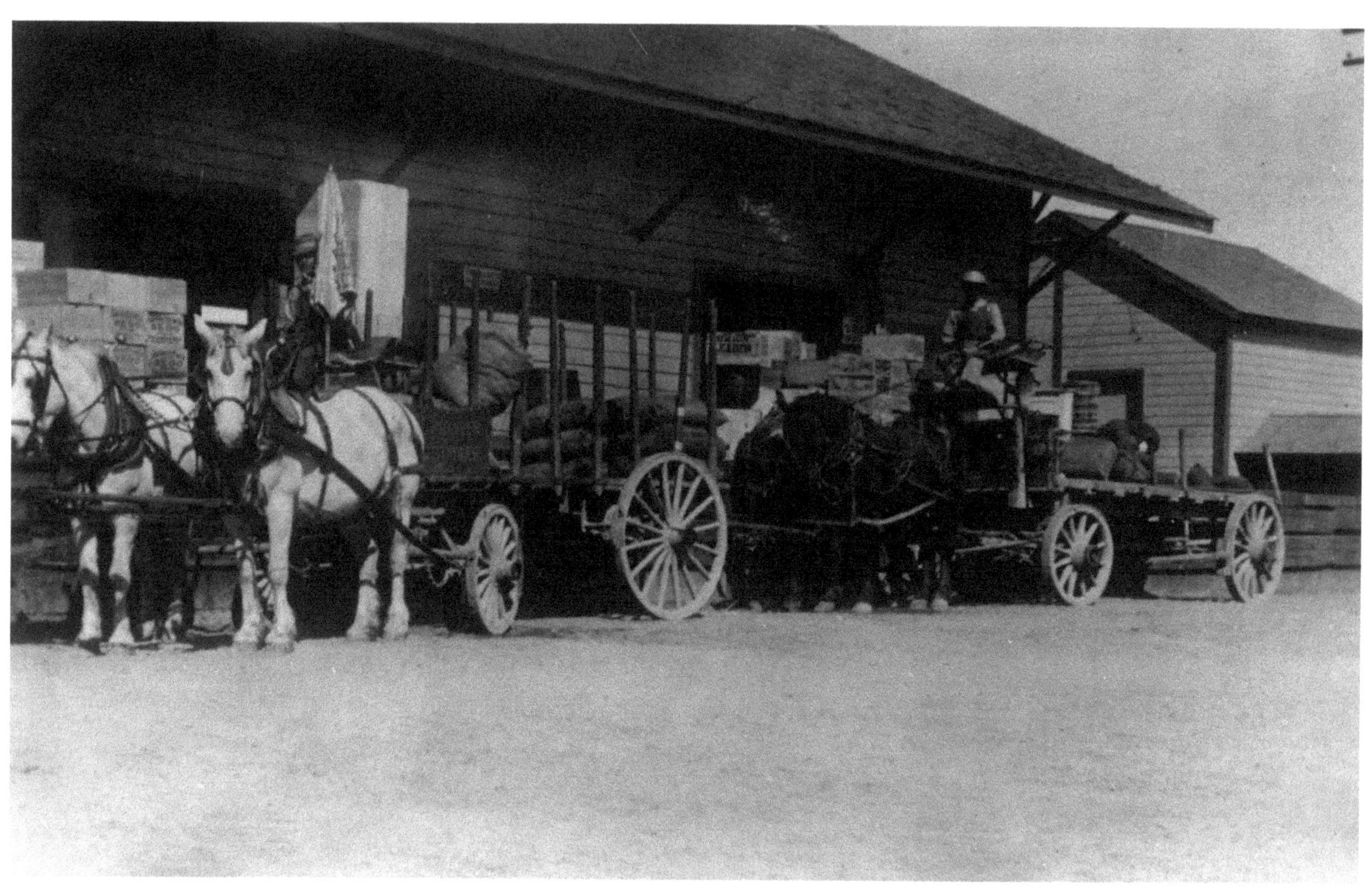

A pair of wagons carry provisions, probably in Gila Bend. The town takes its name from the nearly 90-degree turn the Gila River makes near the town site. When the railroad came through this desert region in 1880, the nearby water supply proved ideal for use by the steam locomotives. The water served other purposes, too—the boxes lining the wall at left in this image appear to contain Sego evaporated milk.

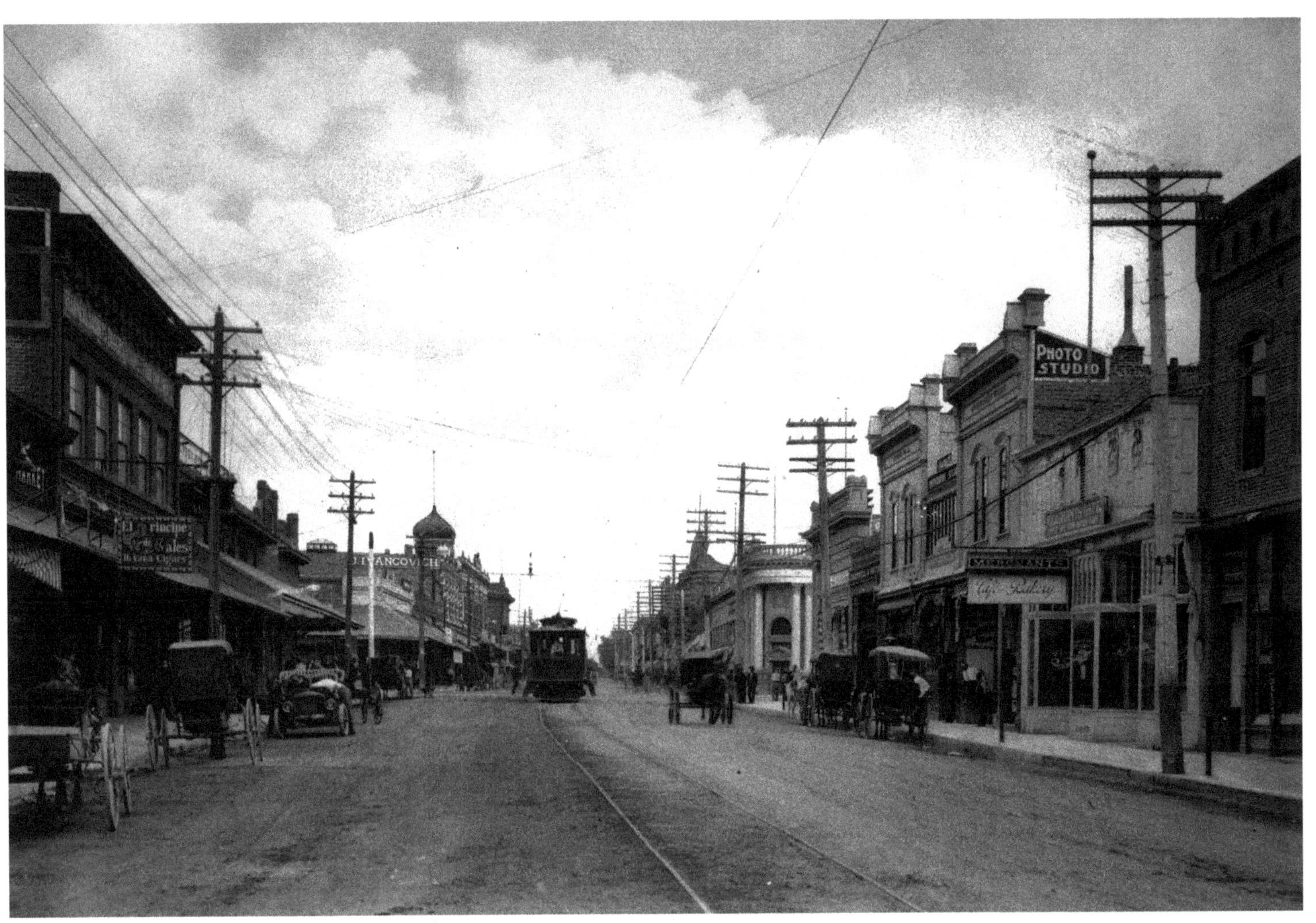

On November 19, 1897, the first horse-drawn streetcar began operating on the streets of Tucson. It cost a nickel to ride. In this early 1900s photo, a streetcar shares the Tucson road with the town's first automobiles. By 1906 the horse-drawn streetcar had given way to the modern electric trolley.

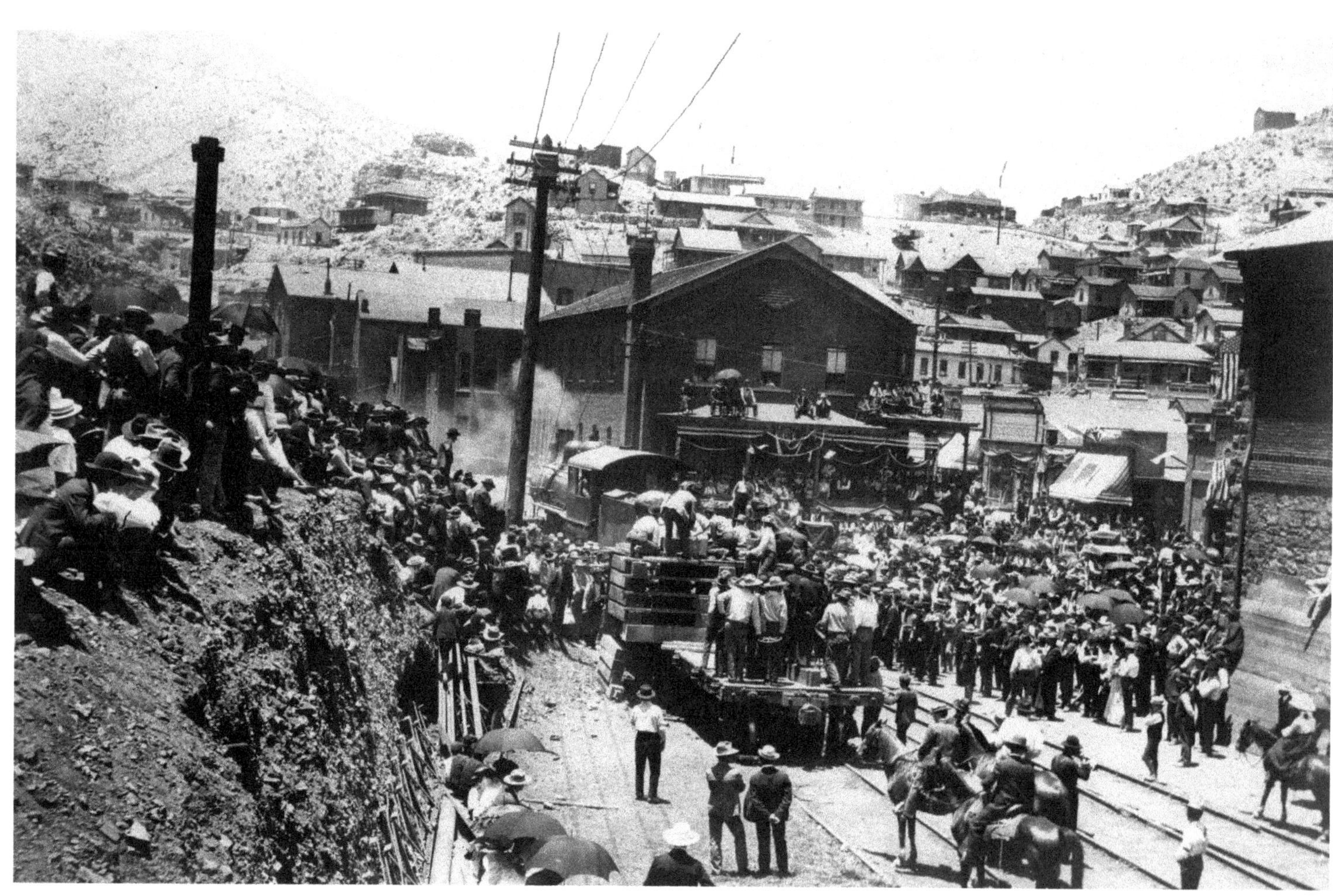

Workers from the Copper Queen mine at Bisbee gather to view a newly arriving ore shovel. Large steam-powered shovels like this one quickly changed how ore was dug from the Arizona copper mines.

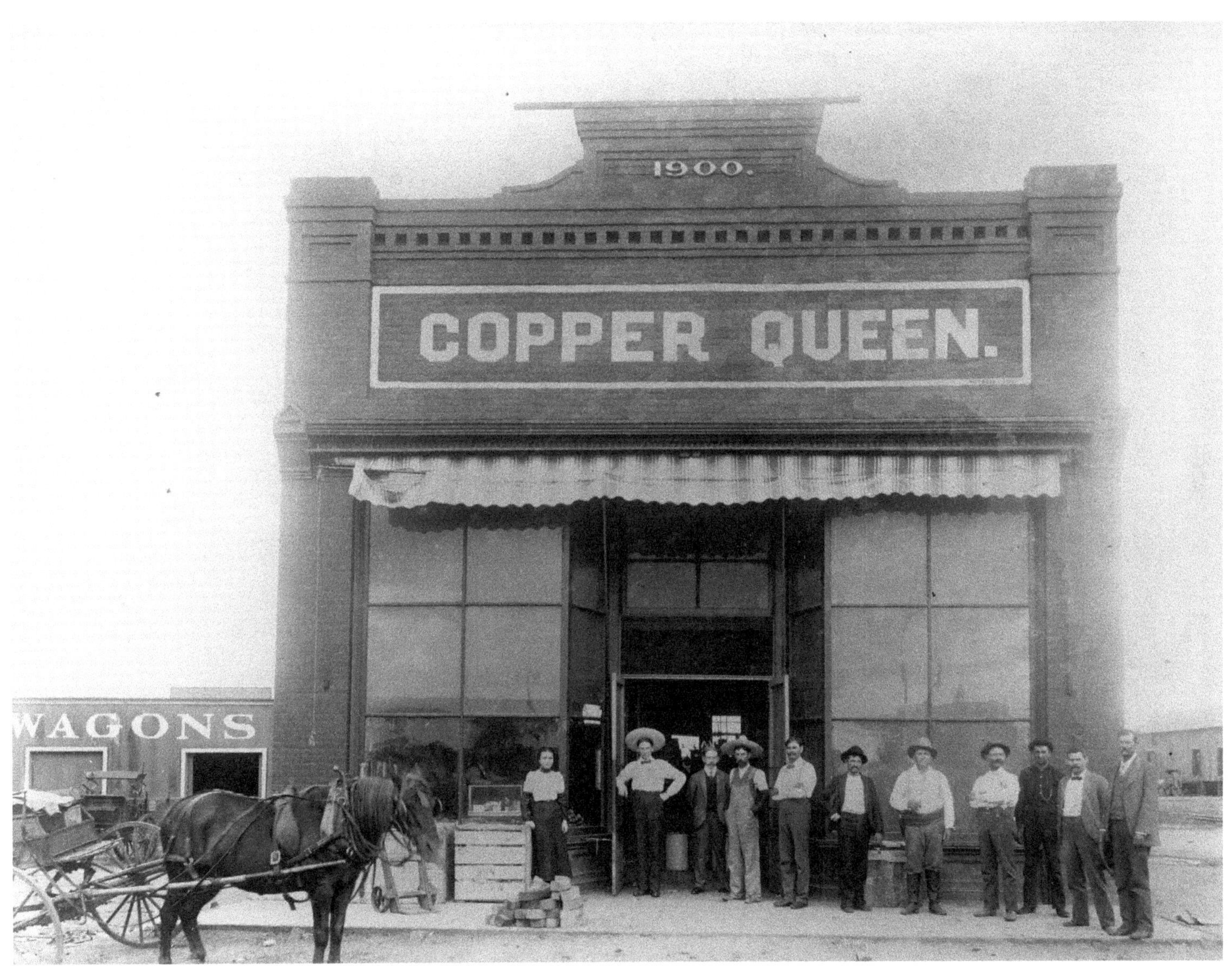

Staff pose in front of the Phelps Dodge Mining Company's Copper Queen Mercantile Store in Bisbee around the turn of the century. As places to receive credit and buy household goods, company stores played an important role in the lives of local miners and their families. Arizona's oldest library was started in the Copper Queen Mercantile Store in 1882 with a collection of several hundred books.

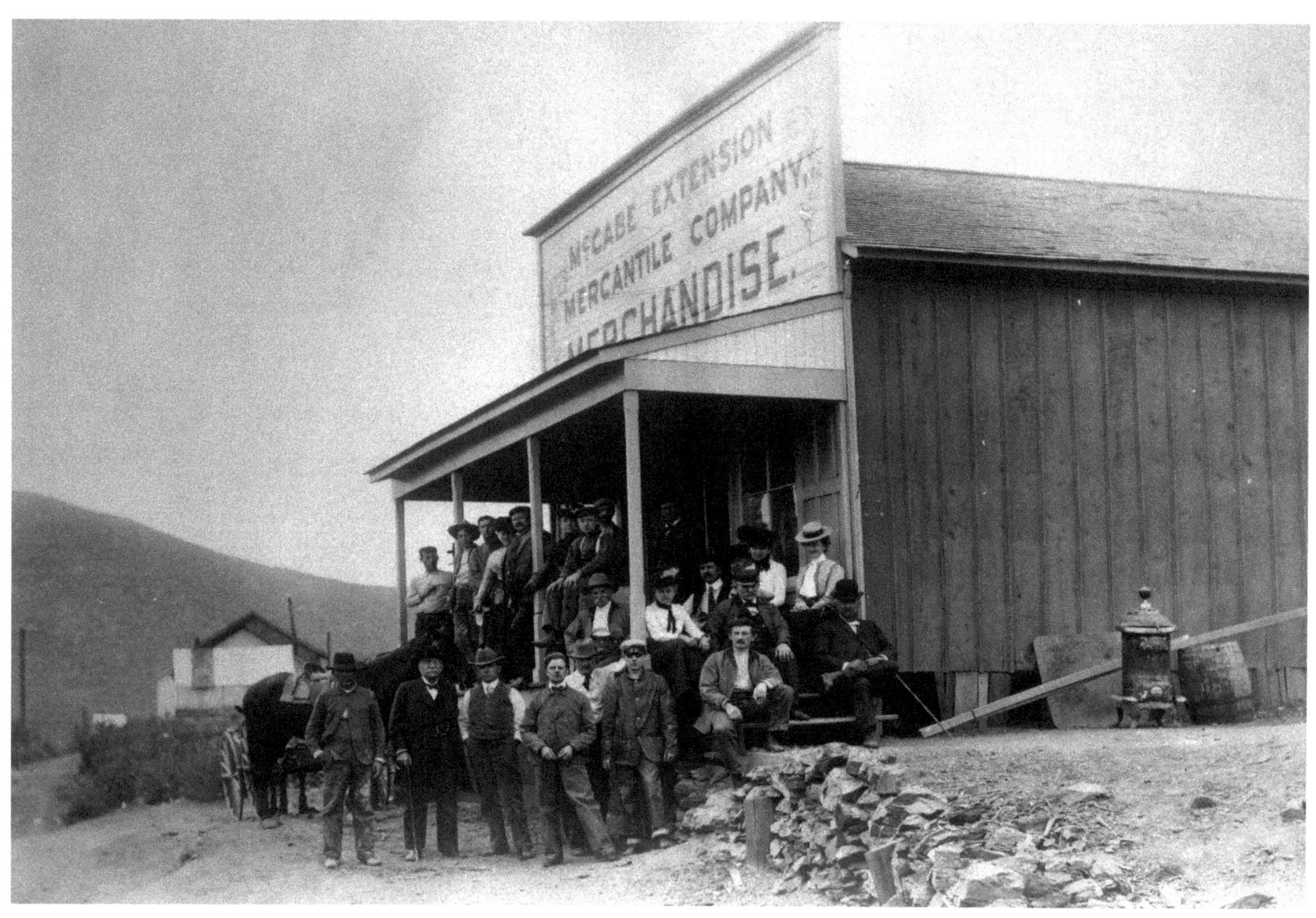

Company stores like the one owned by the McCabe Extension Mercantile Company in Globe provided mining families a place to buy fresh food and supplies, but the monopoly on goods and services held by such stores in the mining camps of Arizona did not always benefit the hardworking, low-paid miners.

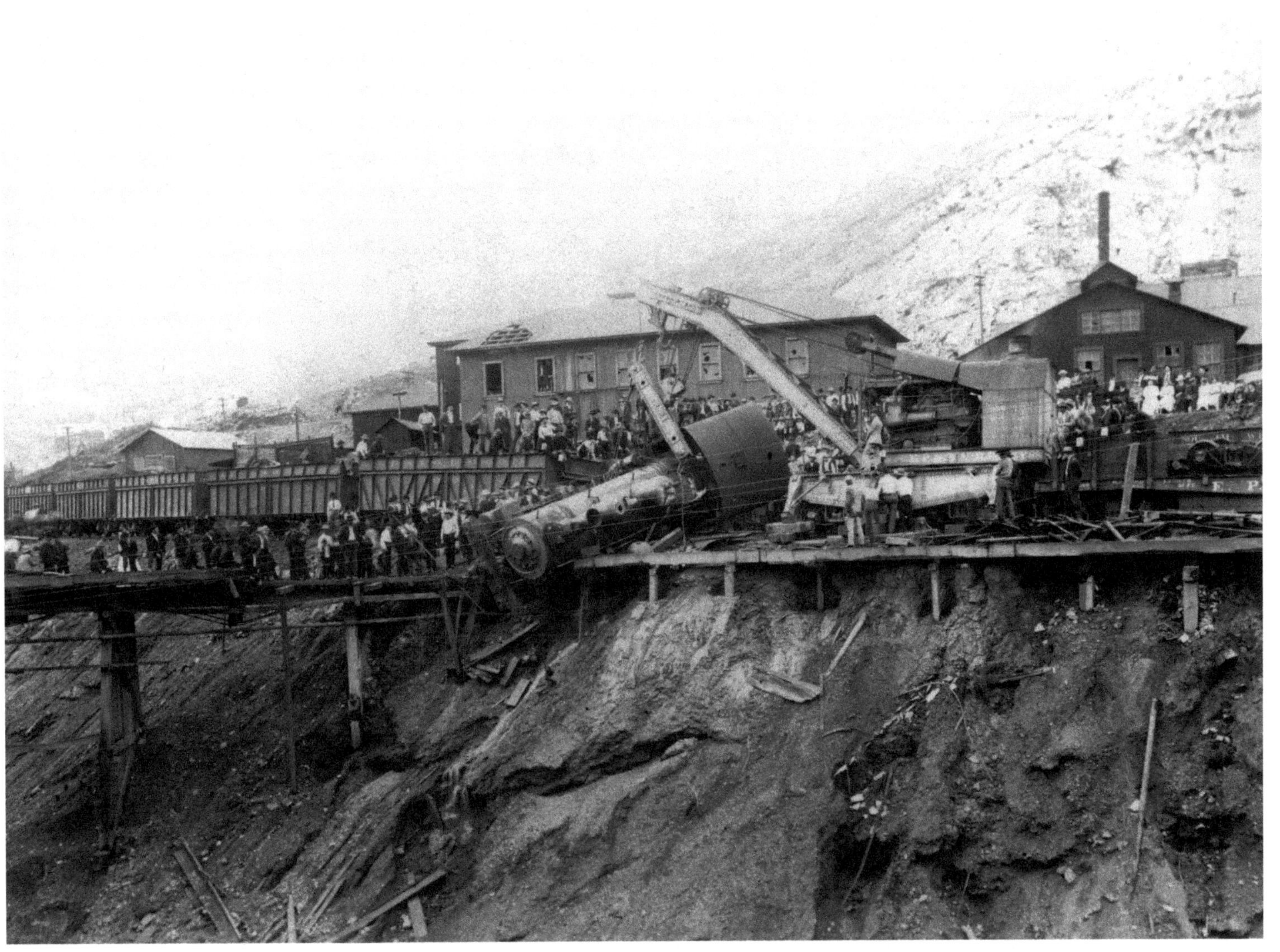

From cave-ins to catastrophes caused by pockets of deadly gas, mining accidents have always been an everyday danger in the lives of Arizona miners. Here an ore train has fallen from the tracks of the Copper Queen mine in Bisbee.

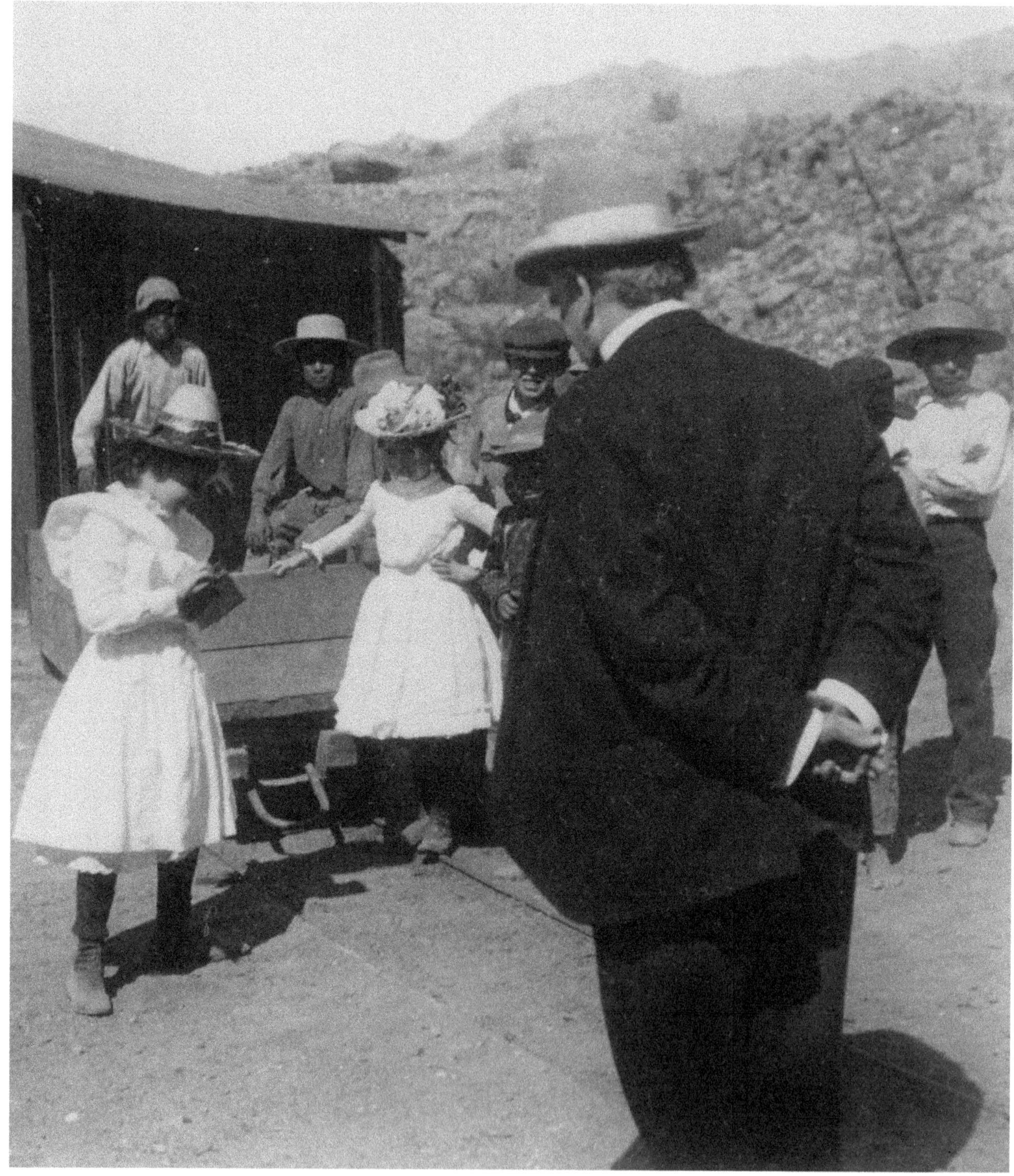

On May 7, 1900, President William McKinley arrived at Congress, Arizona, to visit the Congress Gold Mine, though he declined an invitation to ride to the bottom of the 3,000-foot mine shaft. McKinley was presented with a small gold bar, and each lady of the presidential party was given a gold nugget. Here a daughter of a local miner takes the opportunity to photograph the president.

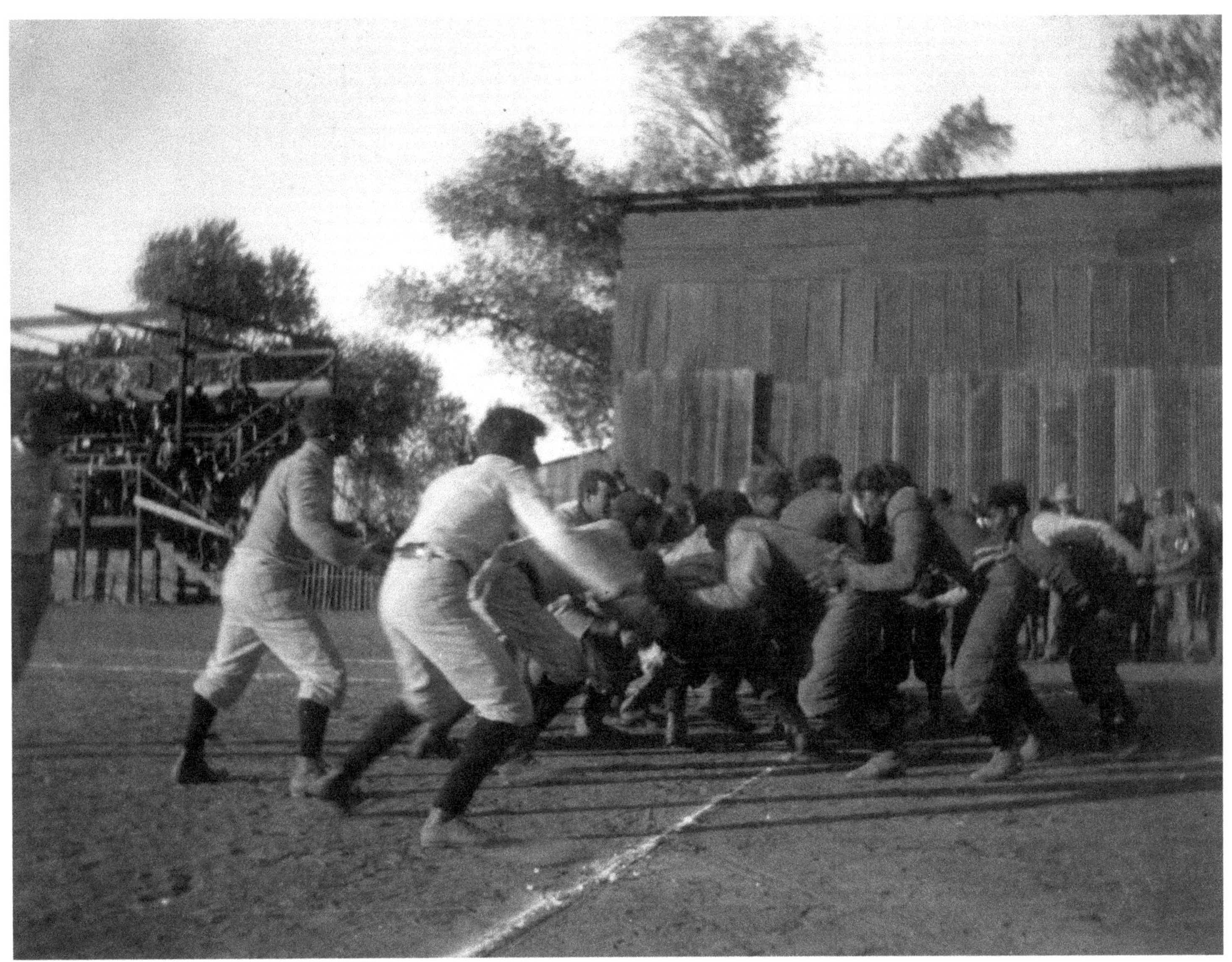

The Tempe Normal School football team, the Normals, battle a gridiron rival in the early 1900s. Tempe Normal School was founded in 1885, through legislation passed by the 13th territorial legislature, and opened on February 8, 1886. The purpose of the institution was to train teachers of "husbandry" (agriculture) and the mechanical arts for work in the territorial public schools. In 1958 this small teaching college became Arizona State University.

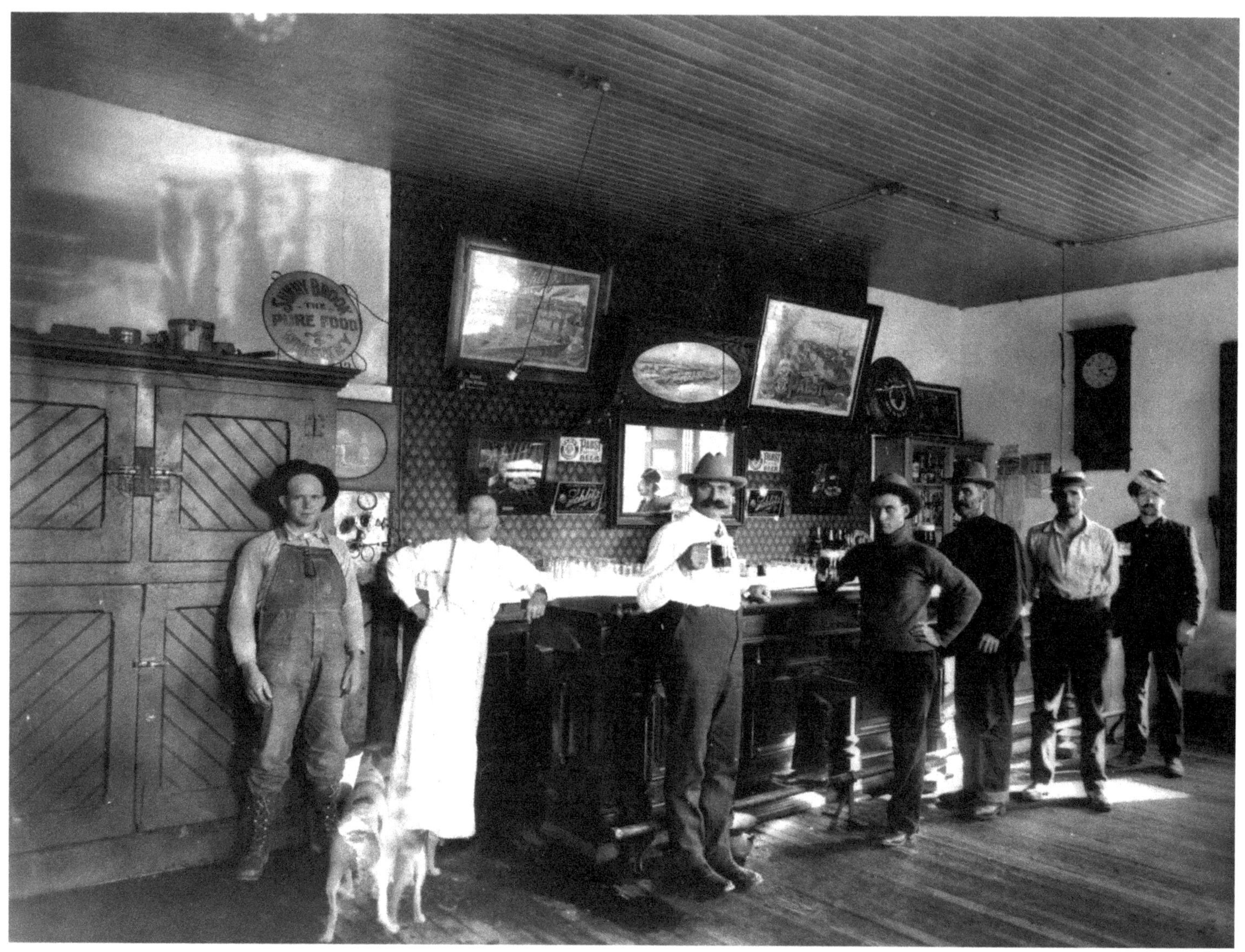

Hard liquor was not hard to come by in the rough-and-tumble Arizona mining towns. With the mines operating three shifts, seven days a week, the saloons stayed open around the clock. These men are at the bar of the Van Slyck & Meyers Whiskey Company in Globe, around 1902.

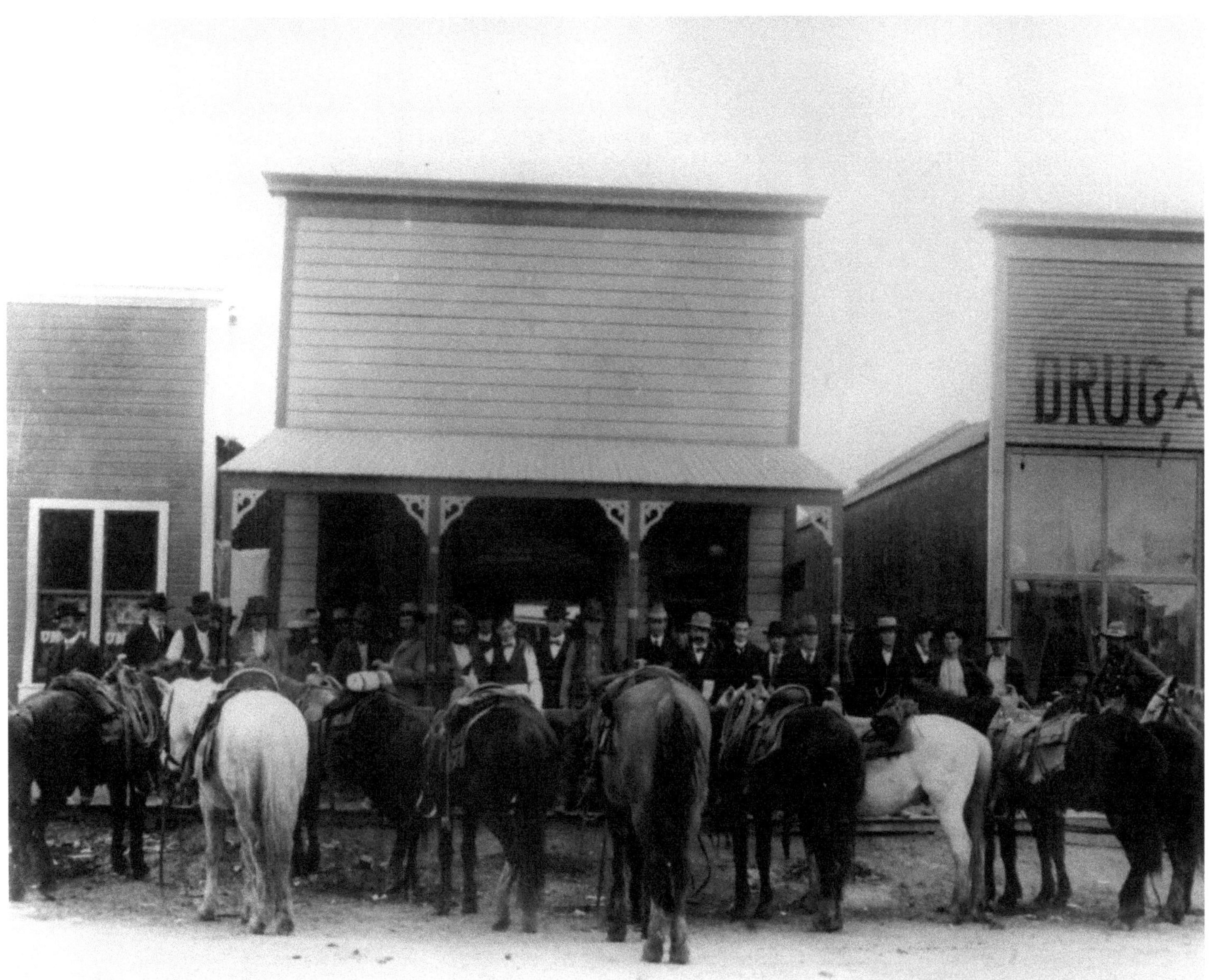

The site of a copper smelter 20 miles east of Bisbee, the town of Douglas was founded in 1900. Named for Dr. James Douglas, president of the Phelps Dodge Mining Company, Douglas was a crossroads where Hispanic, Anglo, and American Indian cultures met, mixed, and prospered. Here a group of local cowboys from the Diamond A Ranch enjoy some leisure time in Douglas.

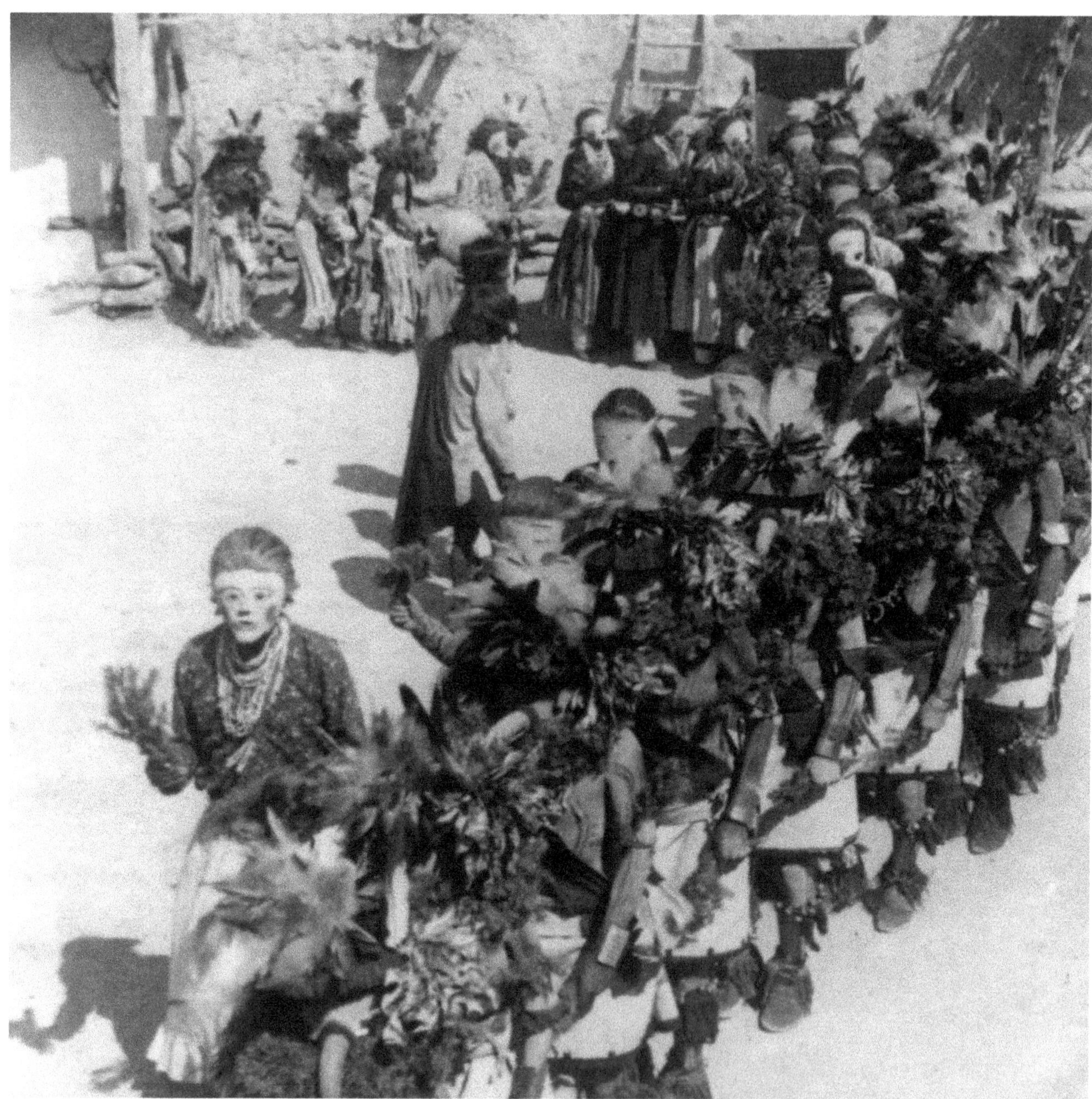

Eleven Hopi villages are located atop and around the base of three northern Arizona mountain mesas. Here a kachina dance is shown being performed at the village of Shungopavi on Second Mesa in 1903. Today most Hopi villages are closed to the public for their kachina ceremonies. Special tribal permission must be obtained to take pictures or make drawings anywhere on the Hopi Nation.

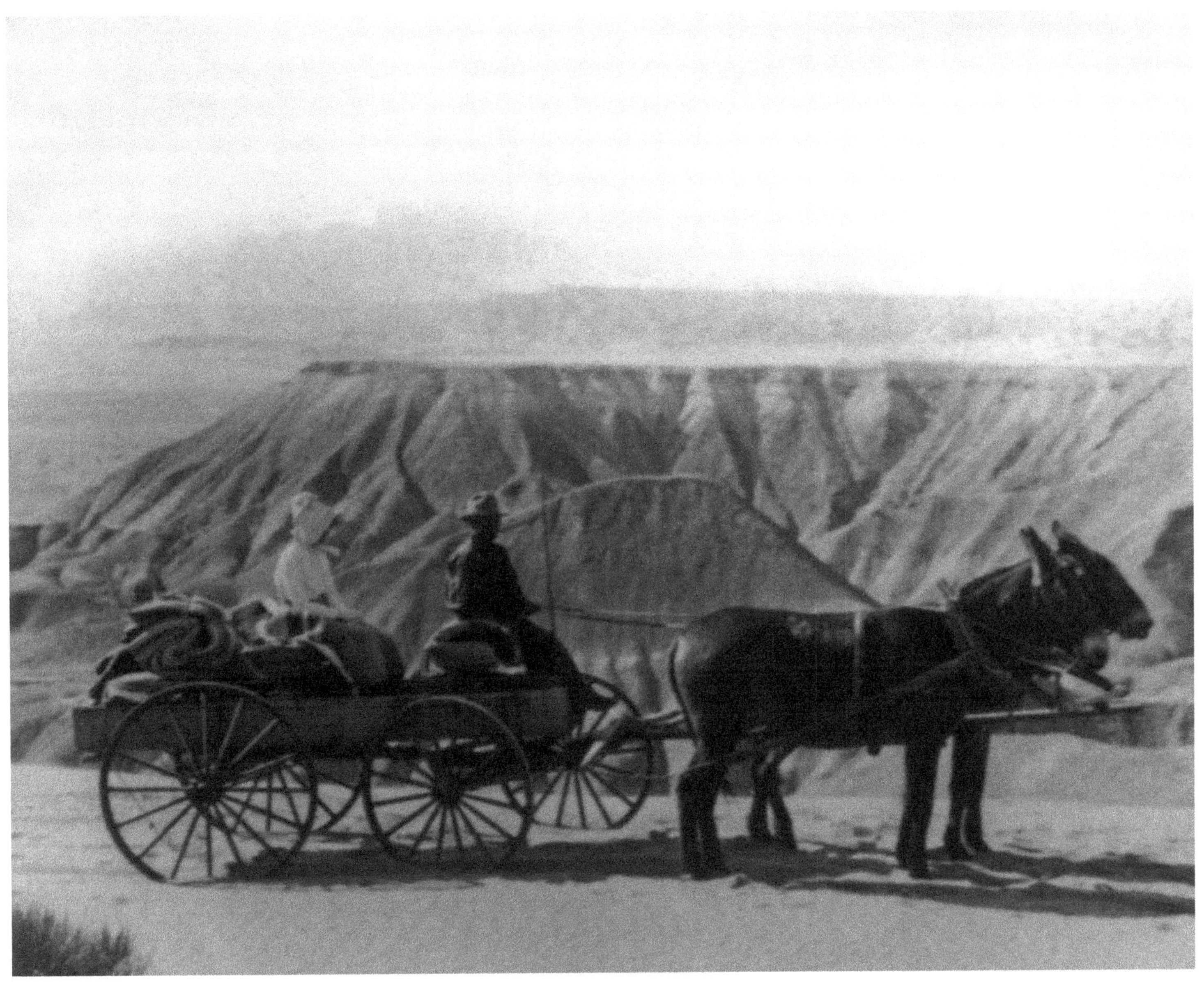

The Painted Desert of northeastern Arizona is a multilayered landscape of many colors and geological textures. It encompasses more than 93,500 acres and extends for over 160 miles. The desert hues range from lavenders to various shades of gray, intermixed with reds, oranges, and pinks. The desert has long been a popular tourist destination, as suggested by this image from around 1903.

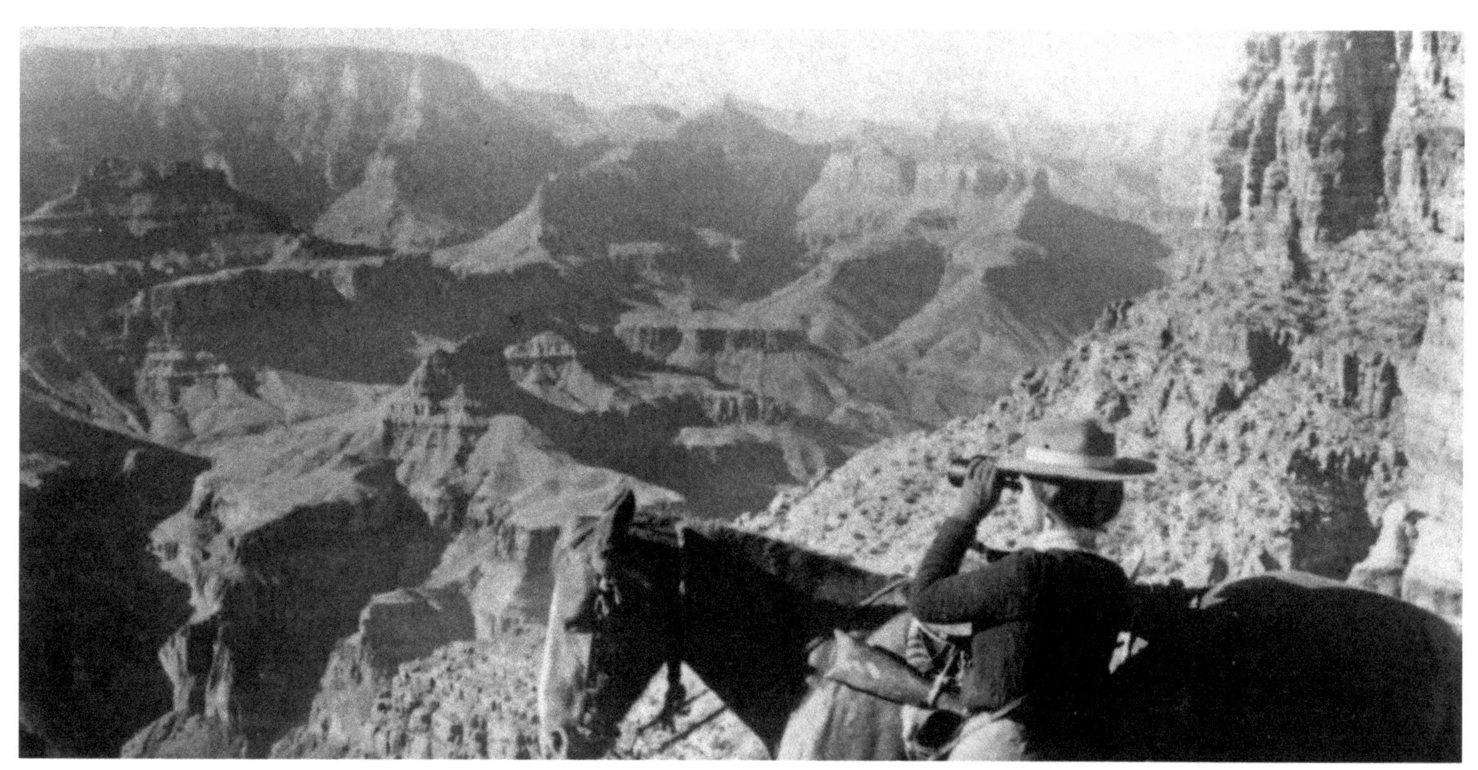

A visitor uses her binoculars to gaze into the depths of the Grand Canyon in 1903. Grand Canyon tourism began in 1882 when stagecoaches from Flagstaff would travel 11 hours to reach the south rim. In 1901 a Santa Fe Railroad spur began bringing tourists from Williams, Arizona, to the Grand Canyon Village. The 64-mile trip cost $3.95. That same railroad spur still brings tourists to the Grand Canyon today.

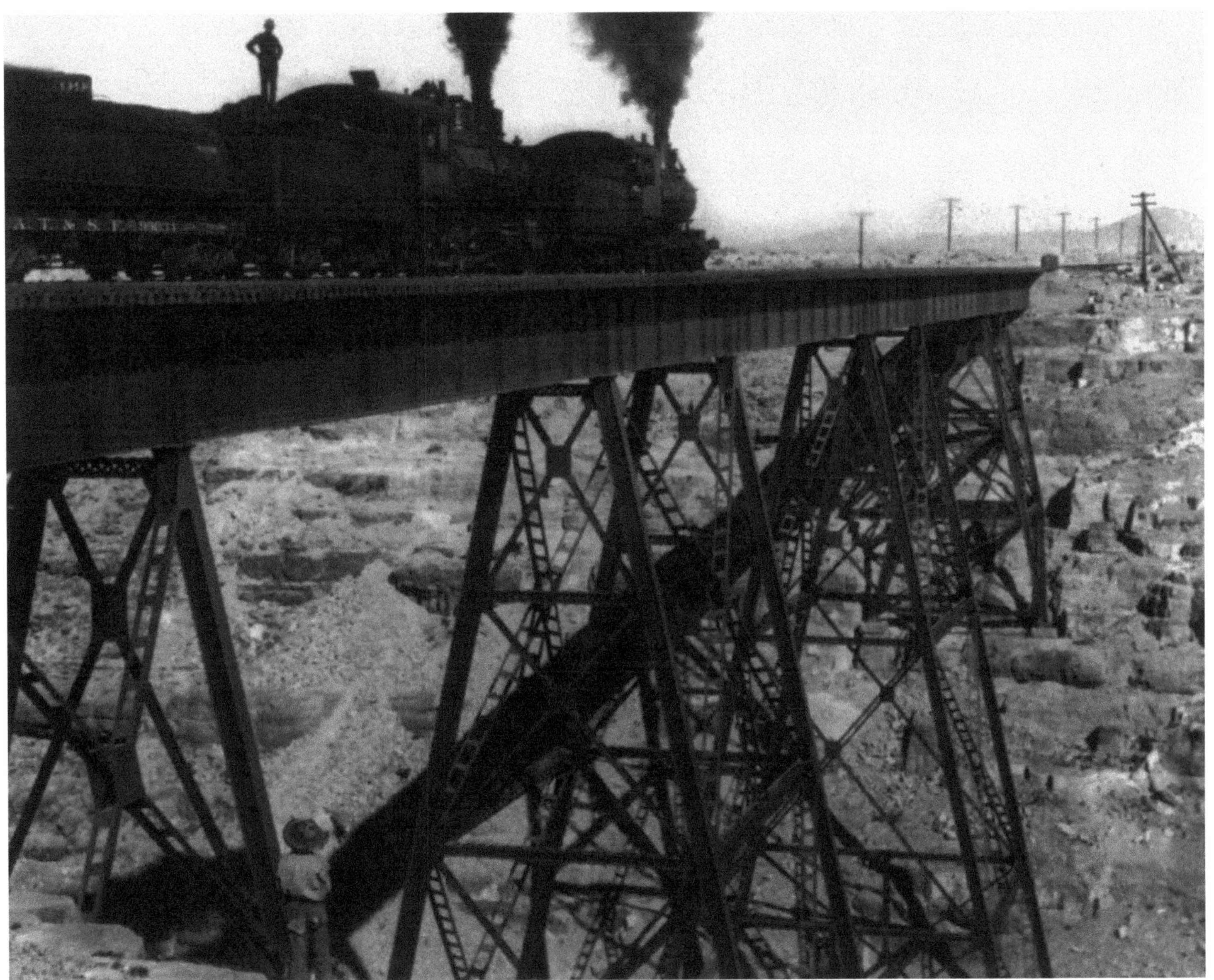

A steam locomotive passes over the railroad bridge built by the Atlantic and Pacific Railroad at Canyon Diablo in northern Arizona. Completed in 1890, the bridge successfully spanned a 255-foot-deep chasm. The wooden timbers were precut and assembled elsewhere, but a mistake in measurement resulted in the bridge coming up short by three feet. Correcting the error delayed the opening of the bridge seven months.

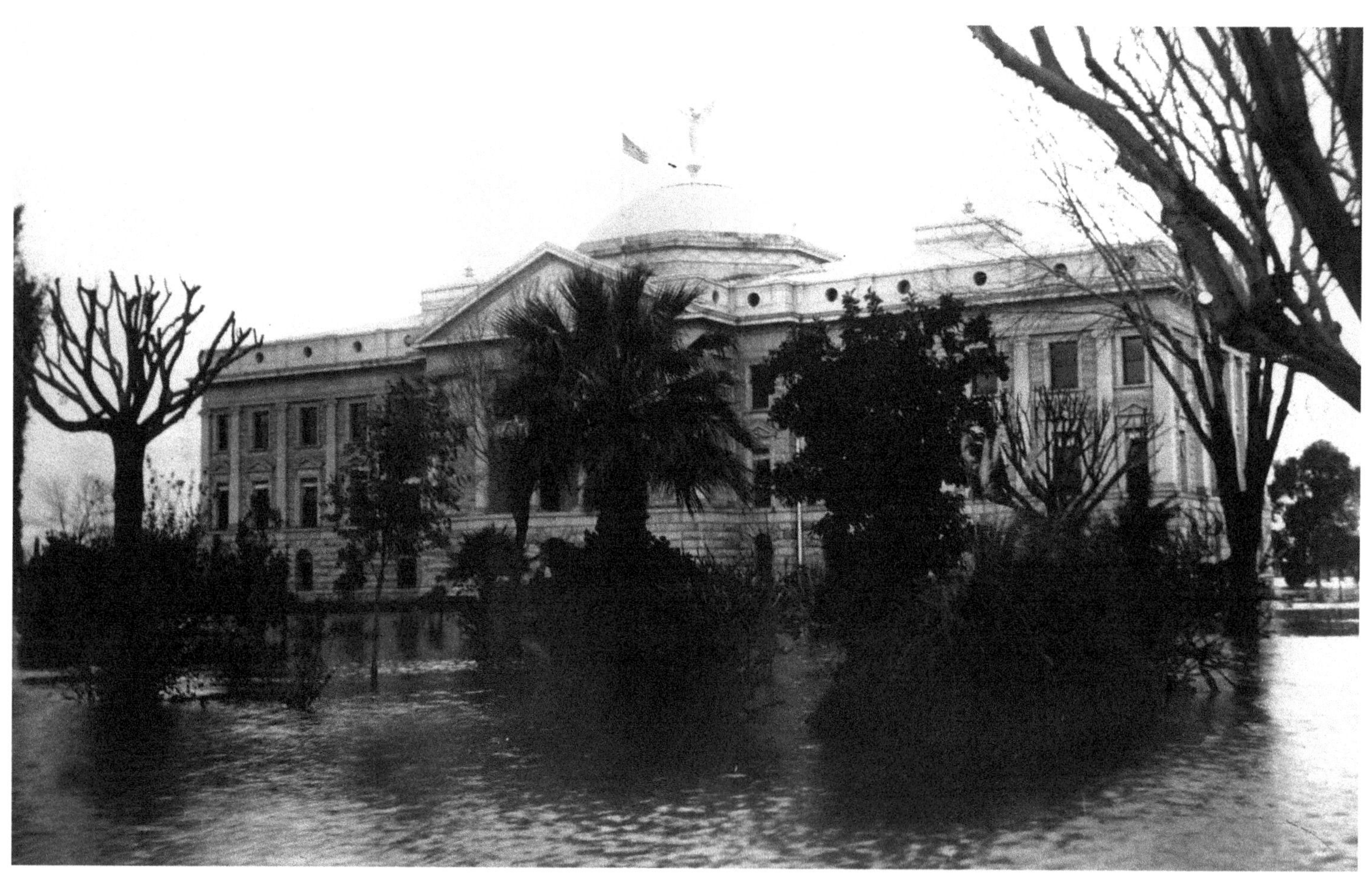

It does rain in the Sonoran Desert, and when the rains are heavy, the desert rivers can quickly overflow and flood surrounding areas, as this 1905 image of the Arizona Territorial Capitol in Phoenix shows. Cycles of drought followed by flooding motivated Phoenix residents to form the Salt River Valley Water Users' Association and to build Roosevelt Dam. The dam stored water for times of drought and captured the heavy rains to prevent flooding.

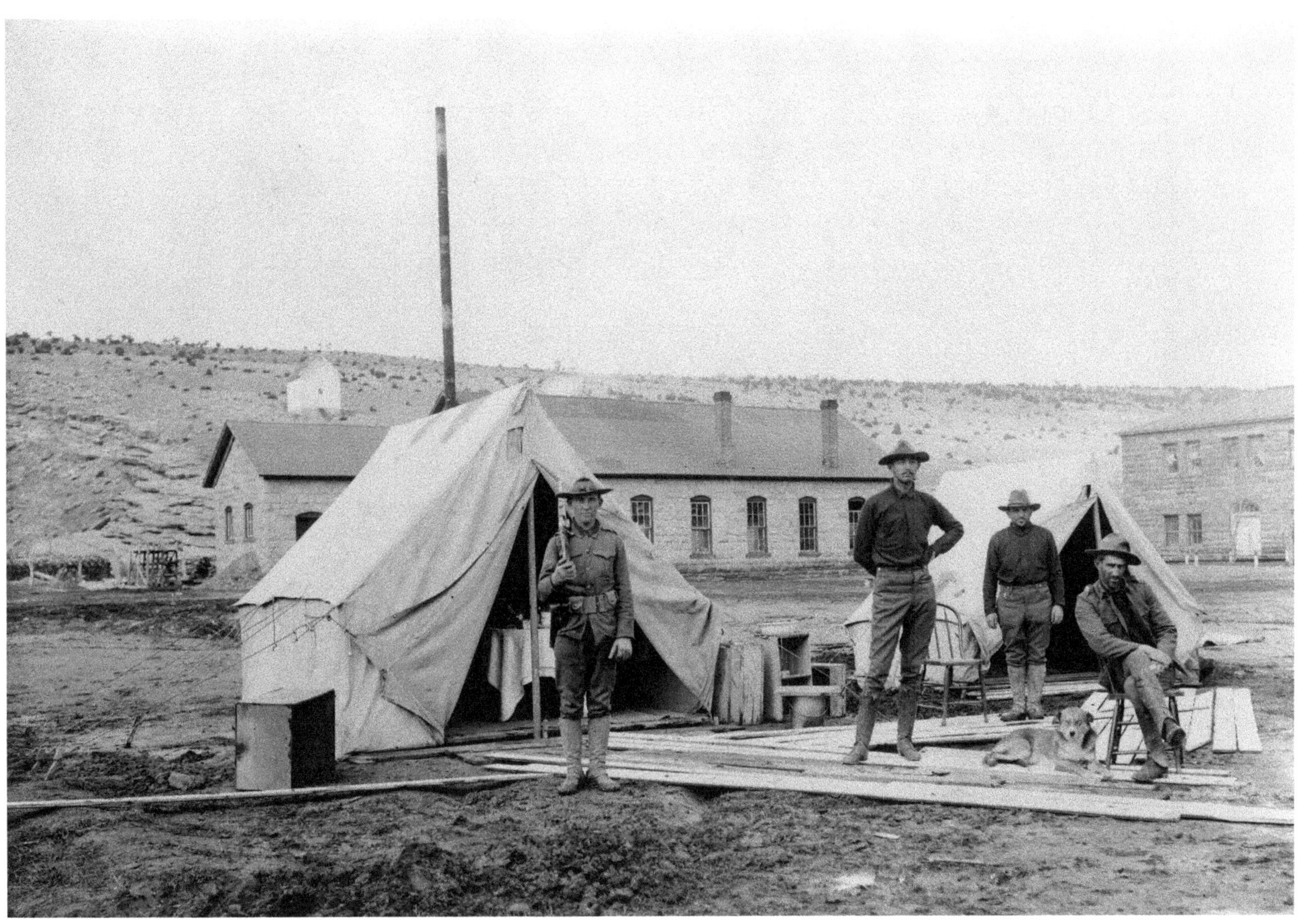

Fort Defiance was established in 1851 to create a U.S. Army presence in the land of the Navajo. The fort lived up to its name, for many horrific battles were fought between the soldiers and the native people. It was from Fort Defiance in 1864 that the forced removal known as the Navajo Long Walk began. In 1868 Fort Defiance was reestablished as an Indian agency, and in 1905 the military was still present, as shown by this photo of the officers' quarters.

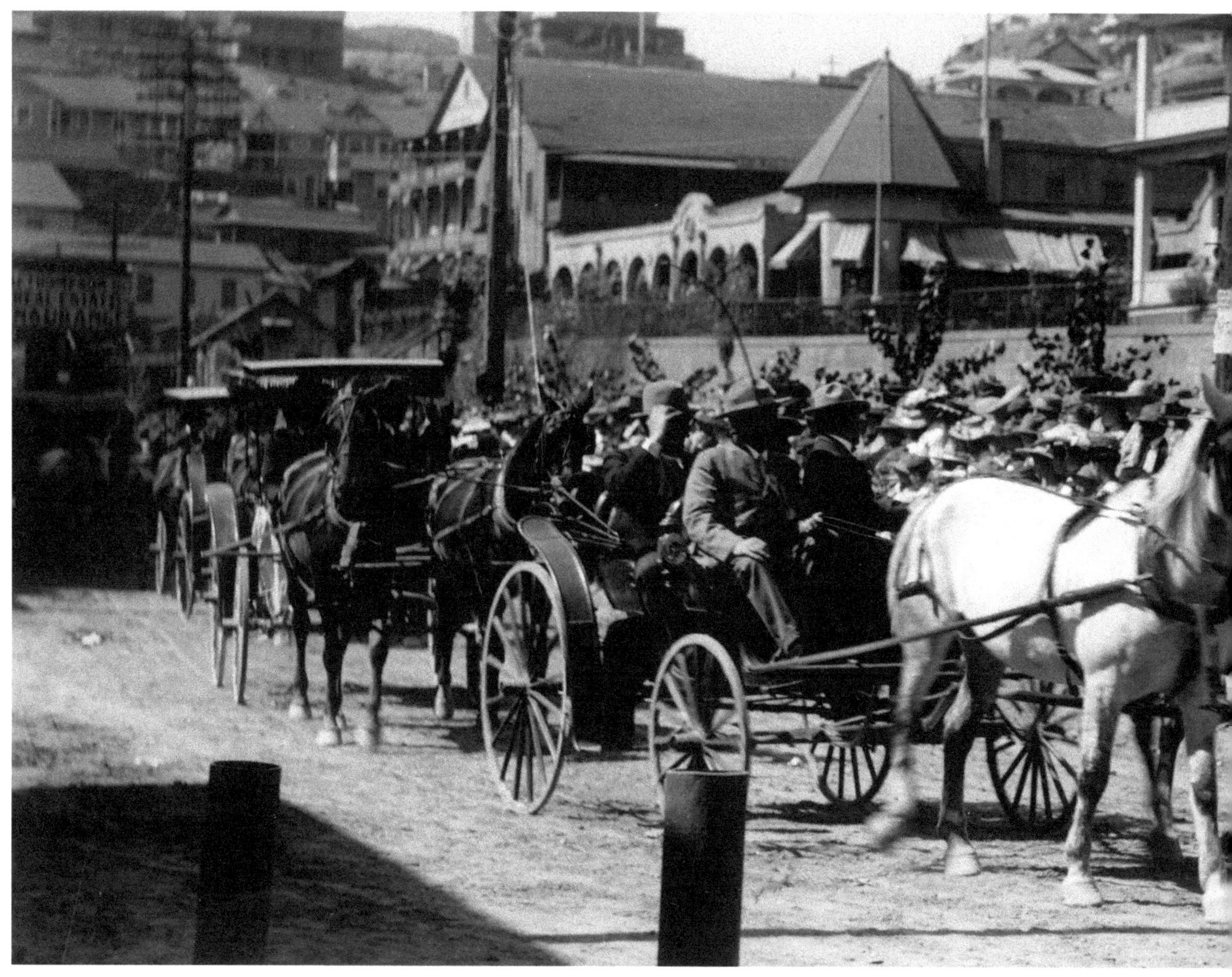

Bisbee in 1905 boasted a population of more than 20,000 residents. The mining town's notorious Brewery Gulch, known for its 47 saloons and its "soiled doves," was called the "liveliest spot between El Paso and San Francisco." But Bisbee was also home to Arizona's first community library and first golf course, as well as the state's oldest ballfields. Here a few of those 1905 Bisbee folks enjoy an old-fashioned community parade.

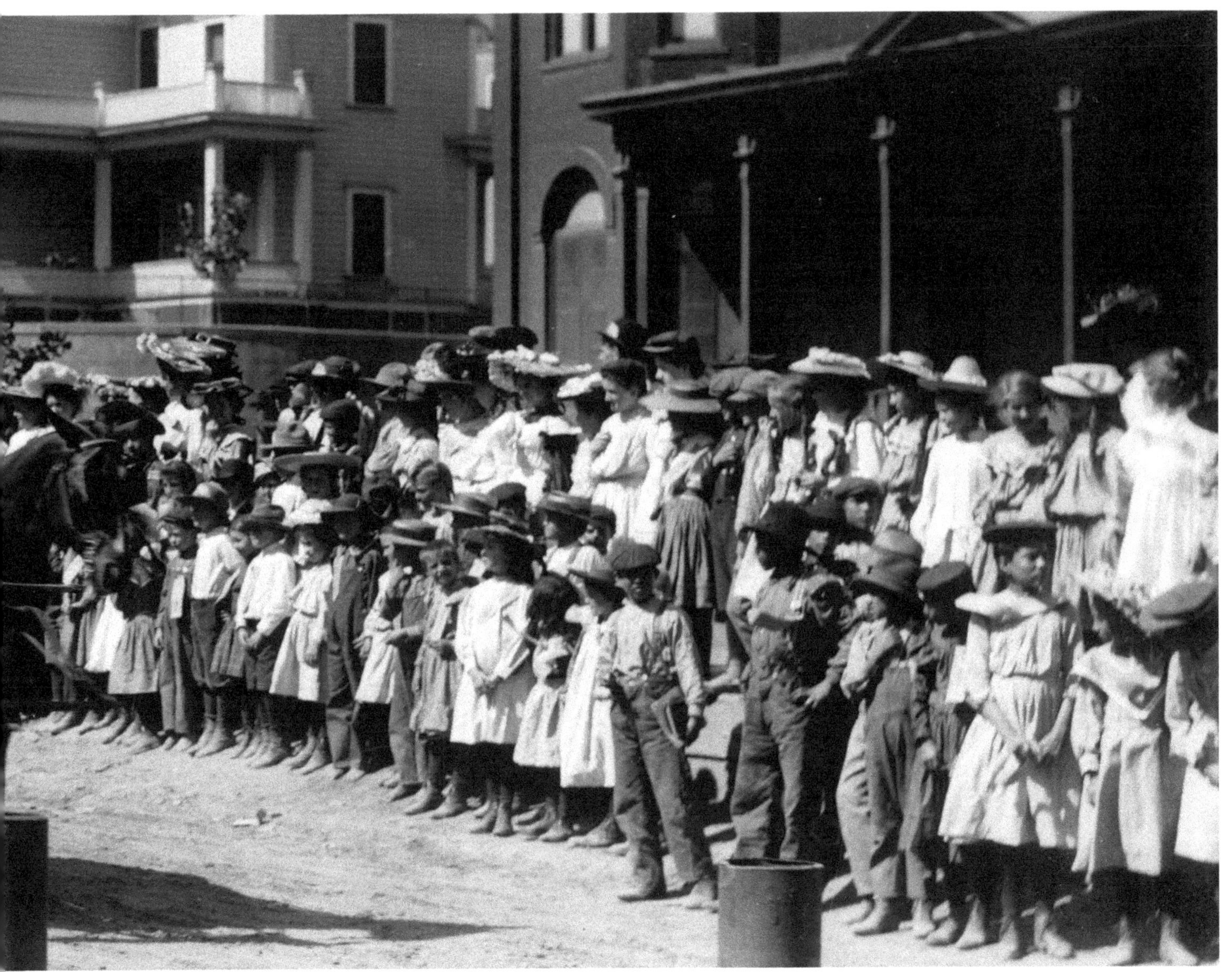

Edward S. Curtis was one of the great photographers of the American West. His 30-year North American Indian Project attempted to capture and preserve images of American Indian people living as they had before contact with the Anglo culture. His life's work cost him his marriage and his health, but he left a photographic masterpiece. These four Hopi women of the village of Walpi were photographed by Curtis in 1906.

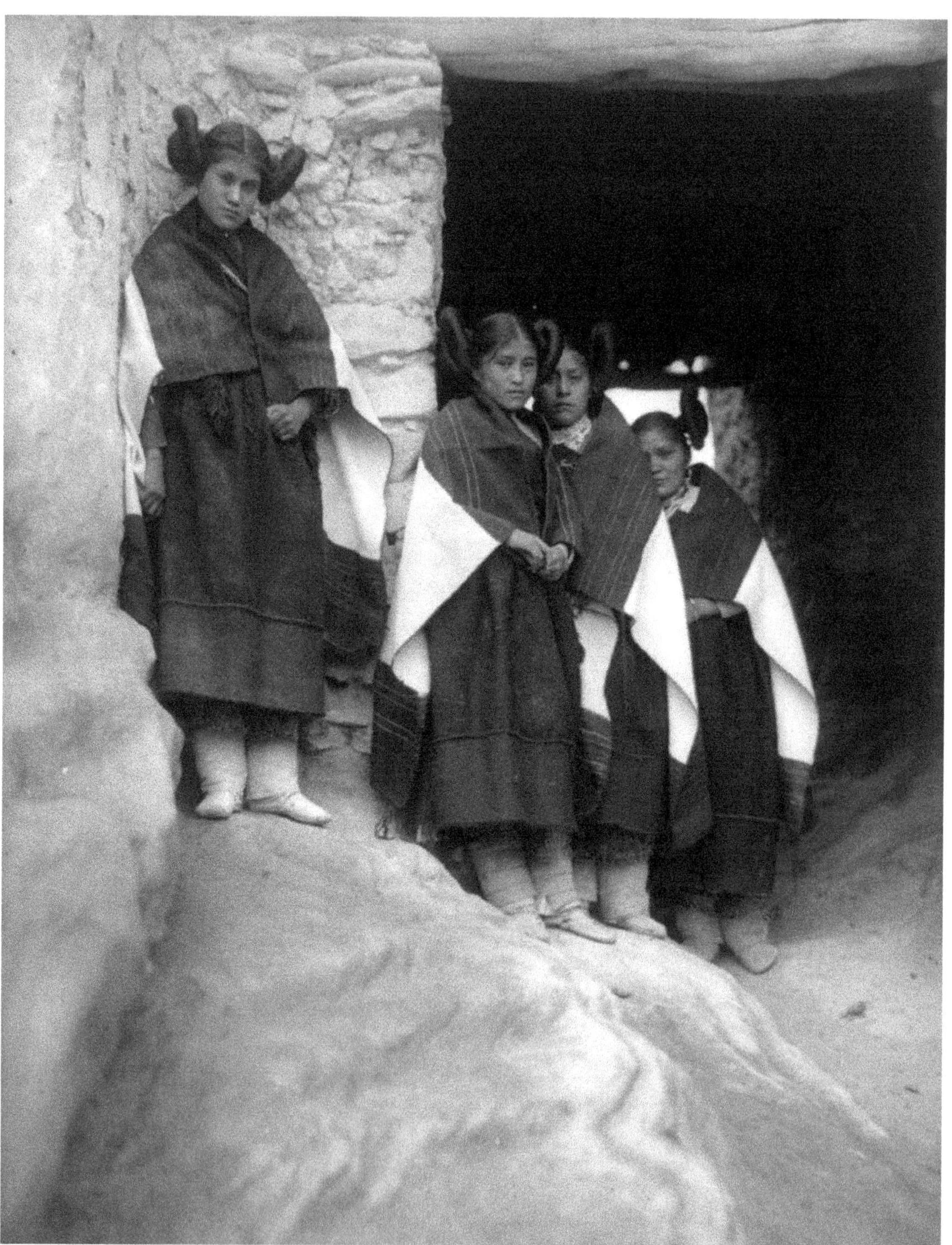

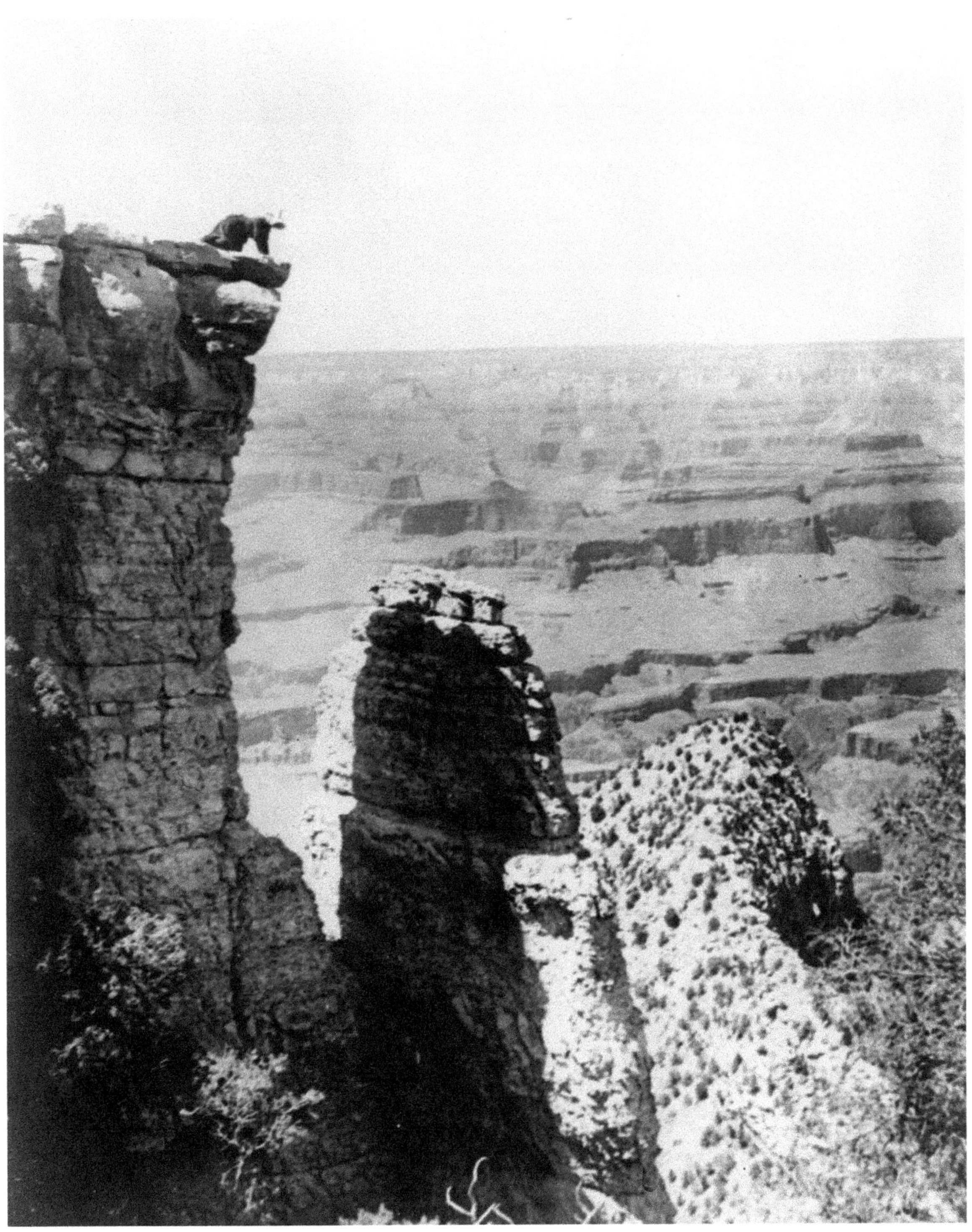

Tourists have been overcoming their fears in order to gaze into the mile-deep Grand Canyon since the early 1880s. Even today there are many places along the rims of the canyon that contain no guardrails or protection from falling. In this 1907 photo, a woman has crawled on her hands and knees to the canyon's edge to peer into the giant gorge.

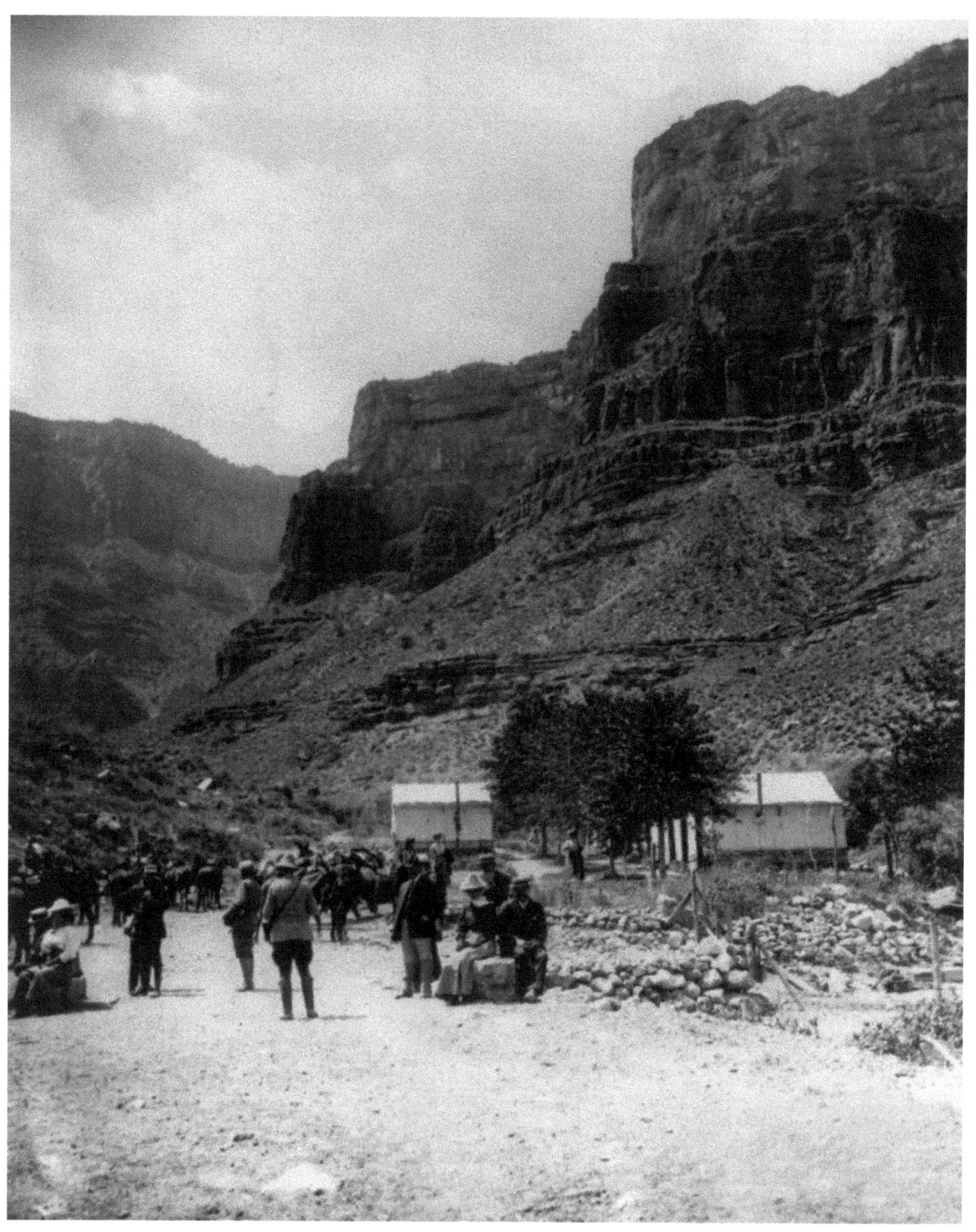

In 1902, while working for the U.S. Geological Survey, F. E. Matthes began to map the Grand Canyon. By 1905 he had created the first topographic maps of the Vishnu, Bright Angel, and Shinumo quadrangles. Perhaps benefiting from Matthes' work, these tourists in 1907 have descended to a canyon campsite 3,100 feet below the south rim.

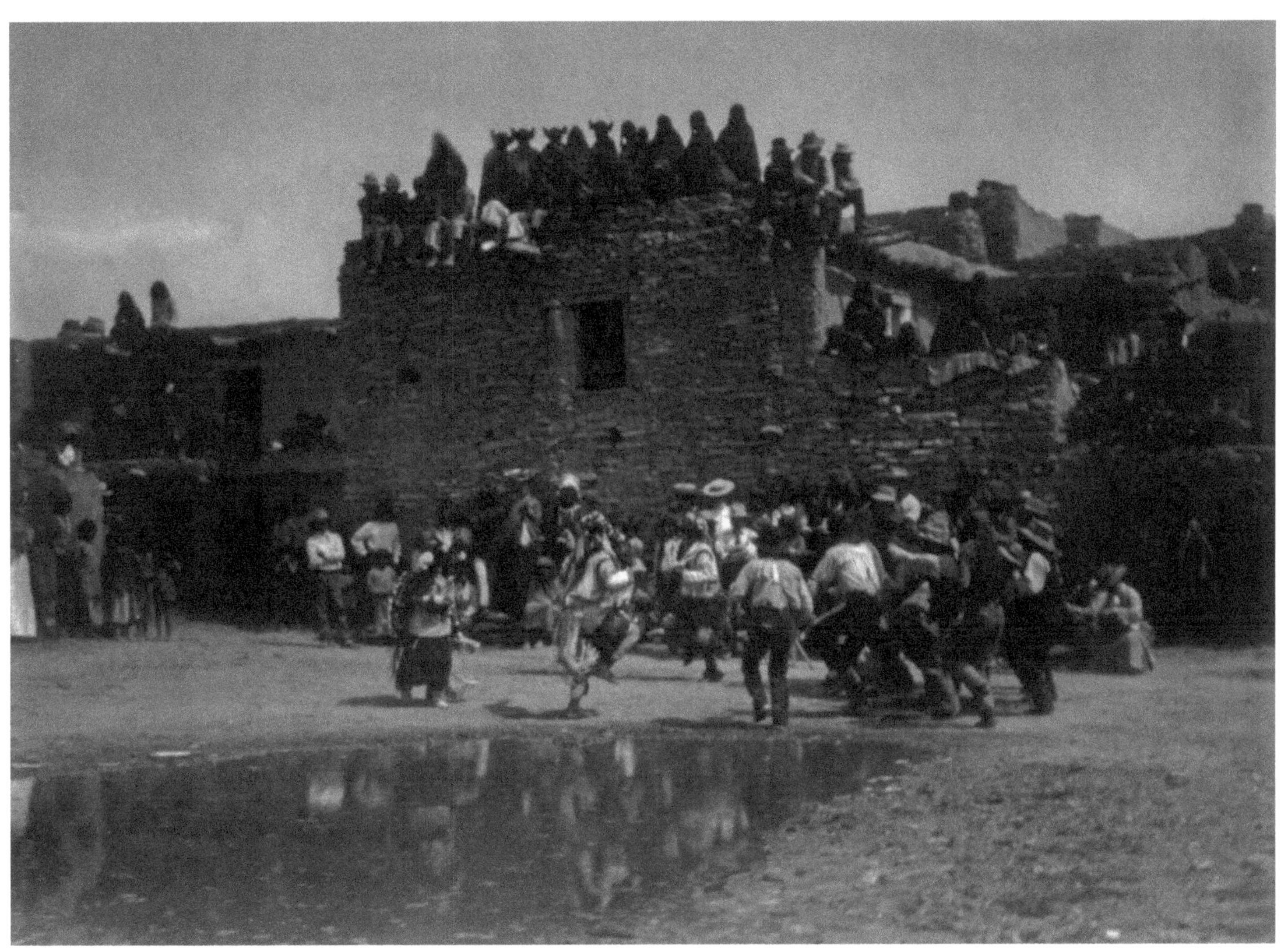

This 1905 photo shows a buffalo dance at the Tewa village of Hano. The Tewa-speaking people of Hano first fled their New Mexico pueblo when the Spanish conquistadors arrived in the early seventeenth century. In 1696 they were invited by the Hopi to settle at the north end of First Mesa. The men of Hano acted as guards of the trail that led to First Mesa and the Hopi villages of Sichomovi and Walpi.

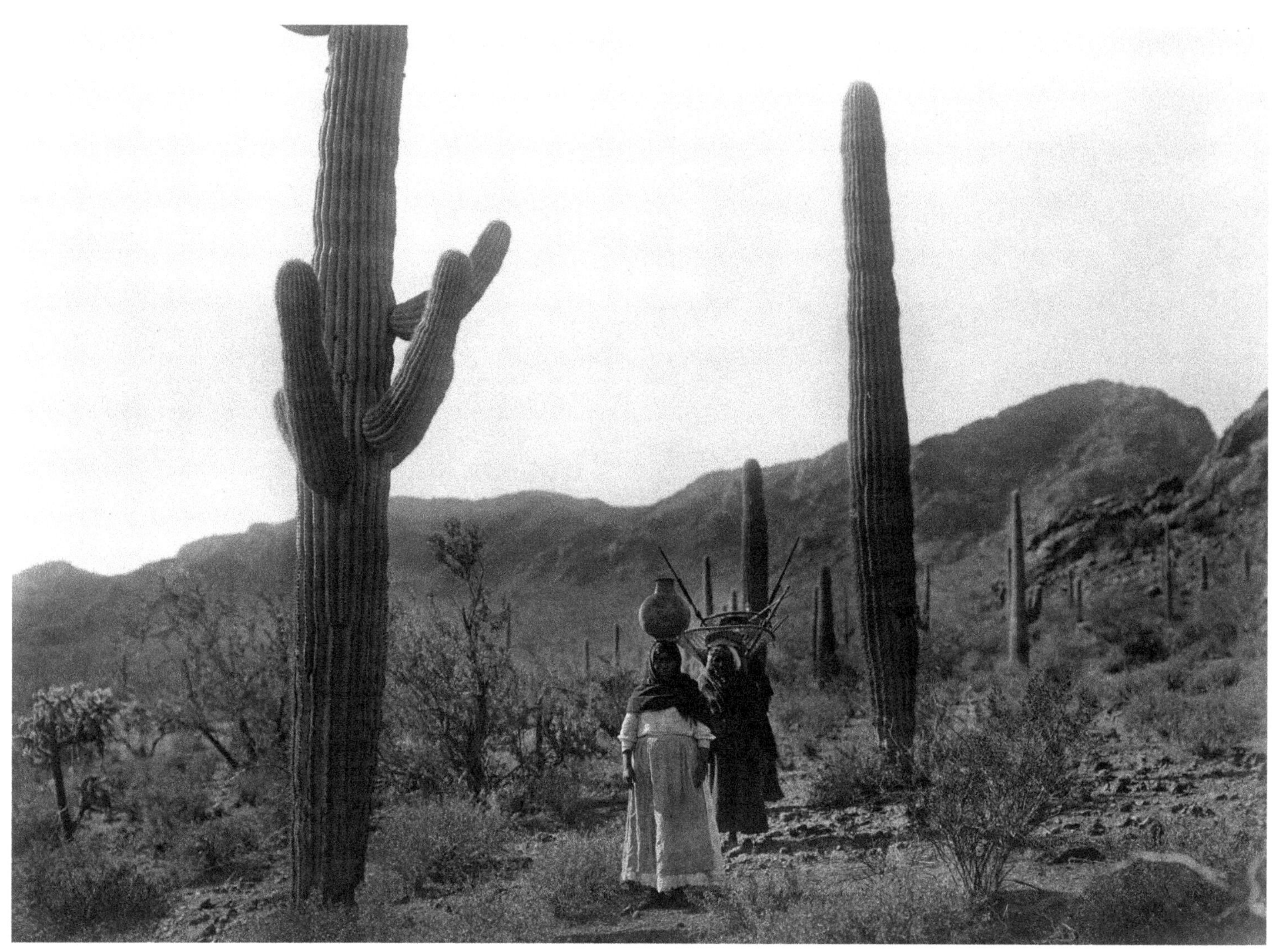

Edward S. Curtis photographed these three Tohono O'odham women—two with burden baskets called "kiho carriers," the third with a ceramic jug—in the Sonoran Desert of southern Arizona in 1907. The tribal name Tohono O'odham translates as "people of the desert." The conquistadors called them Papago, which translates as "tepary-bean eater." The traditional Tohono O'odham homeland extends from southern Arizona into northern Mexico.

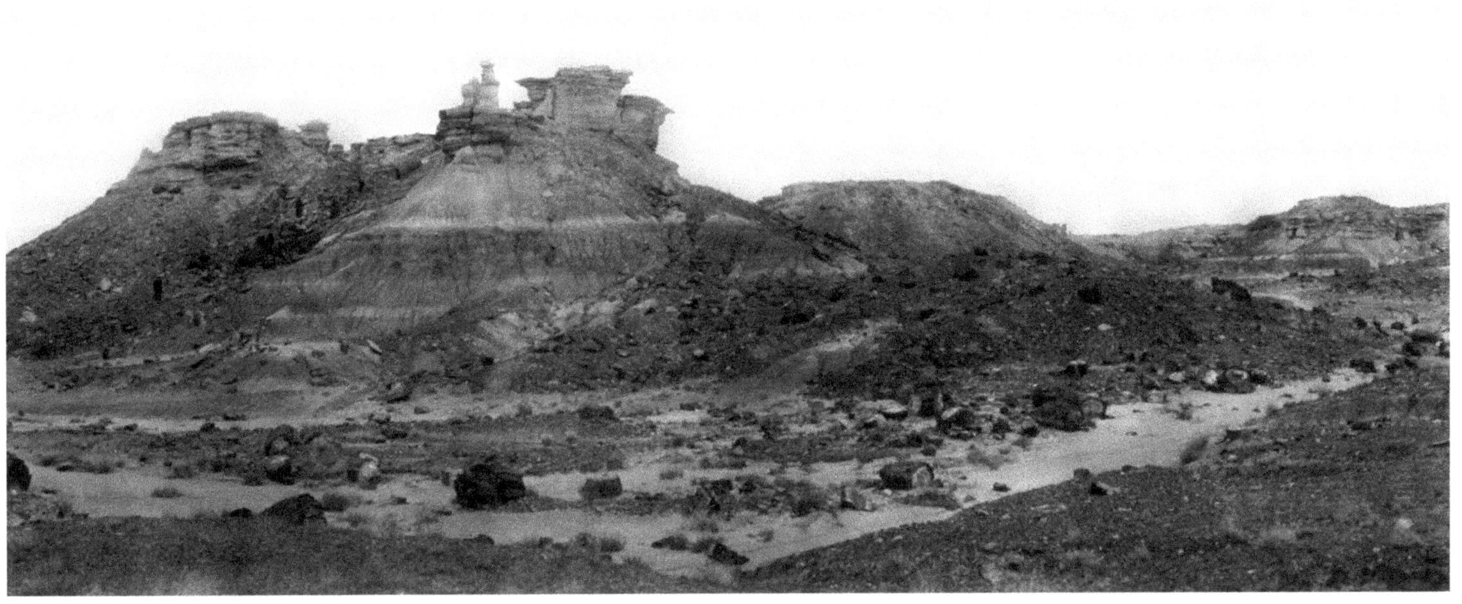

The Petrified Forest of northern Arizona contains one of the largest concentrations of petrified wood found anywhere in the world. This 218,553-acre national park was brought under federal protection in 1906. Today the Petrified Forest National Park is recognized as a treasure trove of Late Triassic fossils, grassland ecosystems, human history, and beautiful scenic vistas. This view shows the unspoiled landscape in 1908.

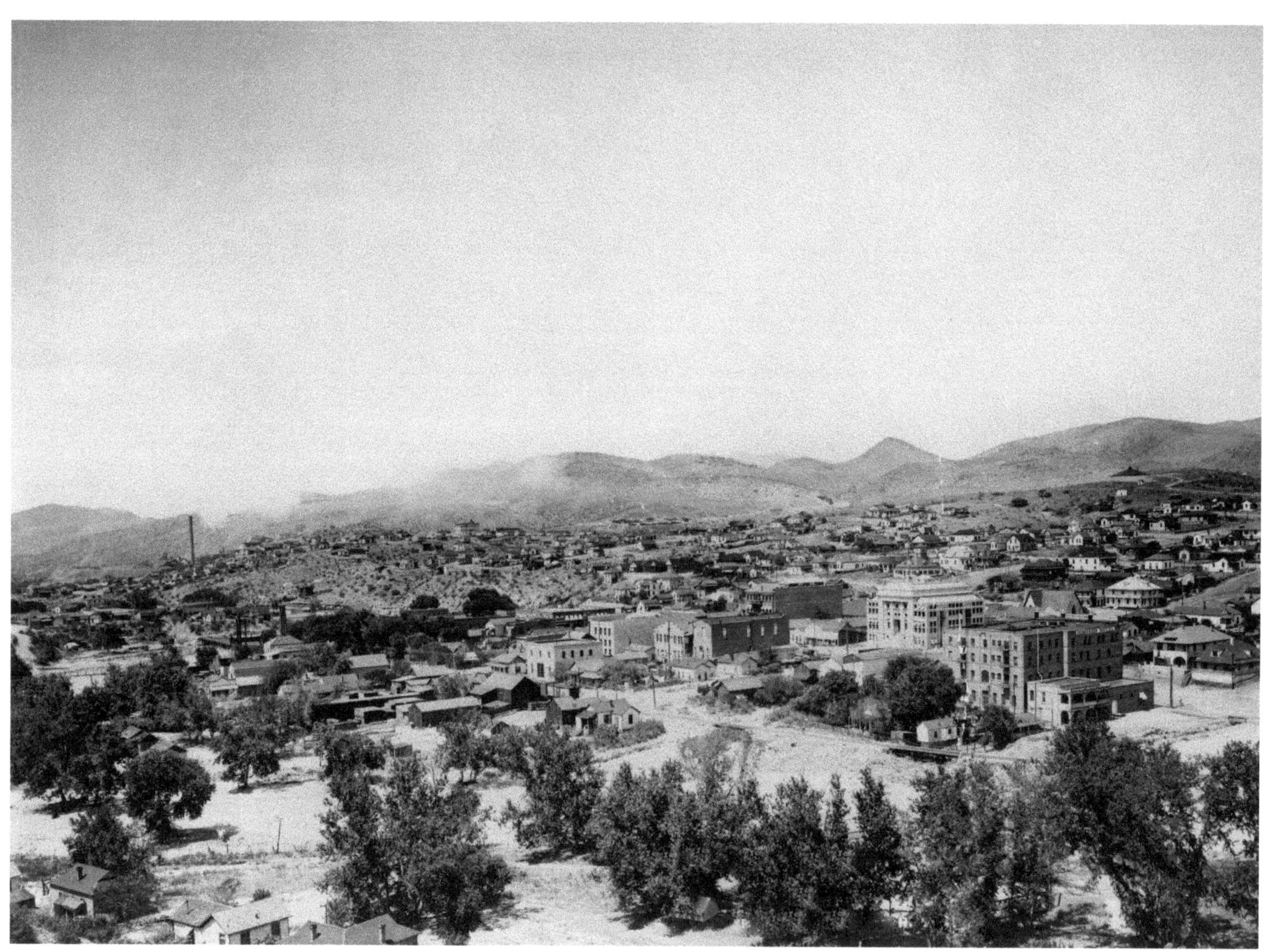

This is how downtown Globe appeared in 1909 when a visitor calling himself William T. Phillips came to the Arizona mining town accompanied by a new bride, Gertrude Livesay. Many historians believe Phillips was really Richard LeRoy Parker—better known as Butch Cassidy, who was thought to have died in Bolivia in 1908. In 1910 William Phillips left Globe for Spokane, Washington, where he died in 1937, leaving questions about his true identity to be debated to this day.

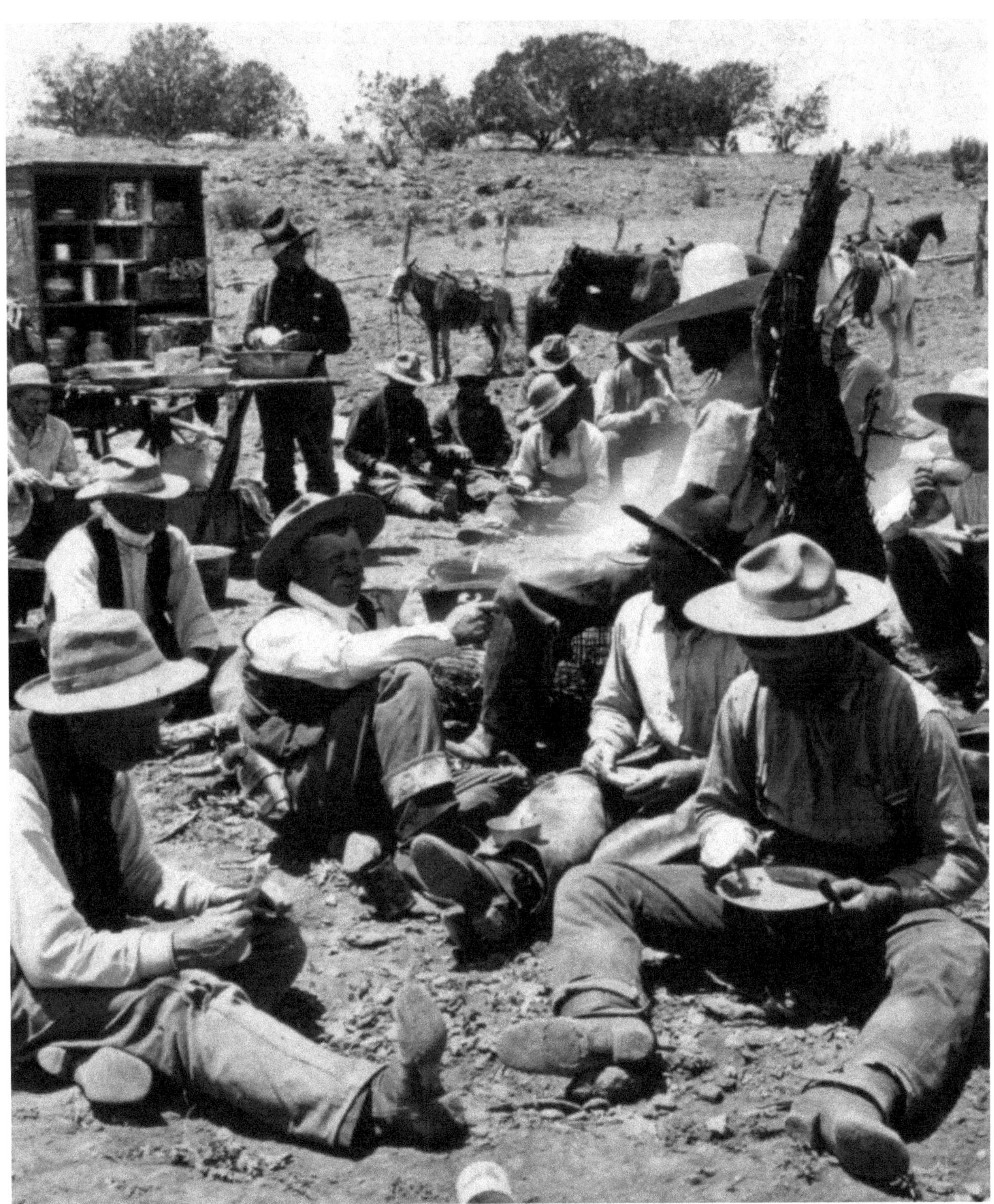

Charles Goodnight invented the chuck wagon in 1866 when he and Oliver Loving were preparing to drive 20,000 longhorn cattle from Texas to Denver. Goodnight purchased a government wagon and rebuilt it to include a slopping box useful for storing food and to serve as the cook's worktable. To the Arizona cowboys in this 1907 photo, "chuck" was food, the cook's box was the "chuck box," and the wagon was the "chuck wagon."

Following Spread: Seen here in 1908, the El Tovar Hotel was built just 20 feet from the south rim of the Grand Canyon by the Fred Harvey Company. The El Tovar opened its doors in 1905 and is one of the grandest historic hotels found in America today. The view of the Grand Canyon from the El Tovar Hotel is truly spectacular.

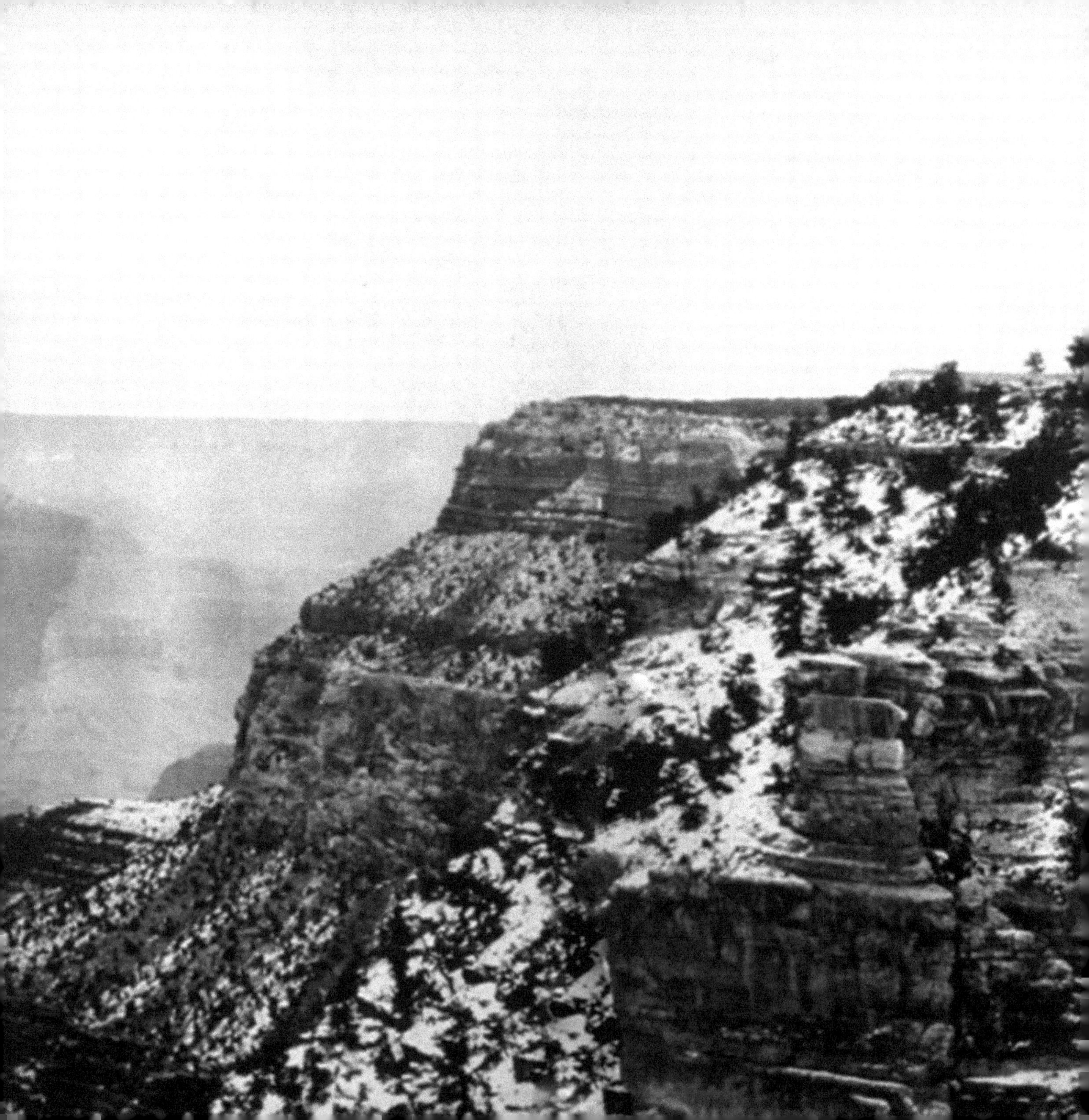

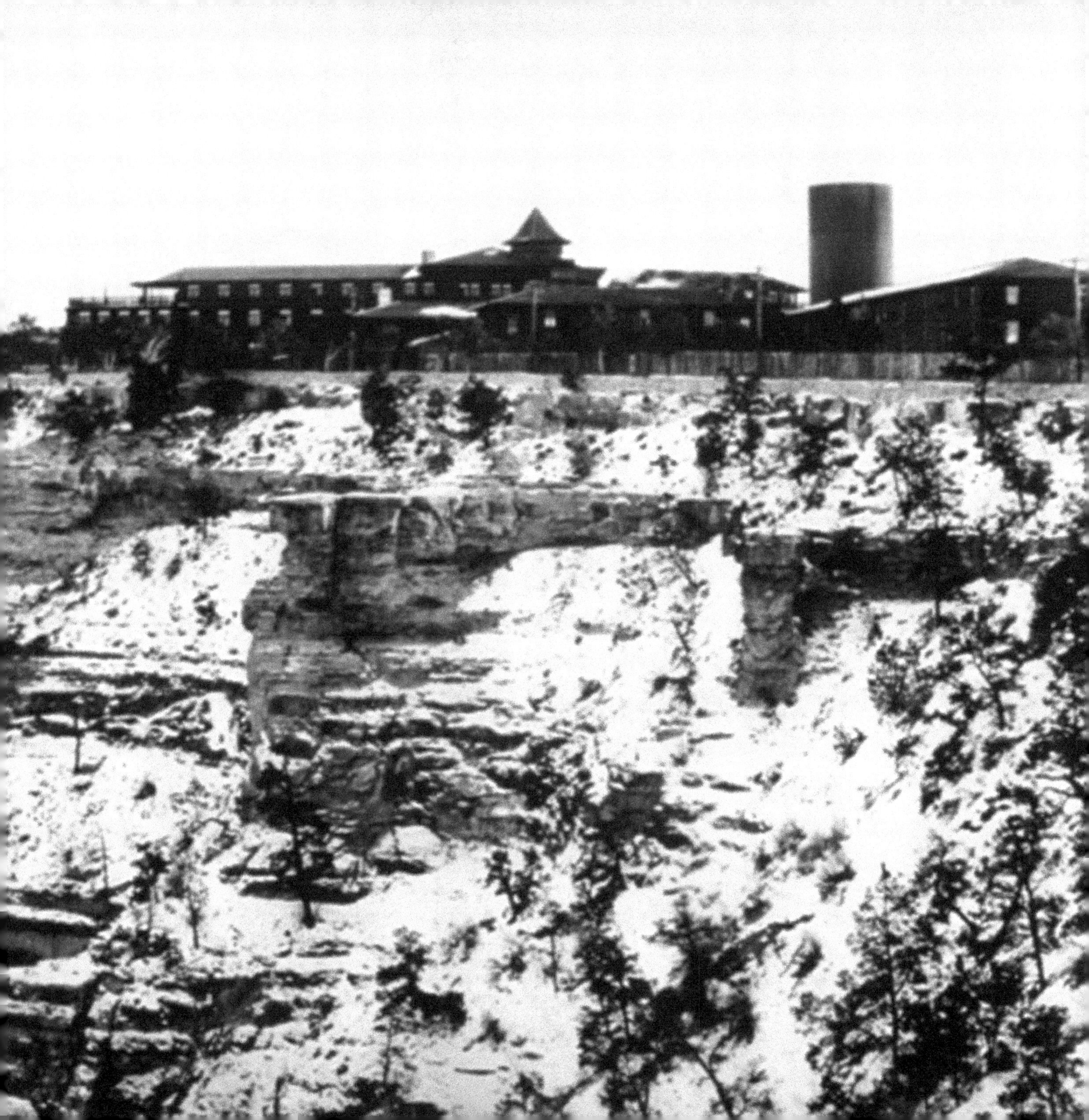

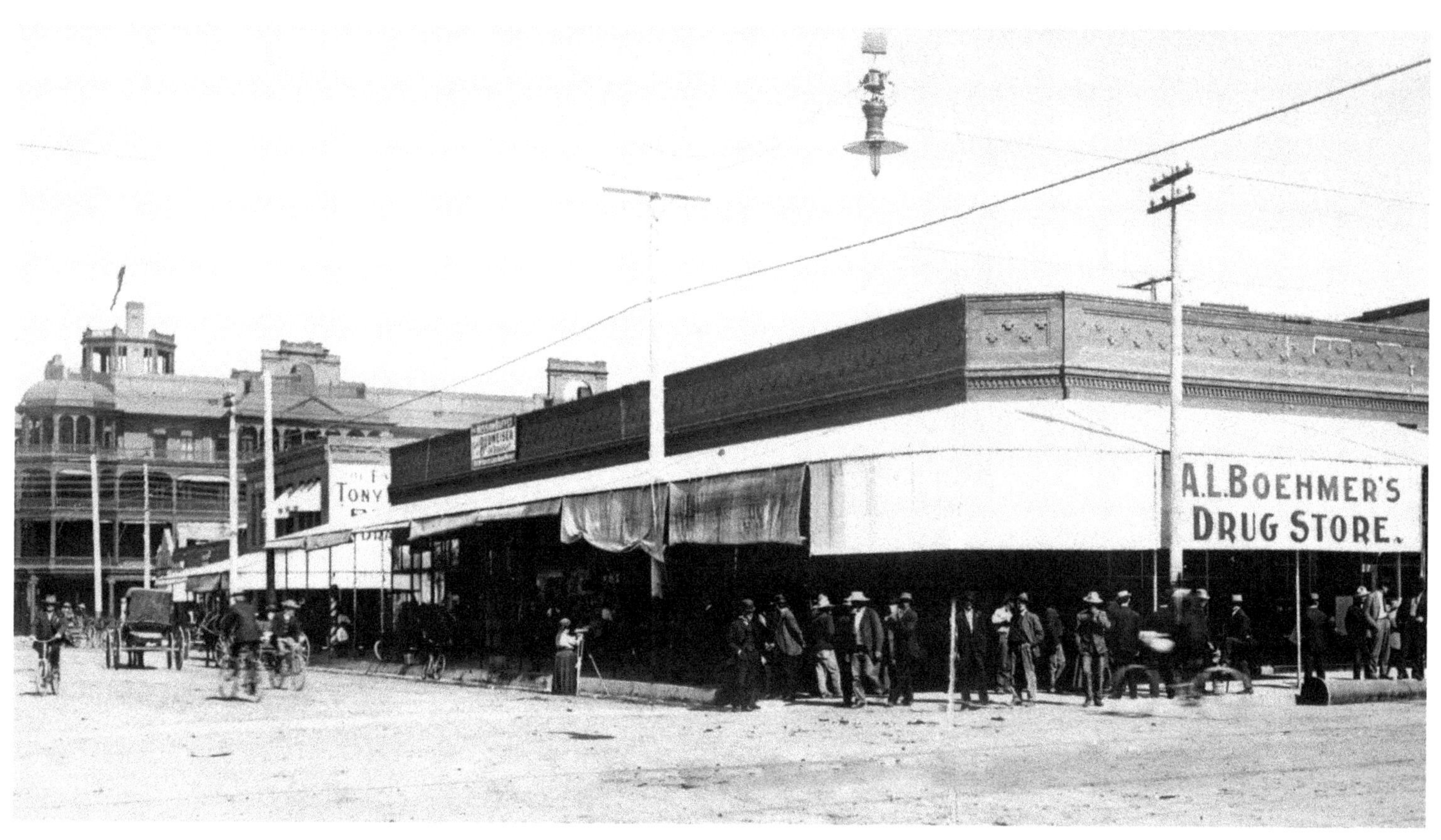

This Phoenix view is facing north on Central Avenue from Washington Street in 1908. A. L. Boehmer's Drug Store stands on the northeast corner, and the famous Adams Hotel is seen in the background.

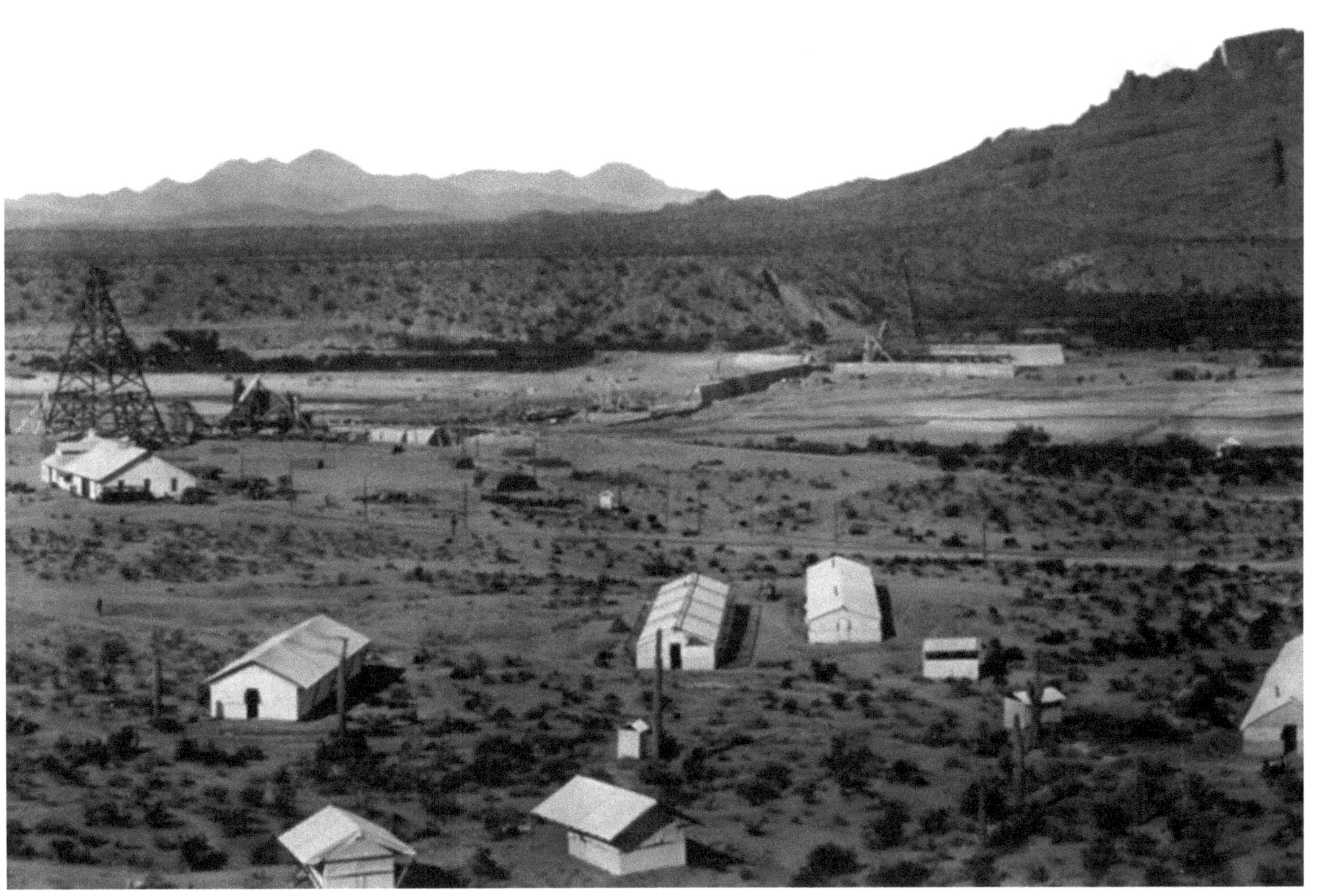

Diversion dams were used by the farmers of the Salt River Valley to bring water from the Salt River into smaller canals to irrigate their fields. Built in 1906 and seen here two years later, the Granite Reef Diversion Dam in Mesa is 29 feet high and 1,000 feet long, and channels water into canals north and south of the Salt River. Red Mountain rises in the background at right.

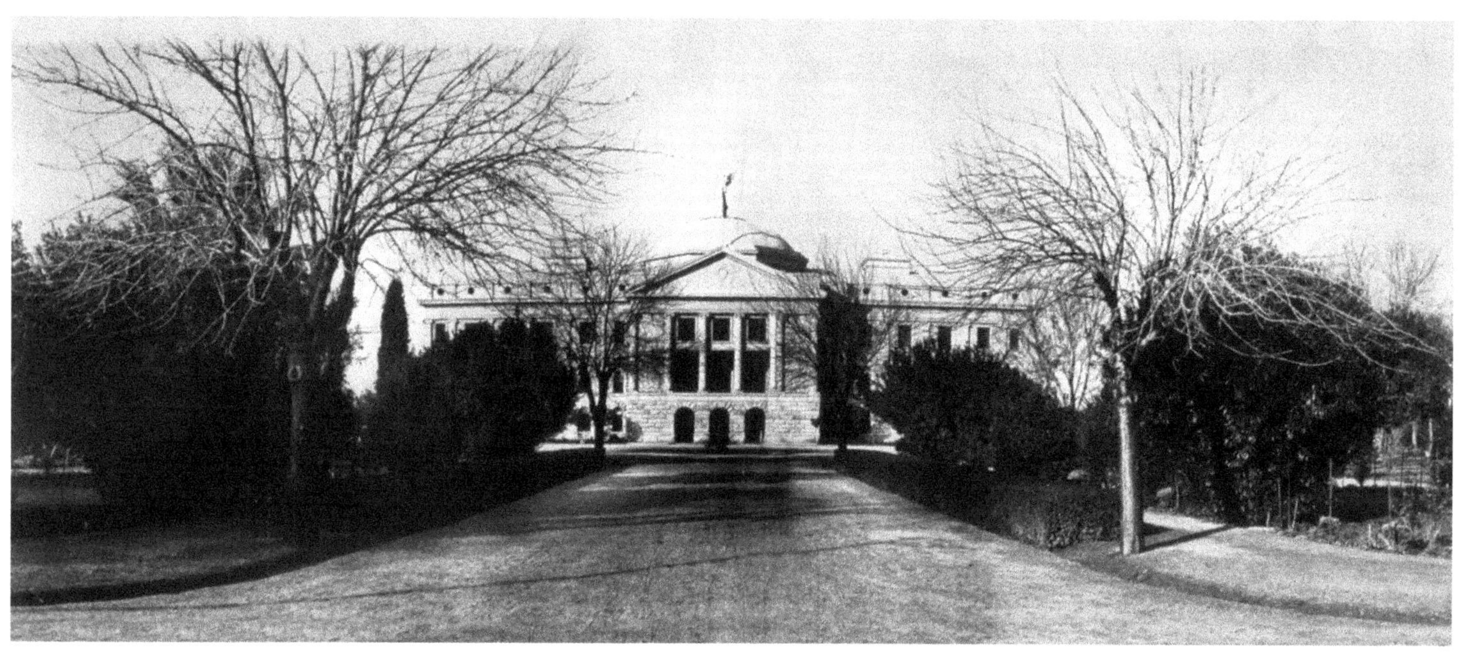

This 1908 view of the Arizona Capitol in Phoenix faces west from Washington Street. Completed in 1901, the Ionic Grecian–style stone building measures 184 feet long and 76 feet high. All of the stone was quarried from Arizona mountains. The Capitol dome features a 7-foot, 600-pound weather-vane statue called *Winged Victory.*

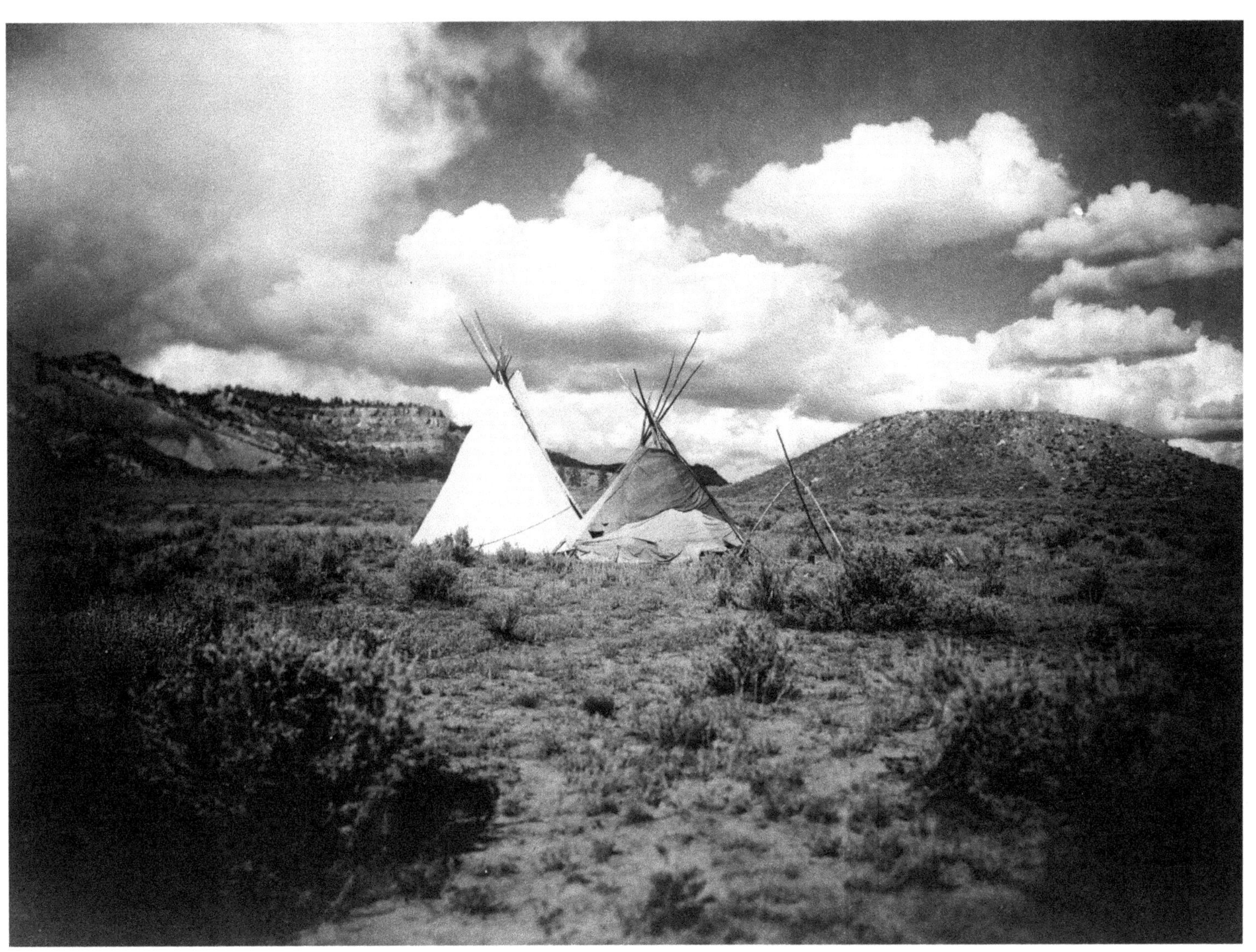

Although this photo made in 1909 by the Fred Harvey Company is titled "Two Apache Indian teepees in a hilly landscape of Arizona," the Apache people of Arizona traditionally did not use the tepee, as it was too cumbersome for their nomadic lifestyle. The tepee and other nontraditional Indian items began to show up in Arizona when the Fred Harvey Company began bringing tourists who wanted to have their pictures taken in the "Wild West."

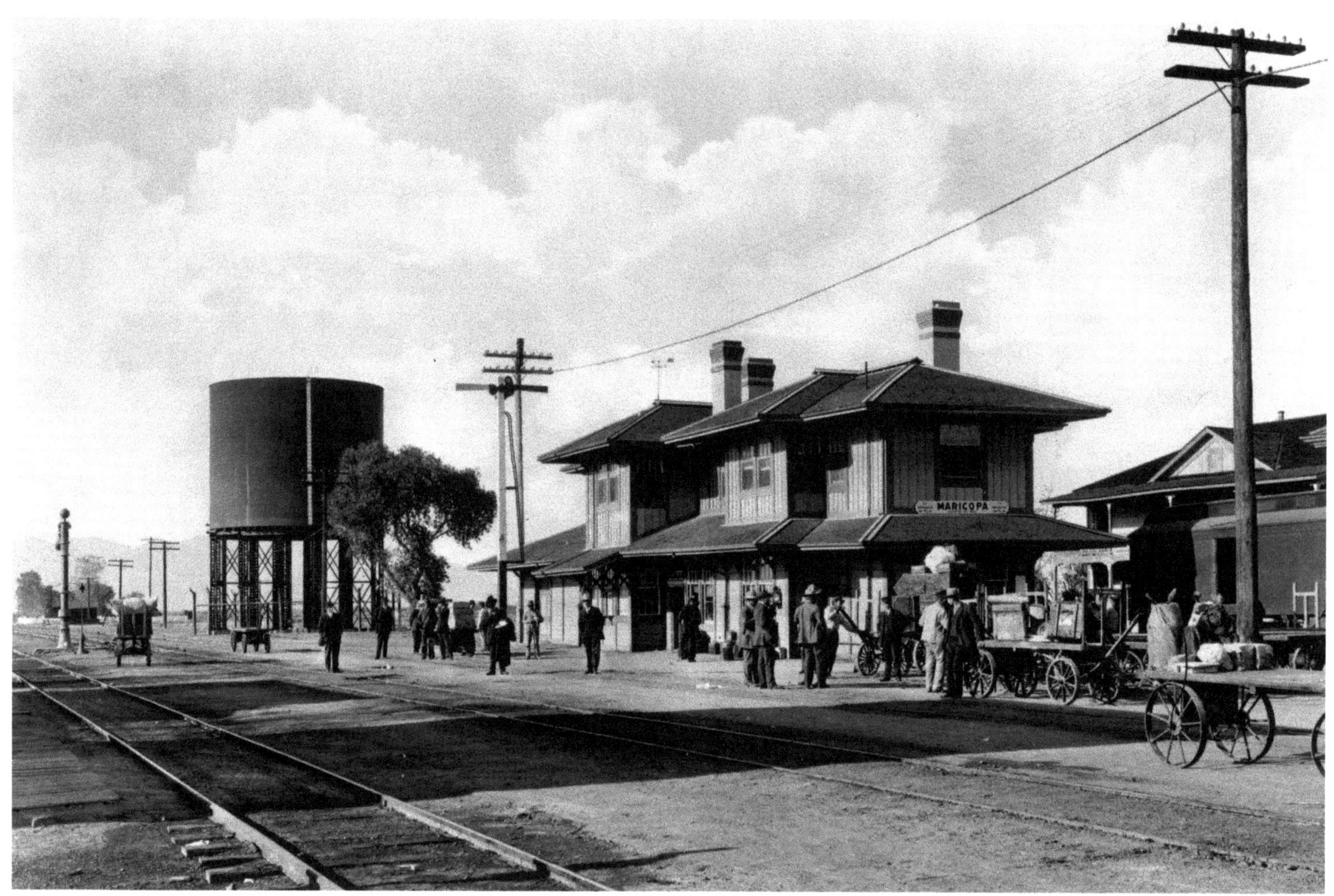

Passengers at the Maricopa depot await the arrival of the next train. The town developed around natural springs located in the middle of the Sonoran Desert. When the Southern Pacific Railroad came through Arizona in 1879, Maricopa Wells served as a much needed water stop for the steam locomotives crossing the hot desert. In 1887 a railroad spur, built from Maricopa Wells, brought the railroad to the small Arizona farming community called Phoenix.

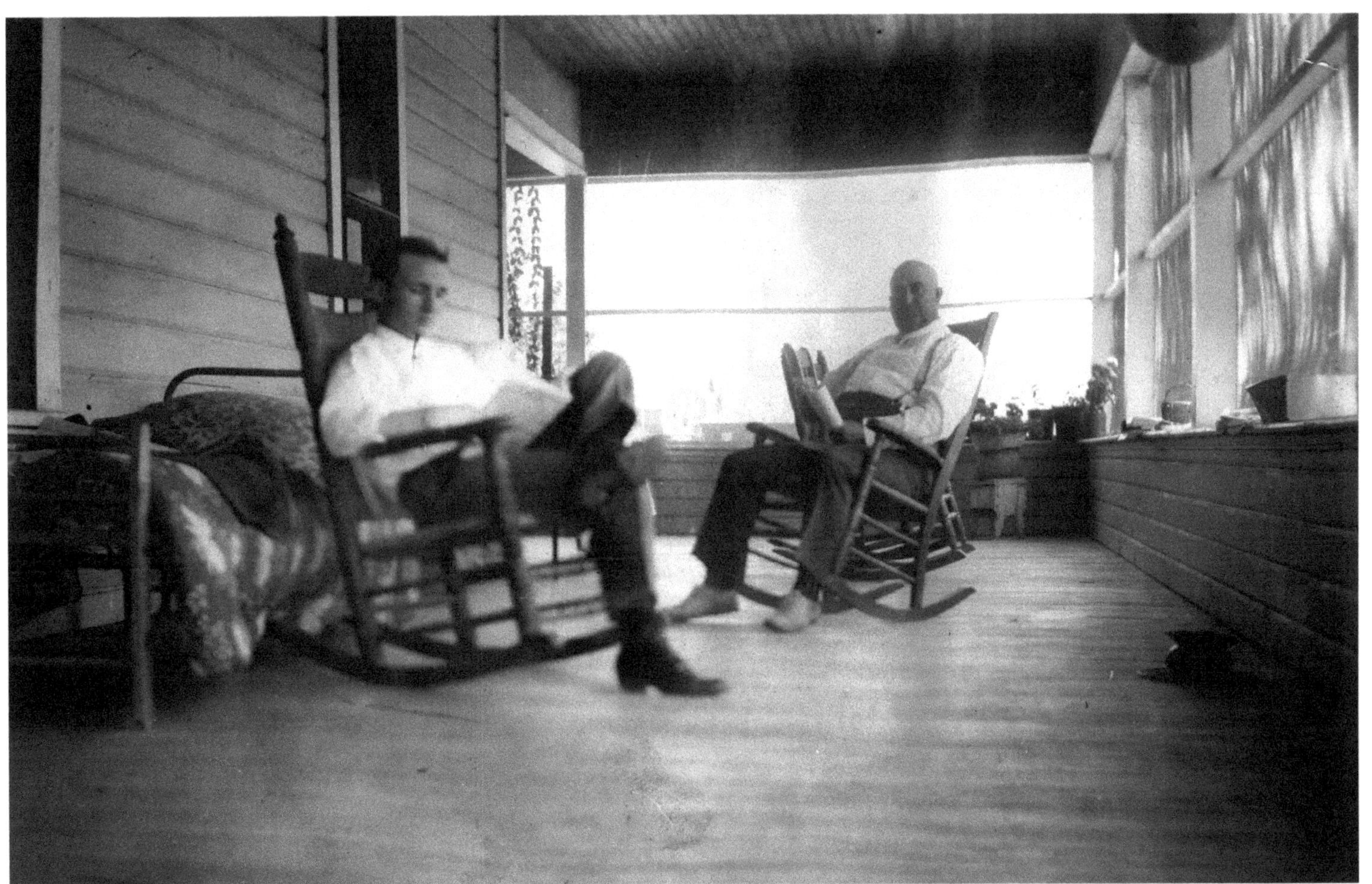

George W. P. Hunt (right) sits on his Globe front porch with a friend in 1909. Born in Huntsville, Missouri, in 1859, Hunt came to Globe as a young man in 1881. Between 1893 and 1910 he became probably the best known and respected politician in the Arizona Territory. He was elected Arizona's first state governor in the election of 1911.

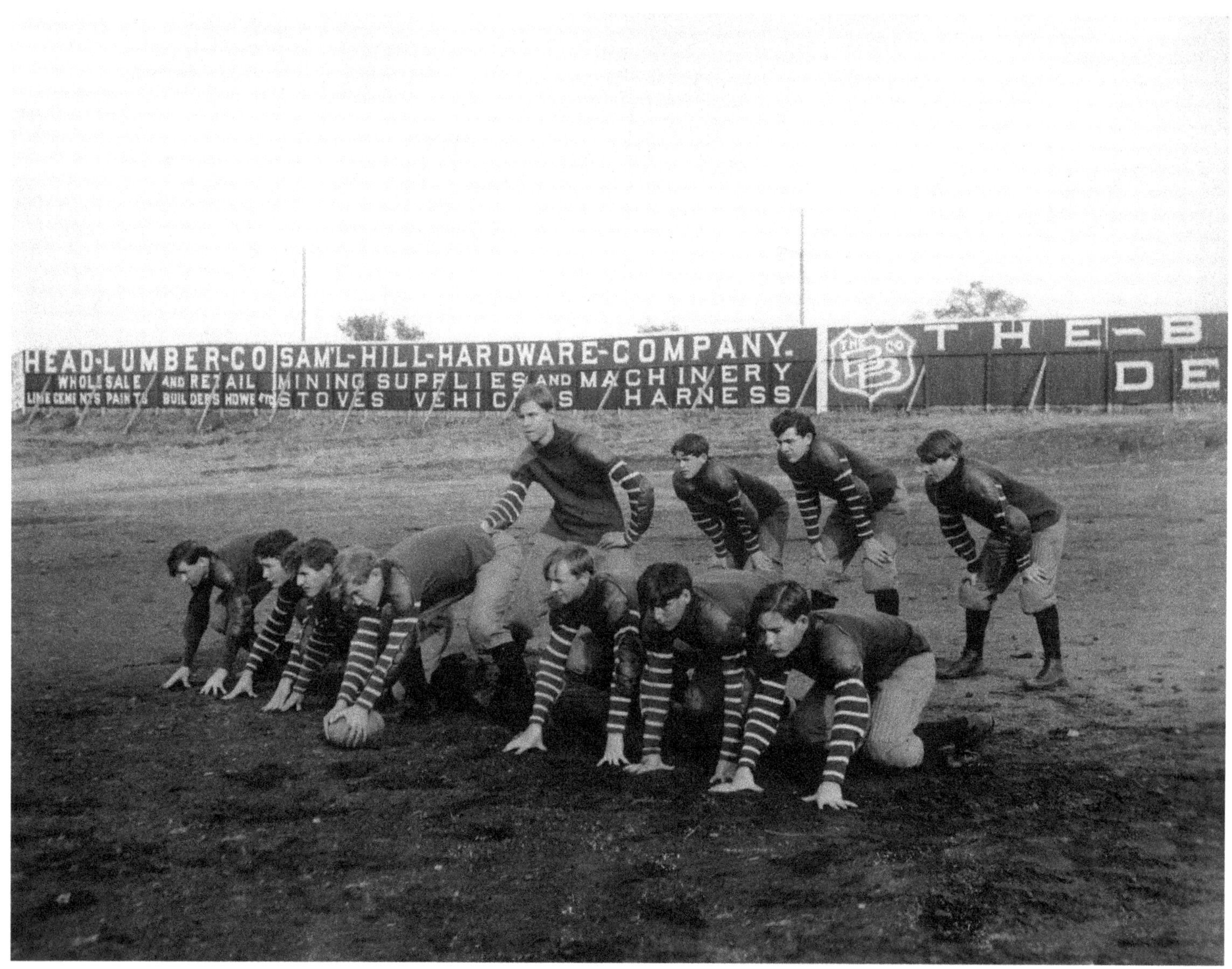

The first Prescott High School Badgers football team strikes a pose in 1910. Sixteen years later, the 1926 Badgers would become the only undefeated football team in the school's history, with an 8-0 record. That year the young boys from Prescott won the Northern Arizona championship, prevailing in a league that included, besides Prescott, teams from Flagstaff, Clarkdale, Williams, Winslow, Jerome, and Kingman. Prescott outscored its opponents by a combined 147-13.

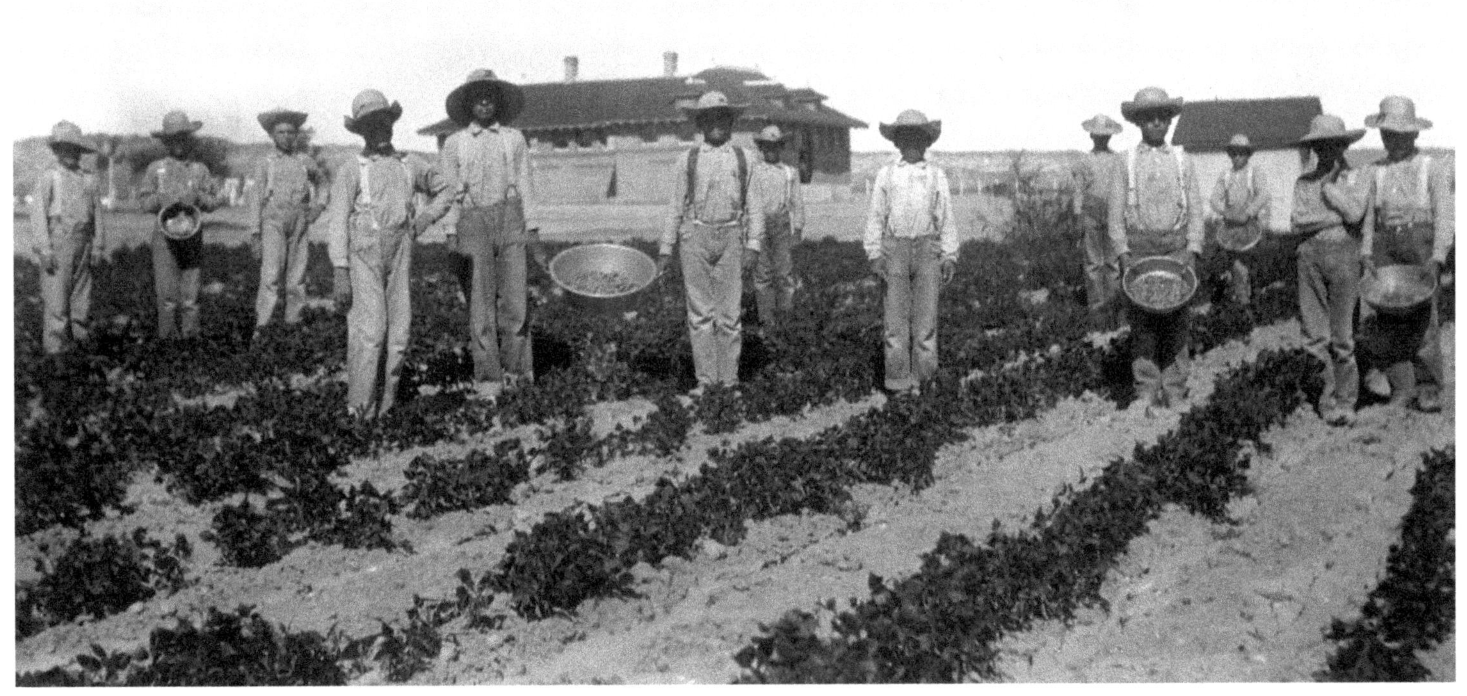

Arizona schoolchildren were long taught that the state was founded on its "five Cs"—copper, cotton, cattle, citrus, and climate. The five Cs provided the economic foundation upon which Arizona grew from a Wild West territory into the 48th state of the Union. This photo from around 1912 shows students working in the cotton fields at the Arizona Industrial School for Wayward Boys and Girls, located at Fort Grant.

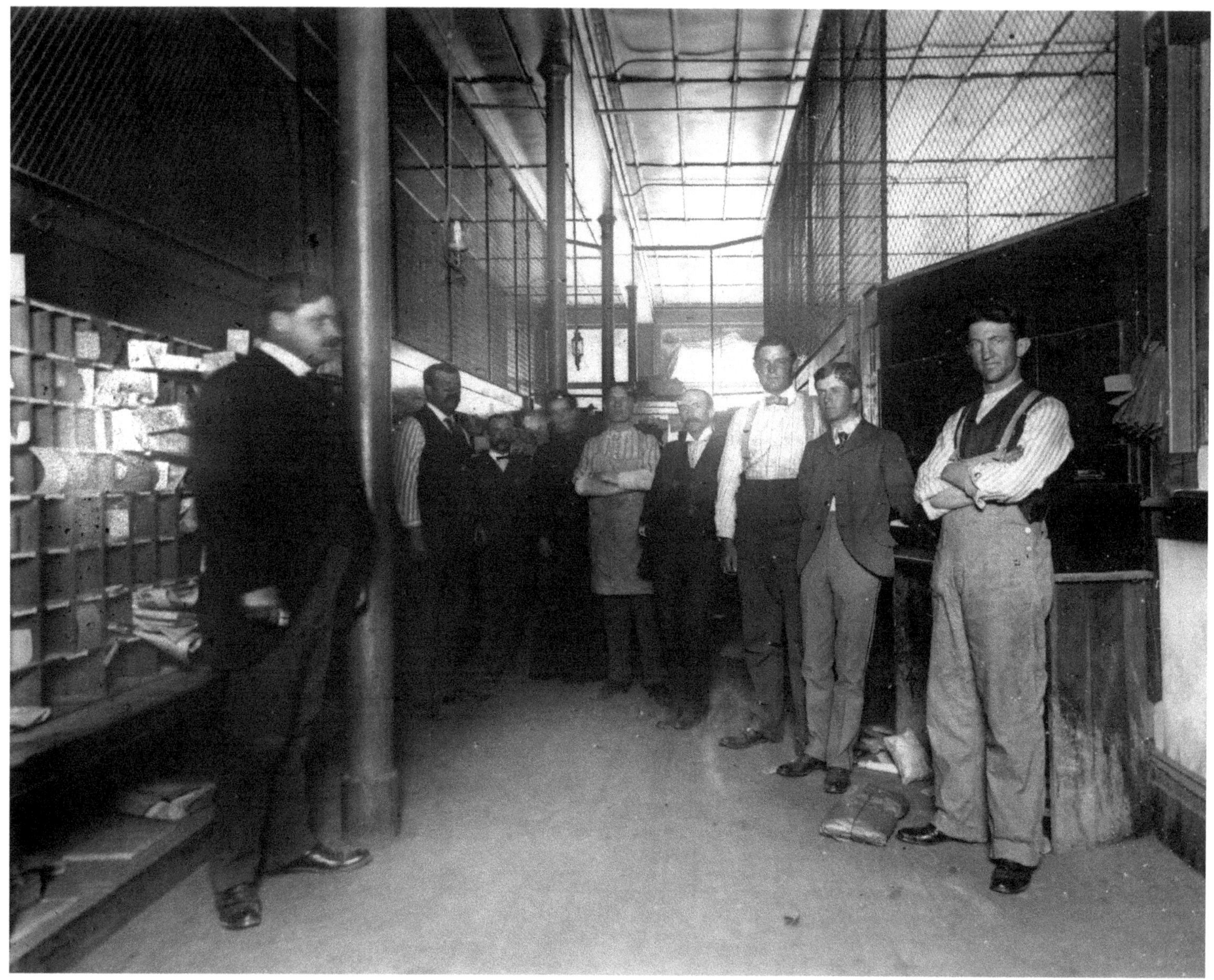

The first post office in Phoenix was established on June 15, 1869, with Jack Swilling as the postmaster. Most historians credit Swilling with founding Phoenix in 1867 when he started the Swilling Irrigation and Ditch Company to reopen the ancient Hohokam irrigation canals and once again bring water to desert fields. Here a later postmaster, James McClintock, and staff stand proudly inside a new Phoenix post office around 1910.

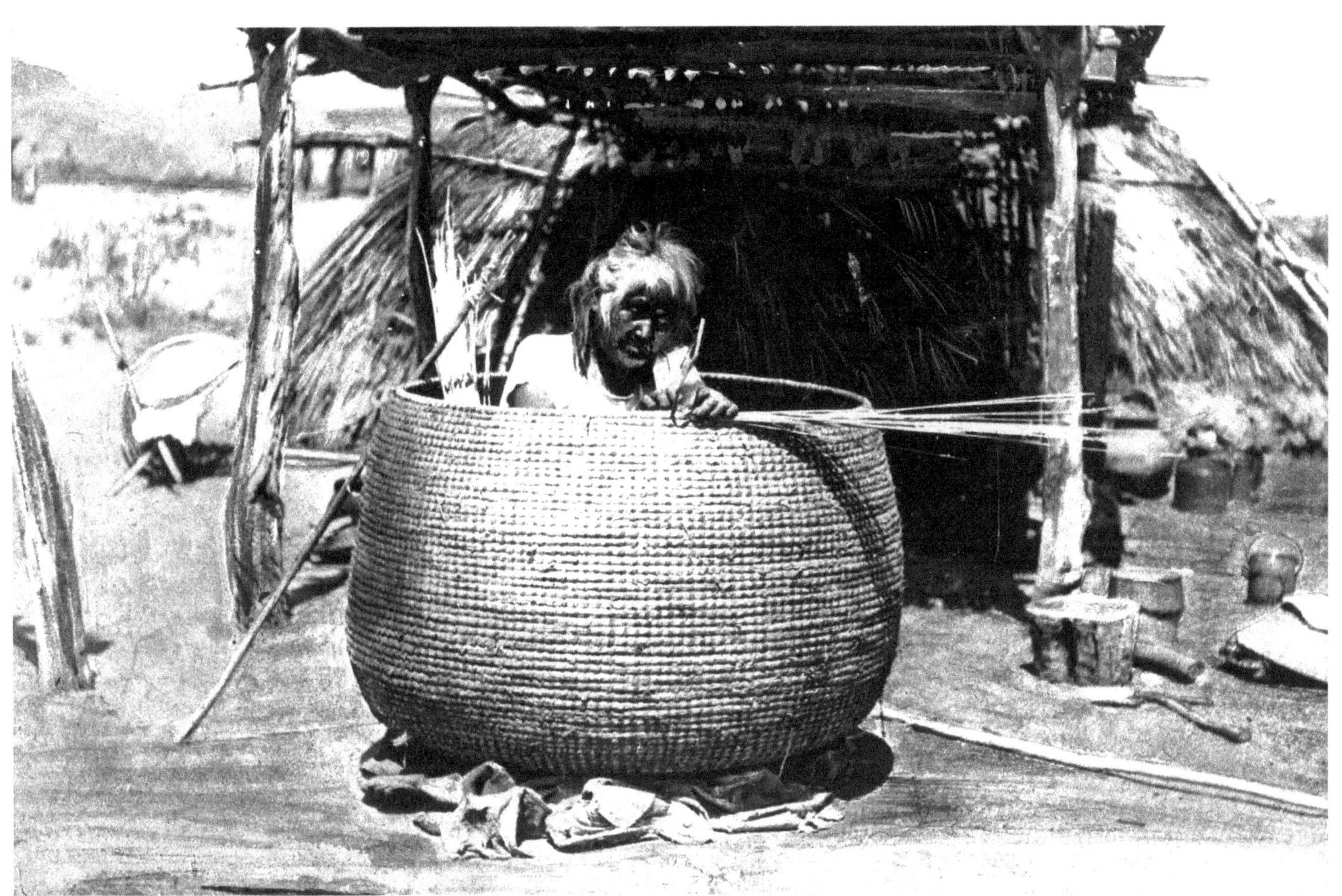

This 1910 photo shows a Pima Indian woman sitting inside a large food storage basket she is weaving. The Pima women are known for their great skill in basket making. Traditionally their beautiful baskets were made using willow and devil's claw sewn over bundles of cattail reed. As time has passed, fewer and fewer Pima baskets have been made, and the old ones have become quite valuable.

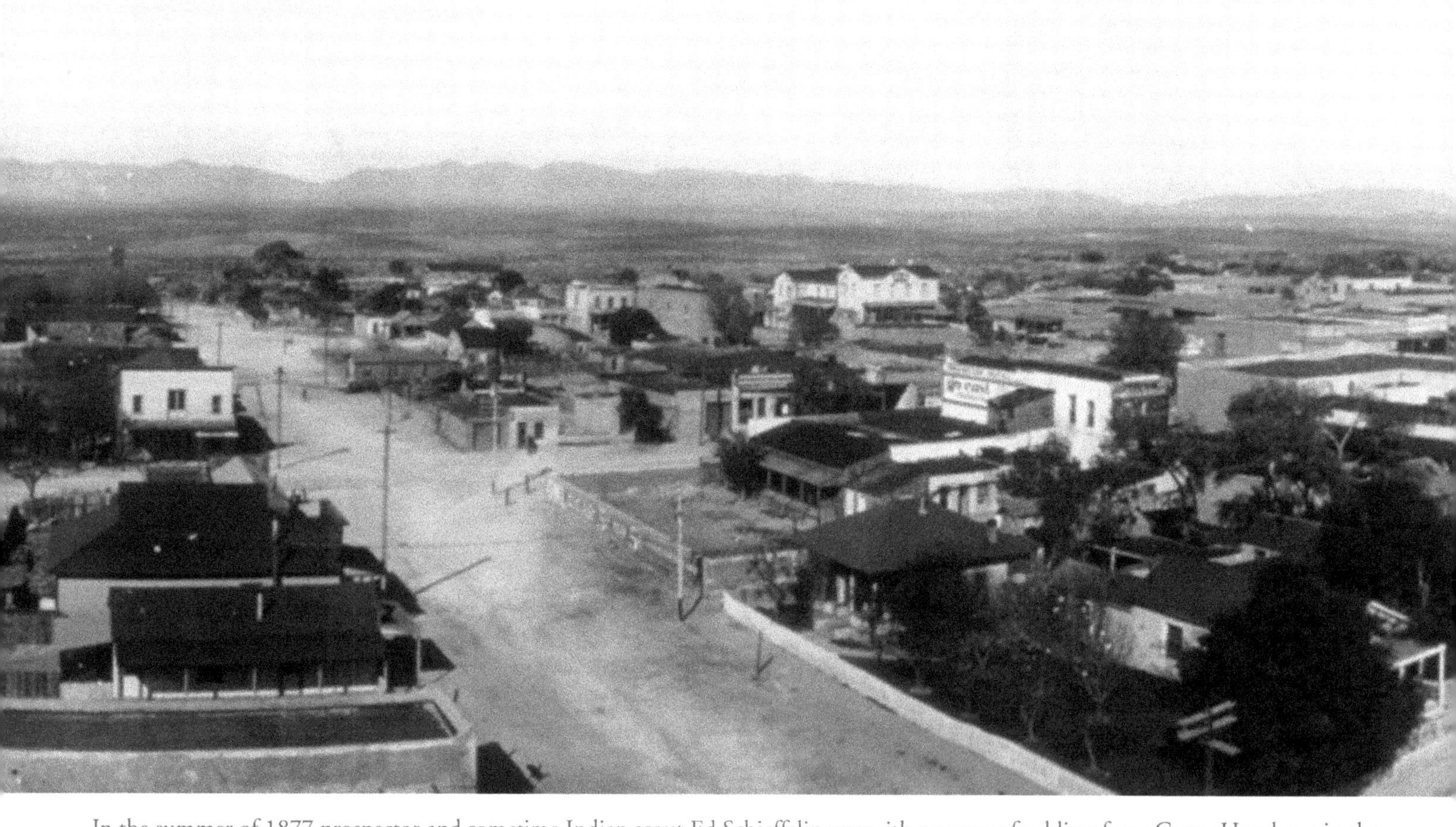

In the summer of 1877 prospector and sometime Indian scout Ed Schieffelin was with a group of soldiers from Camp Huachuca in the desert of southeastern Arizona, when he decided to leave the soldiers to continue his long search for silver. Because of the Apache Indian threat, a soldier warned Schieffelin to be careful or the only stone he would find would be his tombstone, or words to that effect. So when Schieffelin found his silver mine, he named it Tombstone. This photo shows the town that grew up around Schieffelin's strike as it appeared in 1909.

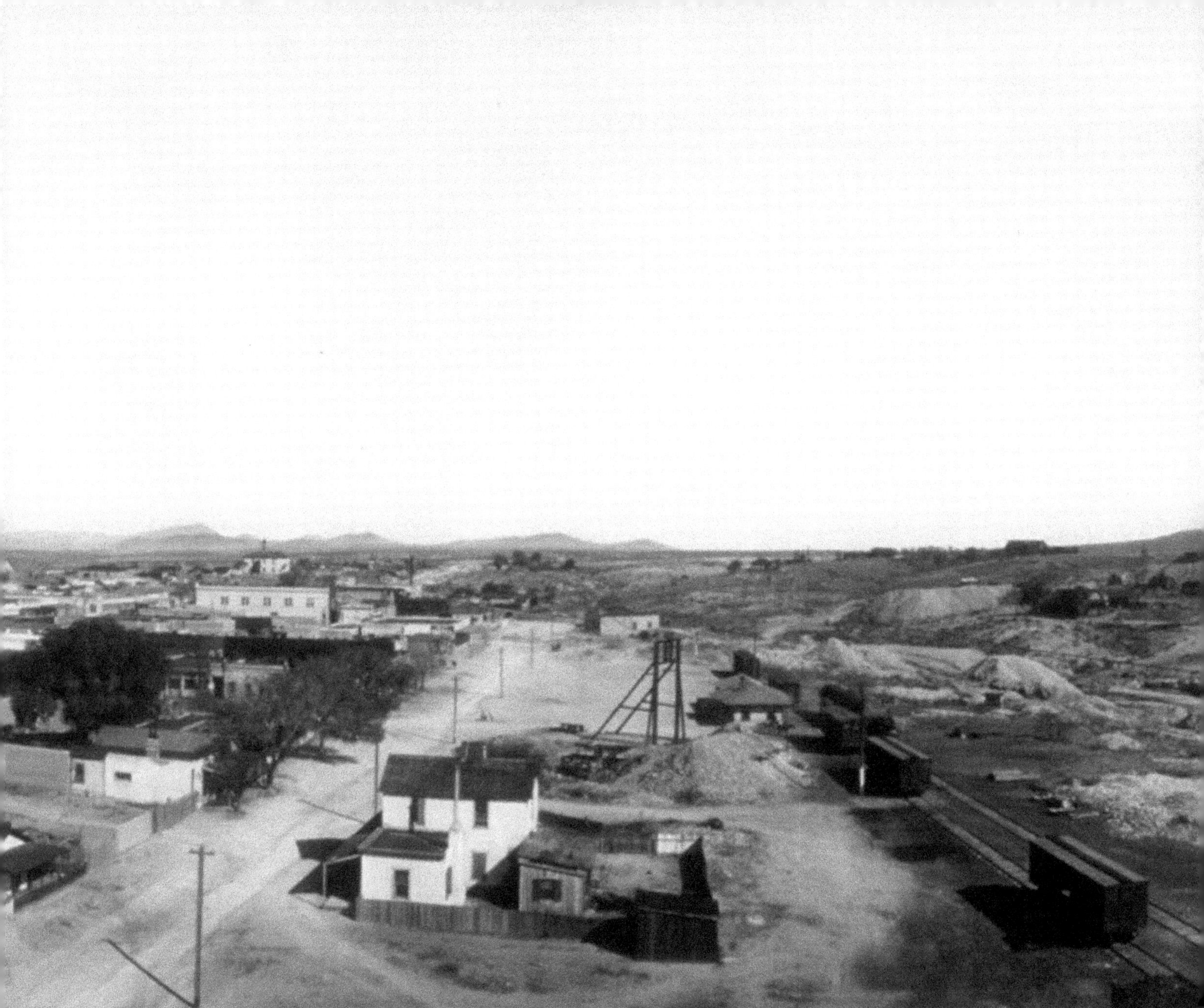

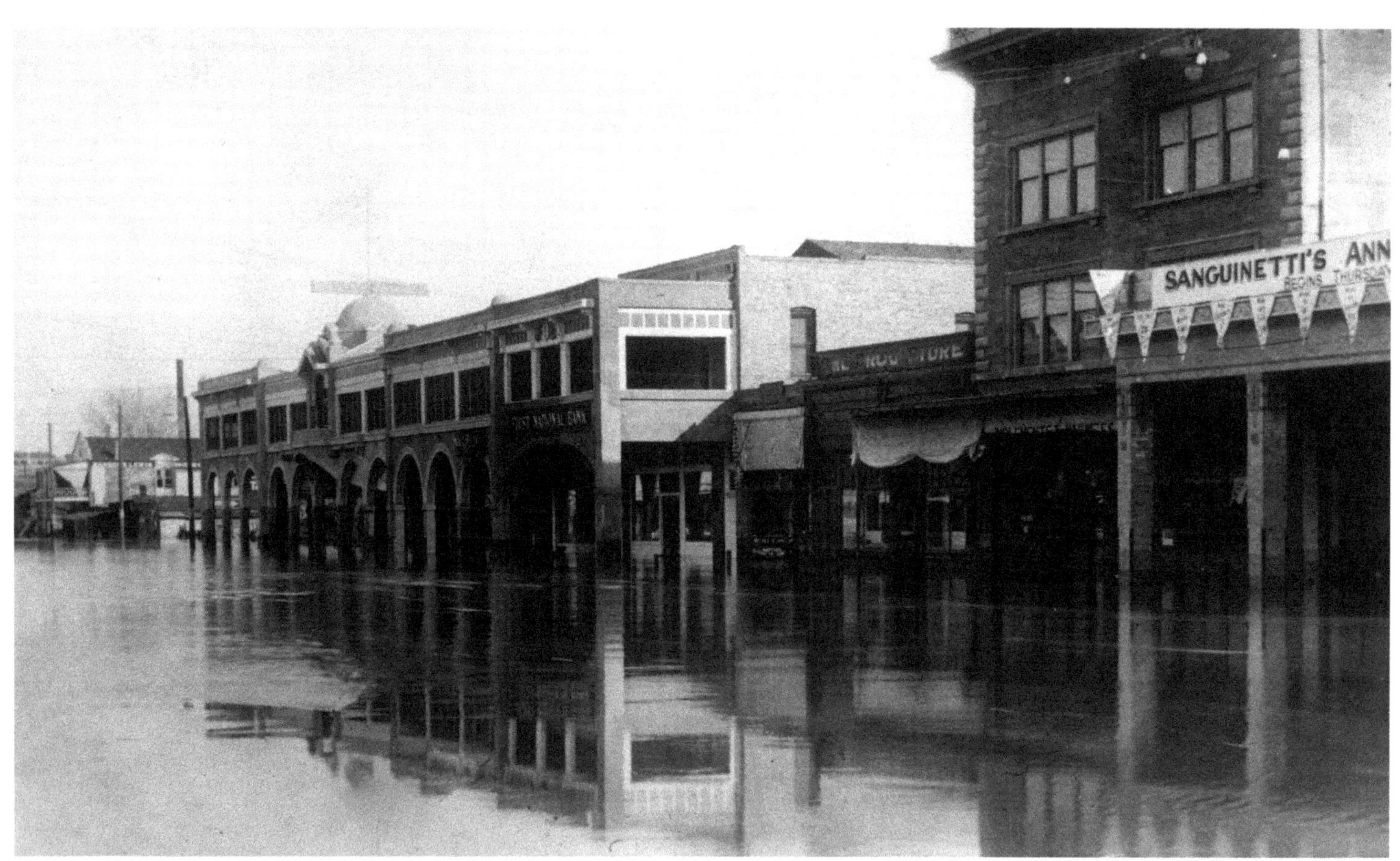

Arizona desert towns needed access to fresh drinking water, so they were always developed close to water sources. However, heavy desert thunderstorms could make creeks, streams, and rivers rage with floodwaters that would overwhelm levees and dams and rush into the towns. Here downtown Yuma has been flooded by the Colorado River—a source of drinking water one day, destroyer of the town the next.

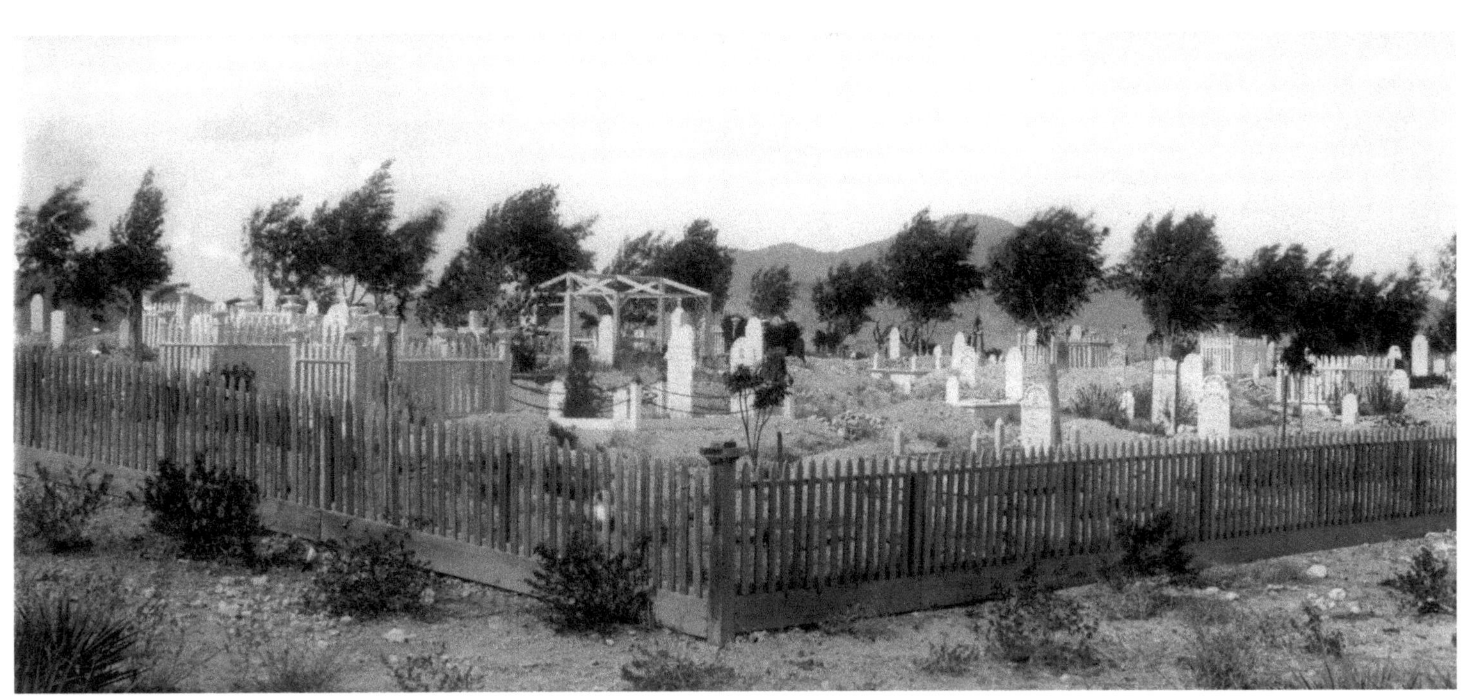

The Tombstone City Cemetery saw its first burial in 1882, even though it did not become an official cemetery until 1884, the year the notorious Boot Hill Cemetery closed. Shown here around 1910, the Tombstone City Cemetery is today in great need of restoration. To quote a local restoration activist: "These are the real people who stopped in this hellhole of a desert to make a life and a town."

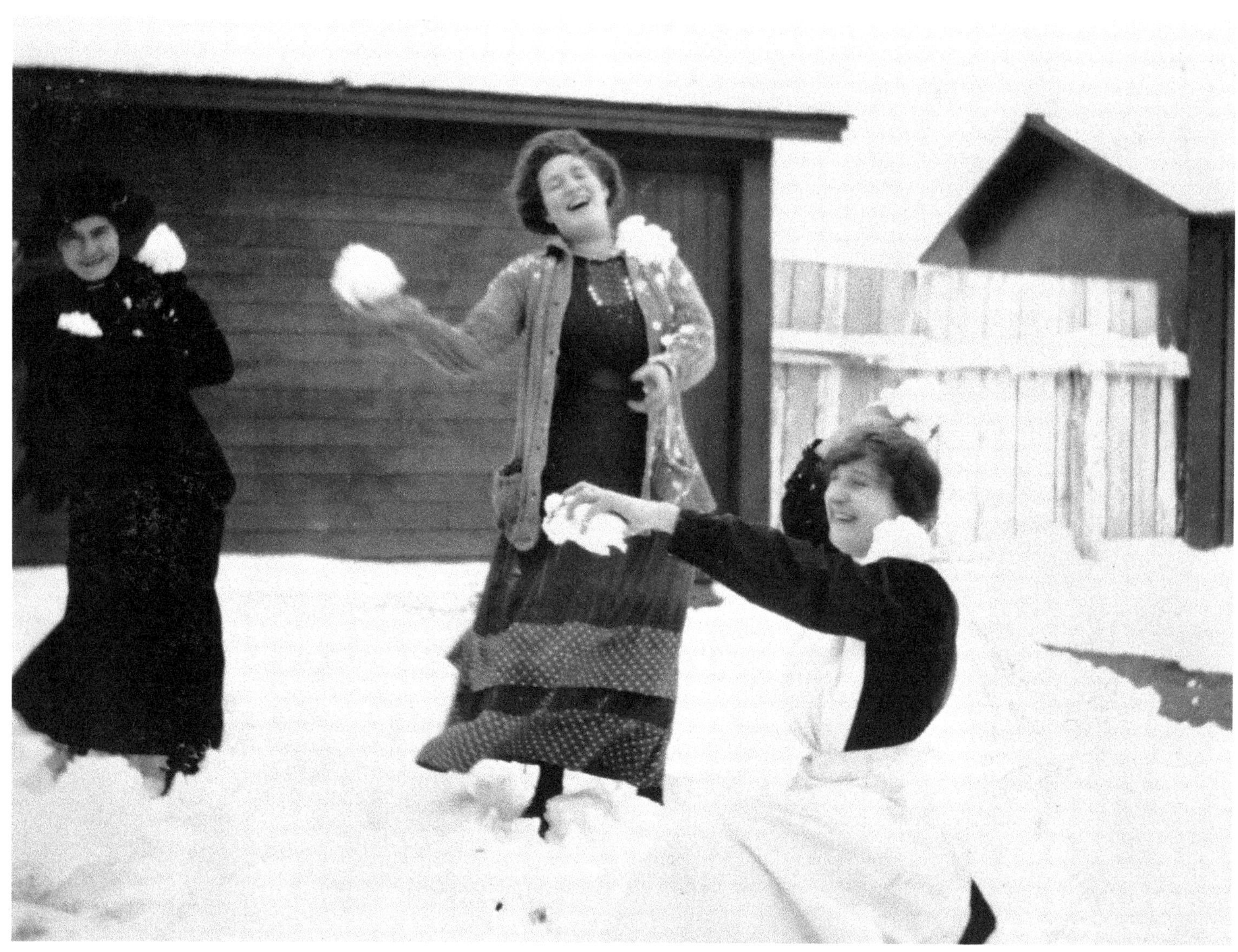

Harvey Girls, usually young women from the East, were employed in the Harvey House restaurants that lined the Santa Fe Railroad from 1876 to the early 1950s. Possibly as many as 100,000 Harvey Girls came to the West in those early years, often becoming the first wives and mothers in the small Western towns where they worked. These Harvey Girls are having a snowball fight at La Posada Resort in Winslow.

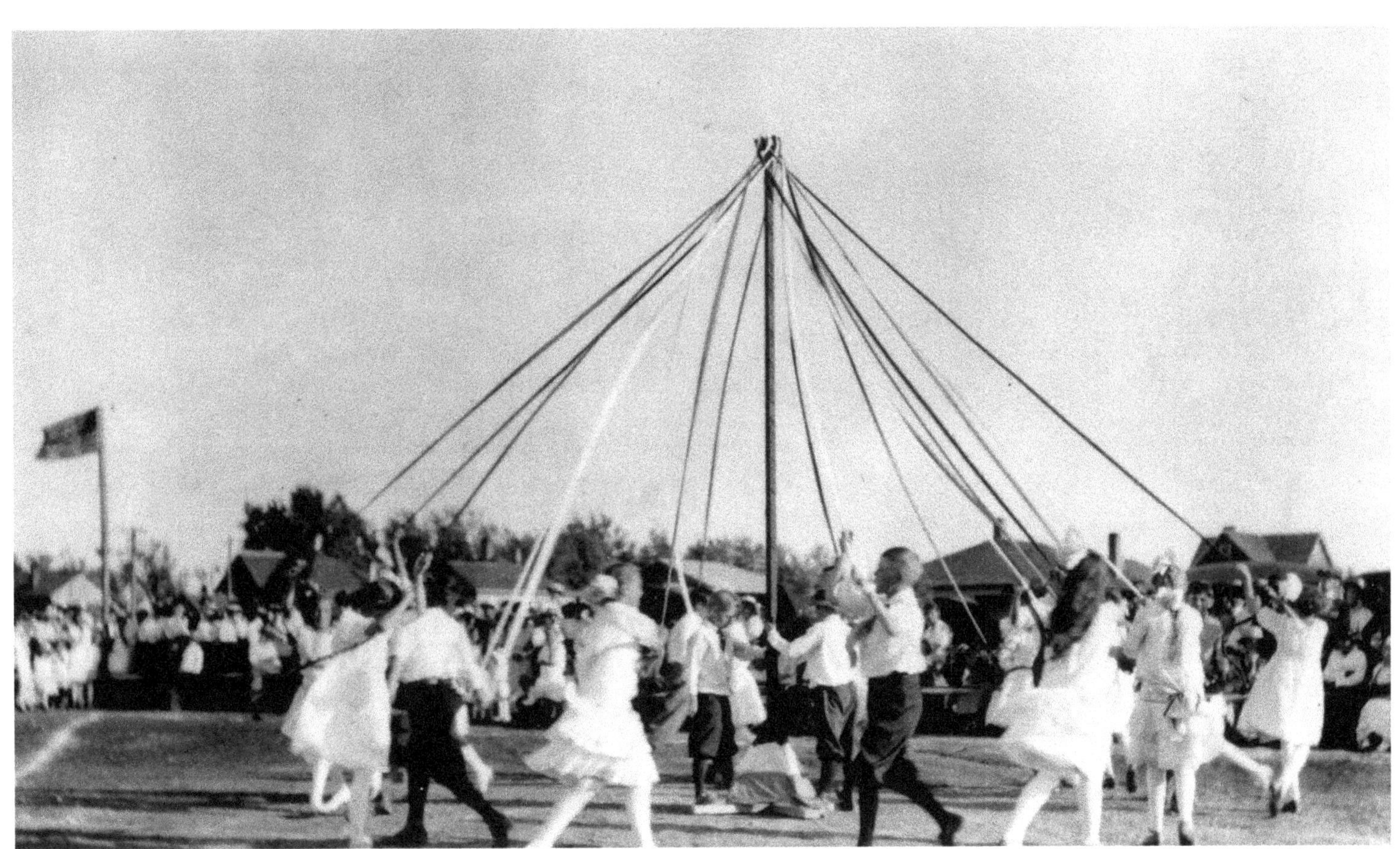

Schoolchildren dance around a maypole in Winslow around 1910. Winslow is one of the many railroad towns established during the 1880s. Most historians believe it was named after General Edward F. Winslow, who at that time was president of the old St. Louis and San Francisco Railroad. The Navajo Indians' name for the town is Beeshsinil, which means "iron lying down."

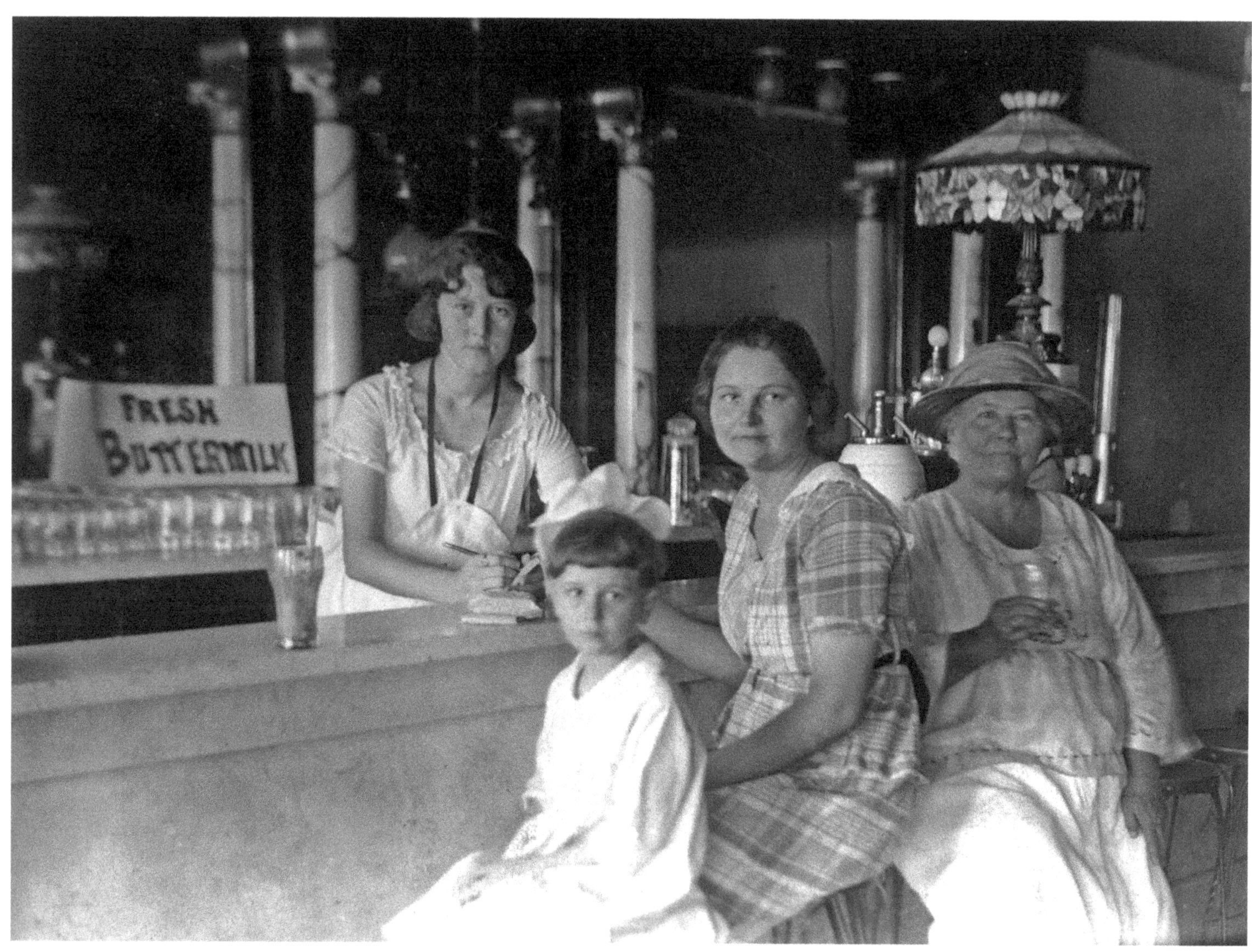

Casa Grande was founded in 1879 at the terminus of a railroad line from the copper mining district. In fact the settlement was first called Terminus, but the name was later changed to Casa Grande in honor of a Hohokam Indian ruin located some 21 miles from the railroad site. By 1910 a local family could enjoy a cool soda at this Casa Grande fountain to help cope with the Sonoran Desert summers.

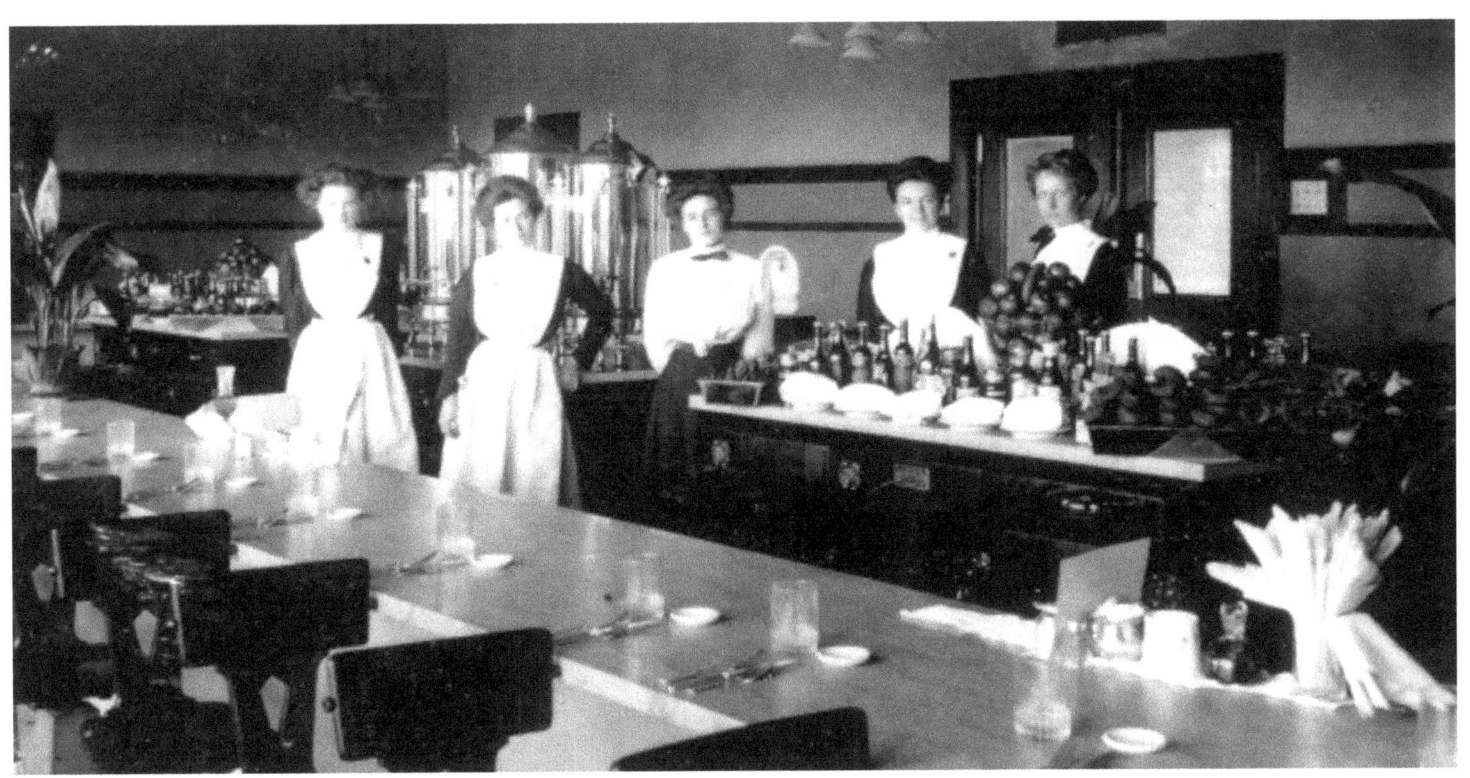

The Harvey Girls of La Posada in Winslow served meals in the last of the great Harvey Houses to be built. La Posada was designed as a Spanish hacienda by Mary Jane Colter and opened in 1930. A virtual Who's Who of America stayed overnight at La Posada when traveling the transcontinental railroad. Today the historic hacienda is restored and offers twenty-first-century guests a chance to experience the "last great railroad hotel."

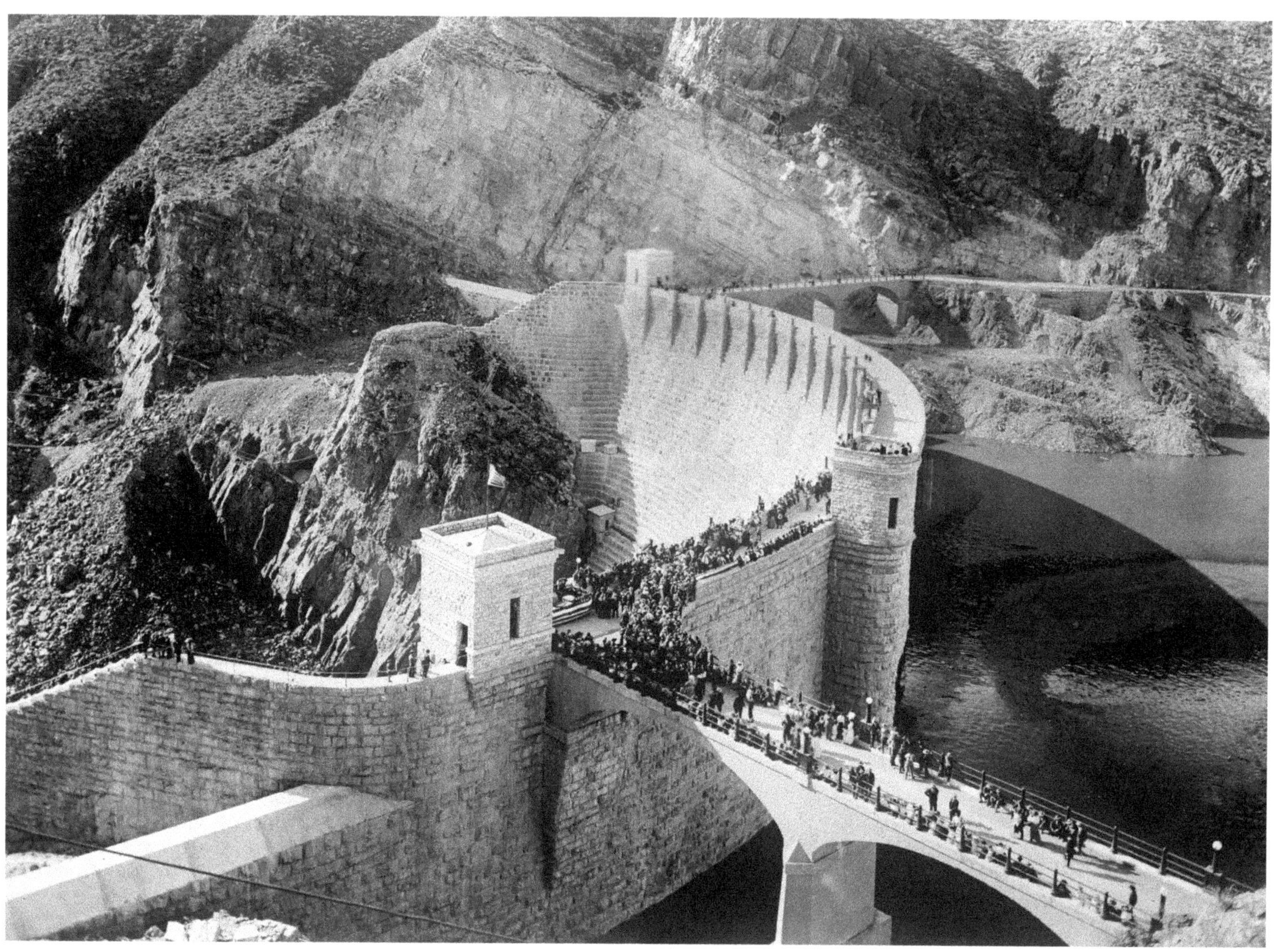

The Newlands Reclamation Act of 1902 provided federal loans to the 16 western states for the funding of irrigation projects. As a result, nearly every major river in the West was dammed. Built across the Salt River, some 40 miles east of Phoenix, Roosevelt Dam was the first Newlands Reclamation Act project in Arizona. The guest of honor at the March 18, 1911, dedication ceremony was Theodore Roosevelt, for whom the dam was named.

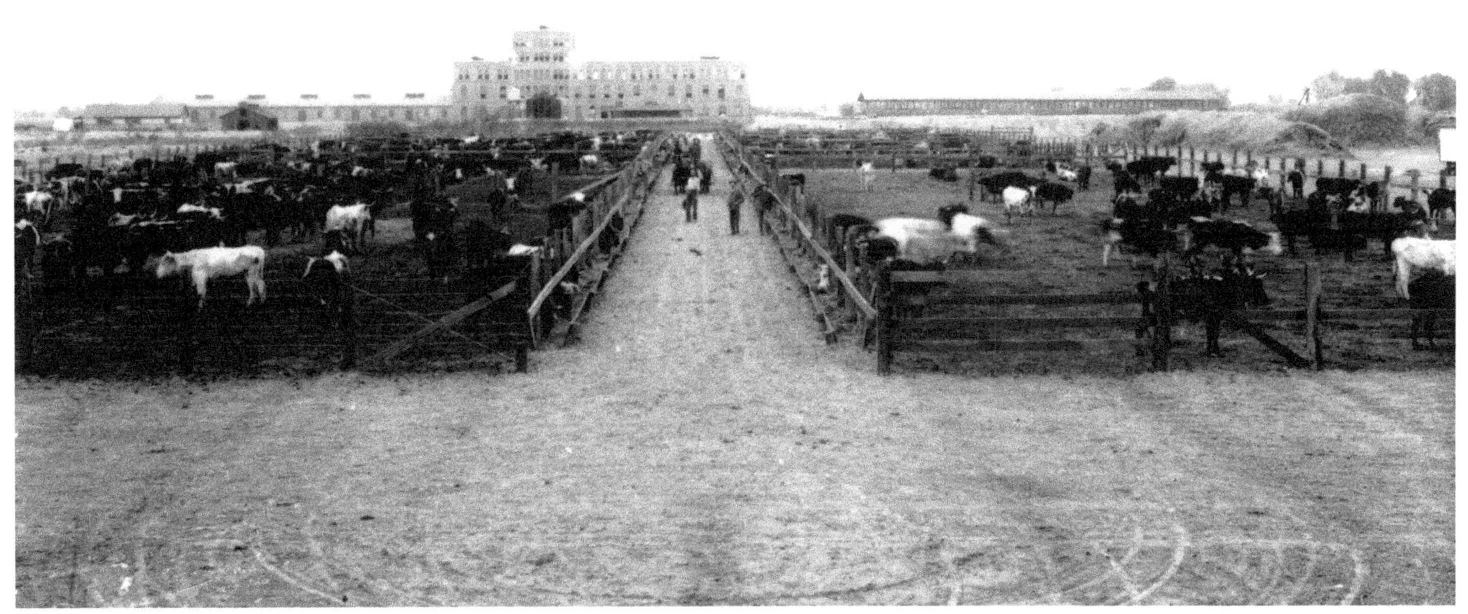

Glendale's official founding date is given as February 27, 1892, the day the New England Land Company surveyed the first residential area for the Church of the Brethren of Illinois. With completion of Roosevelt Dam two decades later, Glendale could count on a stable water supply and became an agricultural paradise, producing lettuce, melons, sugar beets, and cotton. Cattle ranching prospered as well, evident by the size of the Glendale stockyards seen here in 1913. A sugar beet factory looms in the distance.

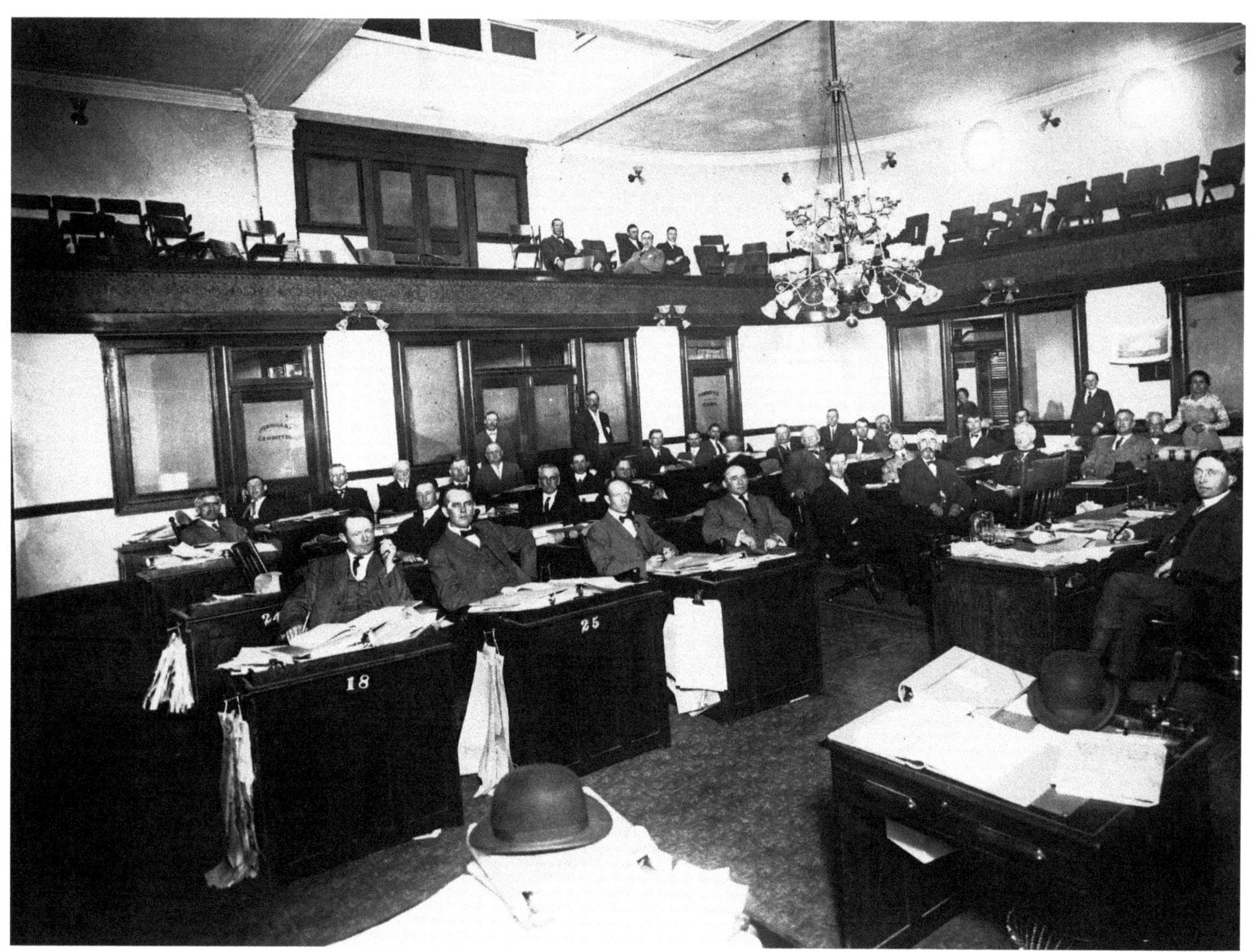

On February 14, 1912, President William Howard Taft signed the Arizona Statehood Act, which made Arizona the 48th state of the Union. In Phoenix, Governor George W. P. Hunt led Arizona citizens in a celebration down Washington Street to the State Capitol, where he gave his statehood address from the second-floor balcony. With statehood achieved, the first Arizona state legislature, shown here in 1913, began its work.

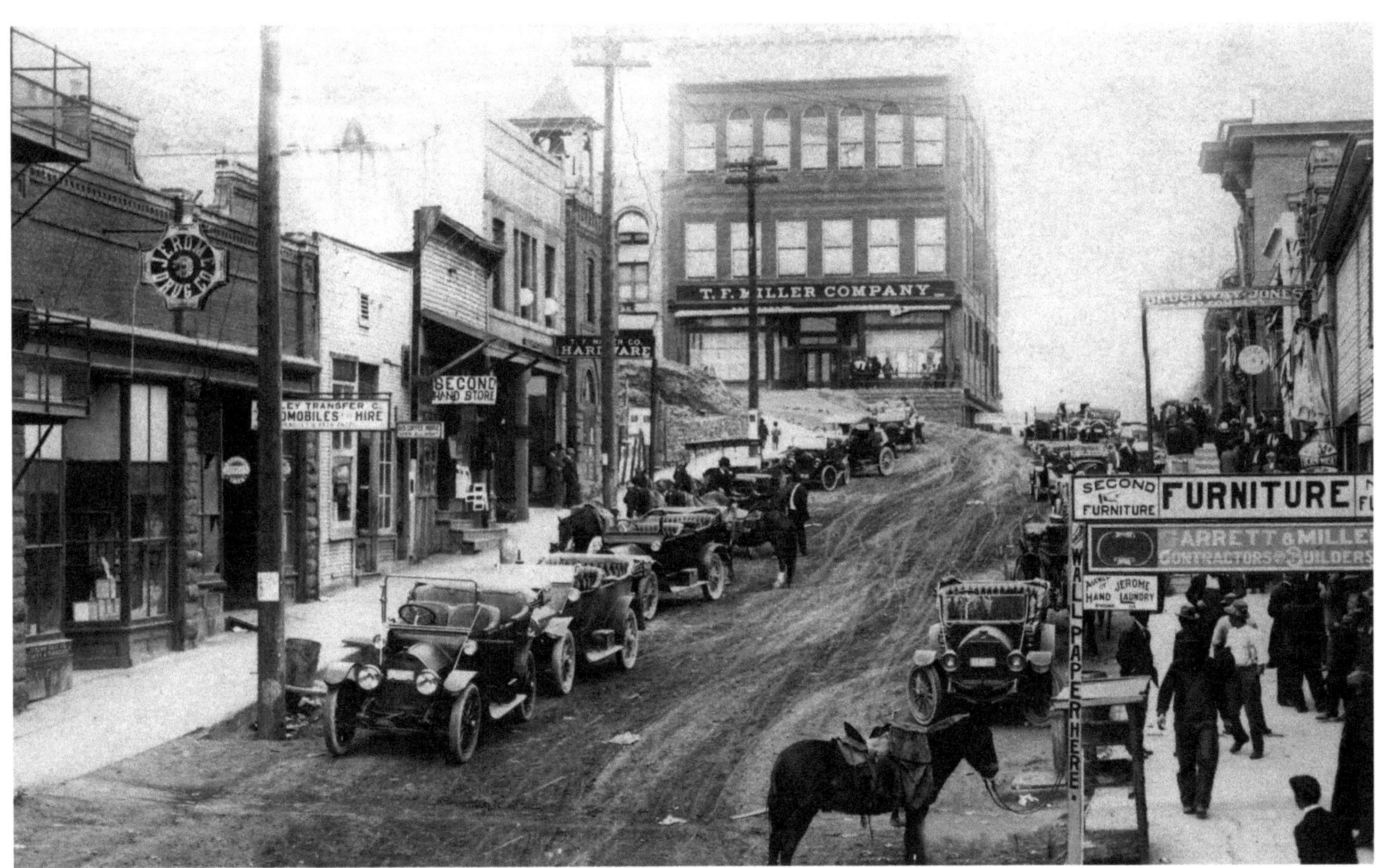

The copper mining town of Jerome was built on the side of Cleopatra Hill in 1883. It was named after New York investor Eugene Jerome, who never visited the town. Jerome's United Verde Mine produced more than $1 billion in silver, gold, and copper during its 70 years of operation. By 1915, when this photo was taken, the population of Jerome had grown to over 2,500 citizens.

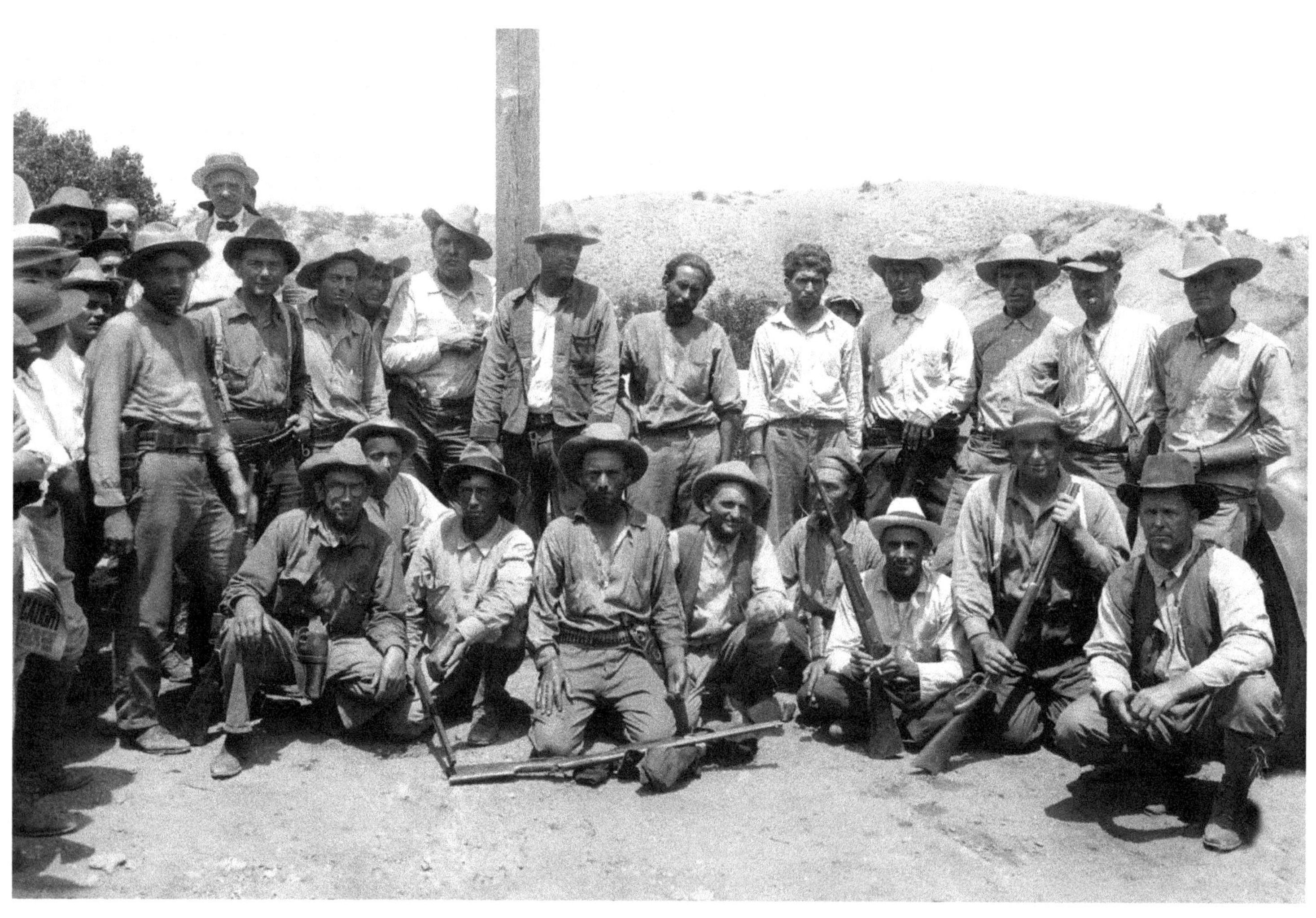

Posse comitatus or sheriff's posse is the common-law authority of a county sheriff to enroll any able-bodied male aged 18 or older to help keep order or pursue a felon. Lawmen of the West often turned to fellow citizens for help under the terms of that authority. This photograph taken around 1915 in Nogales, Arizona, appears to be of a Santa Cruz County sheriff's posse with two prisoners.

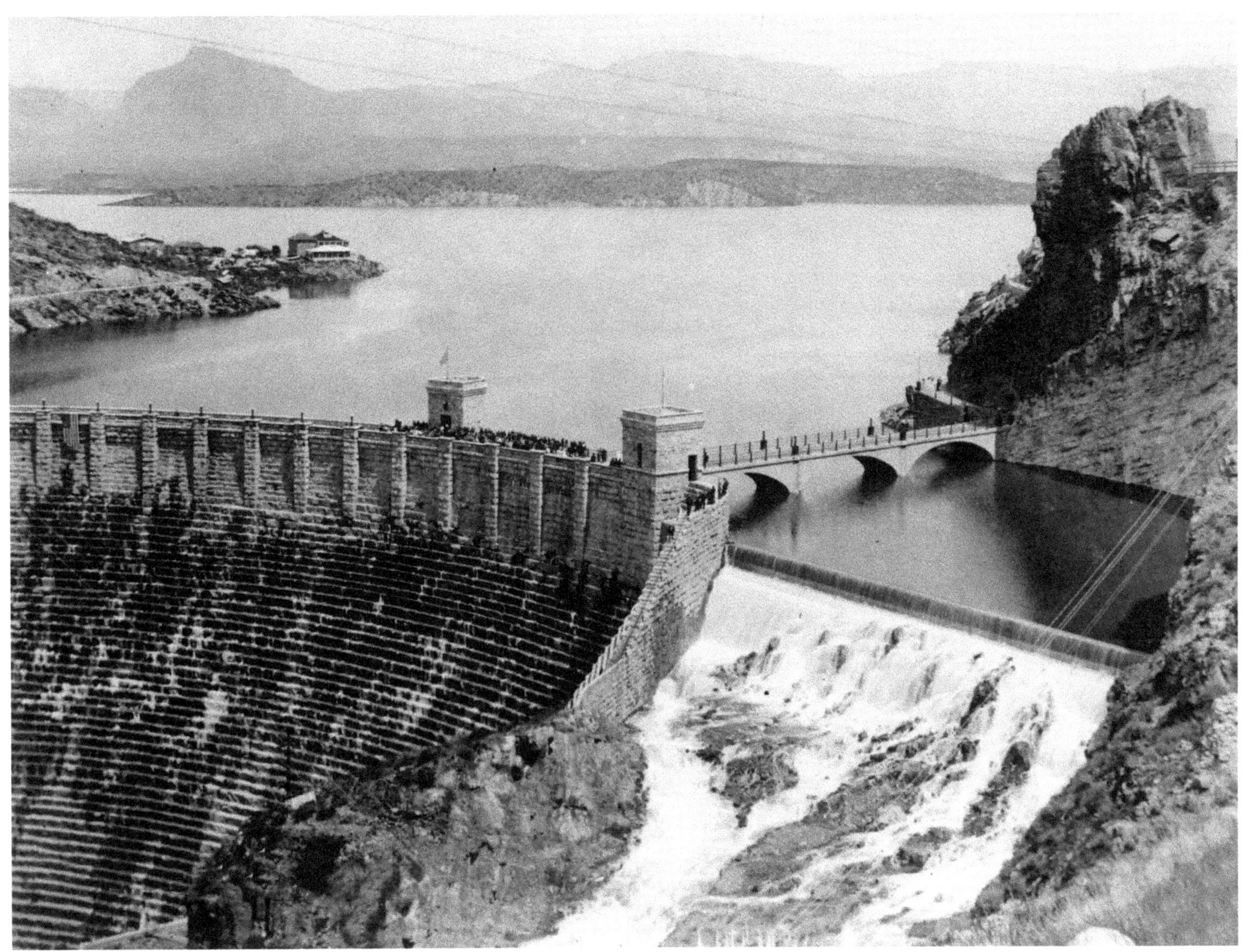

In this winter 1915 image, water from Roosevelt Lake rushes through the overflow spillway of Roosevelt Dam. This marked the first time since the dam's completion in 1911 that the reservoir reached its full capacity, requiring that excess water be released into the Salt River.

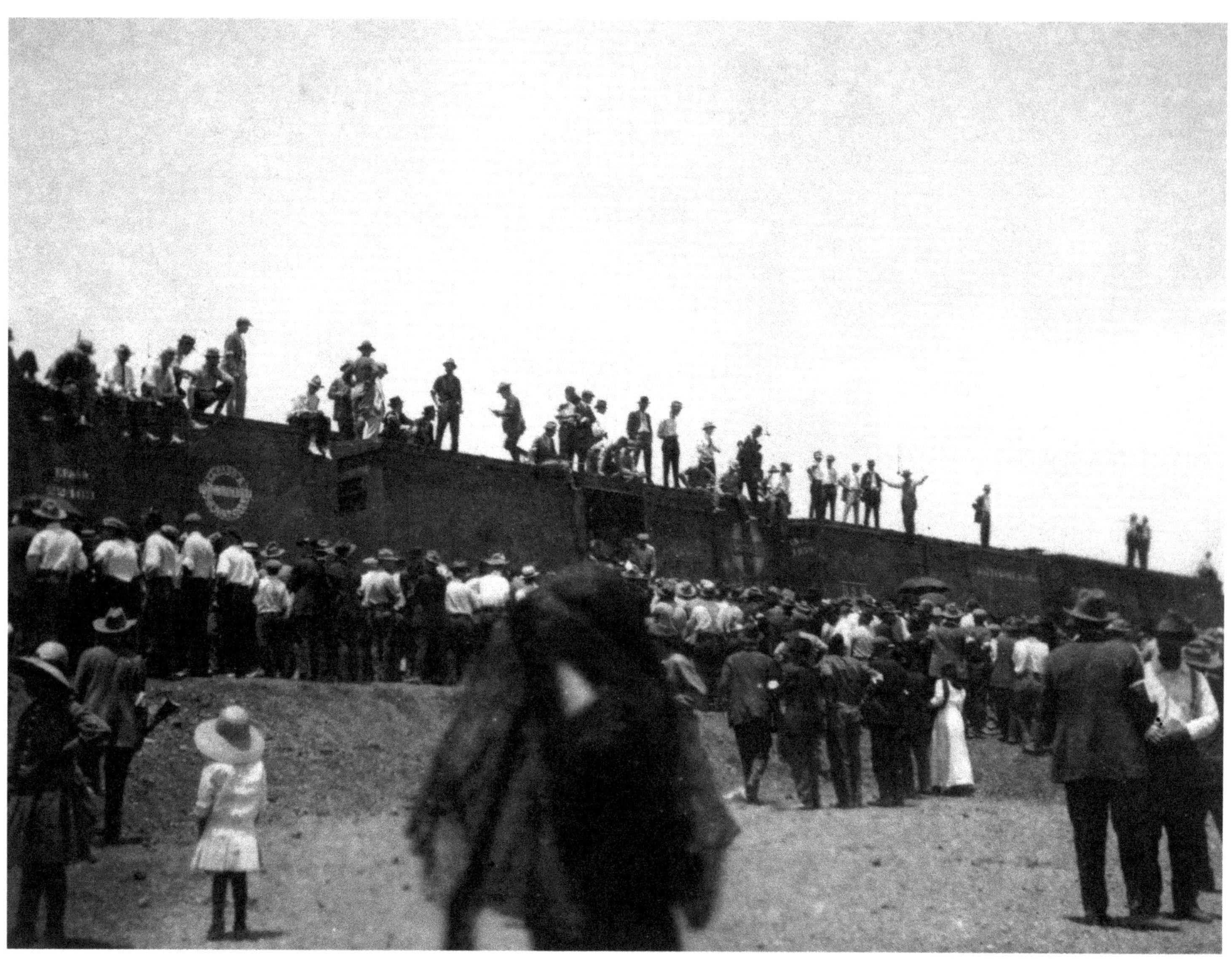

The Bisbee Deportation occurred on July 12, 1917, when 1,186 striking copper miners (or in some cases, men who were thought to be strikers) affiliated with the Industrial Workers of the World were rounded up by fellow citizens and forced into waiting boxcars. The boxcars were then pulled some 200 miles into the New Mexico desert and abandoned. This event not only shocked the miners of Arizona but impacted labor union activities throughout the United States.

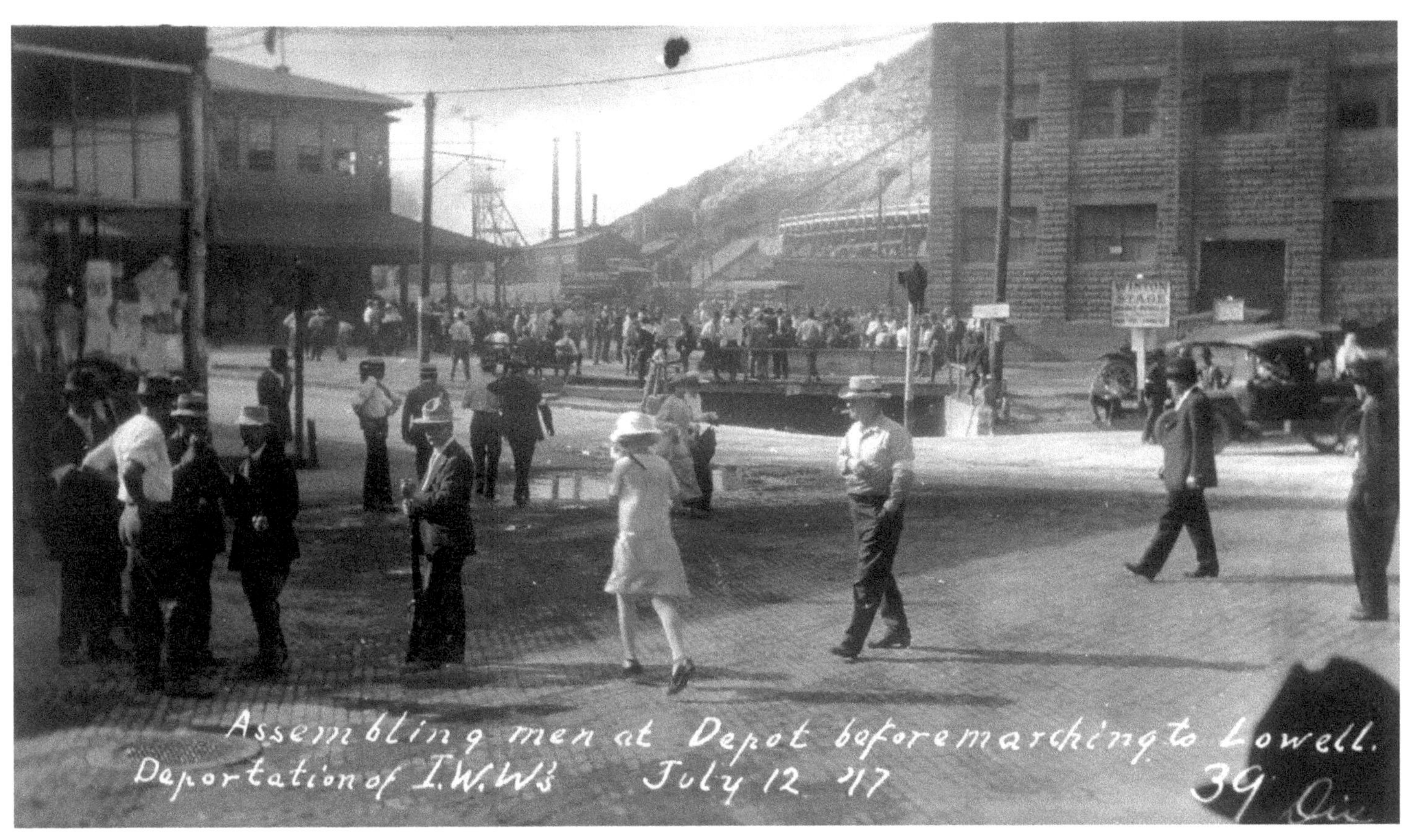

During the Bisbee Deportation, the men involved in rounding up striking miners wore white armbands to identify one another.

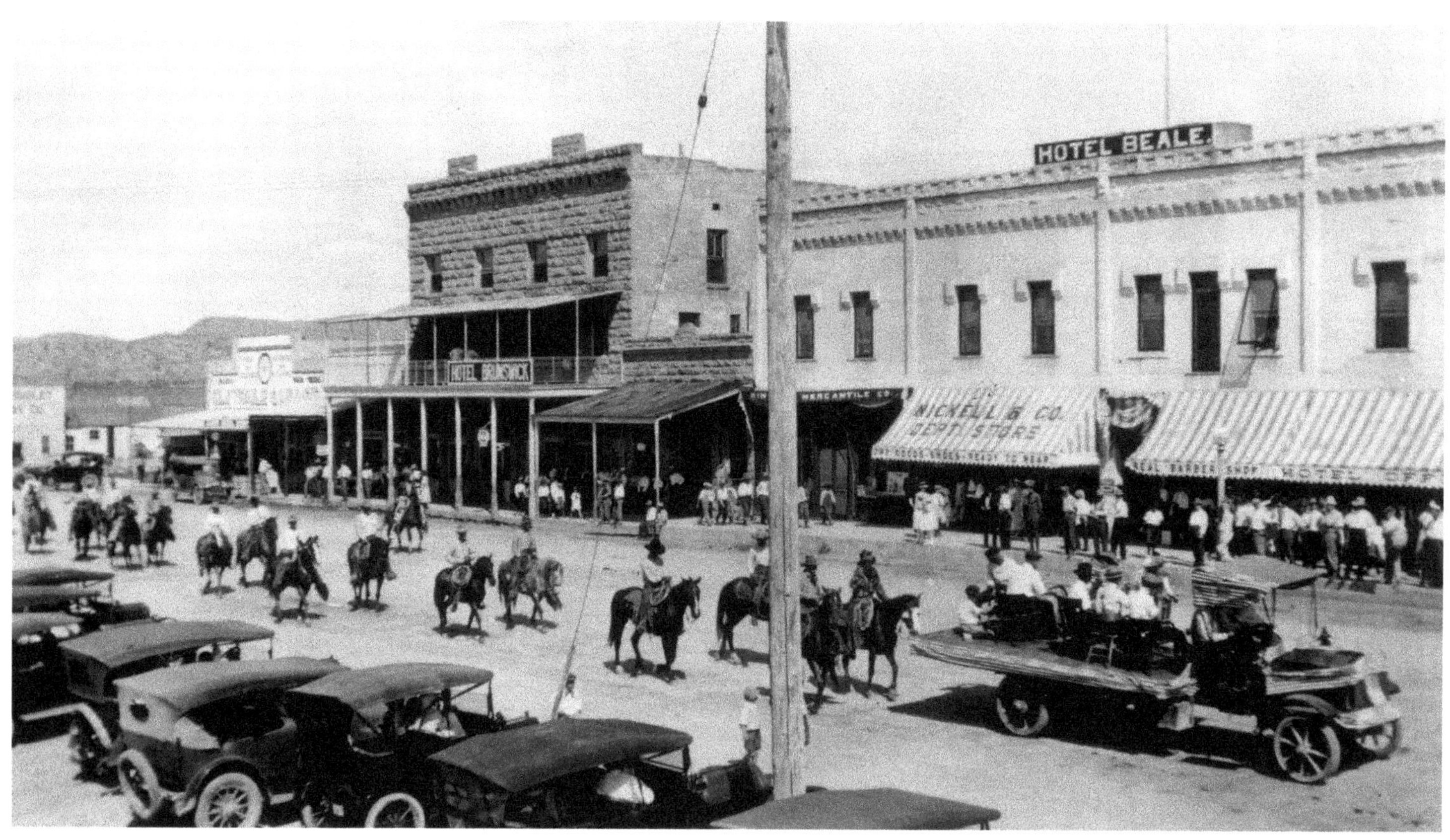

The town of Kingman was founded in 1882 along a newly constructed line of the Atlantic and Pacific Railroad in northwestern Arizona. The rail track followed the alignment for a wagon road first suggested by Lieutenant Edward Beale when he explored the 35th parallel in Arizona for the United States Army in the late 1850s. Beale used camels to help transport his men and goods through this rugged area. By 1919 a parade truck was rolling down the streets of Kingman.

Modern Arizona Takes Shape

(1920–1939)

Arizonans roared into the 1920s thankful that the "war to end all wars" was finally over, but shaken by its toll and by the many other deaths caused by the "Spanish flu" pandemic of 1918-19. As the new decade began, Arizona had 350,000 citizens. The population of the farming community of Phoenix had exploded to 9,300 residents.

Copper prices crashed, as did the demand for cotton, in the early 1920s, since neither product was needed any longer for a war effort. Many of Arizona's miners and farmers lost their jobs and their land in these hard times.

A young Arizona writer named Dick Wick Hall brought attention to the humor and wonders of Arizona through his stories syndicated by the New York–based *Saturday Evening Post.* His death at age 49 in 1926 ended the acclaimed folk humorist's run of these wonderful stories.

In 1929, during another tragic revolution in Mexico, and while trying to bomb a Mexican army in Naco, Sonora, an overzealous Irish pilot named Patrick Murphy accidentally dropped a single bomb onto the mayor's garage on the U.S. side of Naco. This small Arizona border town is still the only town in the continental United States to have been bombed from an airplane.

A young woman named Winnie Ruth Judd was tried for murder in Phoenix in 1931, and news coverage of her trial captivated America. It also resulted in many reporters filing stories about the beautiful weather found in Phoenix during February. Arizona's tourism industry was coming to life.

Steamboat captain Nellie Bush was elected to serve in the Arizona legislature in 1920, and after the stock market crash of 1929, Isabella Greenway assisted World War I veterans threatened with loss of work at her struggling furniture factory by building the Arizona Inn in Tucson, maintaining a need for their skills.

Los Carlistas, an early Latino singing group that featured the future National Medal of Arts winner Lalo Guerrero of Tucson, became so popular they traveled to New York City to perform at the 1939 World's Fair. By that same year, architect Frank Lloyd Wright had established Taliesin West in Scottsdale to continue his teaching and creation of his unique designs.

Modern Arizona was taking shape, but its Wild West roots would always be close to the surface.

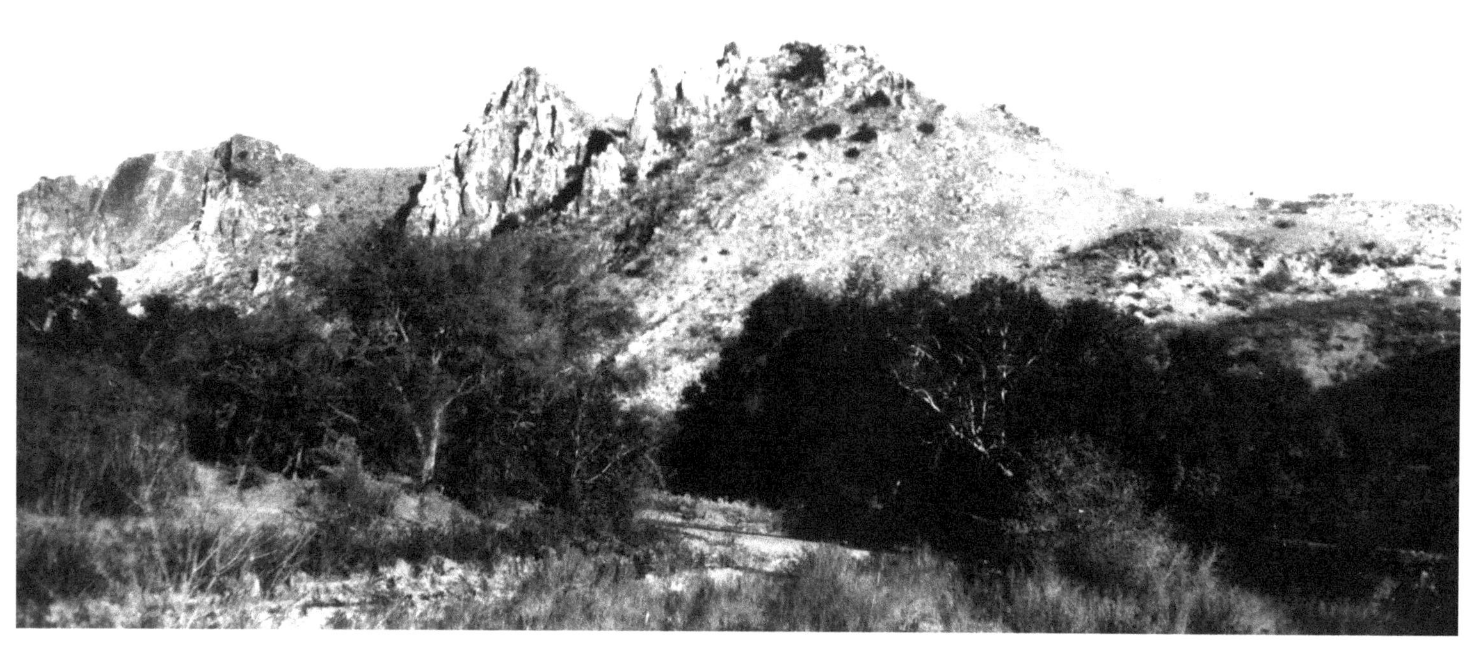

The Sonoita Valley is located on a high plateau in Santa Cruz County. The towns of Patagonia, Sonoita, and Elgin are found there and together are known as the Mountain Empire. Shown here around 1920, the Mountain Empire remains a special place to visit where one can relax and enjoy Arizona's natural beauty.

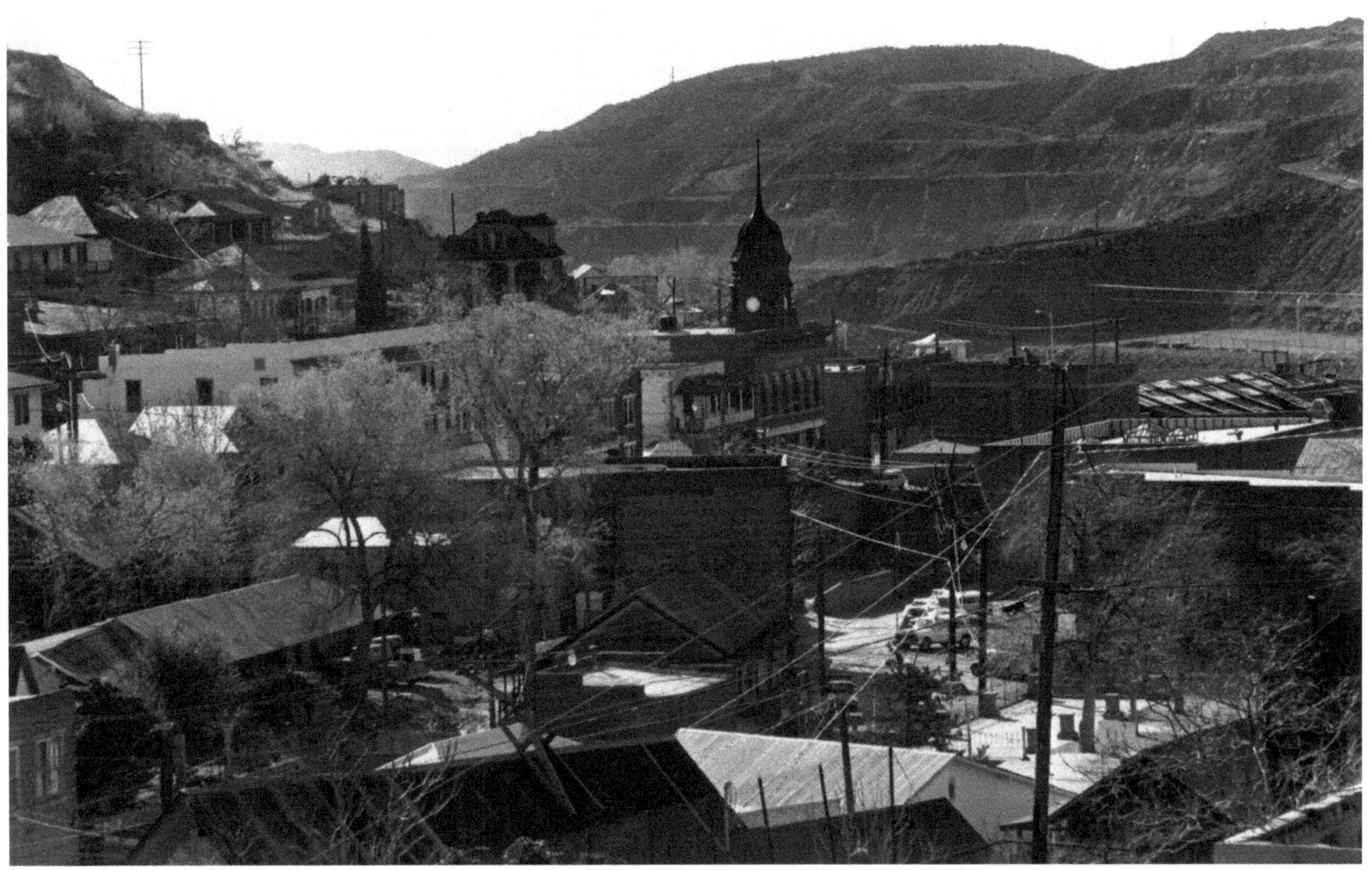

Bisbee was the third-largest town in Arizona in the 1920s. The Phelps Dodge Mining Company still owned the town and influenced every aspect of life in and around it. By the late 1920s, Bisbee had replaced Tombstone as the county seat of Cochise County. The notorious Brewery Gulch saloons had been tamed somewhat but not closed down, since this was the Roaring Twenties.

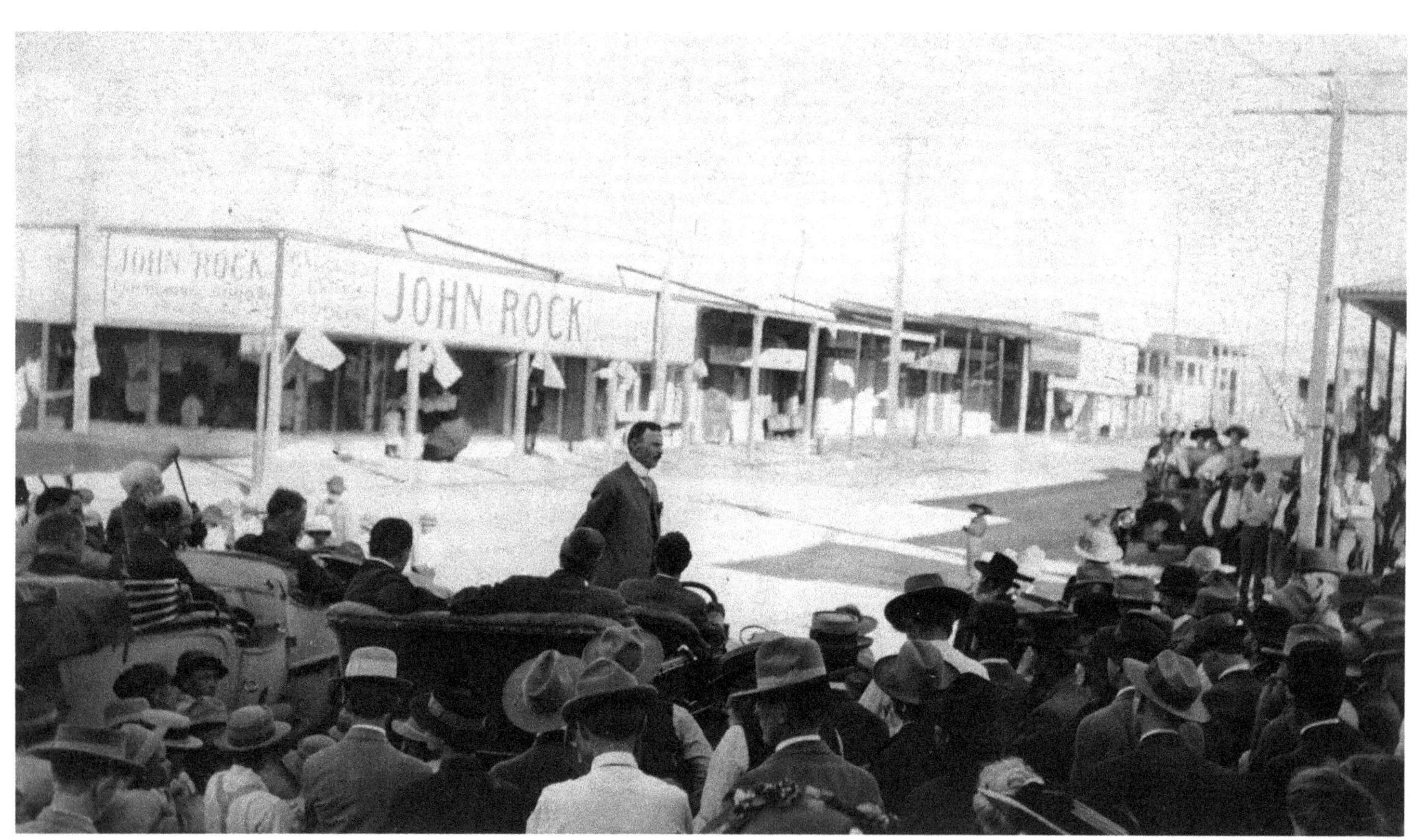

Tombstone was in trouble by the 1920s. The mines had long been flooded, and the "town too tough to die" was struggling to keep its citizens and few remaining businesses. Tombstone's once booming population had dwindled to less than a thousand folks. Here a small crowd of those remaining citizens listen to a local official speak while standing on famous Allen Street.

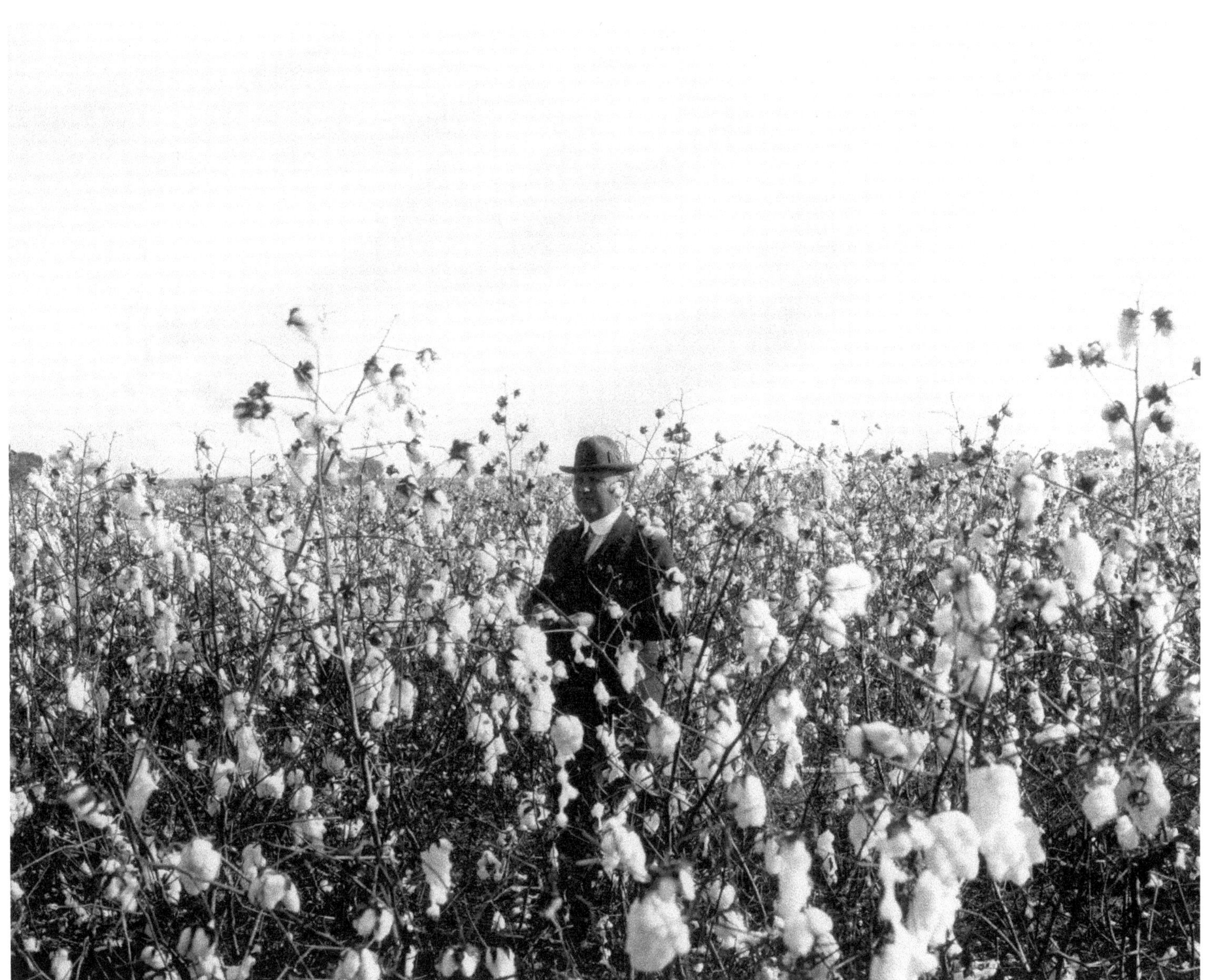

Cotton has been important to mankind for over 7,000 years. The Hohokam Indians, who first inhabited the Salt River Valley in 300 B.C., grew cotton and used it in their daily lives. In 1916 an executive with the Goodyear Tire and Rubber Company, Paul Litchfield, was sent to Arizona to buy several thousand acres of desert land and launch the subsidiary Southwest Cotton Company. The firm grew long-staple pima cotton to be used in Goodyear automobile tires. The man shown here around 1920 is standing in a cotton field in Mesa.

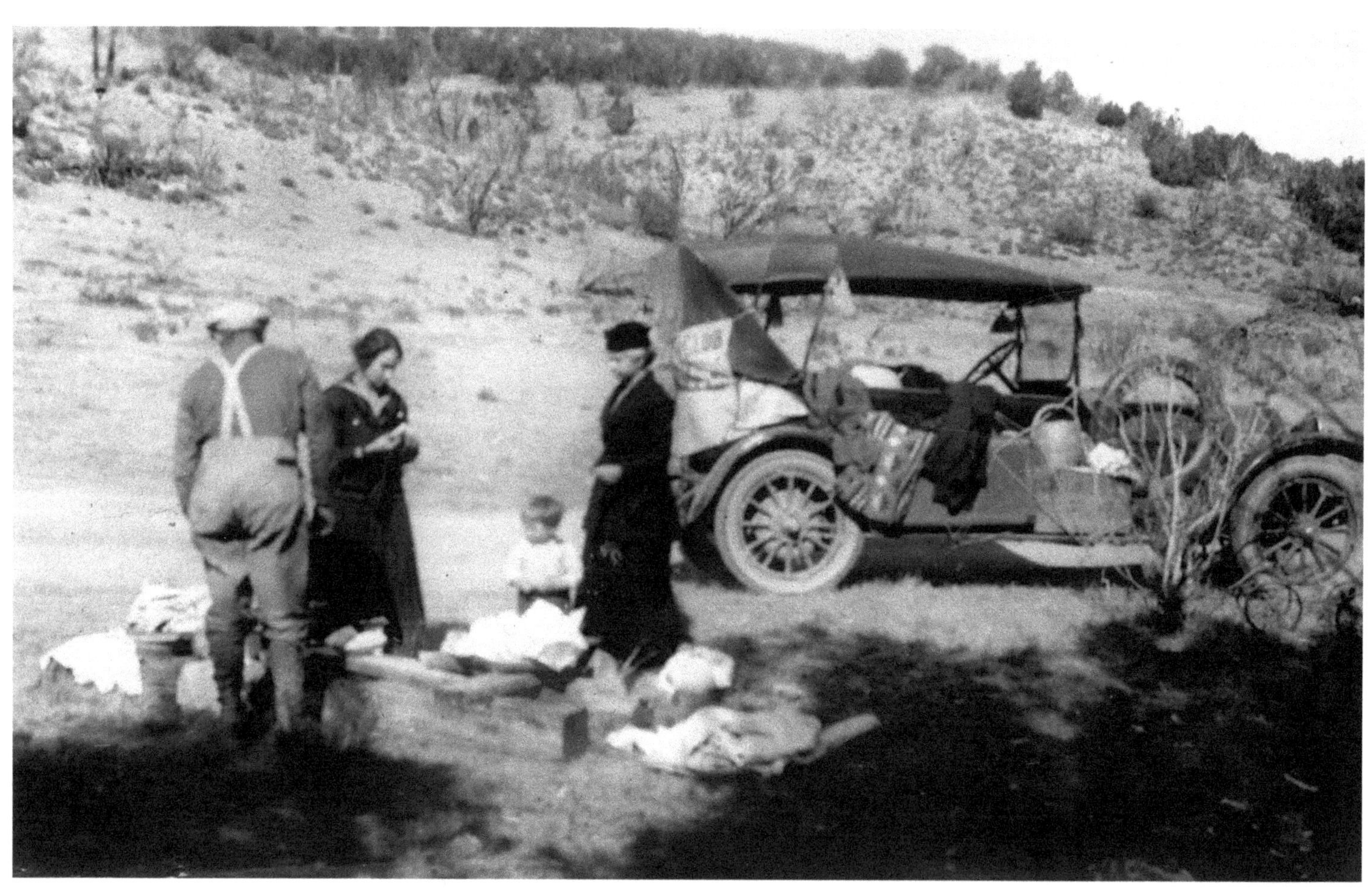

Founded in 1912, Clarkdale was the first master-planned community in Arizona. Named for Senator William A. Clark of Montana, the company town was built by the United Verde Copper Company to provide housing, schools, and other amenities for employees of the firm's copper smelter. Located on the Verde River, the smelter processed copper ore from Jerome from 1913 to 1953. Picnics were a common pastime for Clarkdale families.

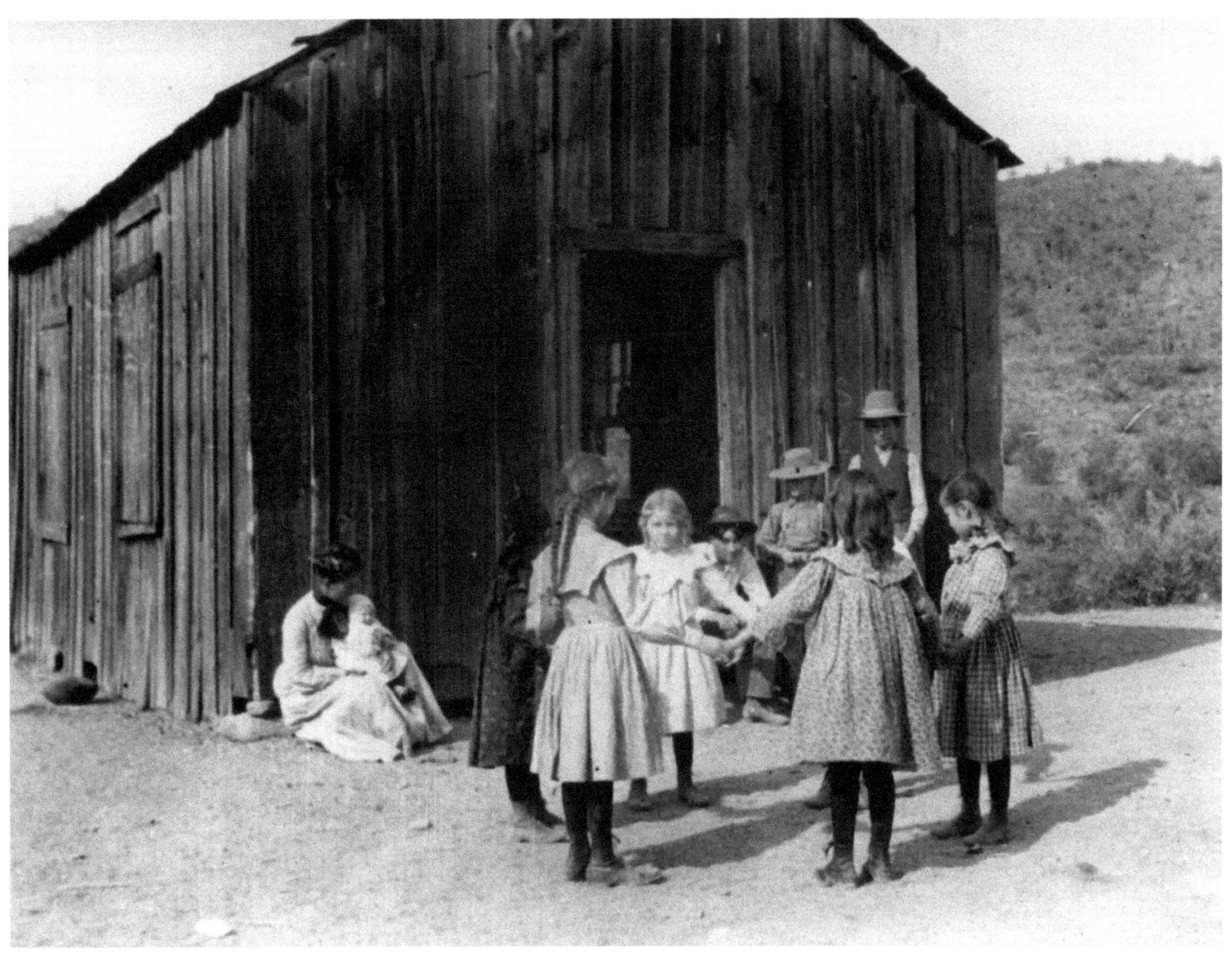

By 1877 Jeriah Wood had built a home along the banks of a small Arizona stream called Cave Creek, where he worked a small cattle ranch and sold goods to miners and travelers. He called his home Cave Creek Station, and a small post office named Overton was maintained there. Other families moved into the area, and by 1886 a one-room schoolhouse was needed. Built beside Cave Creek, the school is shown here around 1920.

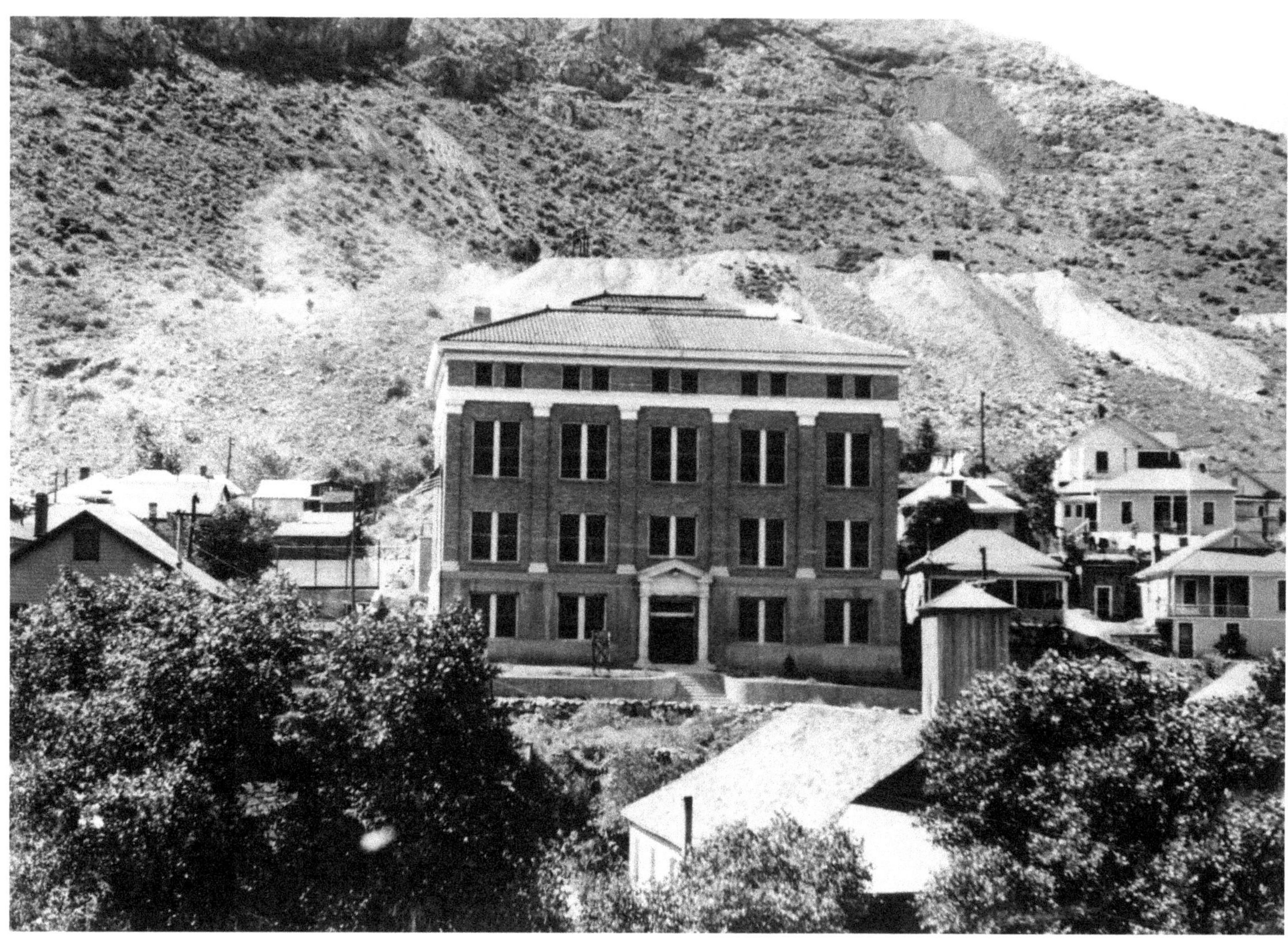

The most surprising Arizona education news in 1920 was the election of a woman as state superintendent of instruction. Elsie Toles was a native-born Arizonan and a member of the first graduating class of Bisbee High School. When she was elected, there were still 282 one-teacher schoolhouses scattered throughout Arizona—though not in Bisbee, where three-story Horace Mann Junior High School was open and in session.

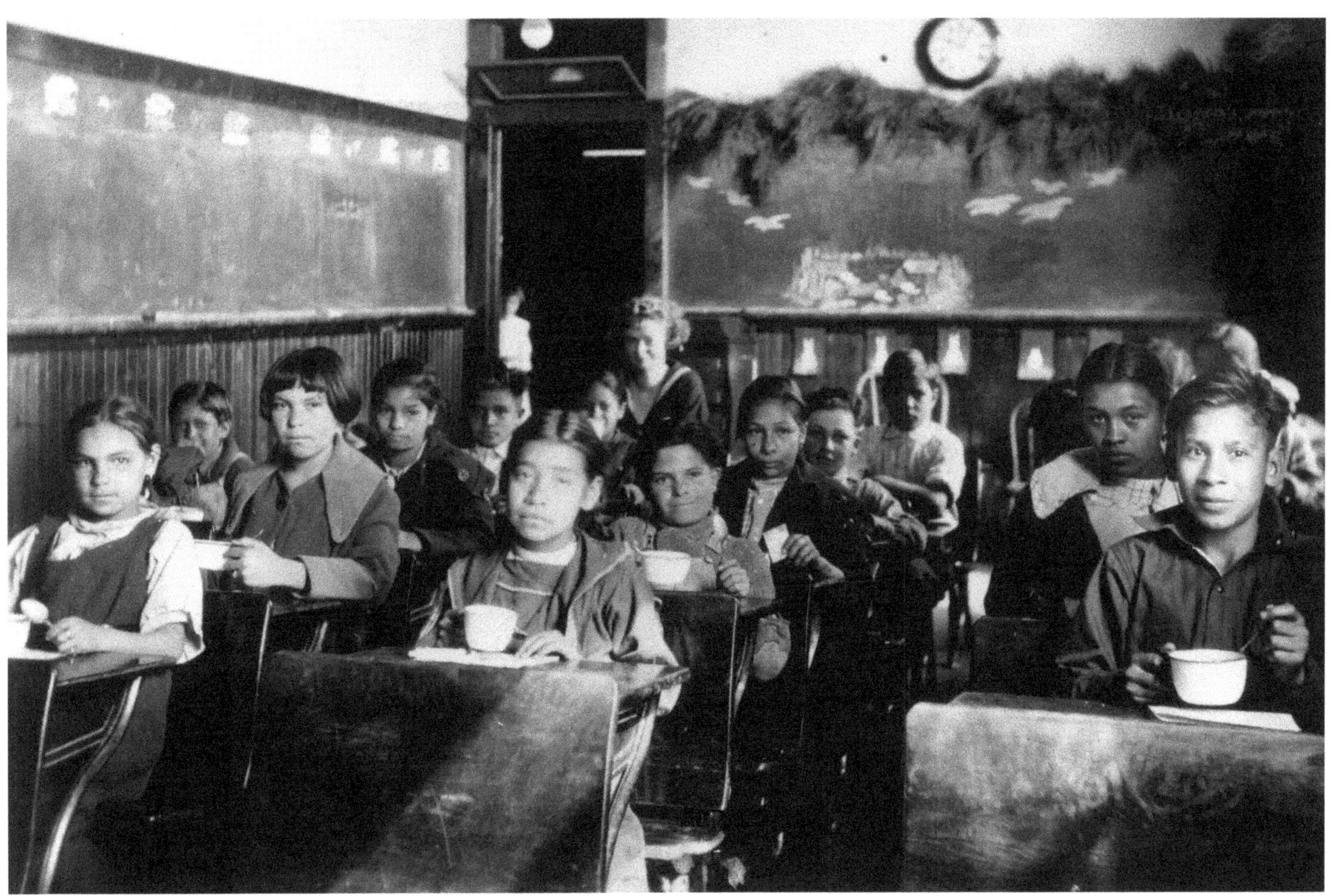

These students with their bowls and spoons are seated in a Flagstaff classroom of the 1920s. Flagstaff's original log-cabin school was built in 1883 and located halfway between the saloons of Old Town and the saloons of New Town. Local citizens built the school far enough away from the two districts' saloons to ensure that no bullets from cowboys firing their guns in "anger or celebration" would endanger the children.

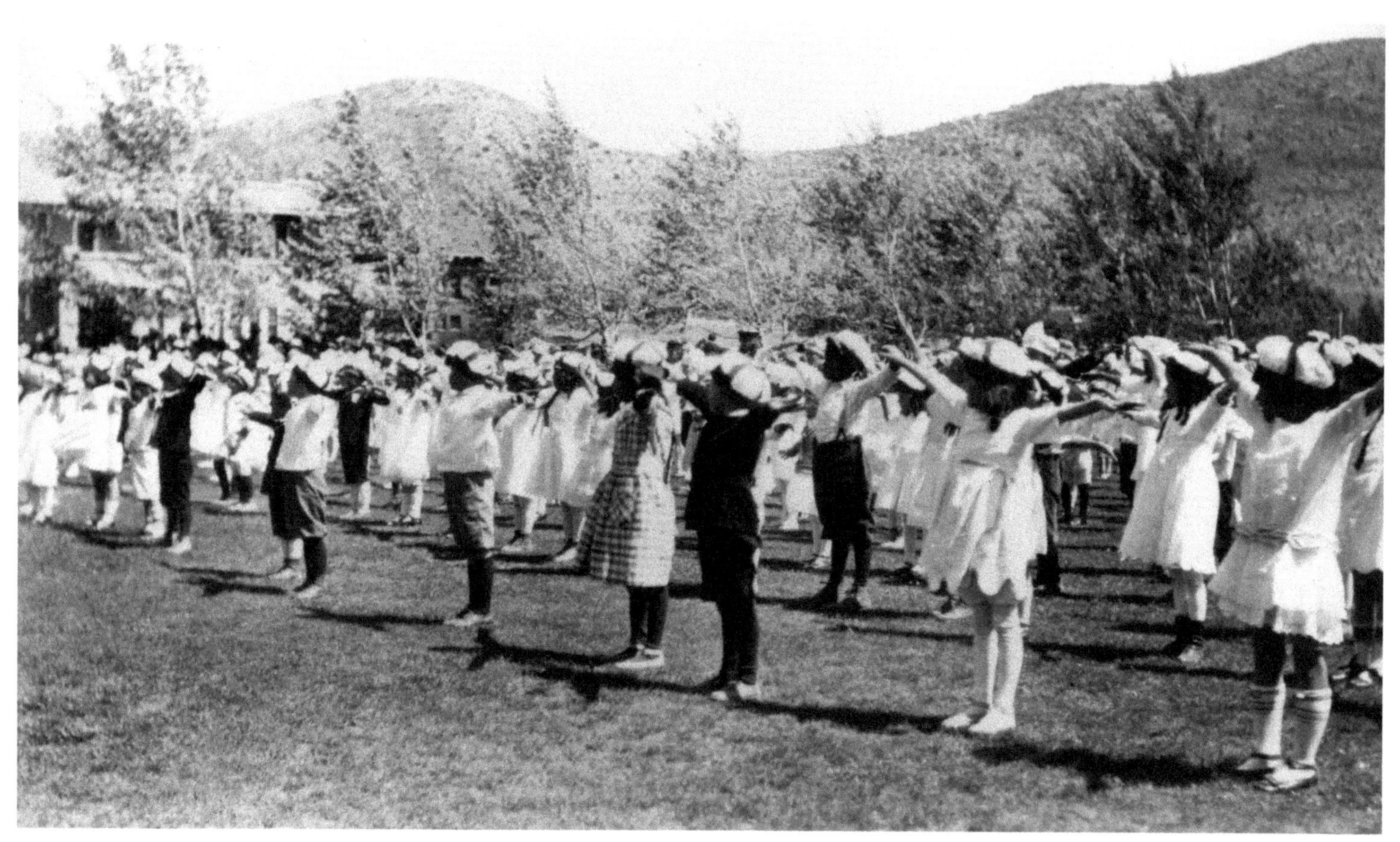

A group of children go through their morning exercises at a school in Bisbee in the 1920s.

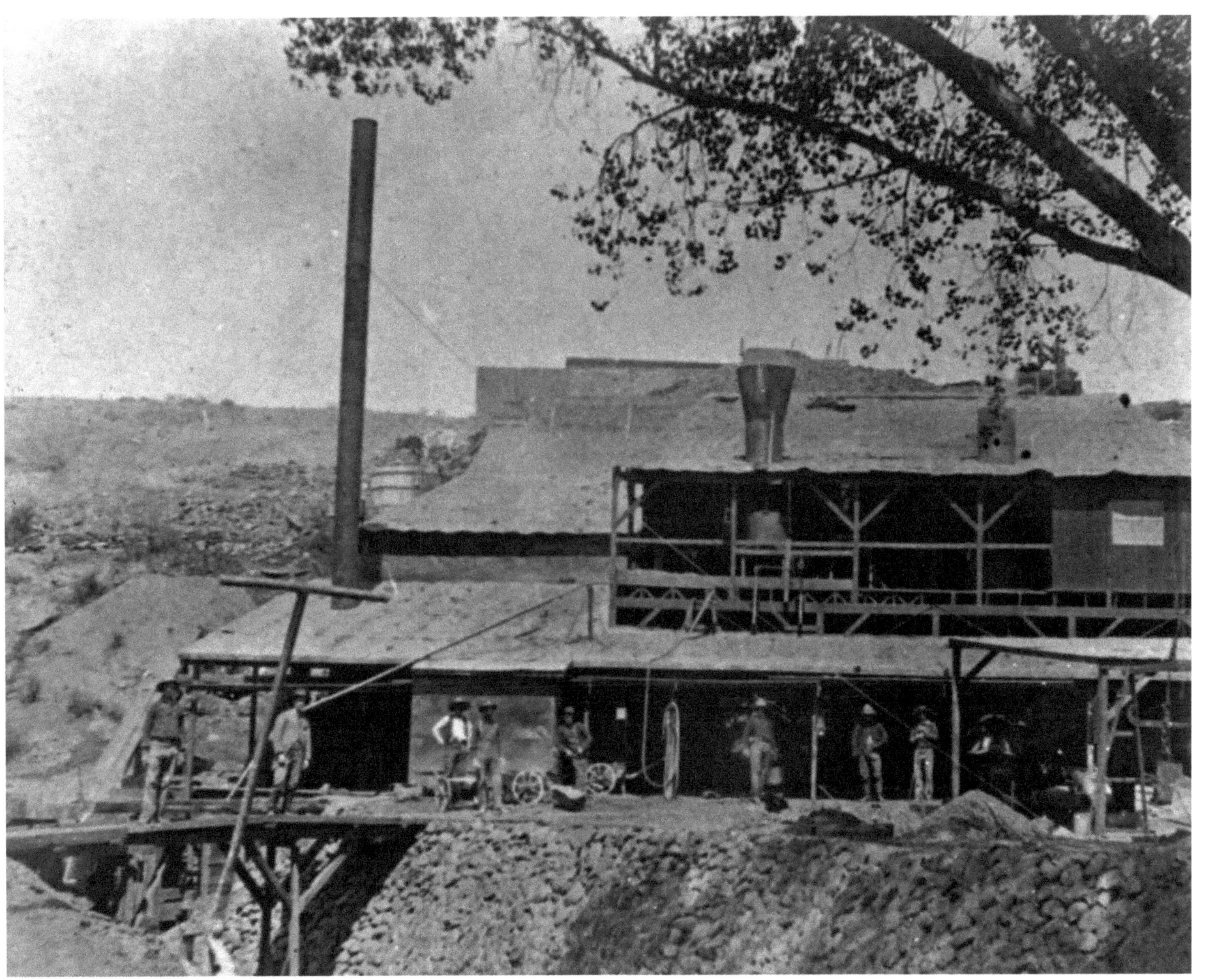

When William Church arrived in the Morenci-Clifton area in 1880, the copper mines were having trouble turning a profit, due to constant Apache Indian raids and an adobe smelter that required rebuilding every few days of operation. The Apache raids ceased in 1886 with the surrender of Geronimo, and the smelter problem ended with the building of the modern Church Smelter, shown around 1920, which used reverberatory furnaces.

A man with a horse and a gun was a common sight in early Arizona. Here a rider near Cave Creek in the 1920s takes a break from the saddle.

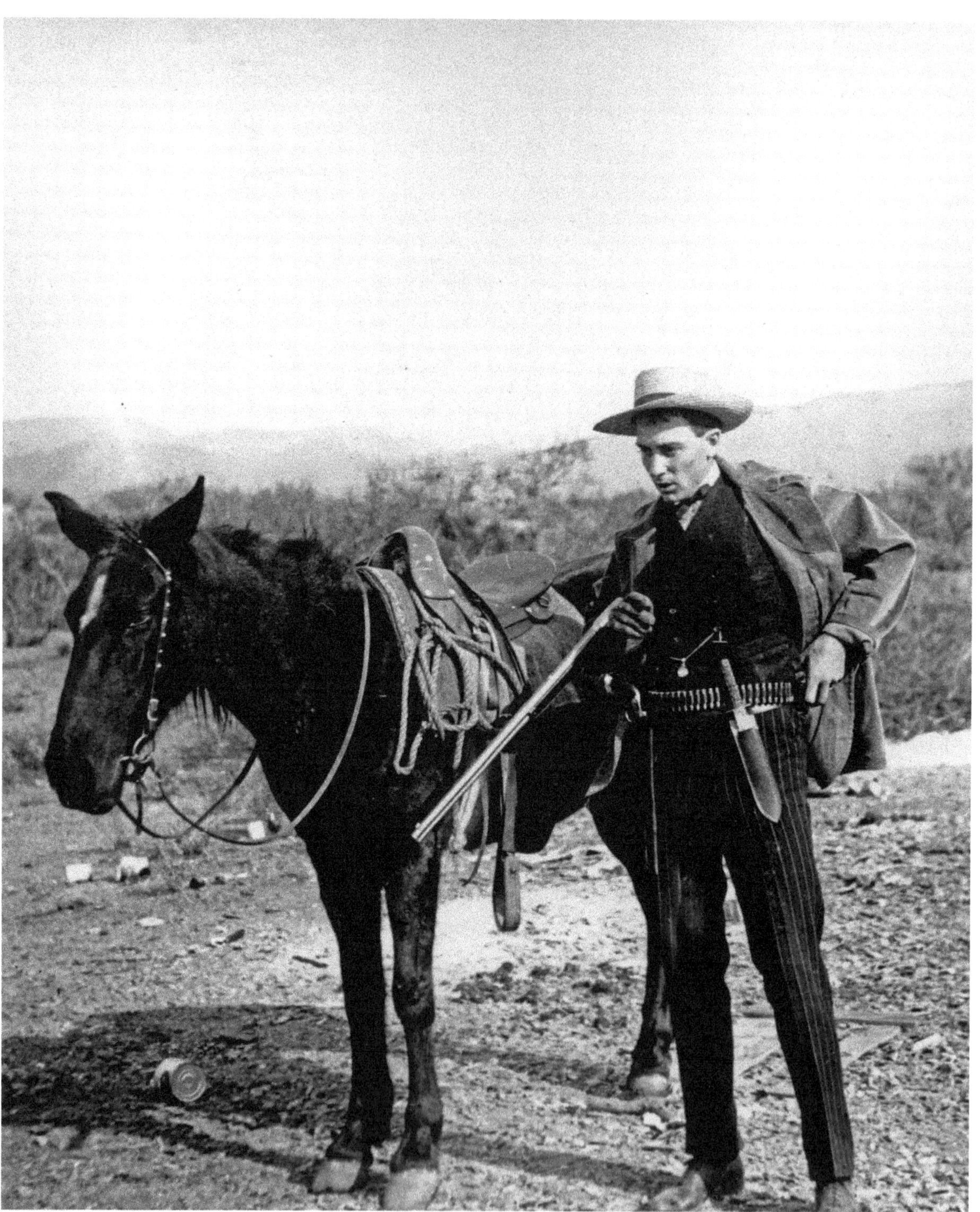

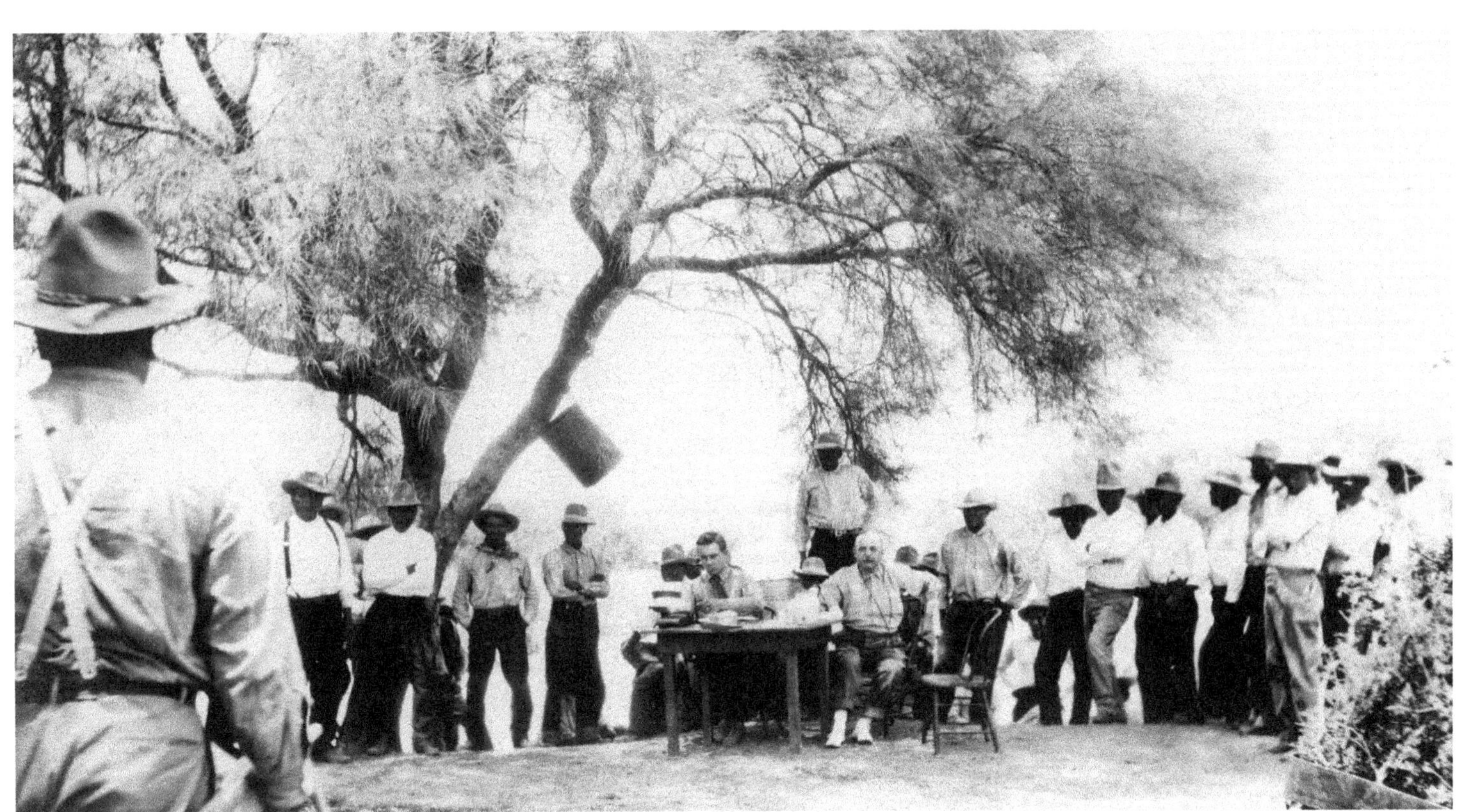

Arizona governor George W. P. Hunt and U.S. commissioner of Indian affairs Cato Sells visit with a group of Tohono O'odham tribesmen south of Tucson in the early 1920s. Sells was well liked and respected by the American Indian people and had helped justify to them why they should volunteer to fight for the United States in World War I. Today the Tohono O'odham Nation town of Sells is named in his honor.

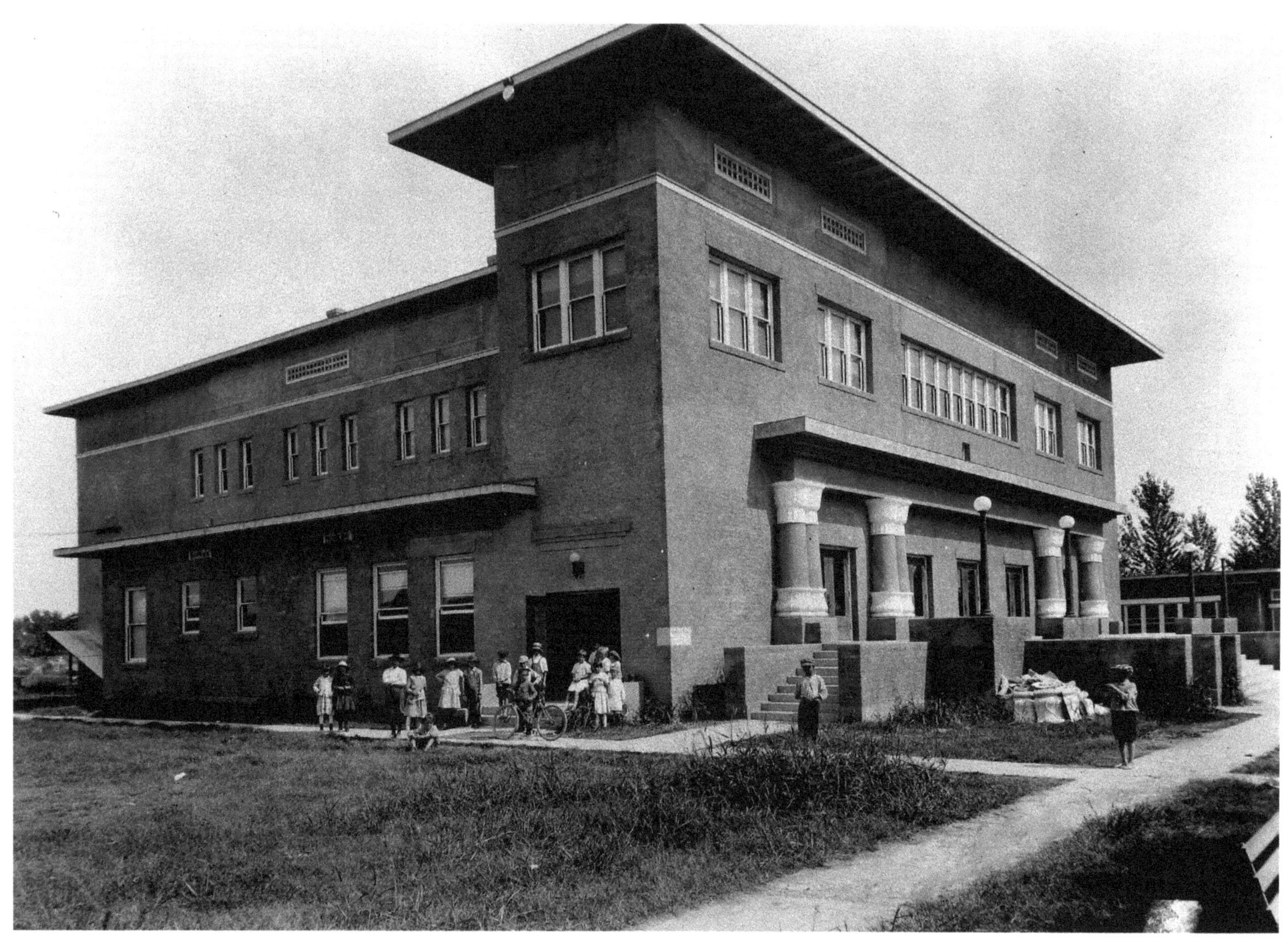

Shown here in the 1920s, Glendale Grammar School opened in 1895 to serve the rapidly growing community northwest of Phoenix. From across the Valley of the Sun, families in search of a better education for their children were drawn to the school. Today Glendale Grammar School is known as Landmark Elementary School and still serves the children of the community.

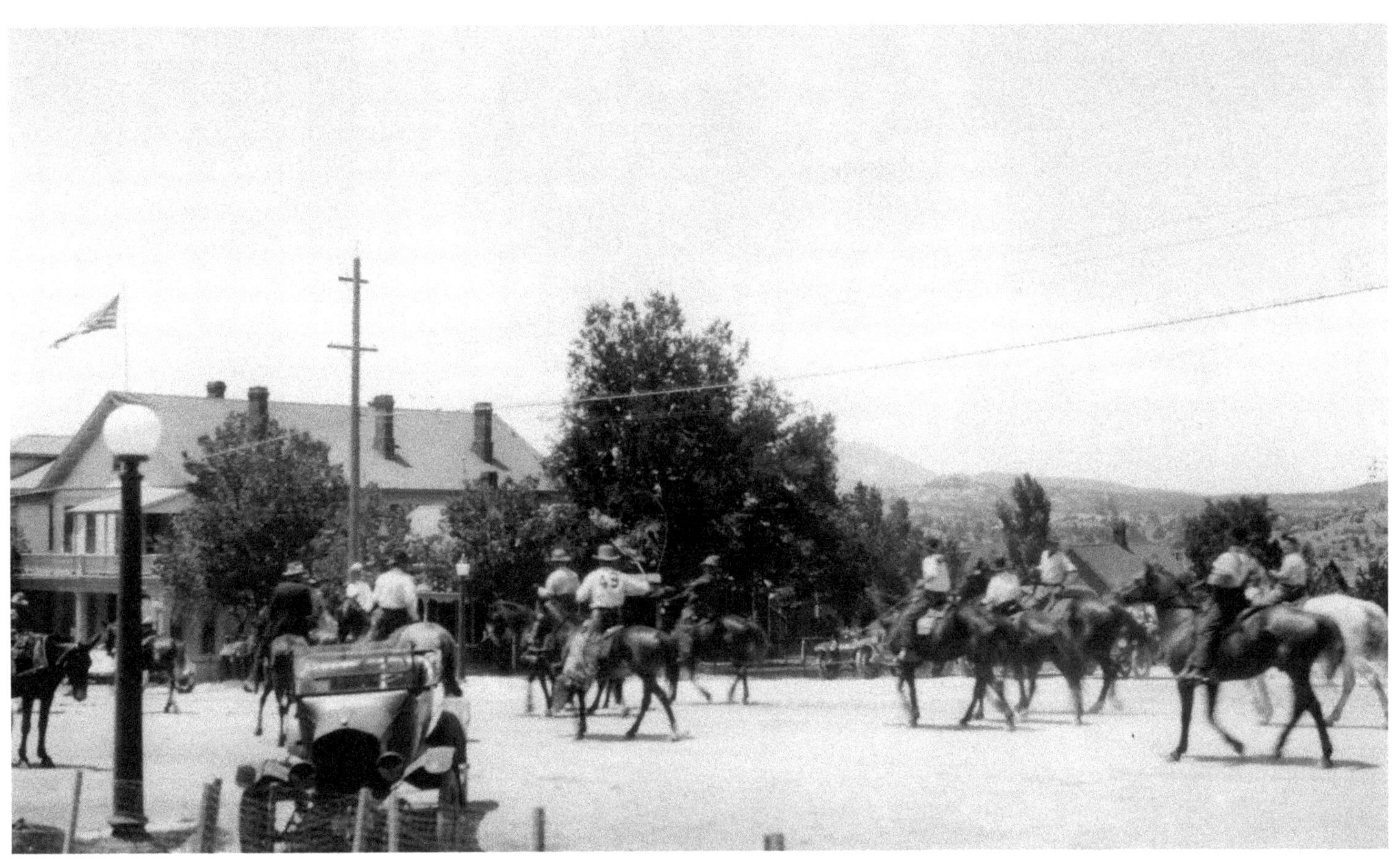

Even though the Prescott rodeo started in 1888, the event was not given the name Prescott Frontier Days until 1913, when the annual Fourth of July "cowboy contest" moved to the Yavapai County Fairgrounds. The word "rodeo," of origins in Spanish, did not come into regular use to signify one of these professional cowboy competitions for many years, and was not applied to the Prescott event until 1924. Here a group of Frontier Days participants parade through Prescott around 1921.

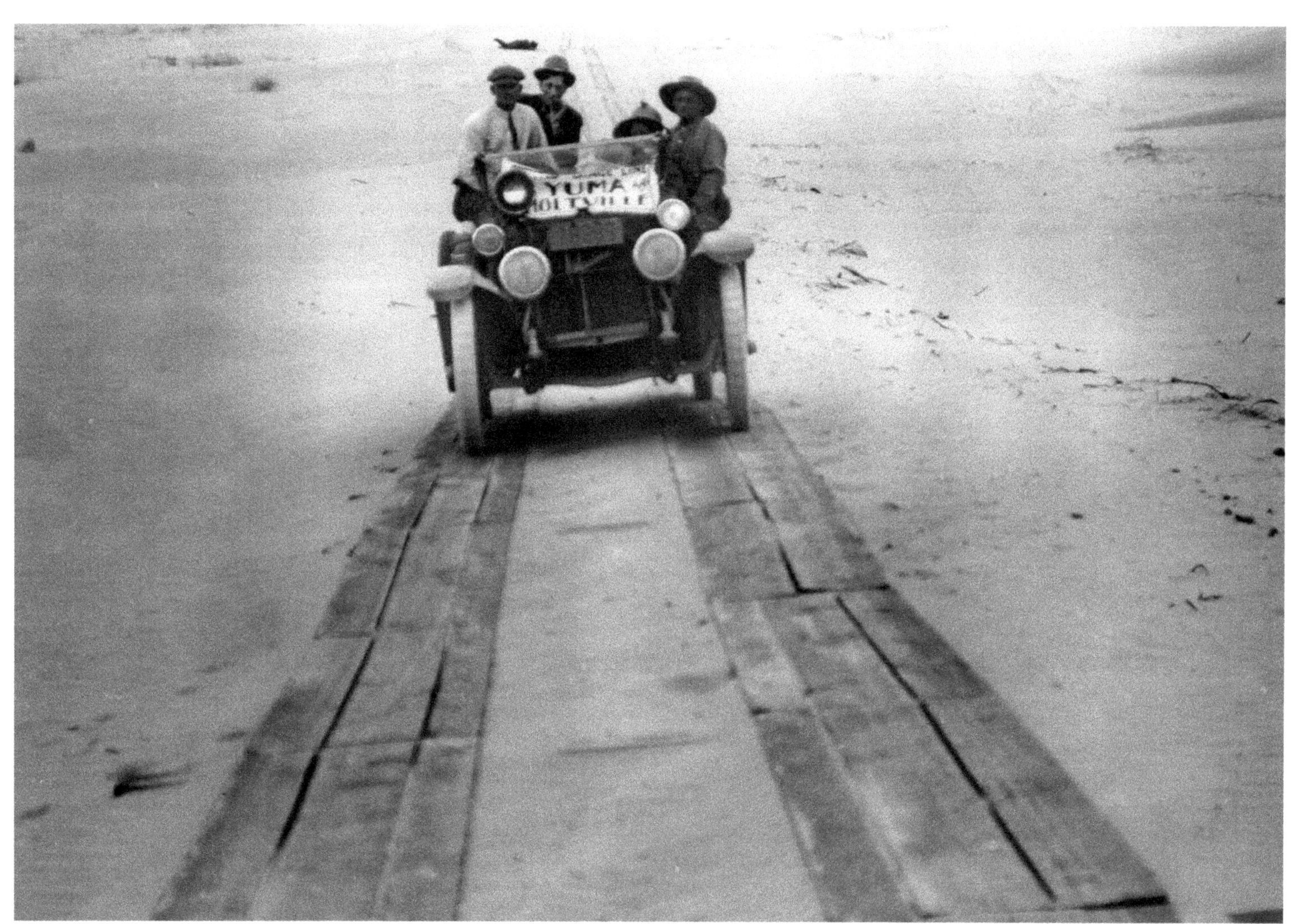

Just west of Yuma, on the California side of the Colorado River, a 40-mile stretch of sand dunes extends into the desert. These dunes posed a significant challenge for early automobile owners wishing to drive from Yuma to San Diego. In 1915 the first plank road across the dunes was built but lasted only one year. A second and better plank road was built in 1916 and was used until a paved road was laid across the dunes in 1926.

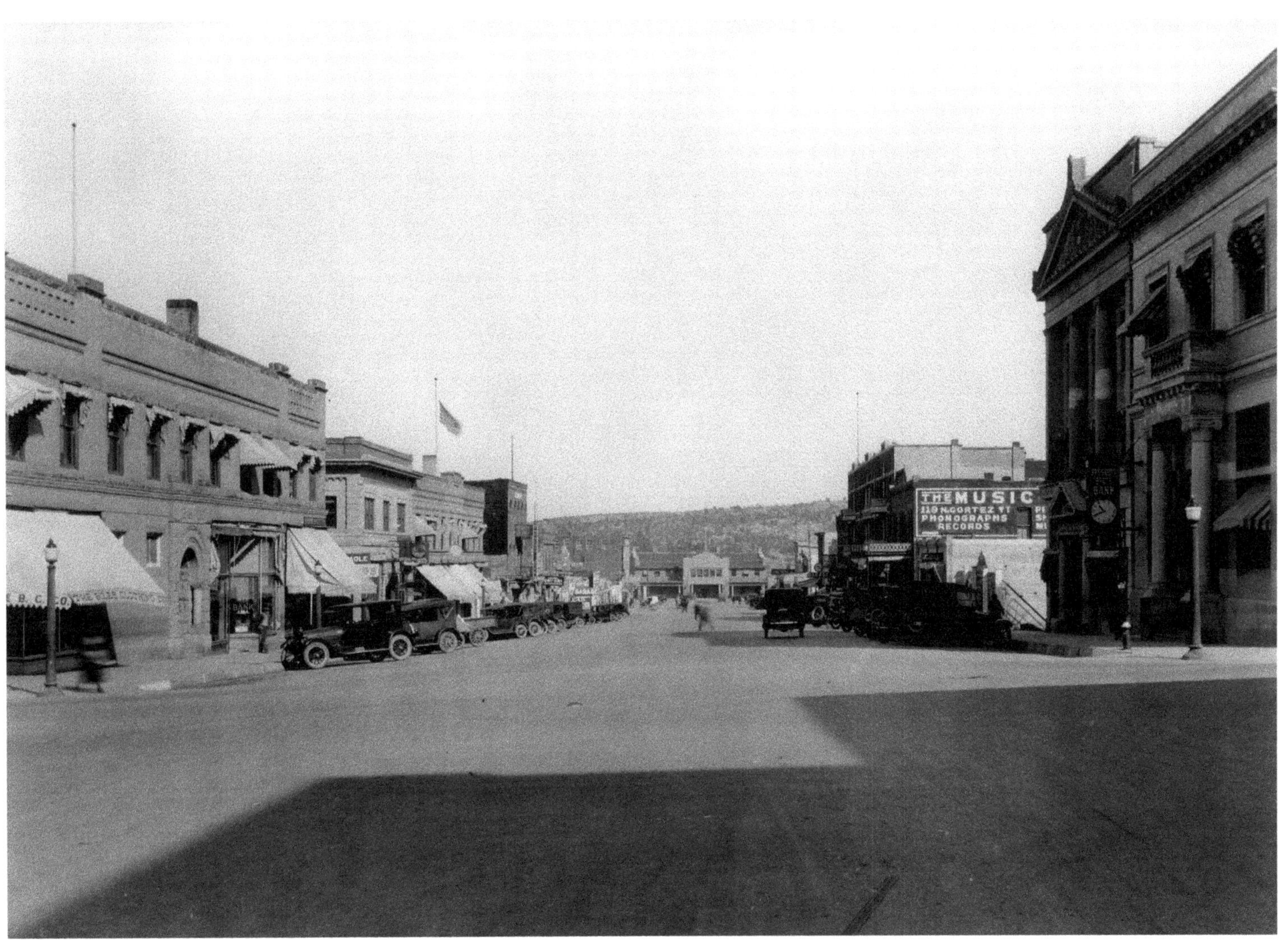

LeRoy Anderson, a local attorney from Prescott, started a community-spirit movement in 1923. The "jewel in the mountains," as Prescott was then called, needed to cultivate the arts and promote local interest in developing city parks, and also invest in infrastructure such as hospitals and good roads, Anderson advised. This view shows Prescott around that time.

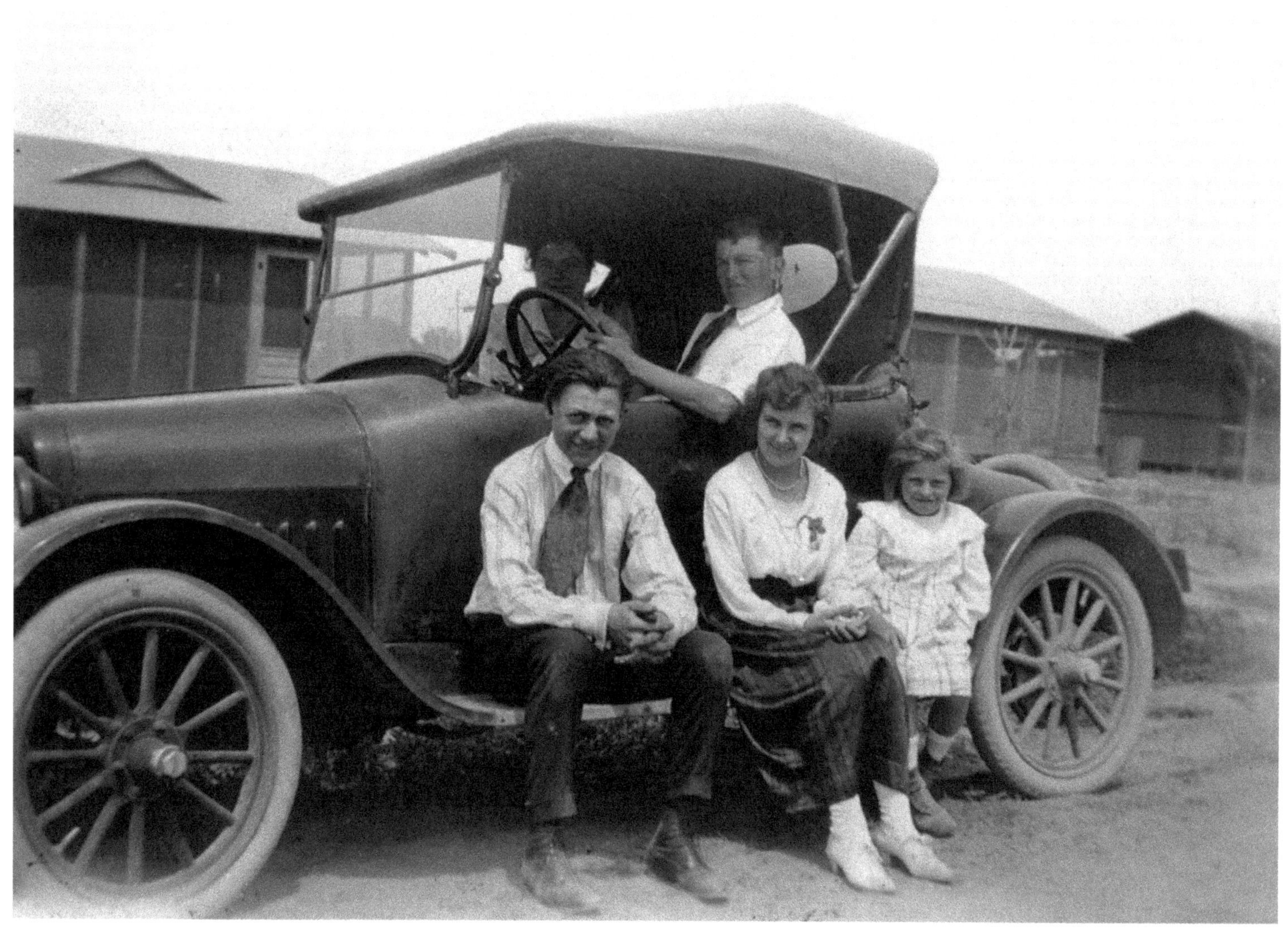

By the 1920s the automobile was well entrenched in Arizona communities such as Glendale, where these folks were most likely photographed. Established in 1892, Glendale was located just a few miles west of where William H. Bartlett homesteaded a 640-acre fruit farm in 1886.

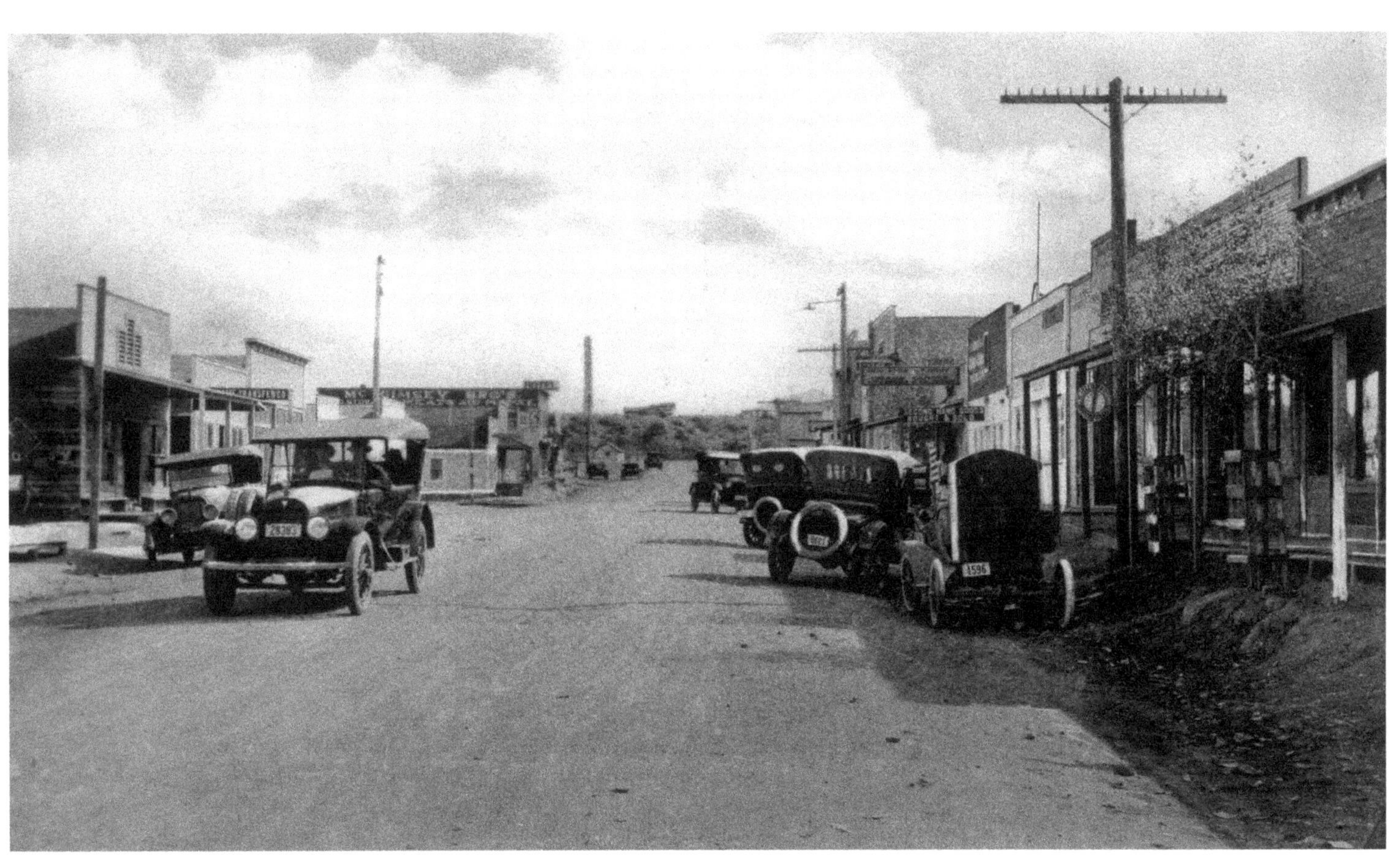

In 1874, a group of soldiers were quartered in an adobe house along the Verde River some 20 miles from Fort Verde. A cluster of 16 cottonwood trees stood near the house, about a quarter mile from the river, and when the time came to name the settlement that developed around the old adobe, Cottonwood was selected. By 1923 Cottonwood had become a prospering town with many newfangled automobiles.

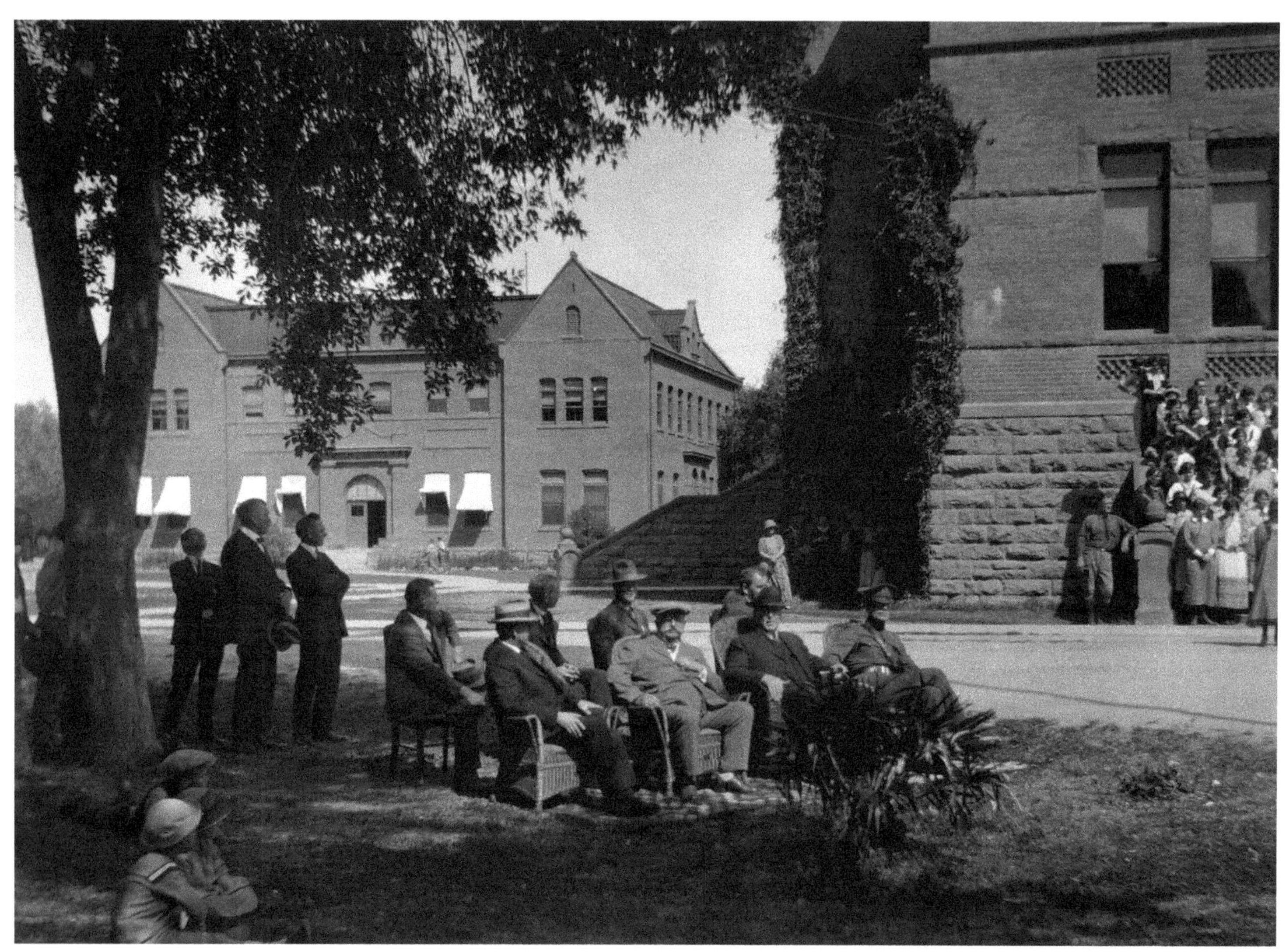

Governor George W. P. Hunt (second from left in the front row of chairs) and a group of Tempe businessmen visit the Tempe Normal School. By the time this 1924 photograph was taken, Hunt was serving his fourth two-year term as governor of Arizona. He would serve a total of seven terms.

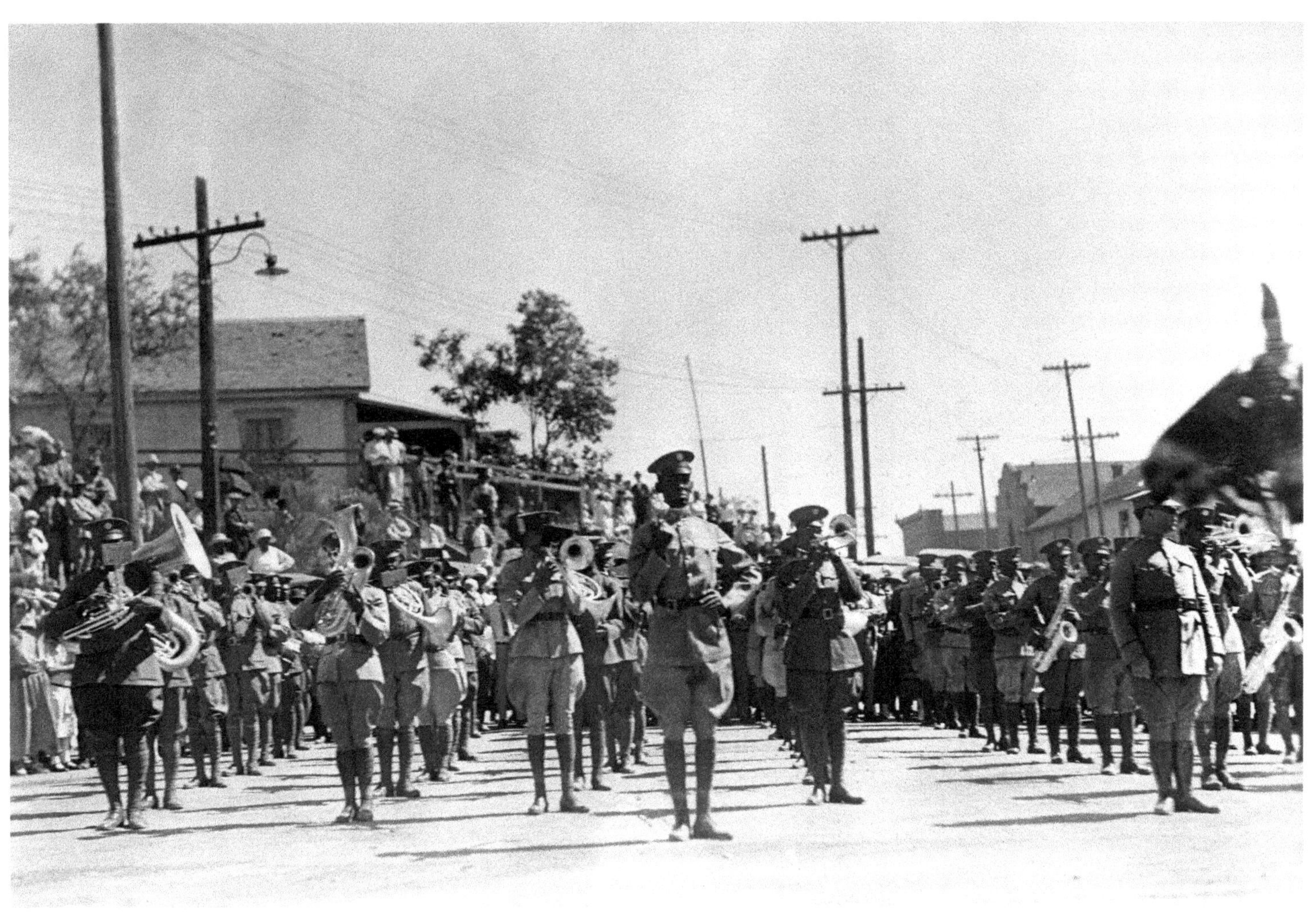

Nogales, Arizona, shares the international border with its sister city of Nogales, Sonora. It was here that the railroad from Mexico met the railroad from Arizona, and the two prosperous communities known as Los dos Nogales grew up together. In this 1924 scene, the 25th United States Infantry Regimental Band, representing an African American unit formed in the nineteenth century, parades through Nogales, Arizona.

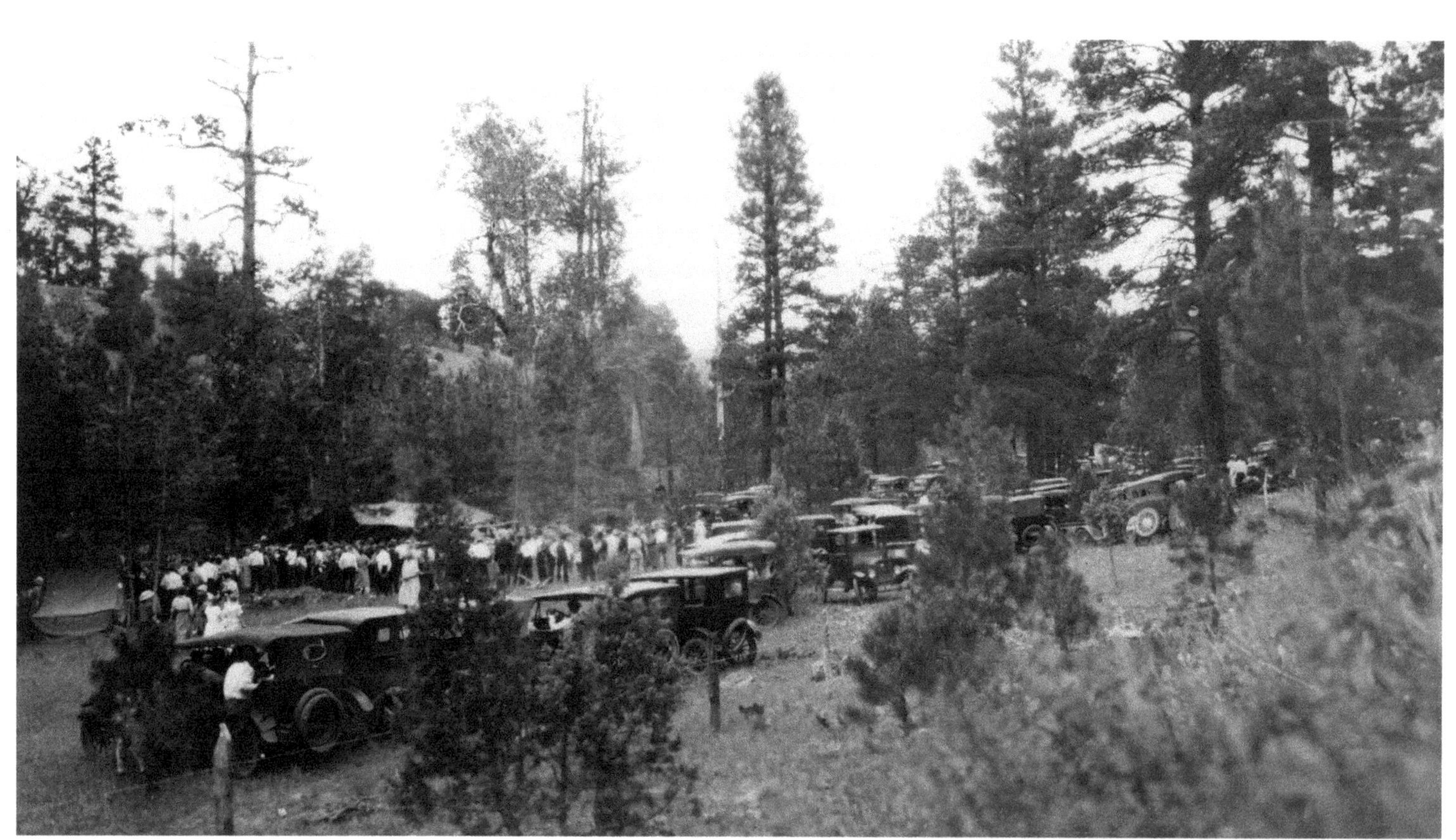

The Arizona community of Springerville grew up on the banks of the Little Colorado River at the eastern base of the White Mountains. In 1879 Henry Springer's Trading Post provided goods and supplies for the ranchers and lumberjacks of the area. The surrounding area is known as Round Valley and is just ten miles north of the Apache-Sitgreaves National Forest, no doubt the location of this 1924 barbecue.

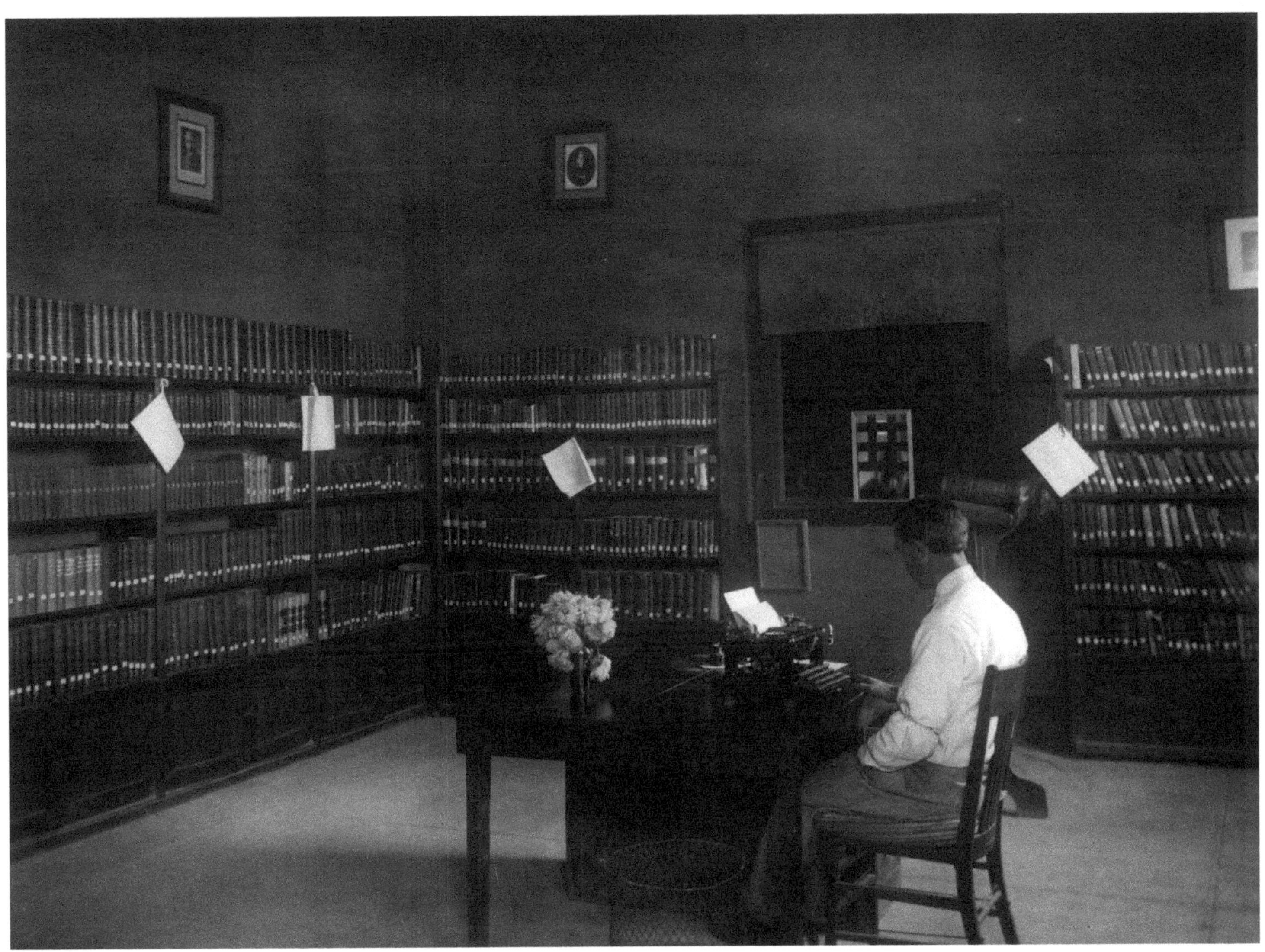

The Arizona State Prison at Florence was opened in 1908 to replace the infamous old Yuma Territorial Prison. Unlike the prison at Yuma, the new Florence Prison had no dungeons, no solitary confinement, and no snake hole (a cave for rebellious prisoners). However, it did have a death chamber—a room with a trapdoor through which a prisoner would fall into a room below when hanged. The Florence facility also had a prison library, shown here in 1924.

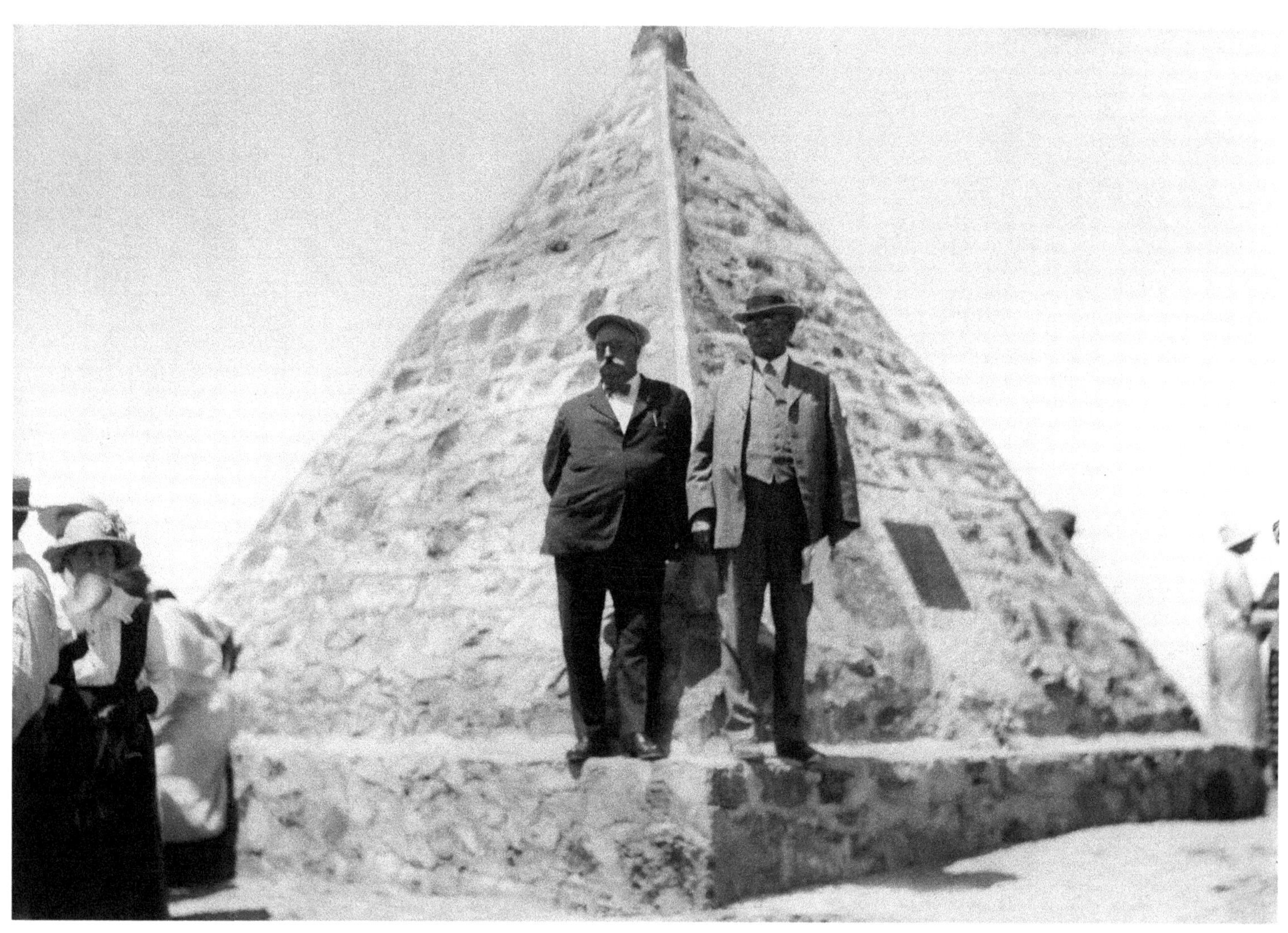

Charles Poston is known as the "Father of Arizona" for his efforts in persuading the United States Congress and President Abraham Lincoln to create the Territory of Arizona. When he died in 1902, Poston was buried under a concrete pyramid near Florence overlooking the Gila River. In this 1925 scene, Governor George W. P. Hunt (left) is visiting Poston Butte, the burial site of the Father of Arizona.

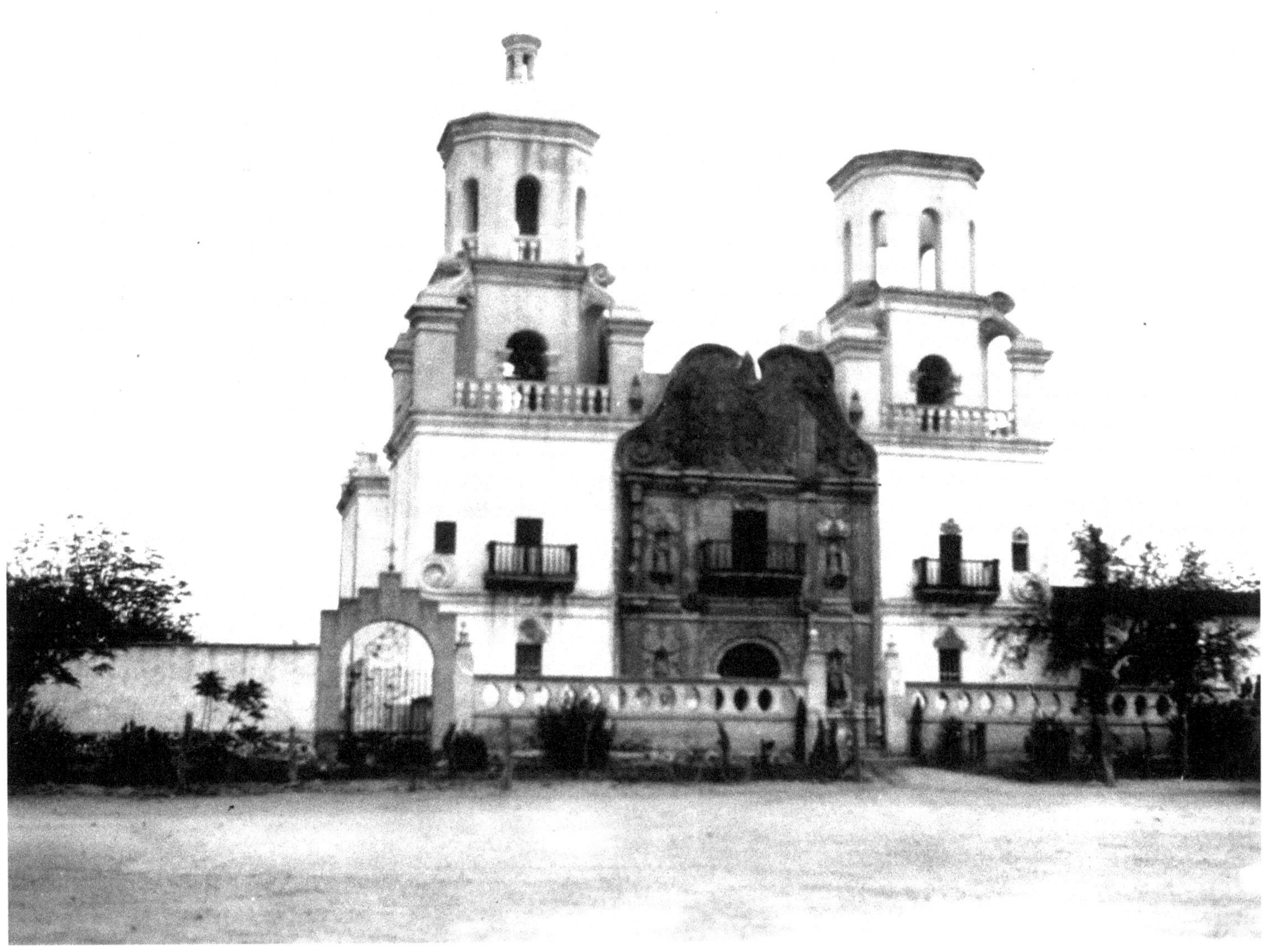

The domes and arches of San Xavier del Bac Mission, and the spectacular paintings that adorn its interior walls, surround and enhance the religious ceremonies that have taken place there for more than 200 years. Franciscan friars at Bac continue to serve the needs of the Tohono O'odham people and the many visitors to the mission, which looks much the same today as it did in 1926.

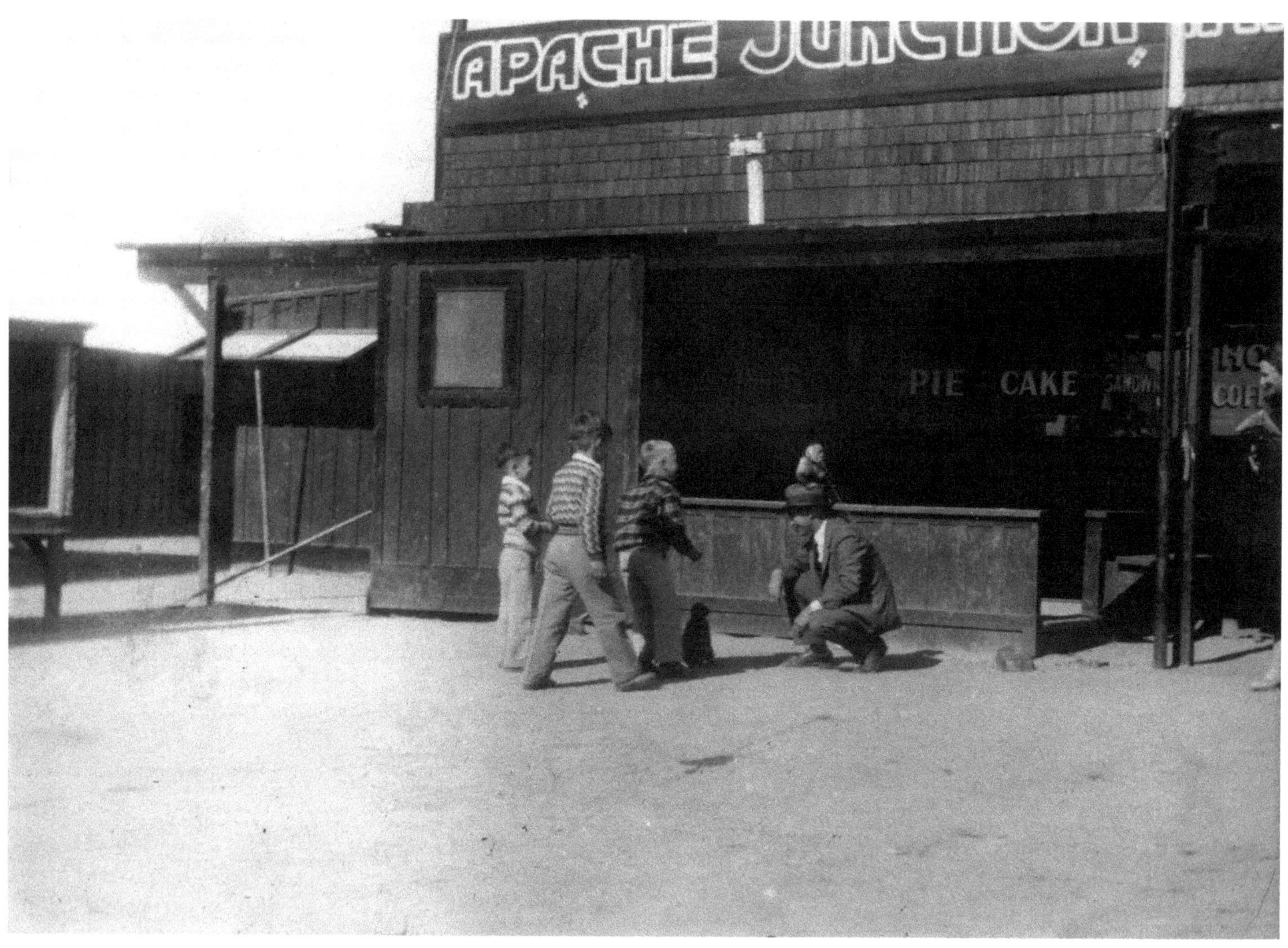

At the junction where U.S. Highway 60 meets the Apache Trail, a small community of stores and gasoline stations called Apache Junction sprang up at the base of the mighty Superstition Mountains. Travelers who followed Highway 60 arrived at the mining towns of Superior, Miami, and Globe. Those who followed the Apache Trail arrived at Roosevelt Dam. Children, too, could enjoy a stop at this oasis junction in 1926.

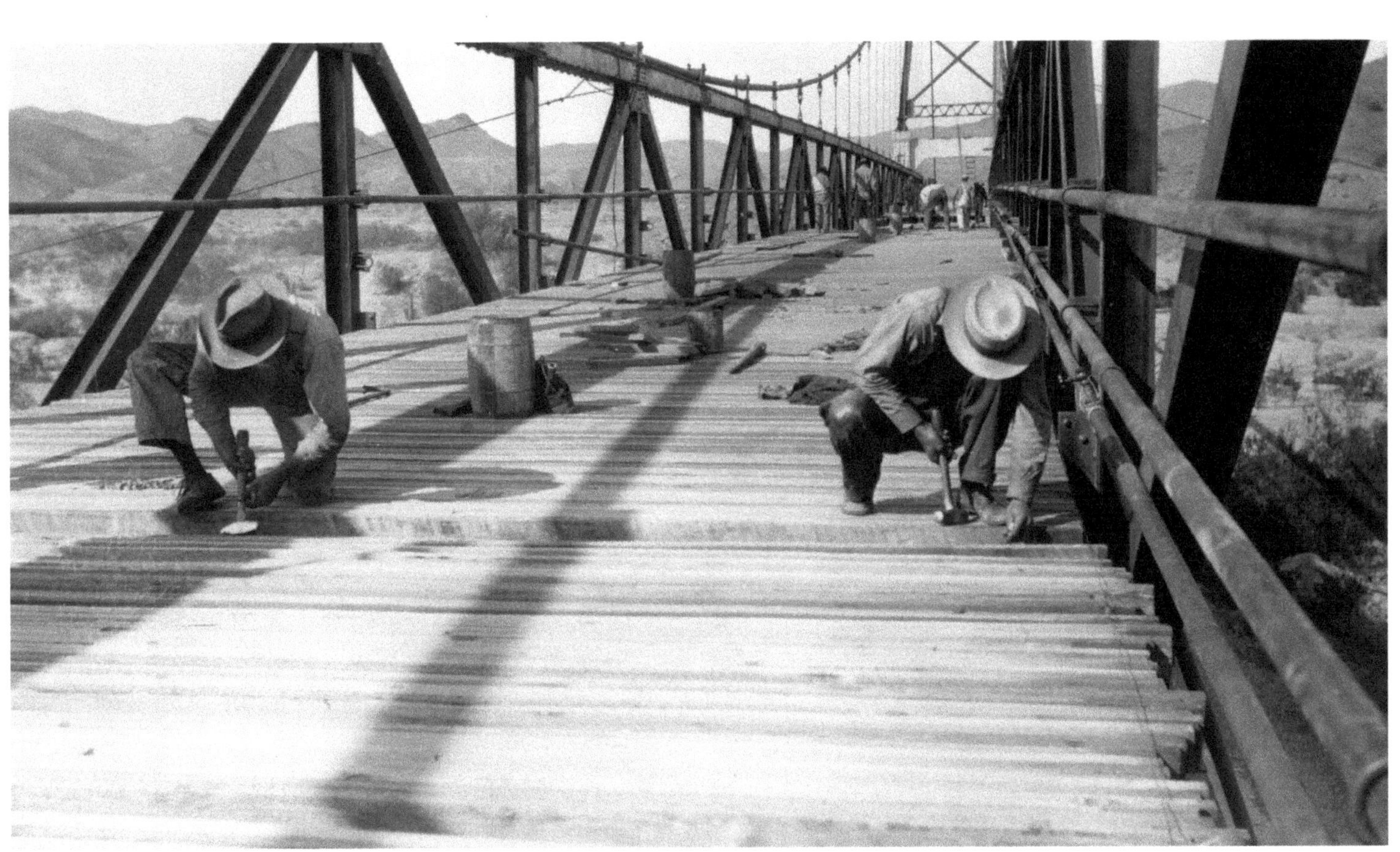

The Dome Suspension Bridge, also known as the McPhaul Suspension Bridge, was built in 1928 to link the towns of Yuma and Quartzsite. It was the longest suspension bridge in Arizona at the time, with the main span extending to 798 feet. The bridge's roadway was made of wooden planks, as shown in this image.

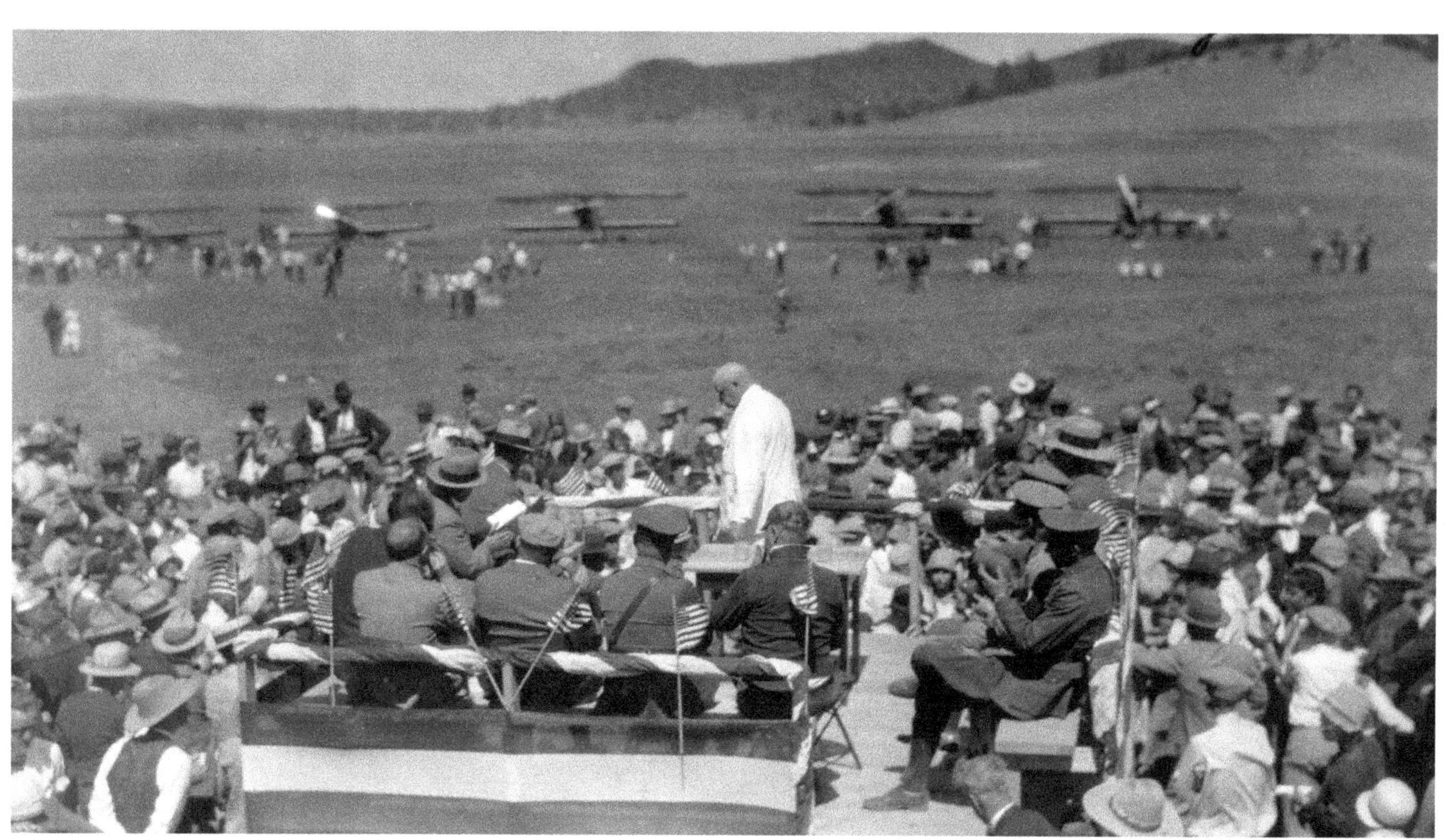

Flagstaff's Pulliam Airport was dedicated in 1928, the year Flagstaff became incorporated. The airport is located four miles from the downtown business district. Here Governor George W. P. Hunt and the citizens of Flagstaff celebrate the opening of the new airport.

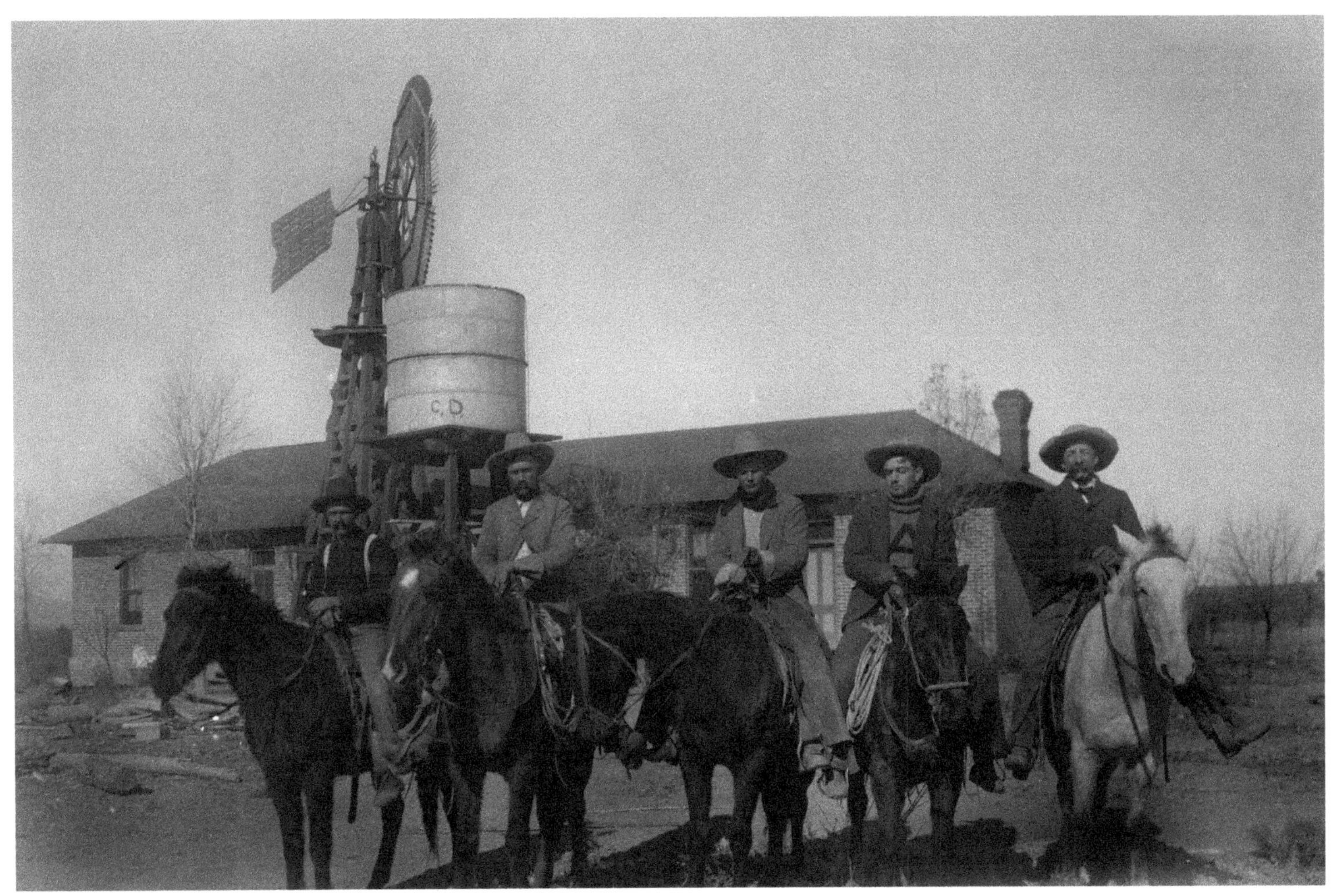

The Lazy B Ranch near Duncan, Arizona, straddles the Arizona–New Mexico border. Growing up on the Lazy B, a young girl named Sandra Day learned the ways of a 1920s Arizona ranch. In 1981, Sandra Day O'Connor became the first woman to serve as a justice of the United States Supreme Court. This photo shows her father, H. C. Day (at far right), and some of the ranch cowboys.

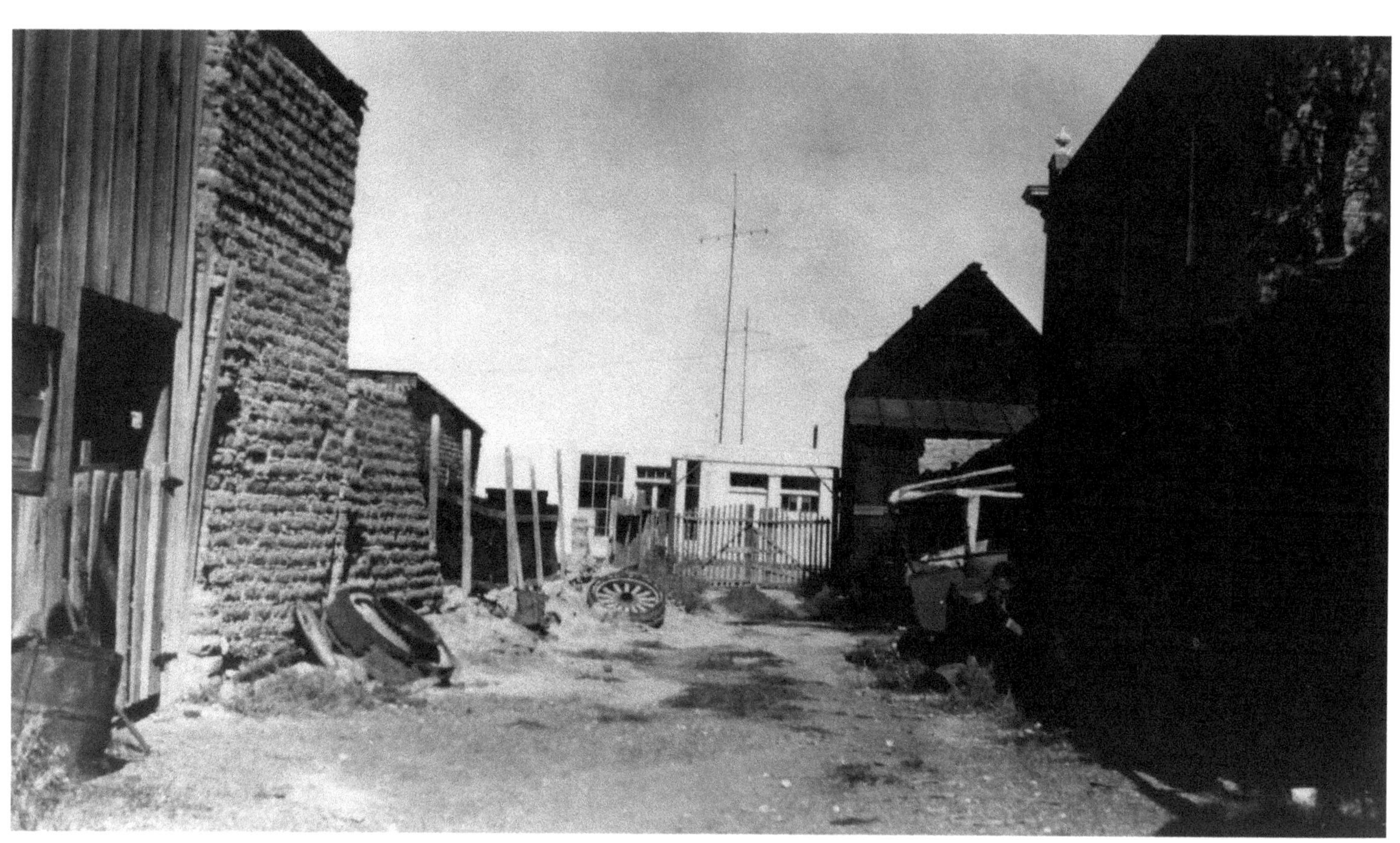

By the early 1930s the population of Tombstone had dropped to less than 150 people. The "town too tough to die" was truly at death's door. This 1930s photo shows the broken-down streets and dilapidated buildings of the most famous of Arizona's Wild West towns.

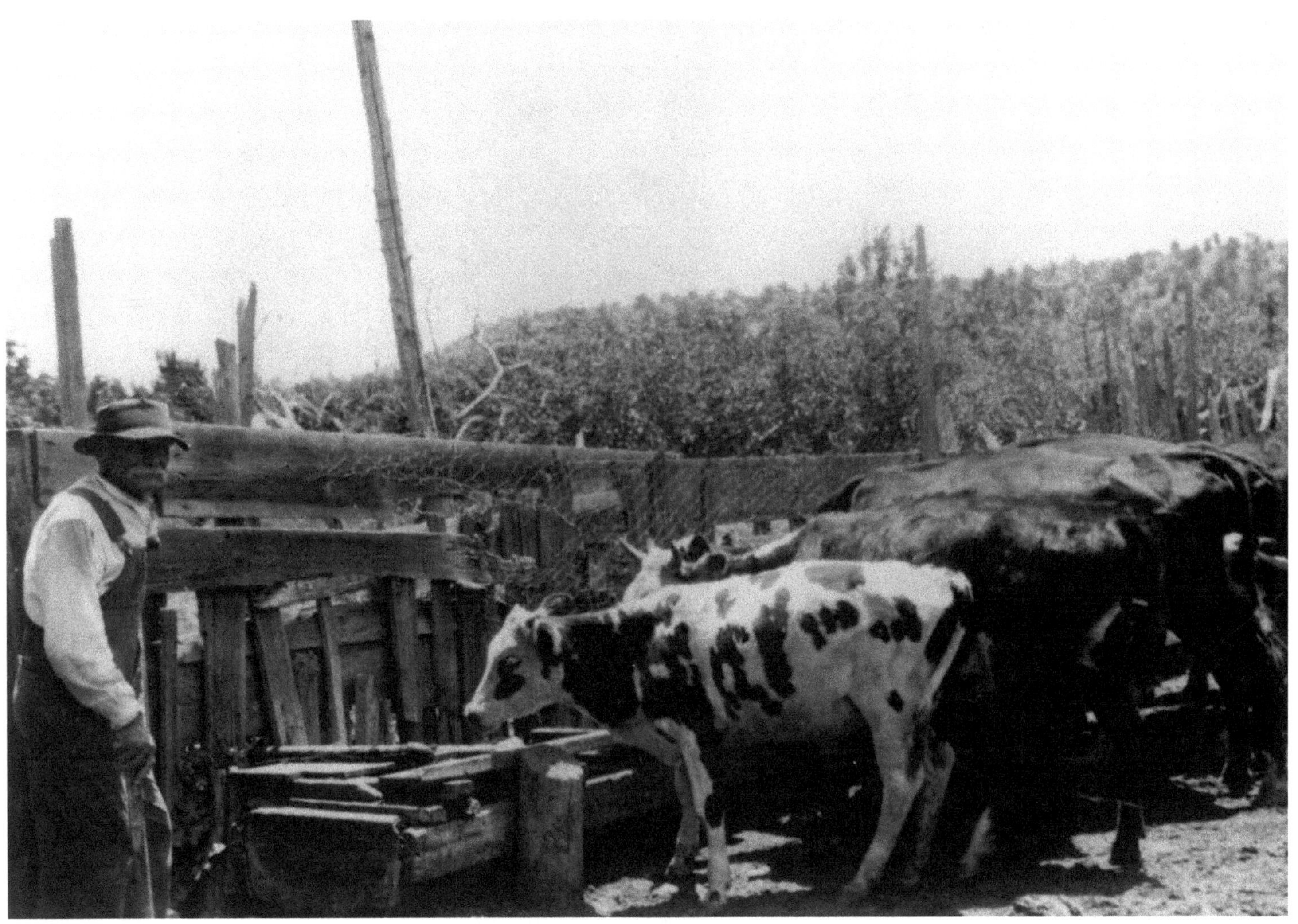

Prescott's early economy was based on cattle ranching and mining. This 1930s photo shows a cowboy still working his cattle. By that time the look of the city was much changed. The old town had burned almost to the ground in a 1900 fire, and when the city was rebuilt, bricks laid with mortar were used instead of wooden frames with adobe, and a charming architectural style arose. Today more than 500 buildings in Prescott are on the National Register of Historic Places.

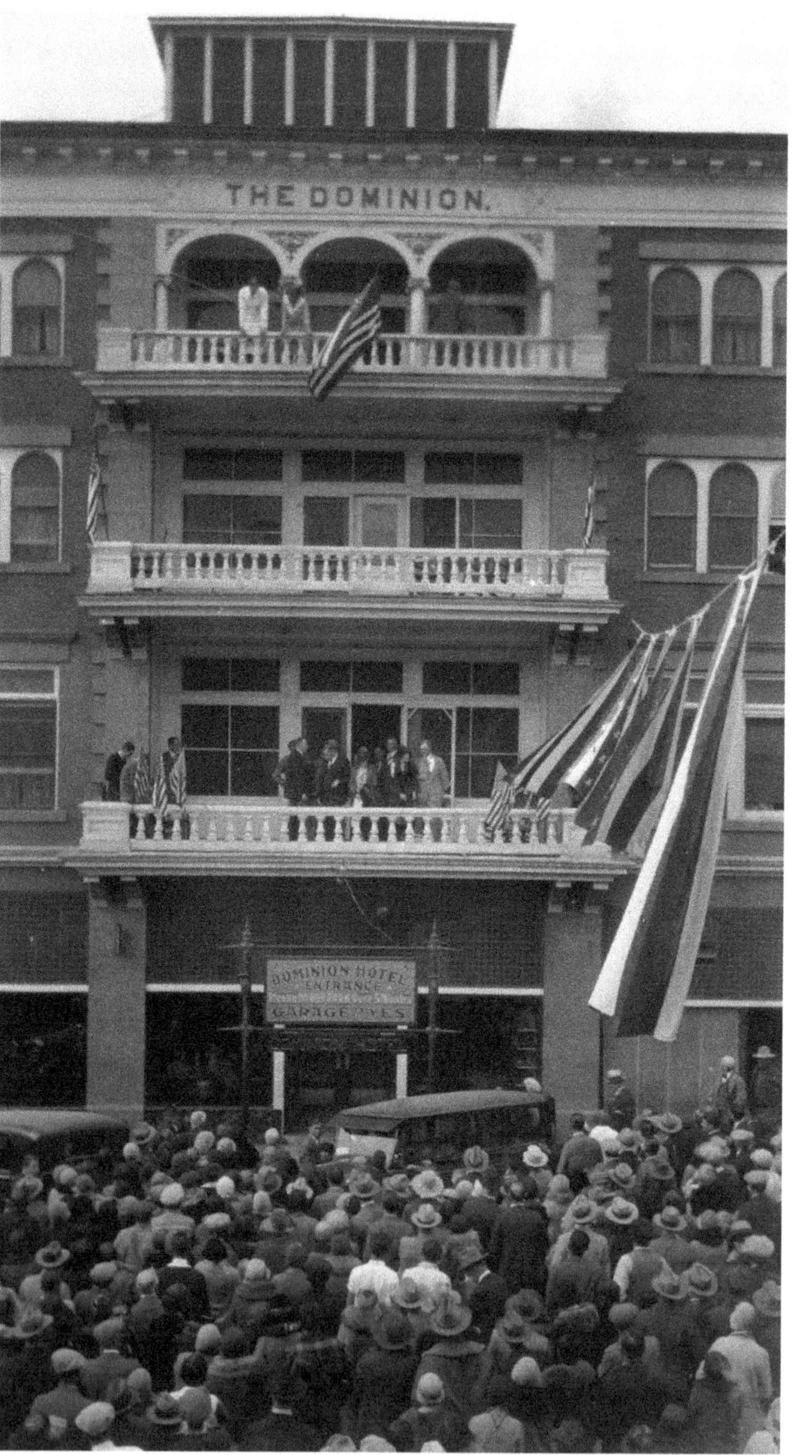

On March 4, 1930, President Calvin Coolidge addressed a crowd of citizens in Globe after dedicating a nearby dam named in his honor. Coolidge Dam stopped the flow of the Gila River and created San Carlos Lake some 31 miles from downtown Globe. The dam is located on the San Carlos Indian Reservation and was a part of the San Carlos Irrigation Project.

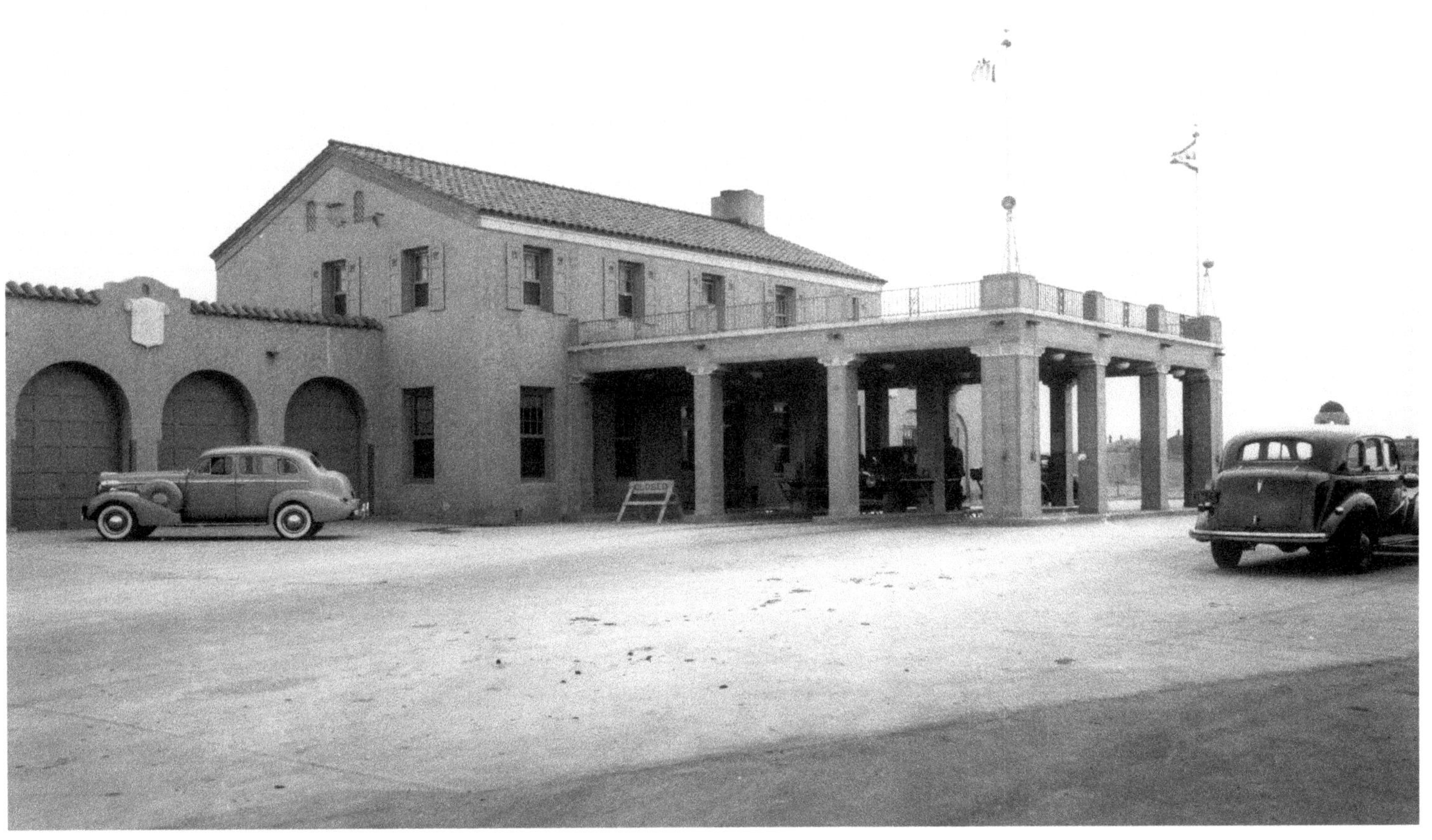

Six Arizona towns serve as ports of entry between the United States and Mexico. Most of them were established shortly after the Gadsden Purchase of 1854 and, with few exceptions, have been sites where commercial entities, families, and friends have always crossed peacefully. This border station and customs house in Douglas was one of the points where United States and Mexico citizens moved back and forth during the 1930s.

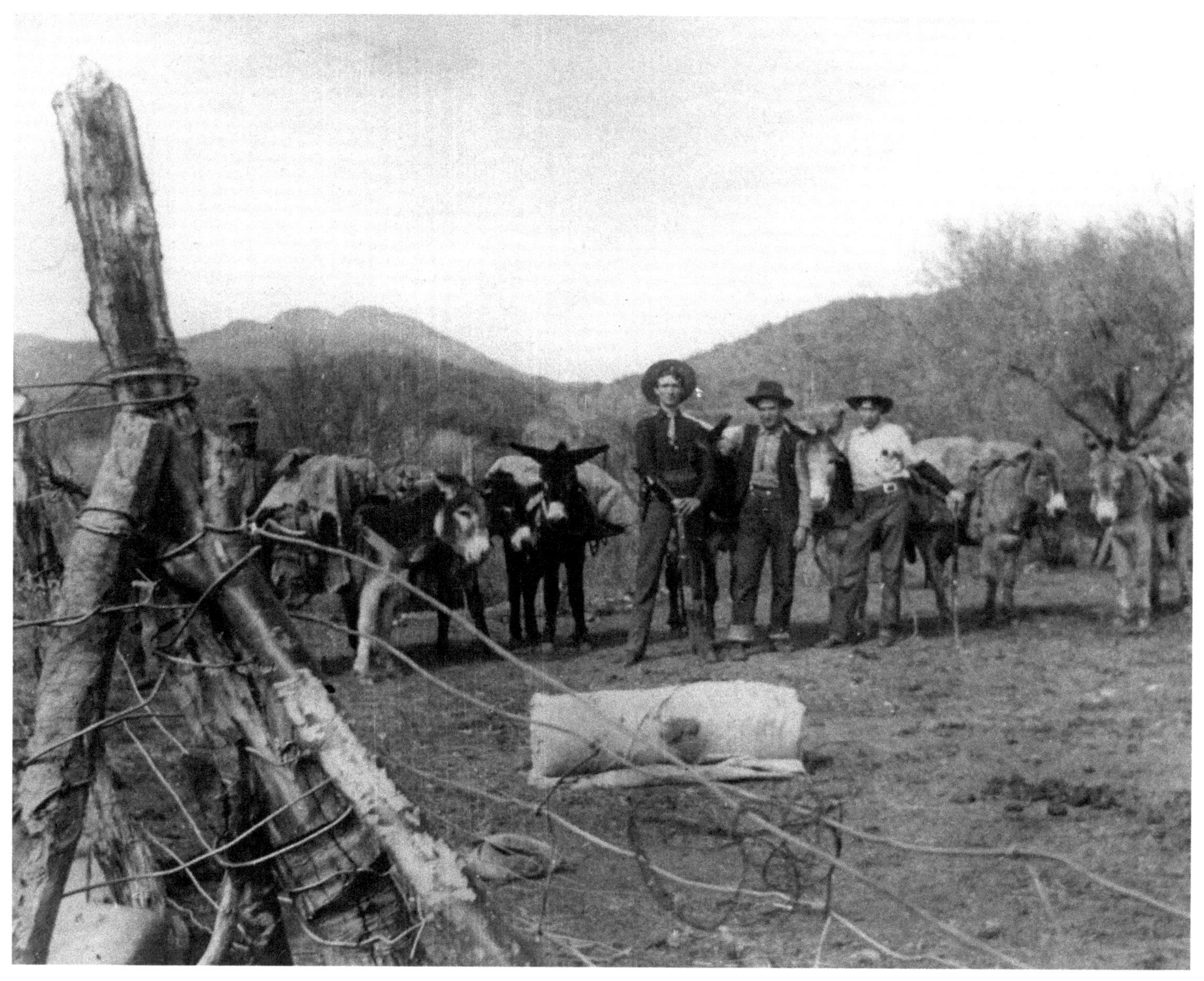

These cowboys with their burros inspect a barbed-wire fence line in the desert around Cave Creek in the 1930s. Most historians credit barbed wire, the railroad, and the influence of mothers in western towns with taming the Wild West.

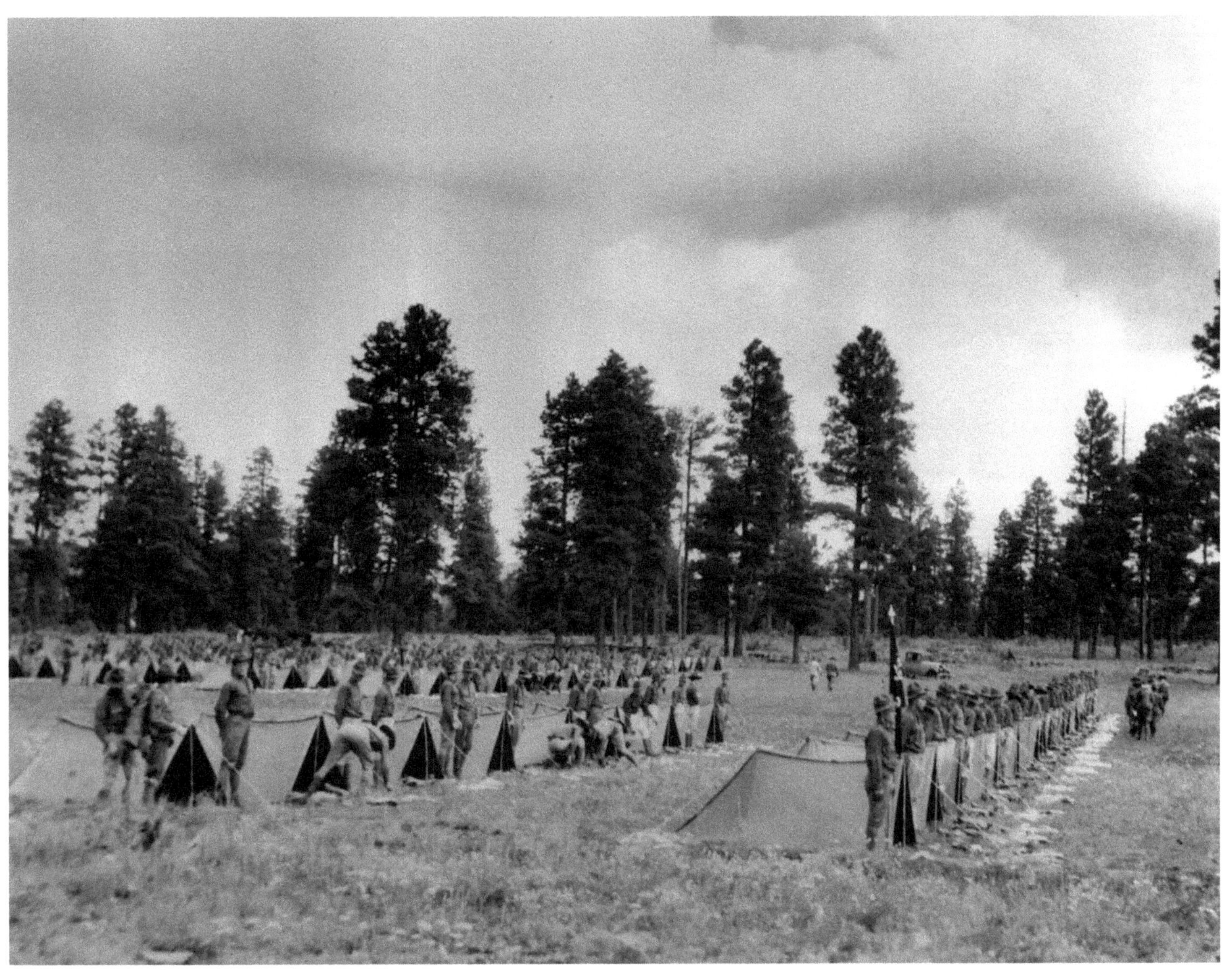

Located three miles south of Flagstaff, Fort Tuthill was constructed in 1929 to serve as a permanent training ground for the 158th Infantry Regiment of the Arizona National Guard. The 158th was deactivated in 1968. One of the original Fort Tuthill buildings, now located on the Coconino County Fairgrounds, has been restored to house a military museum devoted to the fort's history.

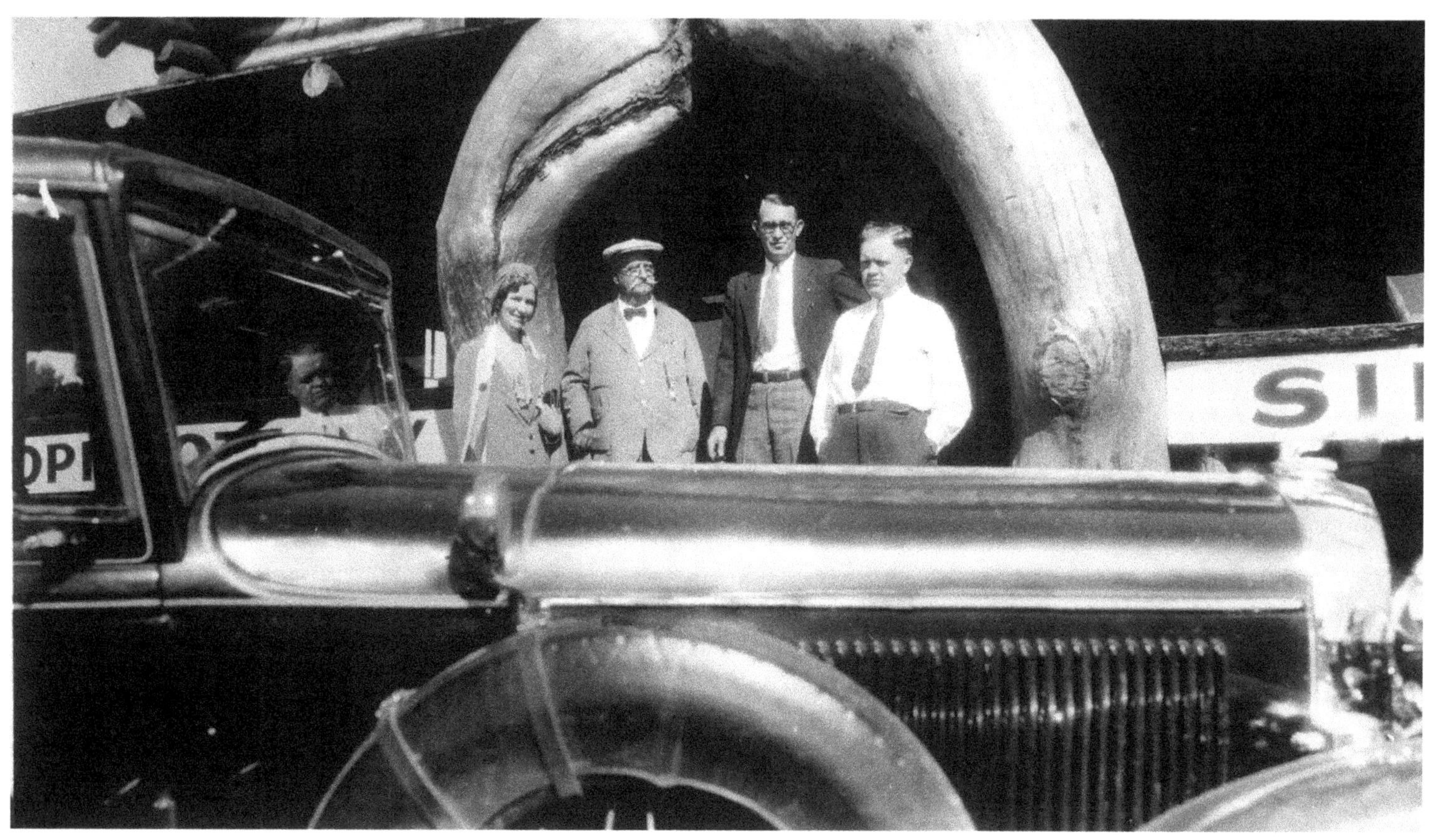

Known for its unique entry under an arching, split tree trunk, the Museum Club of Flagstaff is regarded by many as Arizona's premier roadhouse and western dance club. Built in 1931 along Route 66, the club with its large wooden dance floor has long provided fun outings for both the Arizona cowboy and the politician. Even Governor George W. P. Hunt showed up to celebrate its opening.

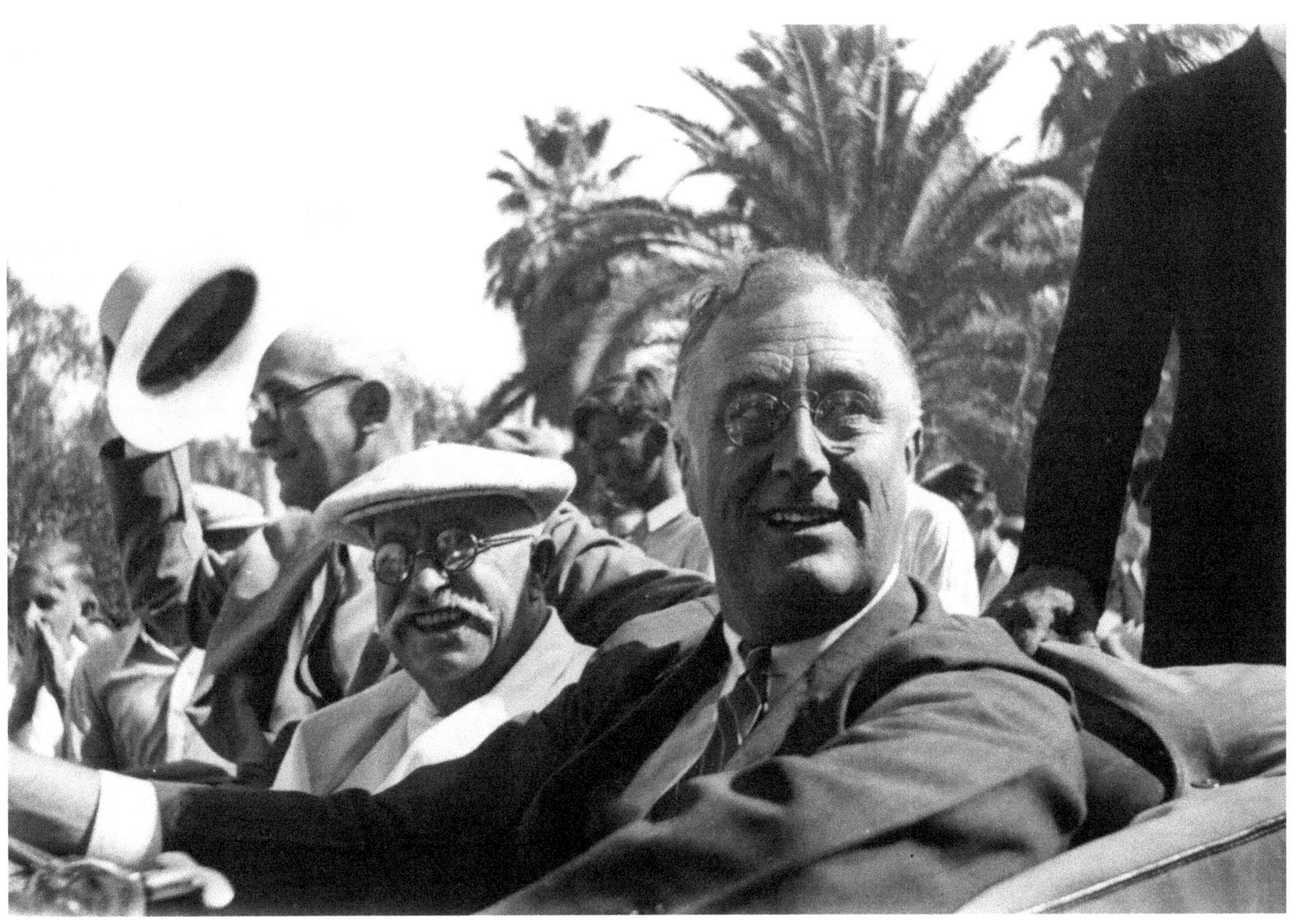

Riding in an open convertible with Governor George W. P. Hunt, presidential candidate Franklin D. Roosevelt greets Phoenix residents during a campaign visit on September 25, 1932.

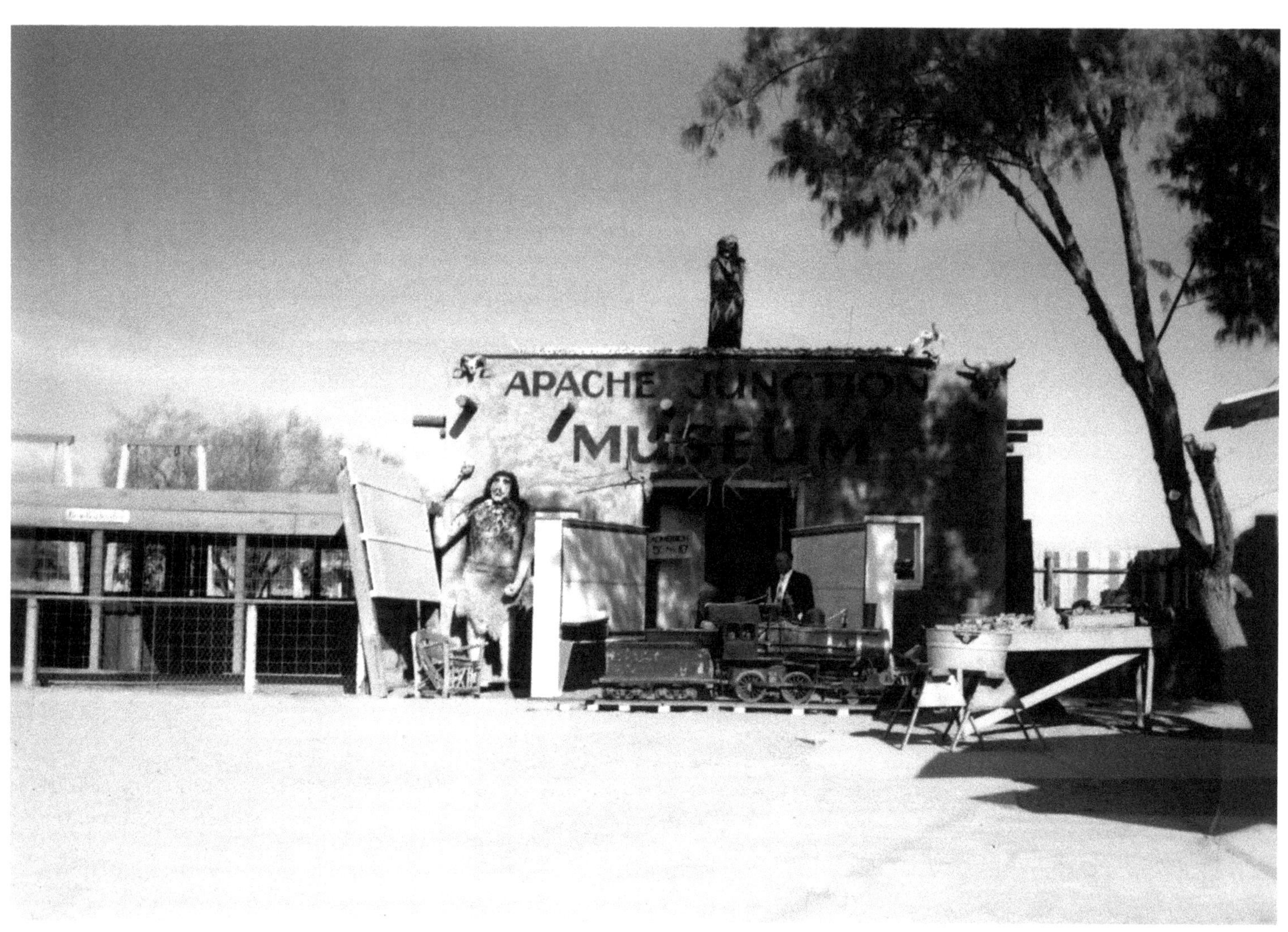

Apache Junction is the starting point and ending point of the Apache Trail. This 120-mile scenic roadway was originally built to move construction materials from Phoenix to the Roosevelt Dam site. In 1915 tourists began using the trail to travel through some of Arizona's most rugged wilderness. A stop at this 1934 museum prepared tourists for the Apache Trail experience.

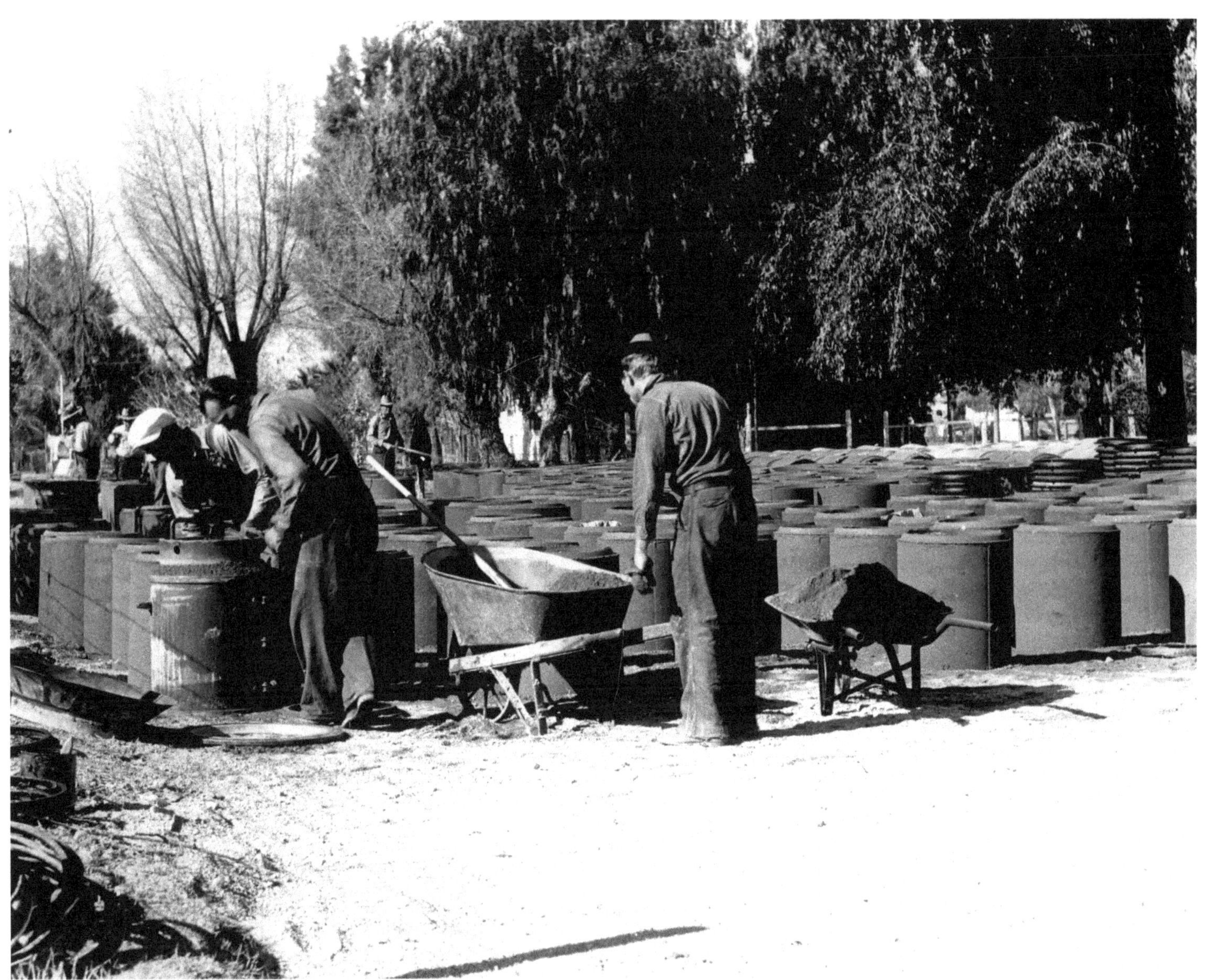

This photo shows men of the Civil Works Administration, a New Deal program started in 1933, hard at work on a project in Glendale. The Civil Works Administration lasted only five months, but a similar program, the Civilian Conservation Corps, completed many projects in Arizona. From the beautiful headquarters of Colossal Cave Mountain Park near Tucson to the trails cut through the Grand Canyon, the CCC built many of the park and recreation facilities enjoyed in Arizona today.

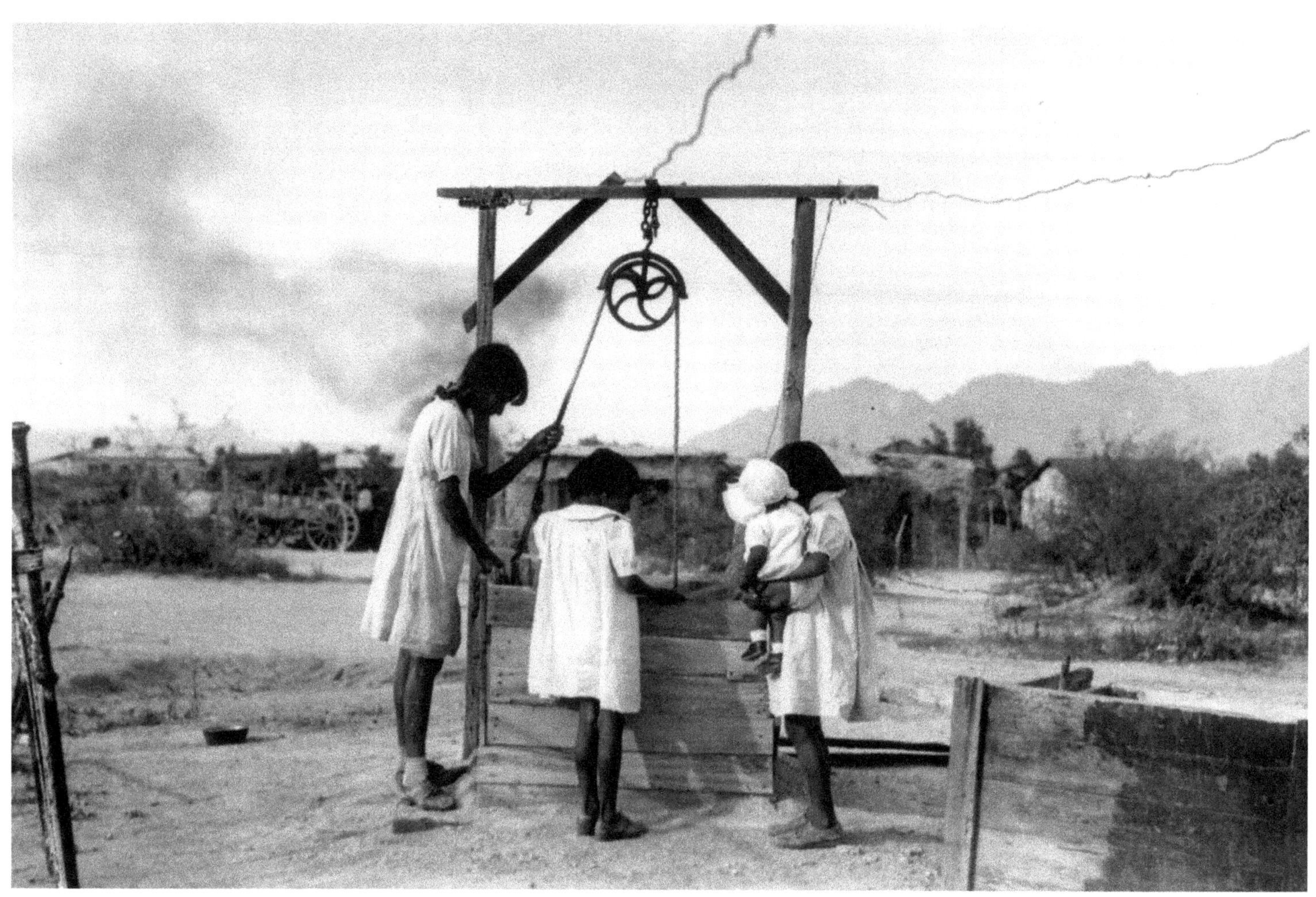

The Works Progress Administration was one of the New Deal programs begun by President Franklin D. Roosevelt during the 1930s. Its mission was to provide jobs and income for the unemployed during the Great Depression. The WPA built many roads and public buildings in the towns and cities of America. These young girls are drawing fresh water from a new well dug by WPA workers on what was then called the Papago Indian Reservation south of Tucson.

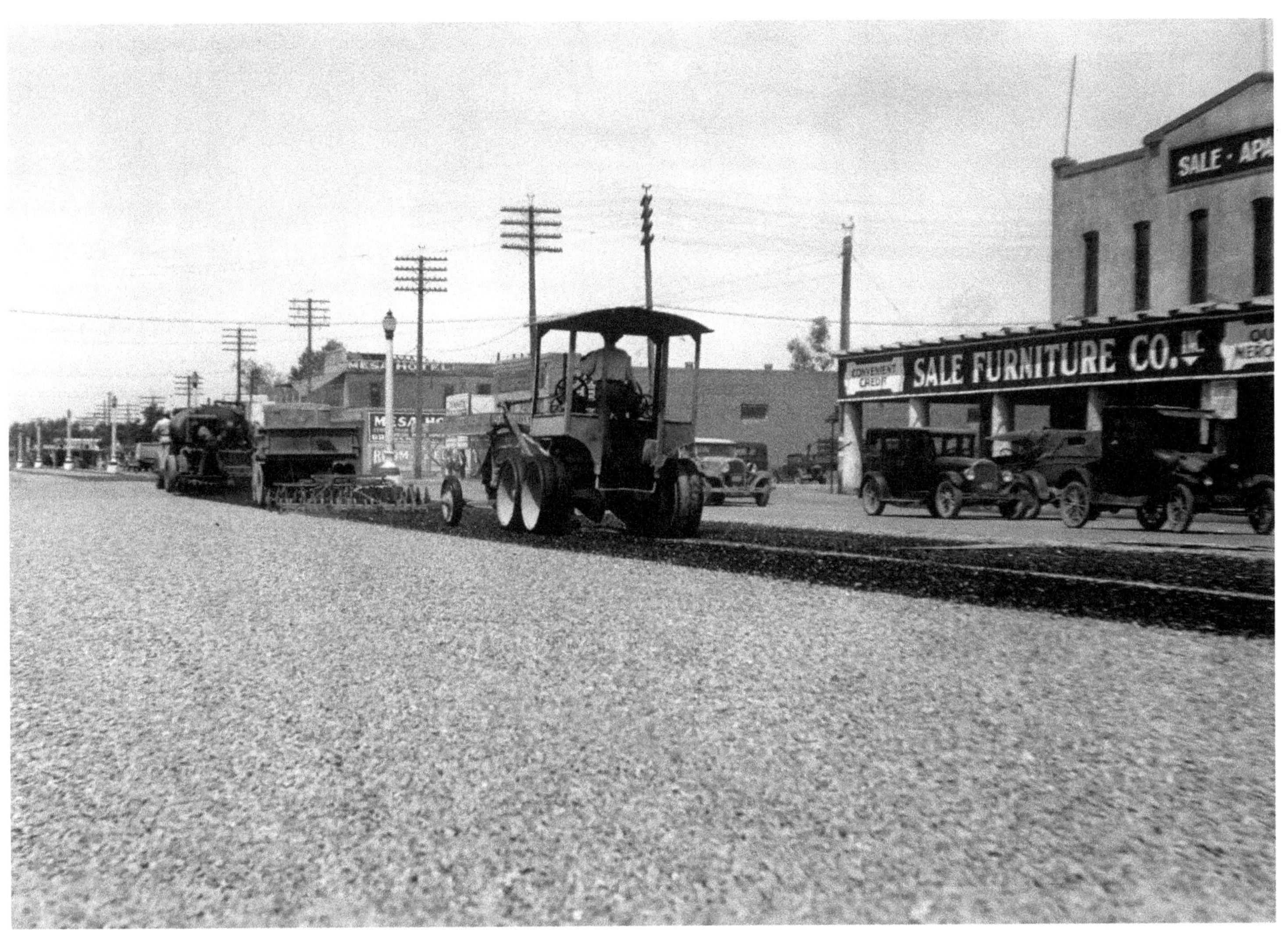

Workers with the Arizona Highway Department pave Main Street in Mesa in 1934. Mesa was founded in January 1878 by Mormon settlers camped along the Salt River east of Phoenix. The name given their settlement was Fort Utah. Other settlers arrived in February and decided to move up onto the nearby mesa, away from the unhealthy river. The town site was officially registered on July 17, 1878, and a post office was established in 1881.

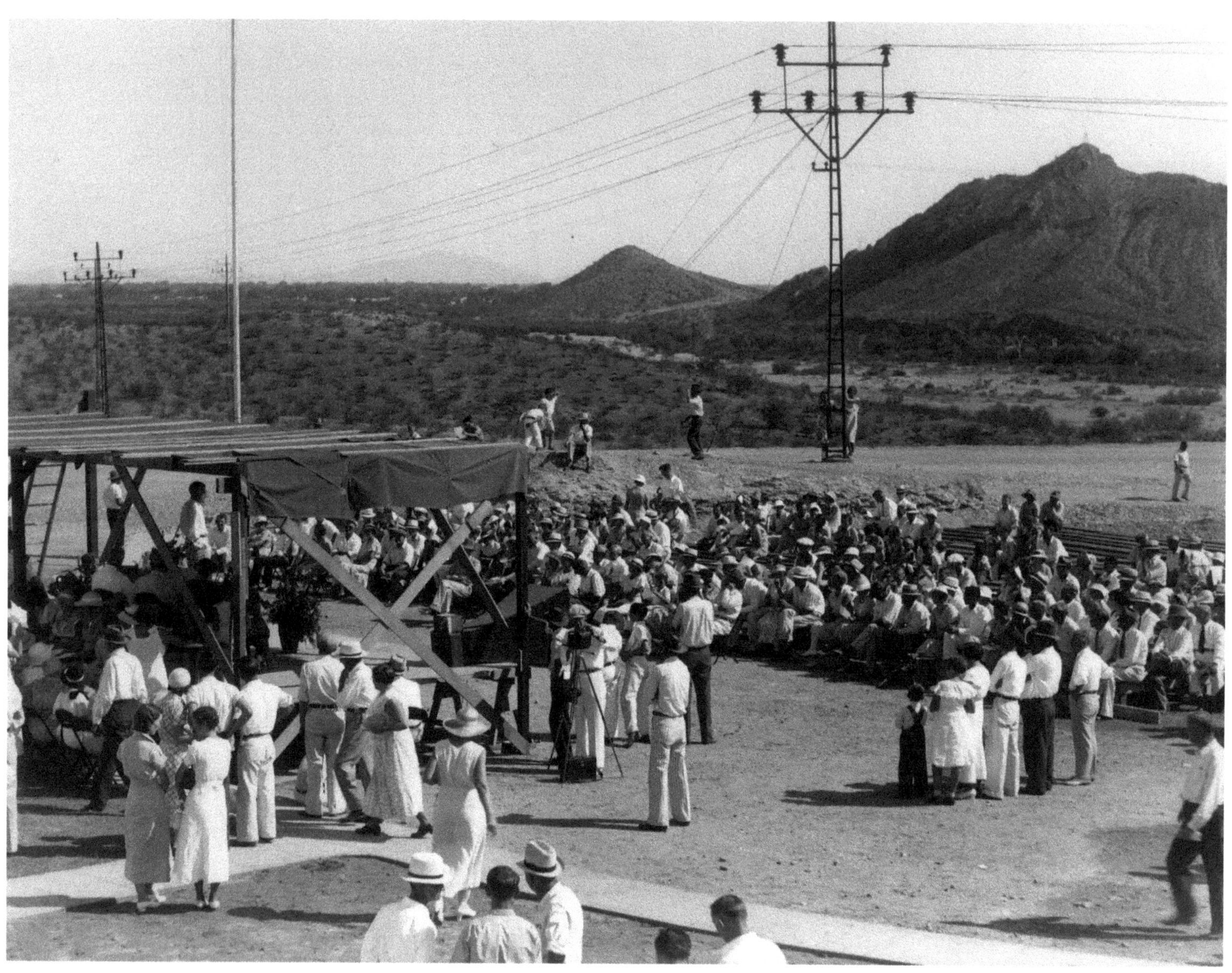

The Tuberculosis Welfare Sanatorium in Tempe was built by the Civil Works Administration and dedicated in 1934, with these folks attending. The 100-bed sanatorium was intended for patients in need of early care or with cases deemed curable. Nationwide the CWA employed a total of 12,942 men and 192 women for work on projects within the National Parks system alone.

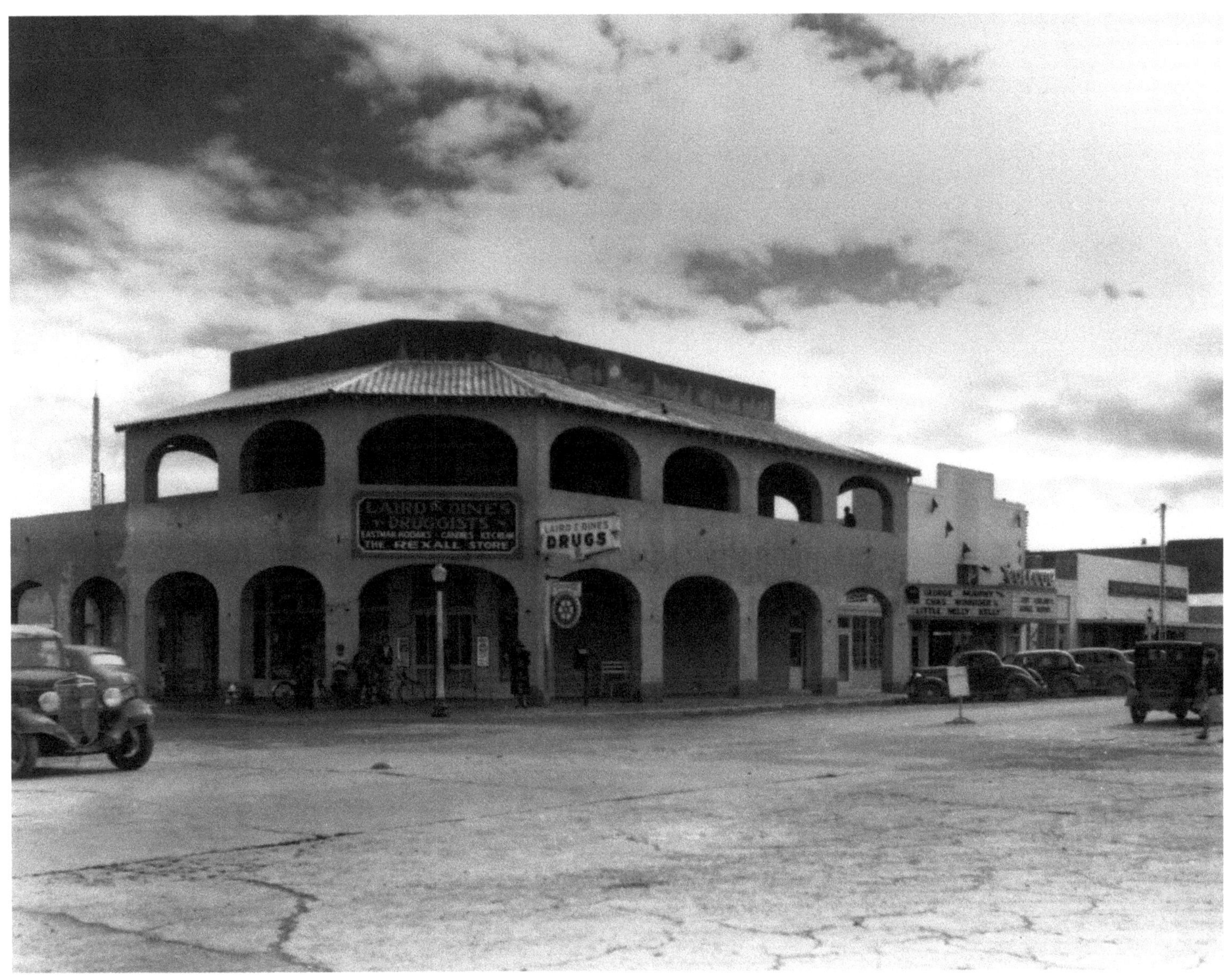

In 1897 Claire Laird of Tempe purchased a dry goods store so that her three boys would have somewhere to work. Dr. James Dines agreed to be Laird's partner and to train her boys as pharmacists. Together they established the Laird and Dines drugstore. The two-story building served the people of Tempe for 63 years. The facade of the old building still stands, but the second floor is now a Hooters restaurant.

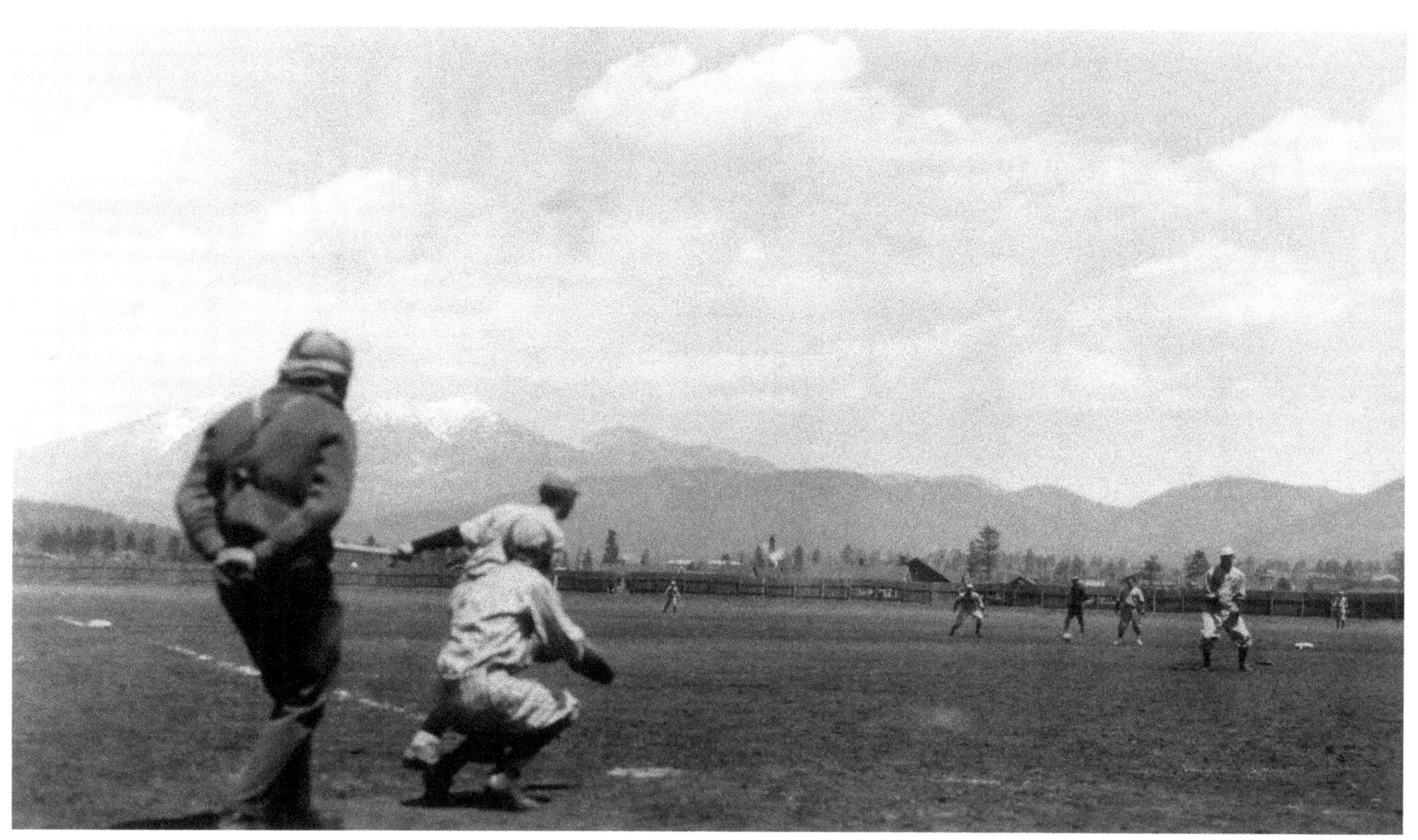

Northern Arizona Normal School's first classes were held September 11, 1899, when twenty-three students with one professor began their academic journey to become public school teachers of the Arizona Territory. Two years later, in 1901, four women made up the first graduating class. In 1925 the school became Northern Arizona State Teachers College, and Northern Arizona University in 1966. The school baseball team, the Lumberjacks, are shown playing a game around 1935.

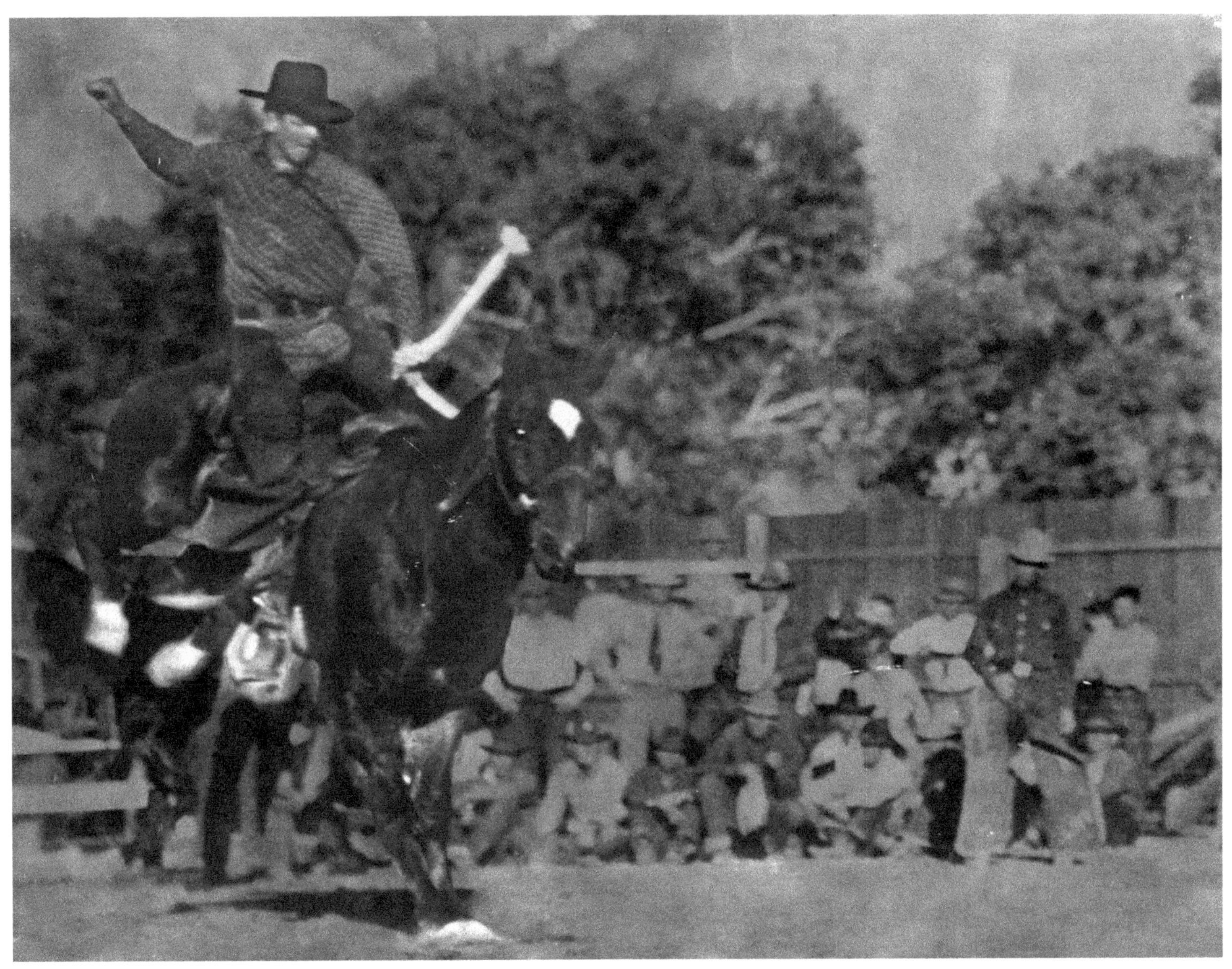

Chandler cowboy Bill Roer is shown riding a bronco in 1936. He might more appropriately have been riding an ostrich, for it was Dr. Alexander John Chandler, a veterinarian with a keen interest in ostrich ranching, who founded this central Arizona town. An annual Ostrich Festival is held in Chandler each March.

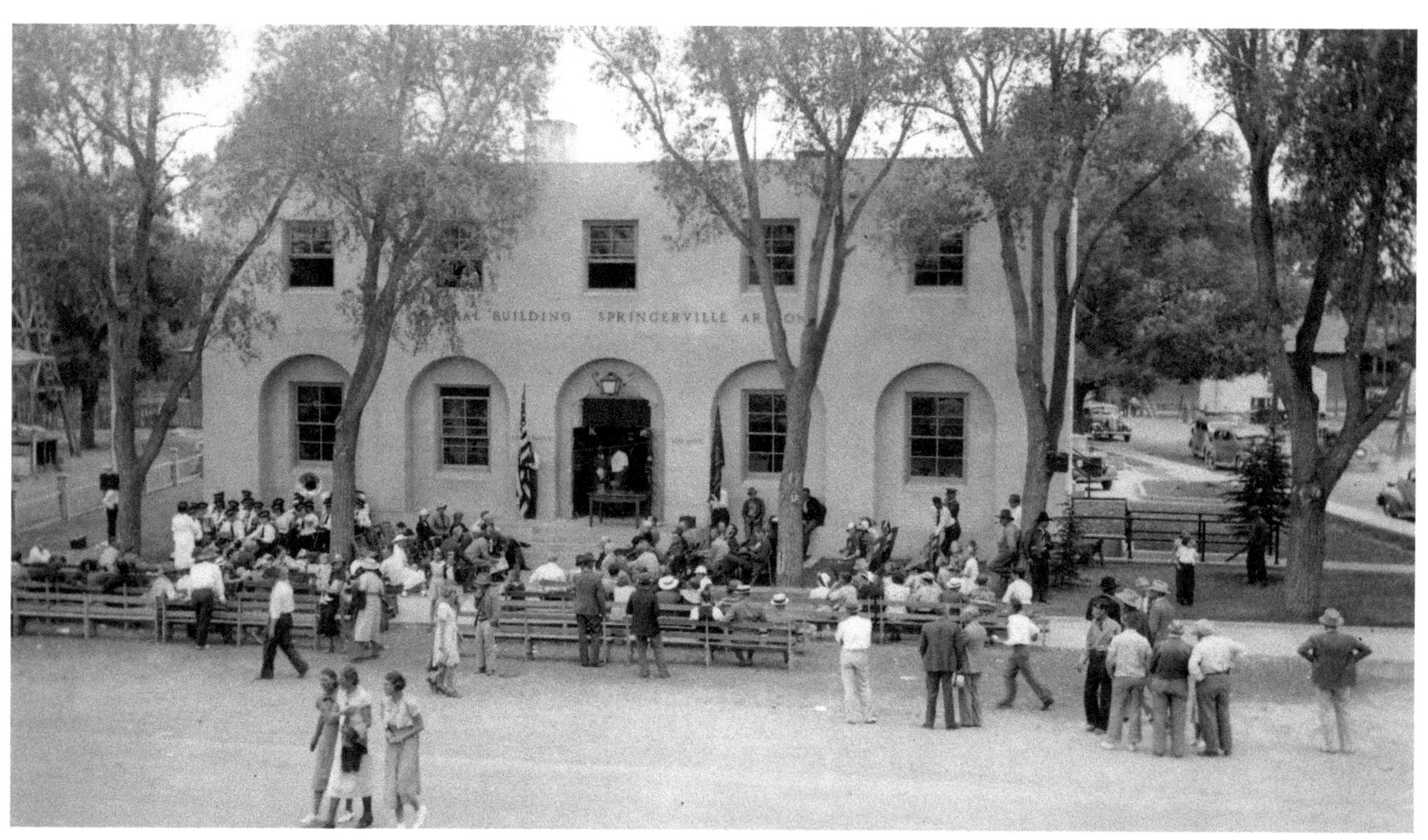

In the late 1930s the owner of the Milky Way candy company came to the Springerville area and started a Hereford ranch. His spread, which he named the Milky Way Ranch, later became part of the 26 Bar Ranch owned by John Wayne and a partner. This Springerville post office, still in service today, must have seen "the Duke" in the lobby on more than one occasion.

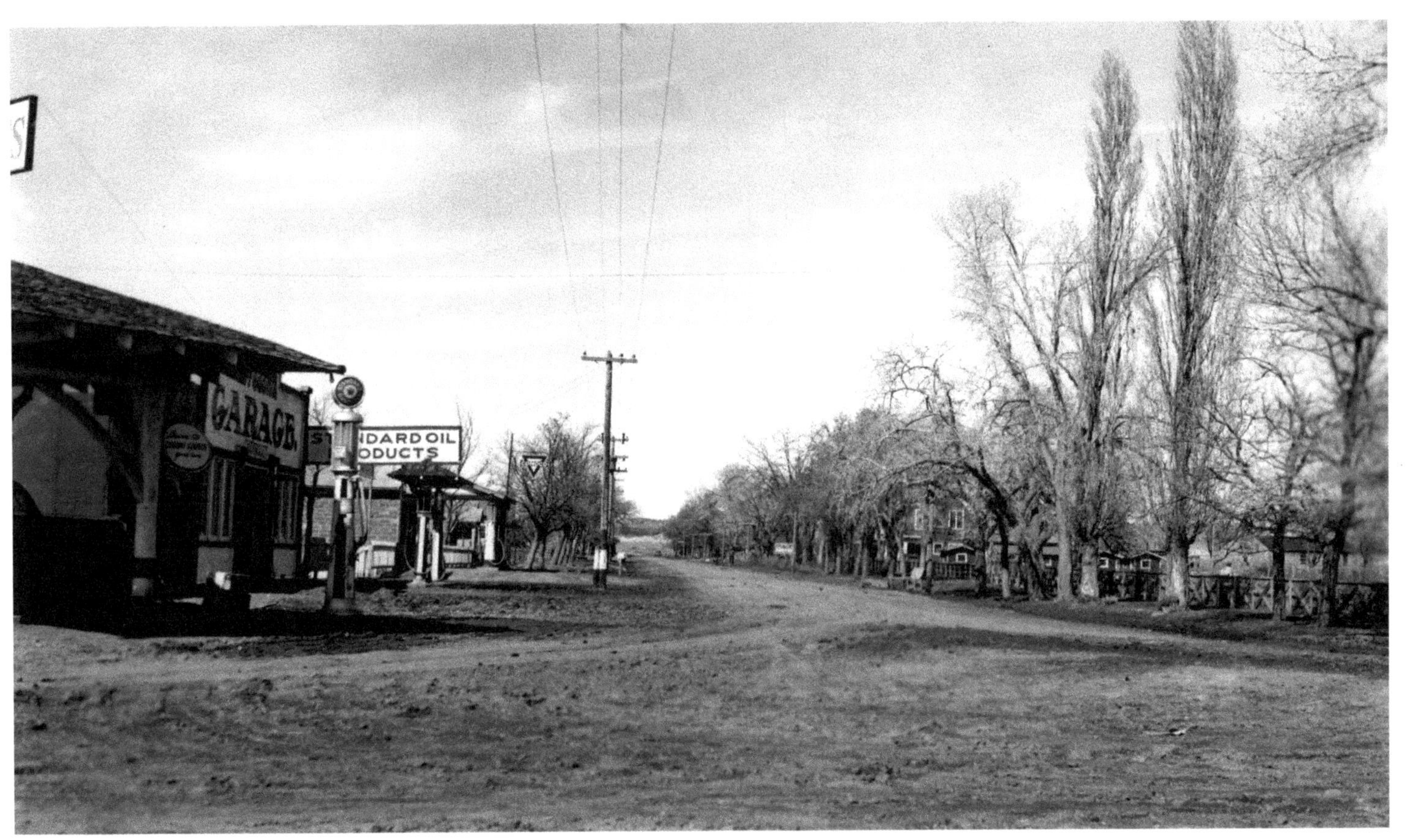

Shown here in Flagstaff in 1937, U.S. Highway 89 was created in 1926 to be a north-south pathway between the Canadian border and Nogales, Arizona. Heading north from Flagstaff through Utah, Idaho, Yellowstone Park in Wyoming, and on through Montana, today's Highway 89 passes through some of the most magnificent scenery of America. It extends 1,685 miles and is often called the "Great Western Highway."

The opening of the Colorado River Bridge at Parker in 1937 ended a 27-year ferry service run by the husband and wife riverboat pilots Joe and Nellie Bush. Nellie Bush was the second woman to serve in the Arizona state legislature and was inducted into the Arizona Women's Hall of Fame in 1982.

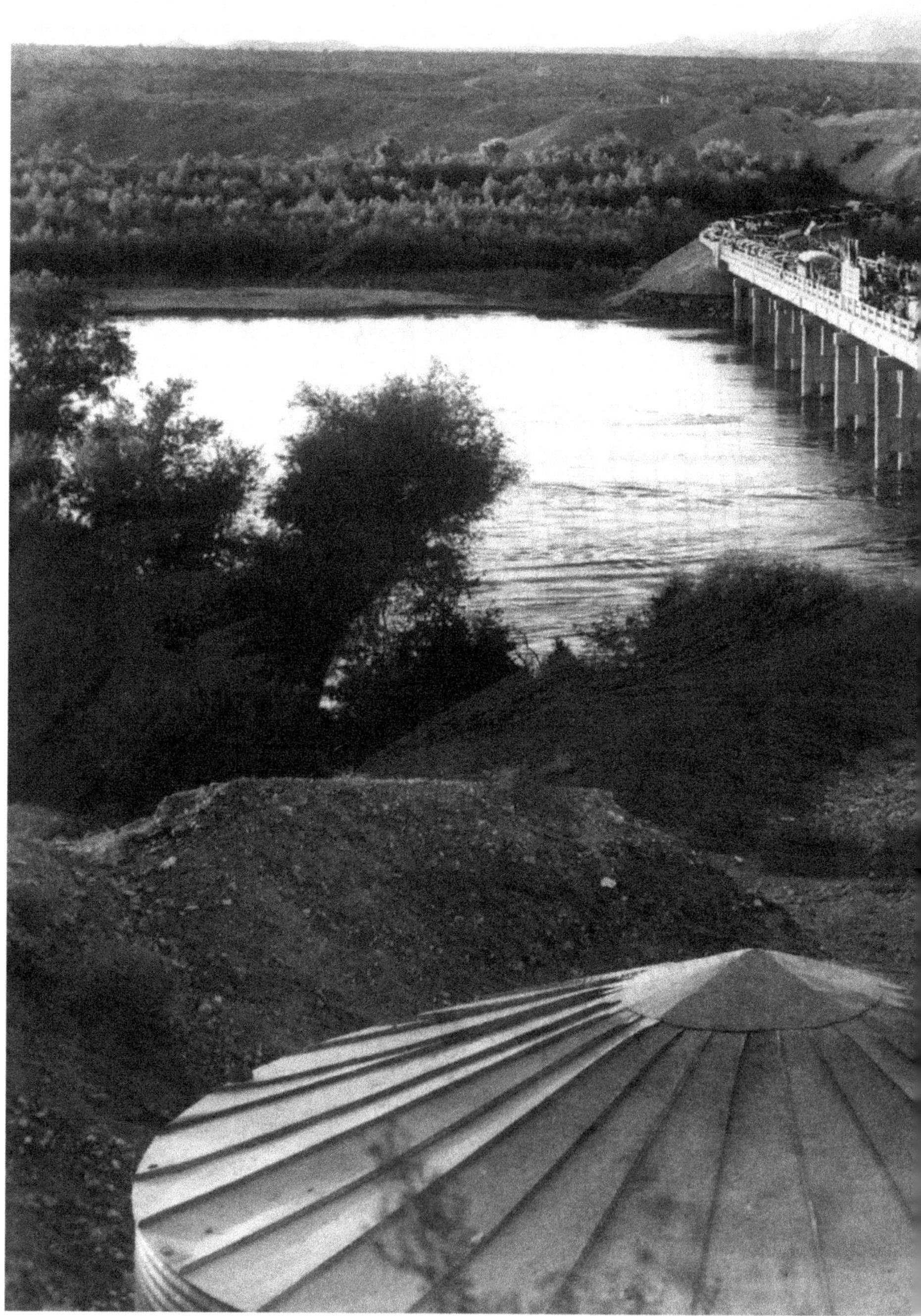

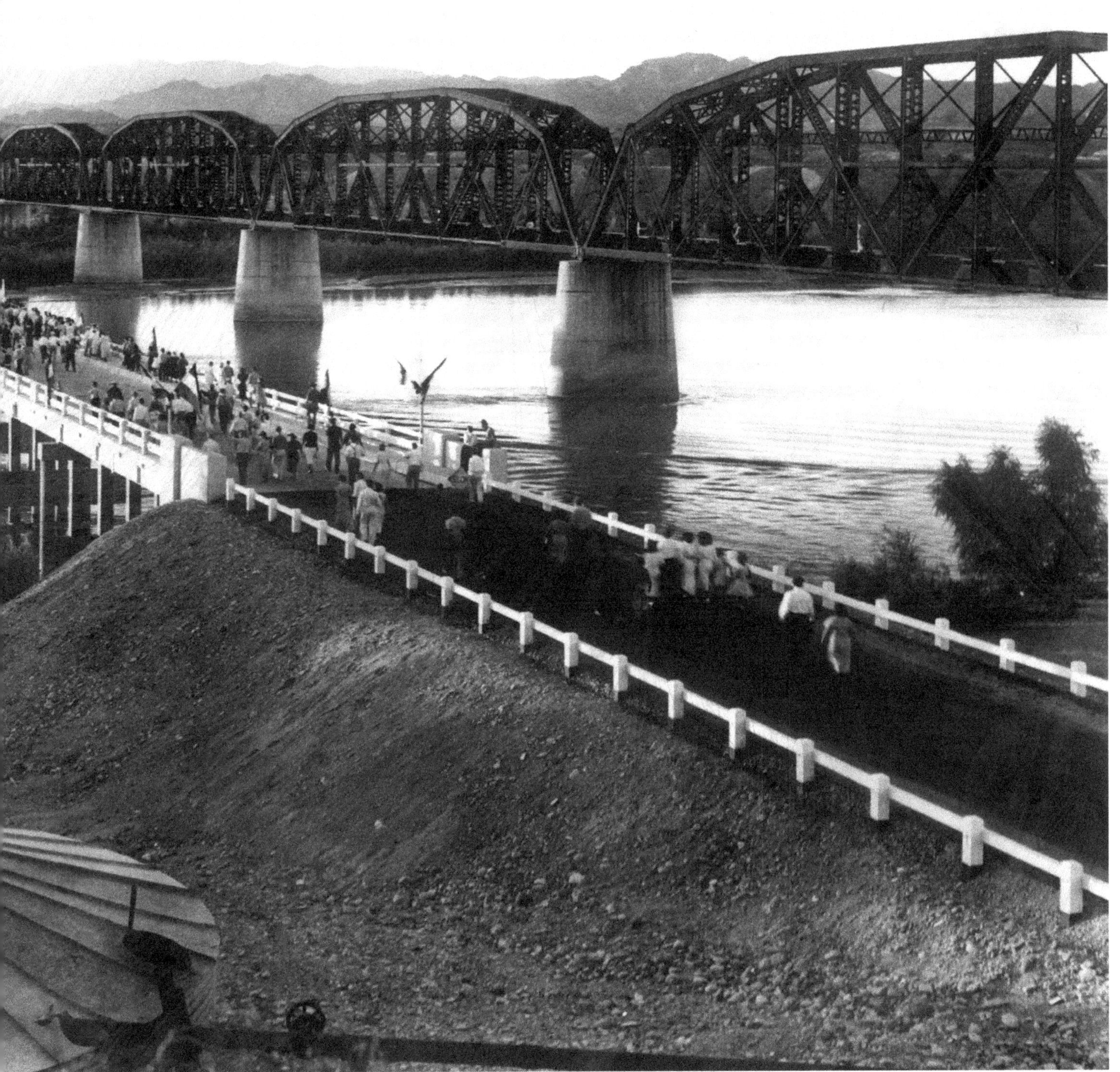

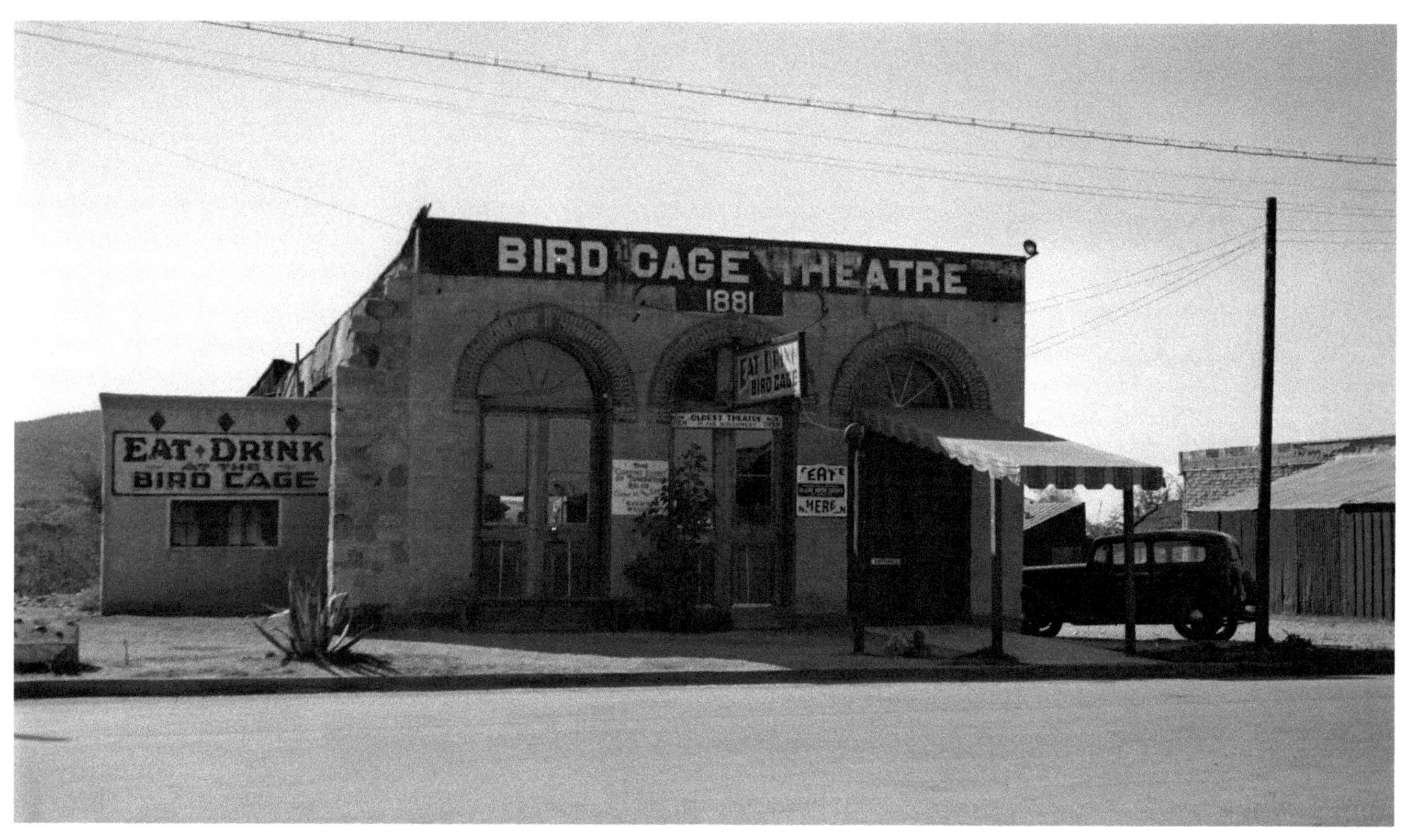

The "wildest, roughest, wickedest honky tonk between Basin Street and the Barbary Coast" is how the *New York Times* once described the Bird Cage Theatre of 1880s Tombstone. The Bird Cage served not only as a theater, but also as a gambling hall, saloon, and brothel. In the Bird Cage's eight years of operation during Tombstone's boom era, 26 people met their death there. This 1933 photo shows the Bird Cage in a quieter time.

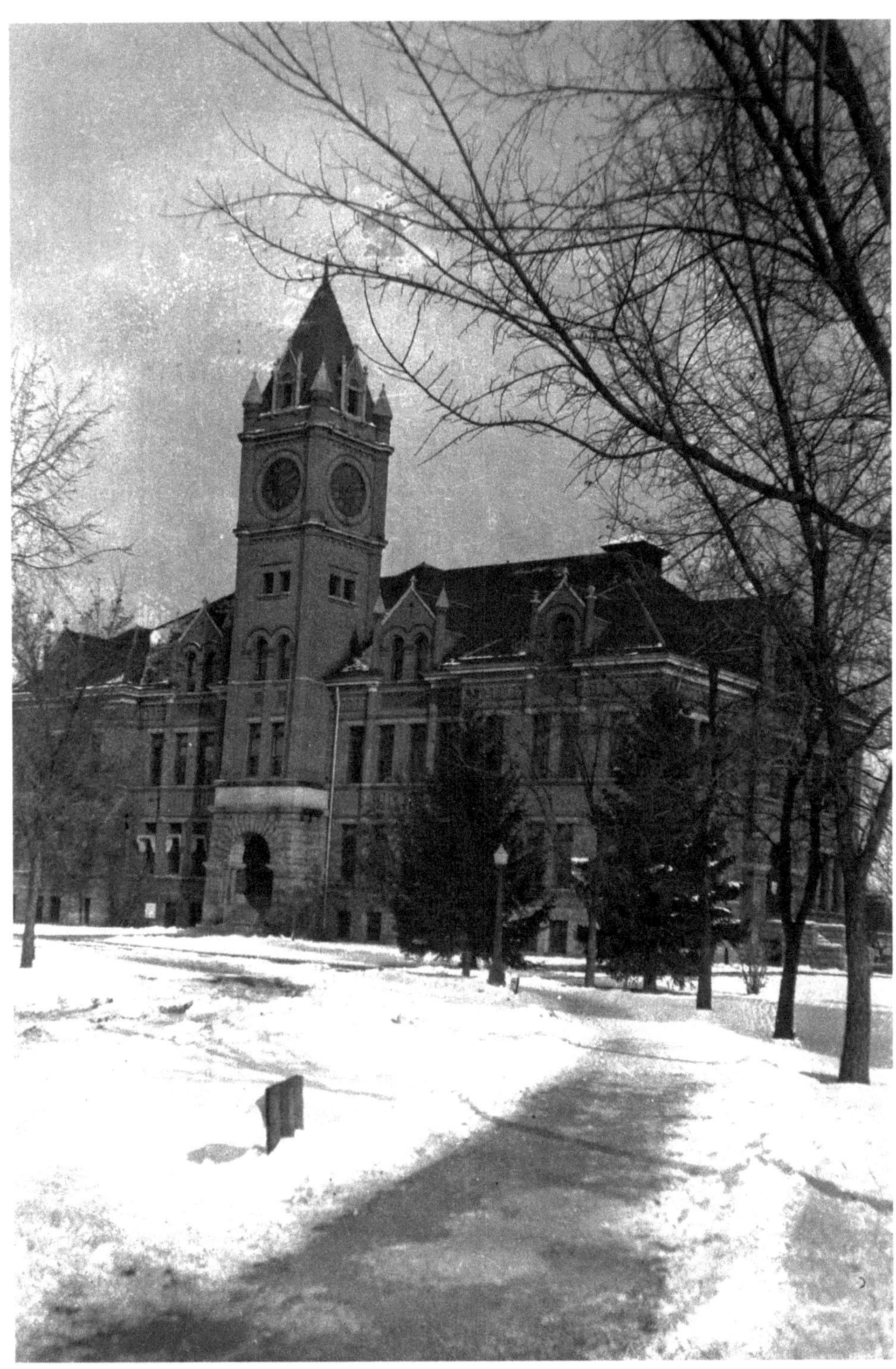

Old Main, on the campus of Northern Arizona University, was built in 1894 to serve as a reform school for wayward youths. When those plans fell apart, the territorial legislature suggested it serve as an insane asylum. Flagstaff citizens opposed that idea, too. The building finally opened on September 11, 1899, as the first classroom building of Northern Arizona Normal School. In 1937, when this photo was taken, it was the administration building.

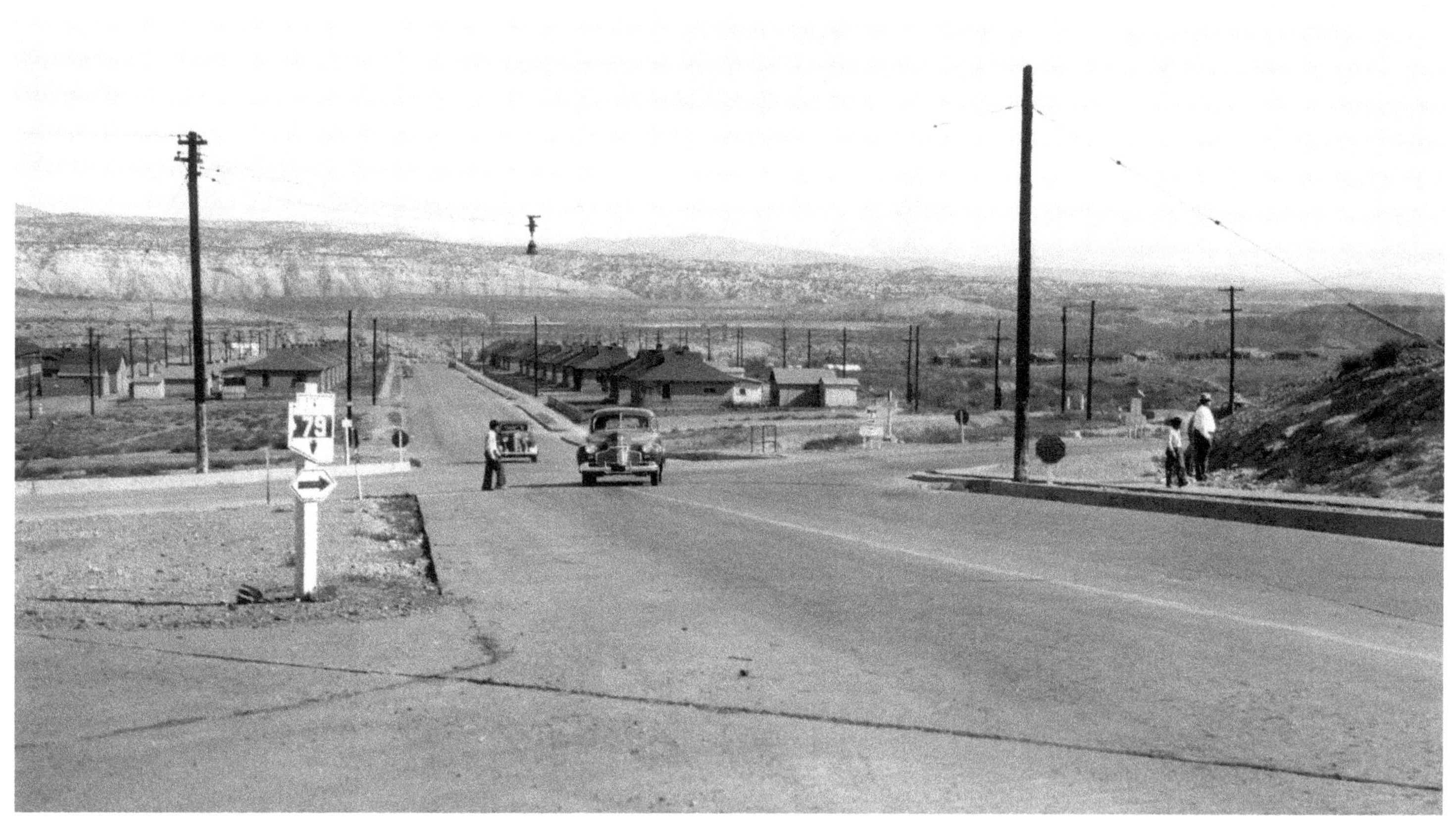

U.S. Highway 89A was first graded in 1927, when the section between Prescott and Clarkdale was completed. By 1938, when this photo was taken near Clarkdale, the 79-mile highway was completed and paved to Flagstaff. Highway 89A passes through some of the most scenic land of Arizona, including Sedona and Oak Creek Canyon.

Desert Airfields and Postwar Growth (1940–1970)

December 7, 1941, the "date which will live in infamy," struck hard at Arizonans, as a great battleship named in the state's honor lay on the ocean floor at Pearl Harbor. World War II was the first American war in which airplanes played a pivotal role, and the beautiful weather at the desert airfields established in Arizona proved ideal for training the pilots.

More than 60,000 flyers were trained at six large bases opened in the desert regions, and more than 150,000 additional military personnel supported those operations. The 6th Army Tank Division, under the command of General George Patton, also trained in Arizona, in the desert north of Yuma, before starting its mission in North Africa.

Many an Arizona woman became a Rosie the Riveter and took a job on an assembly line while the men were away at war. As throughout America, everyone pulled together in the war effort.

Young Navajo men from northern Arizona became United States Marines and brought their unique language to the Pacific Islands to be used for encoding messages. They communicated with fellow marines as they battled across the Pacific and entered into the history books as Navajo Code Talkers.

A young Pima named Ira Hayes also joined the United States Marines and soon found himself helping to raise Old Glory atop Mount Suribachi on a Pacific Island called Iwo Jima.

With the end of World War II, Arizona saw a historic boom in its population. Many of those who settled in the state had first come to this beautiful land to train for war but returned to live in peace and raise their families.

By 1950 Arizona's population had grown to 750,000. In Phoenix, more construction of homes and businesses occurred in one year, 1959, than in the years 1914 to 1946 combined. That unprecedented growth would continue for the next four decades.

Guests ride the range in Wickenburg, known as the Dude Ranch Capital of the World, around 1940. Credited as the first Wickenburg dude ranch, the Bar FX Ranch opened in 1923, to be followed by the likes of the Remudas, Kay El Bar, Rancho de los Caballeros, and Flying E. The latter three ranches still welcome tourists dreaming of being a cowboy—if even for only a week.

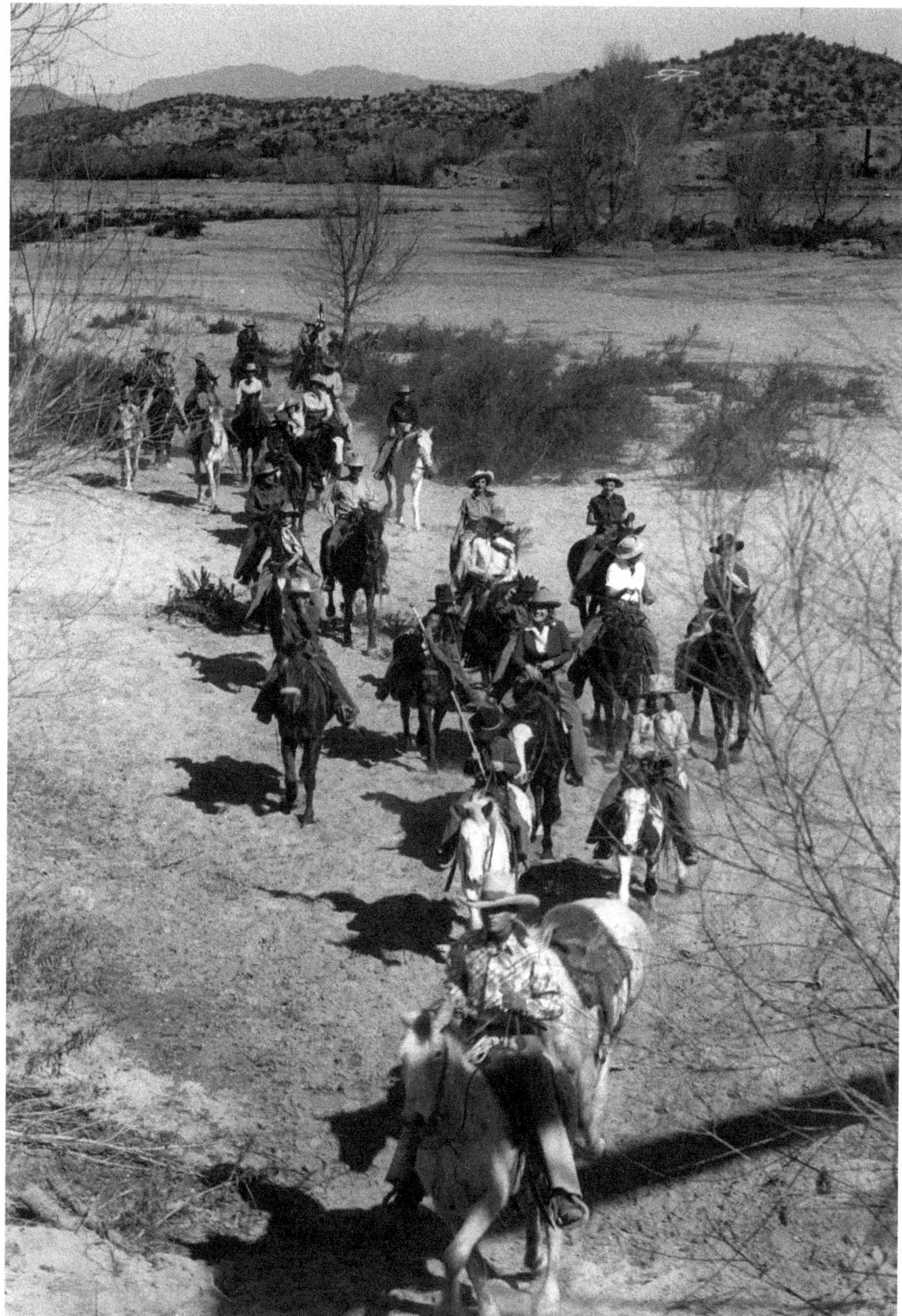

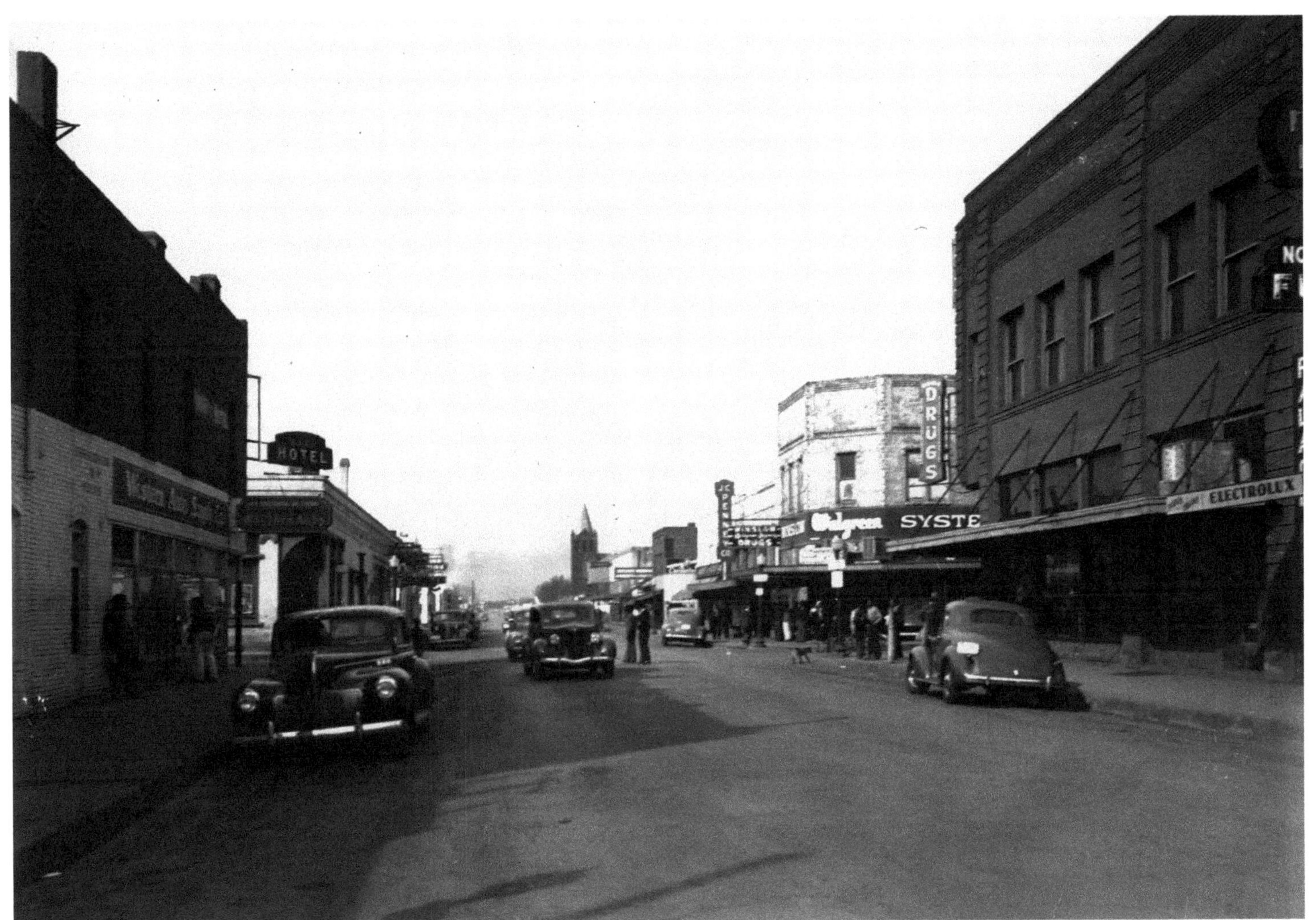

Main Street in 1940s Winslow was part of America's Mother Road, Route 66. Modern travelers can still "get their kicks on Route 66" along the 200 miles of the original road that run through northern Arizona. From the Wigwam Hotel in Holbrook, to "standing on the corner in Winslow, Arizona," to the pine trees of Flagstaff, to the gold mining town of Oatman, Route 66 adventures still await those searching for a time gone by.

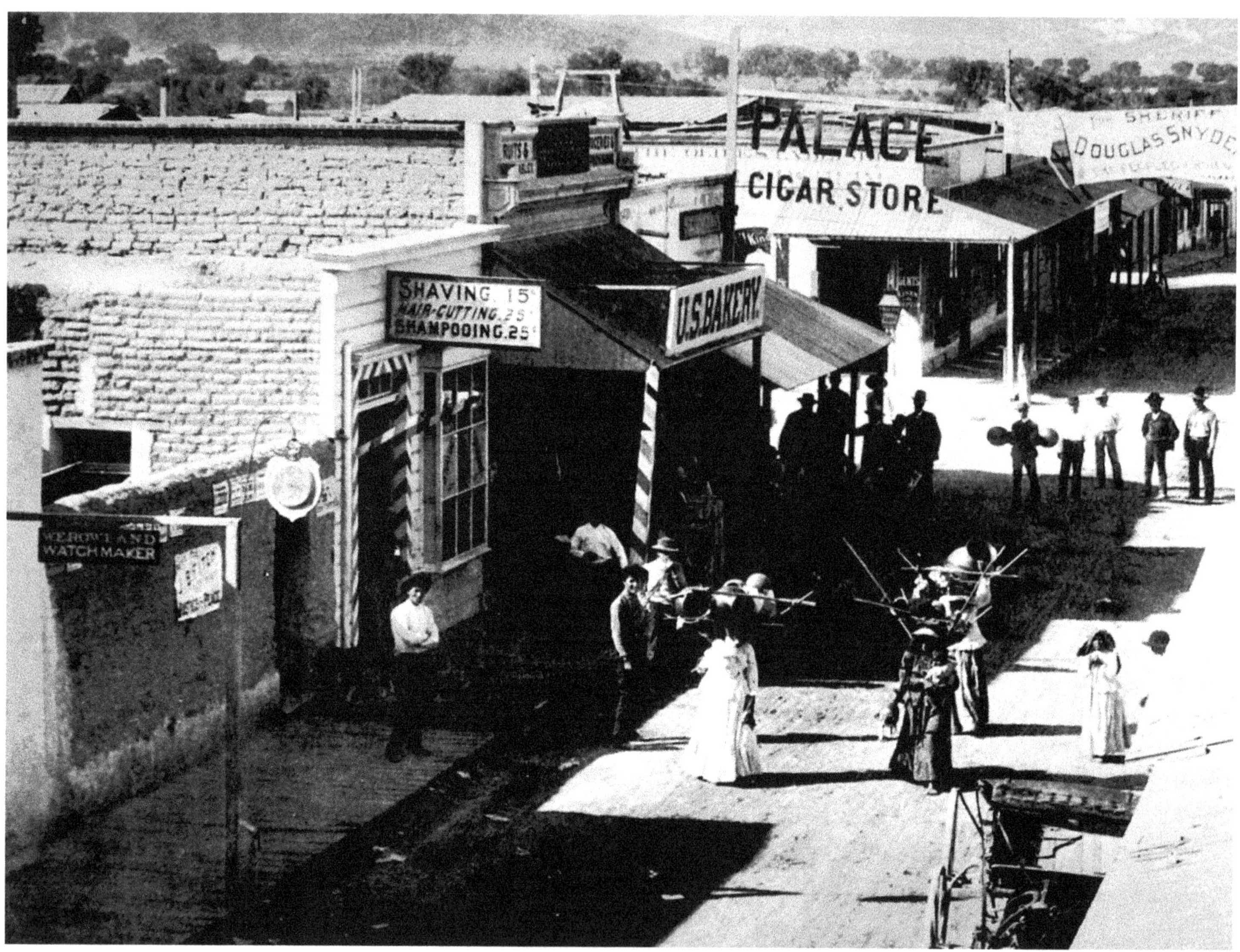

Old Tucson Studios sprang to movie life in 1939 when the management of Columbia Pictures chose a site 12 miles from downtown Tucson on which to build a replica of the town as it might have appeared in the 1860s for the movie *Arizona.* Many westerns have been filmed at Old Tucson in the years since, and the expanded studio now contains a "complete" western town of 75 buildings on a 320-acre set.

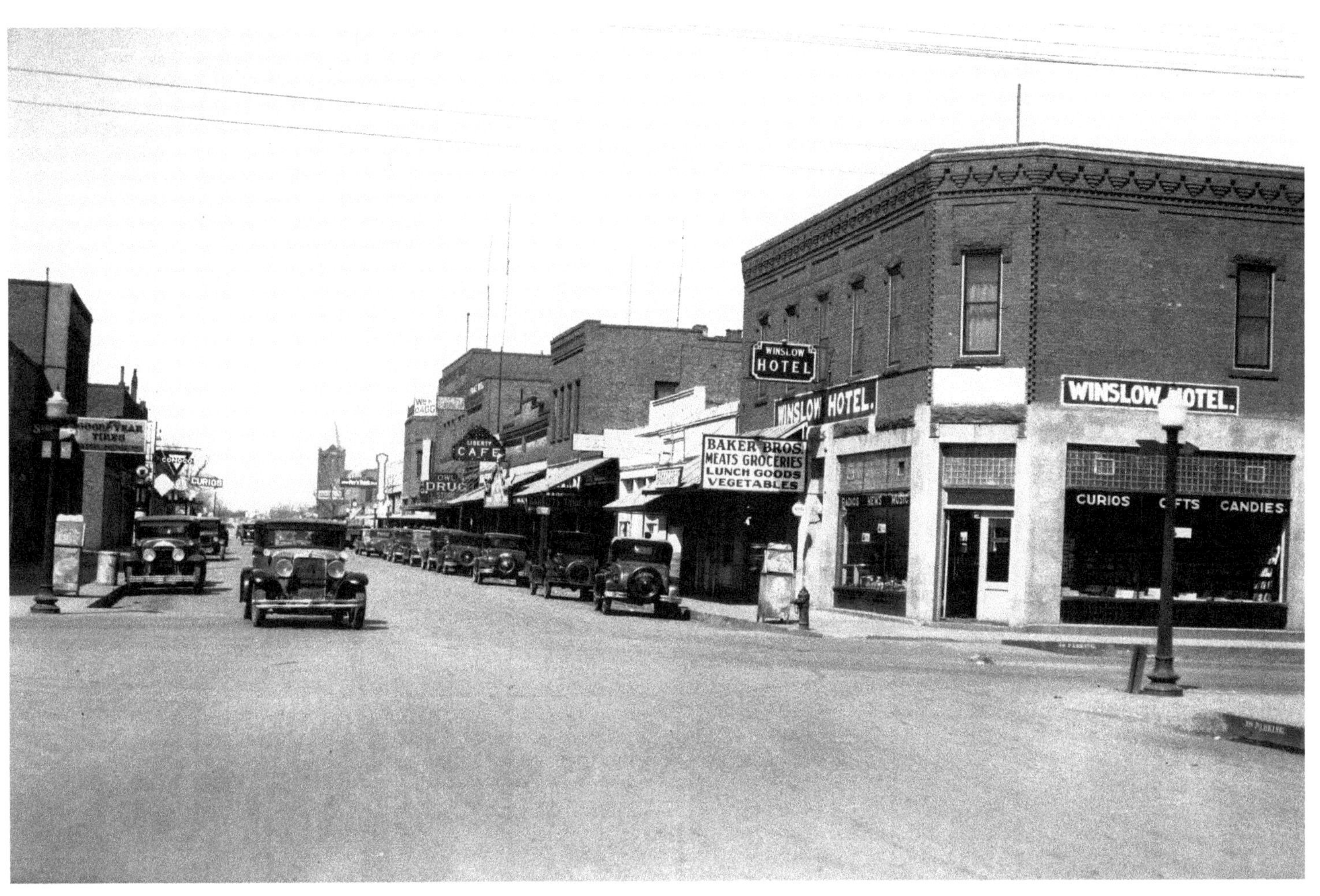

The Winslow Hotel, Liberty Cafe, Owl Drug Store, and other Main Street businesses line the Mother Road, Route 66, in downtown Winslow around 1940.

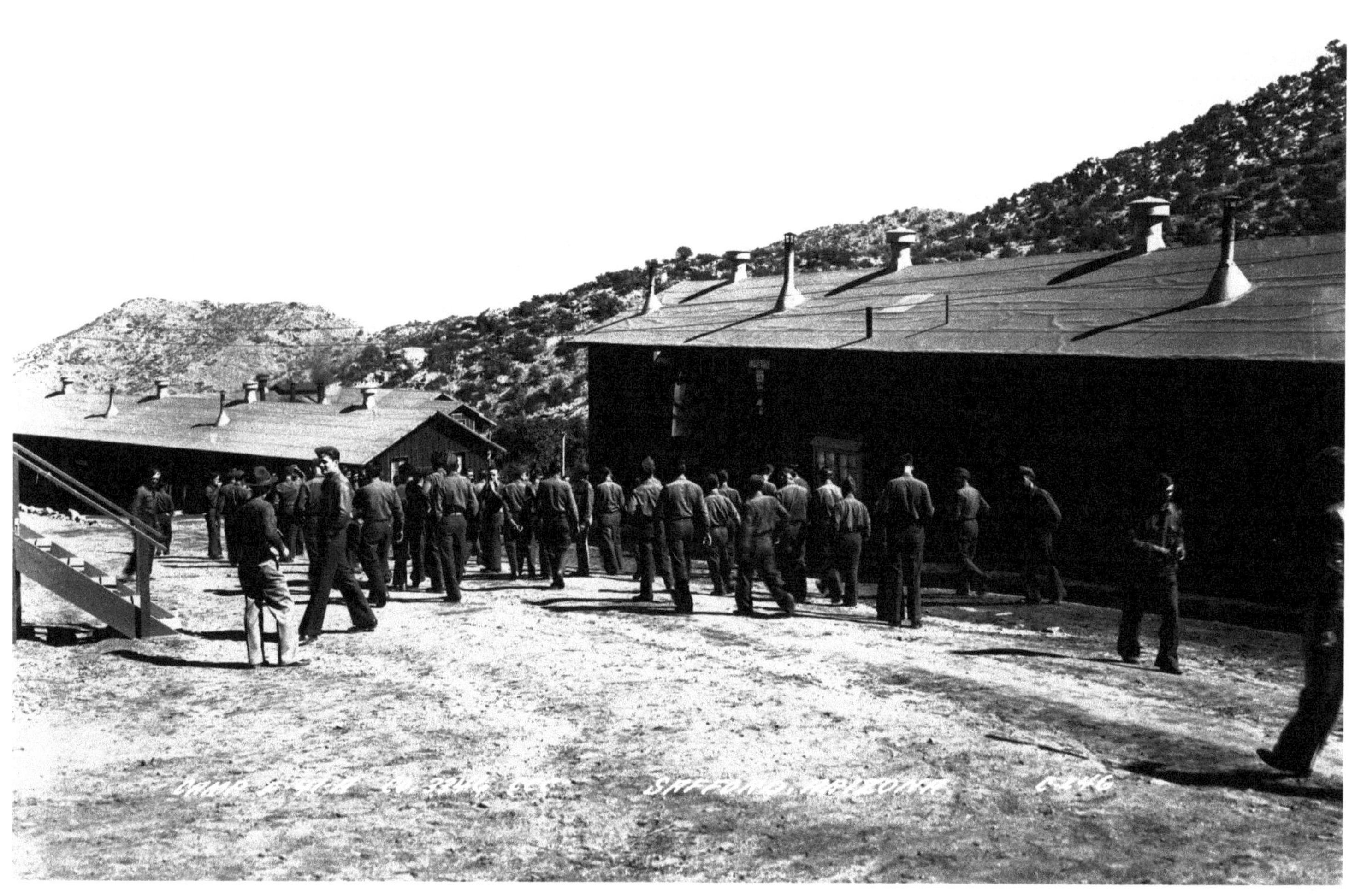

In 1932, half of America's young men ages 15 to 24 were either unemployed or only working part-time. In Arizona, some of those young men were given Civilian Conservation Corps jobs at a camp near Safford. Shown here around 1940, the Safford camp CCC workers helped on a water infiltration project involving state-owned land in the Gila River Valley.

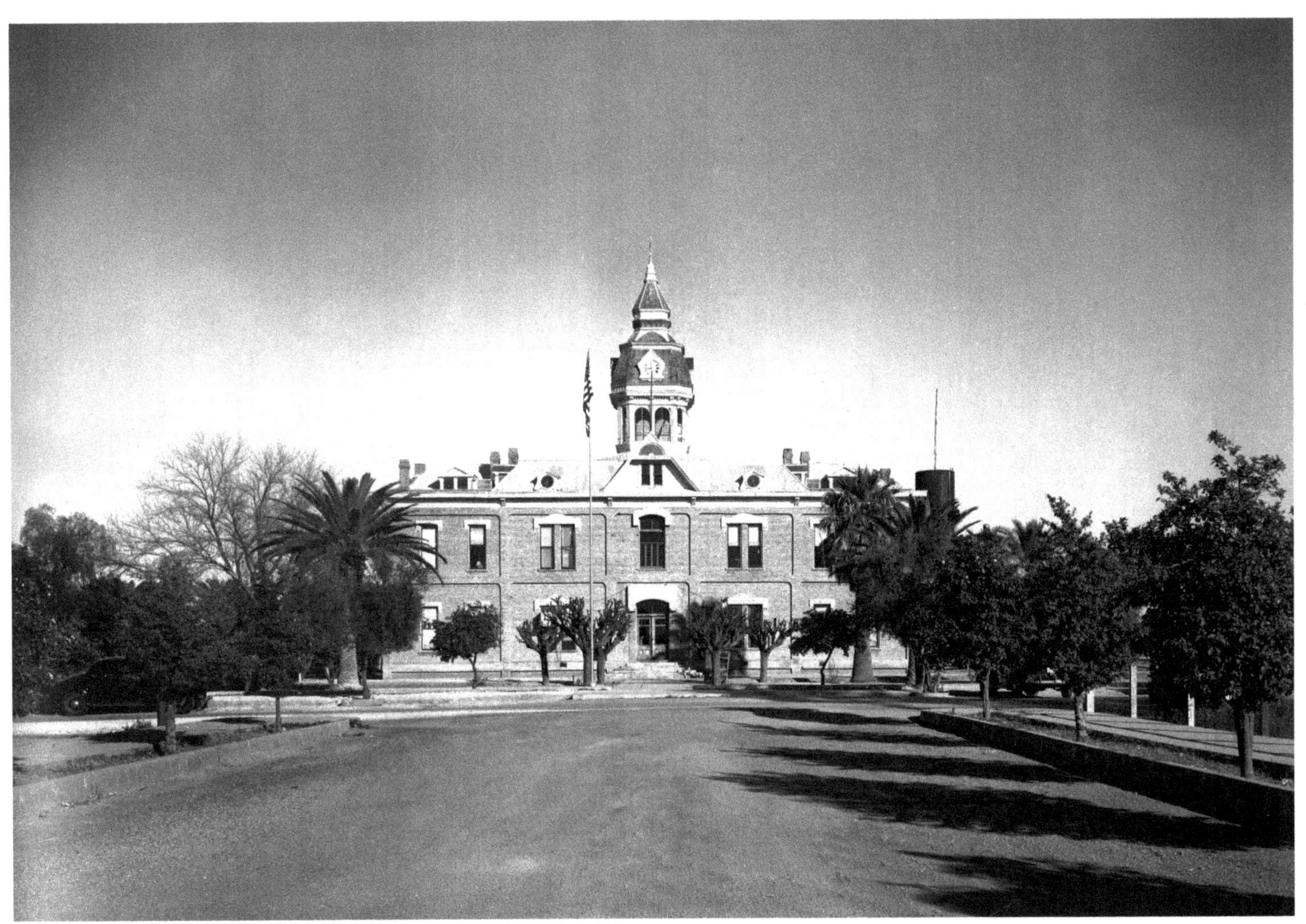

In 1891 Pinal County built a grand courthouse, seen here around 1940, to serve as the seat of county government. The building's $29,000 cost did not leave enough money for a real clock to be placed in the courthouse tower, so a pressed-metal clock face with the time set at 11:44 A.M. was mounted instead. Since the courthouse would close at noon, the 11:44 permanent setting was selected to represent a time of day when citizens coming into town would know they still had plenty of time to get their courthouse business done.

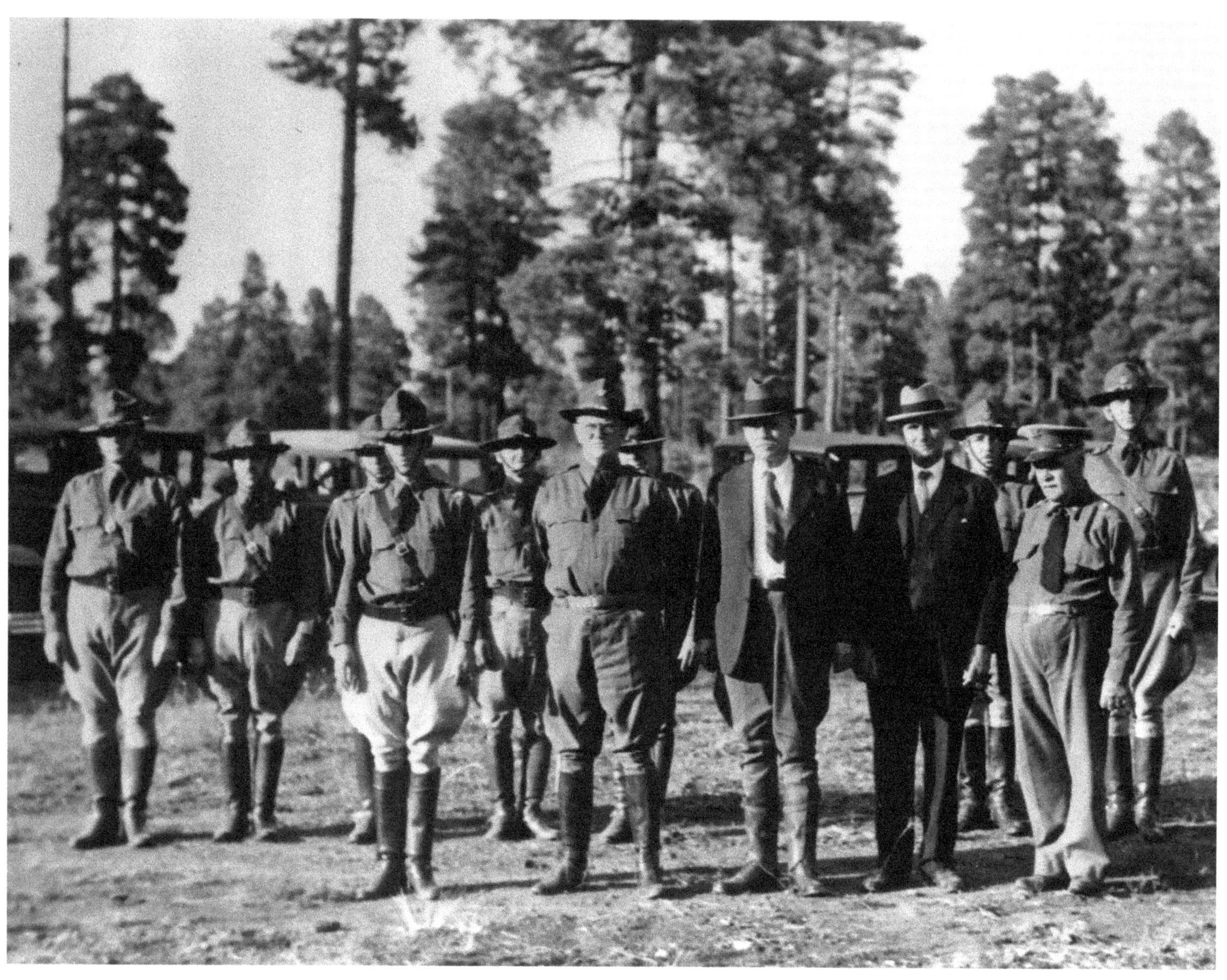

Fort Tuthill, a National Guard training camp, was established in 1929 in the ponderosa pine forest near Flagstaff. It was named for General Alexander M. Tuthill, who is standing in the center of this group of men photographed around 1940. General Tuthill was an industrial surgeon and was also a member of Arizona's constitutional convention.

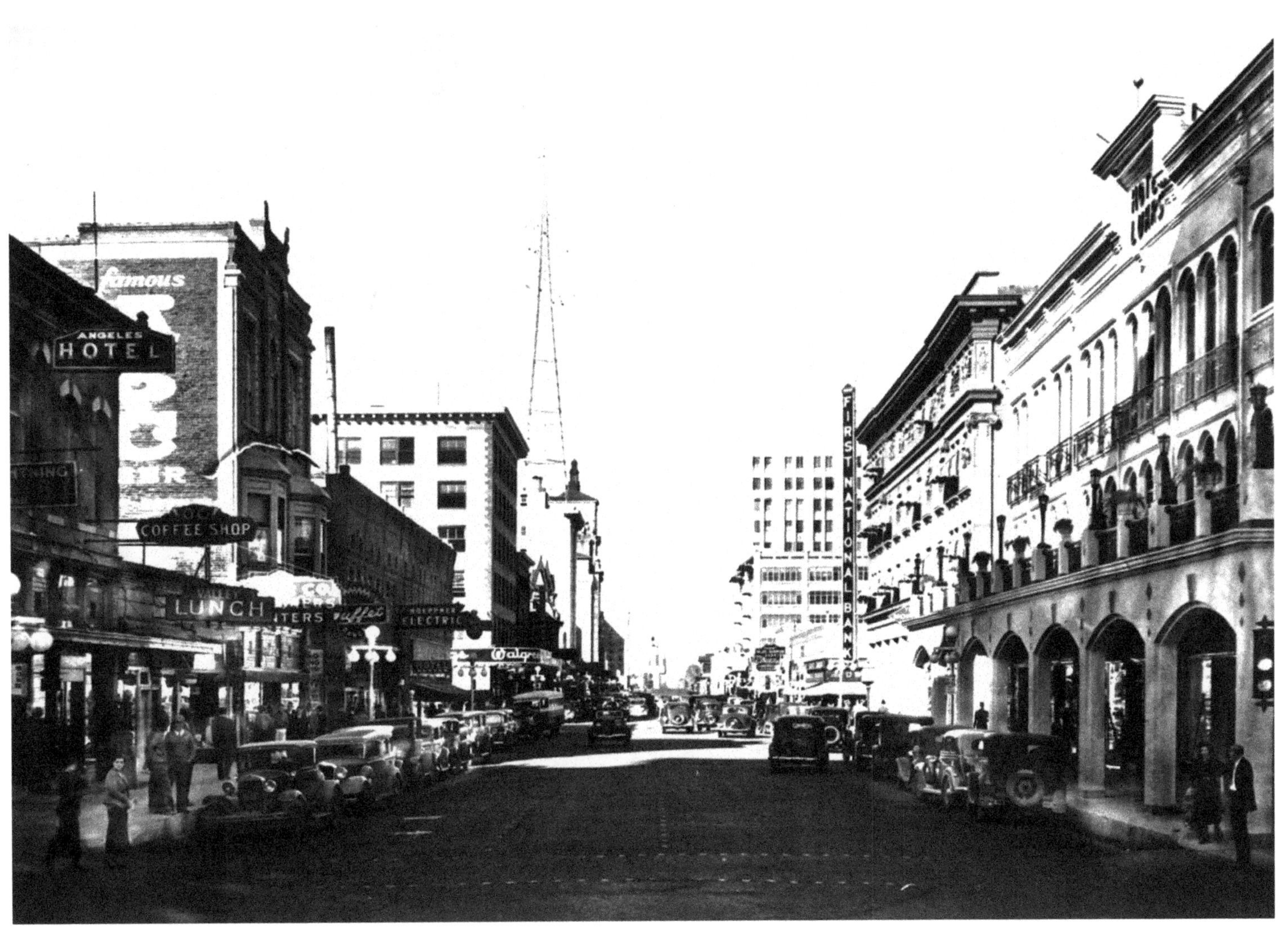

In this morning view facing north on Central Avenue in Phoenix around 1940, the city's Hotel Luhrs can be seen at right.

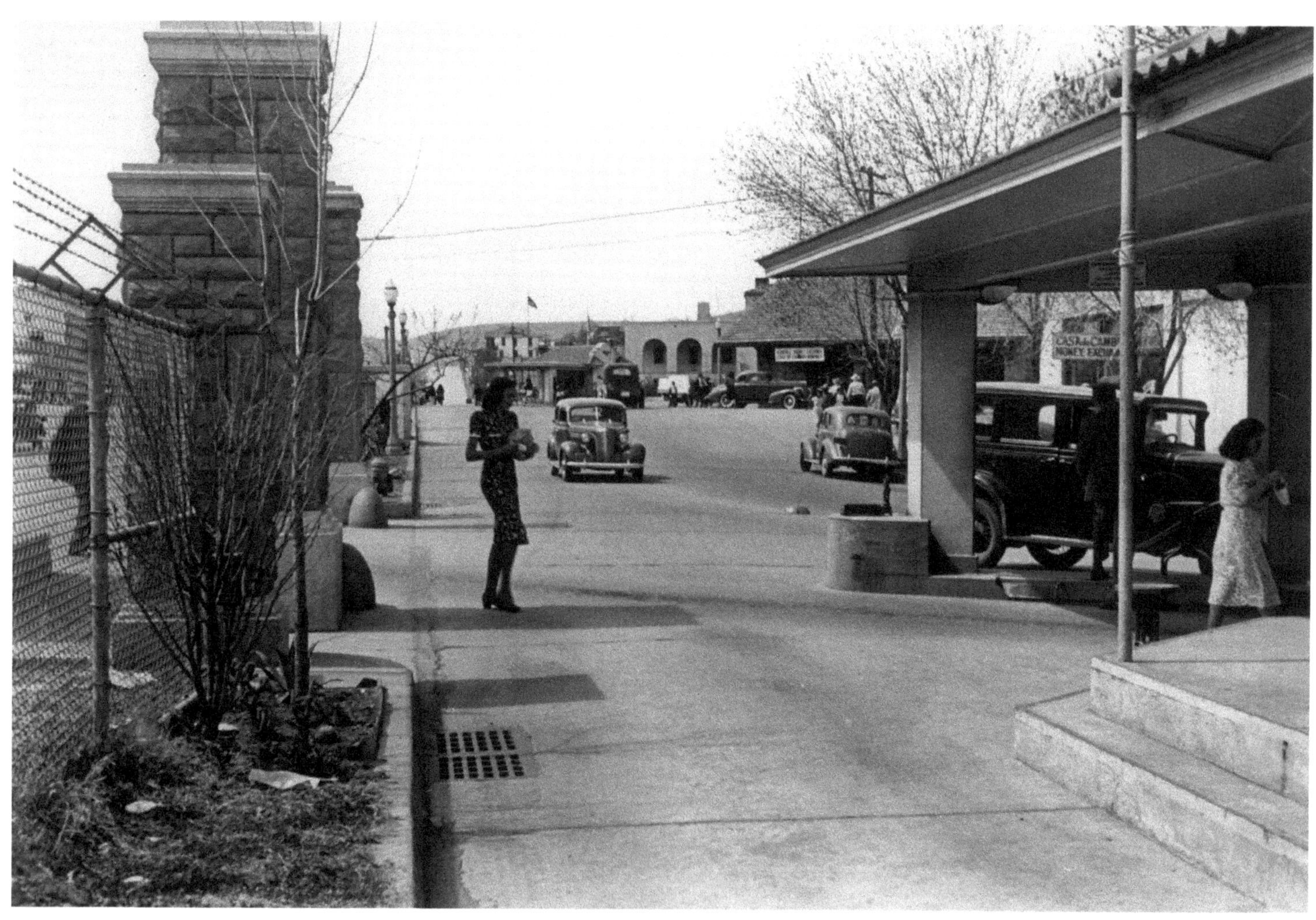

This 1940s view faces Mexico at the border crossing in Nogales, a major port of entry for commerce and people traveling between Mexico and the United States.

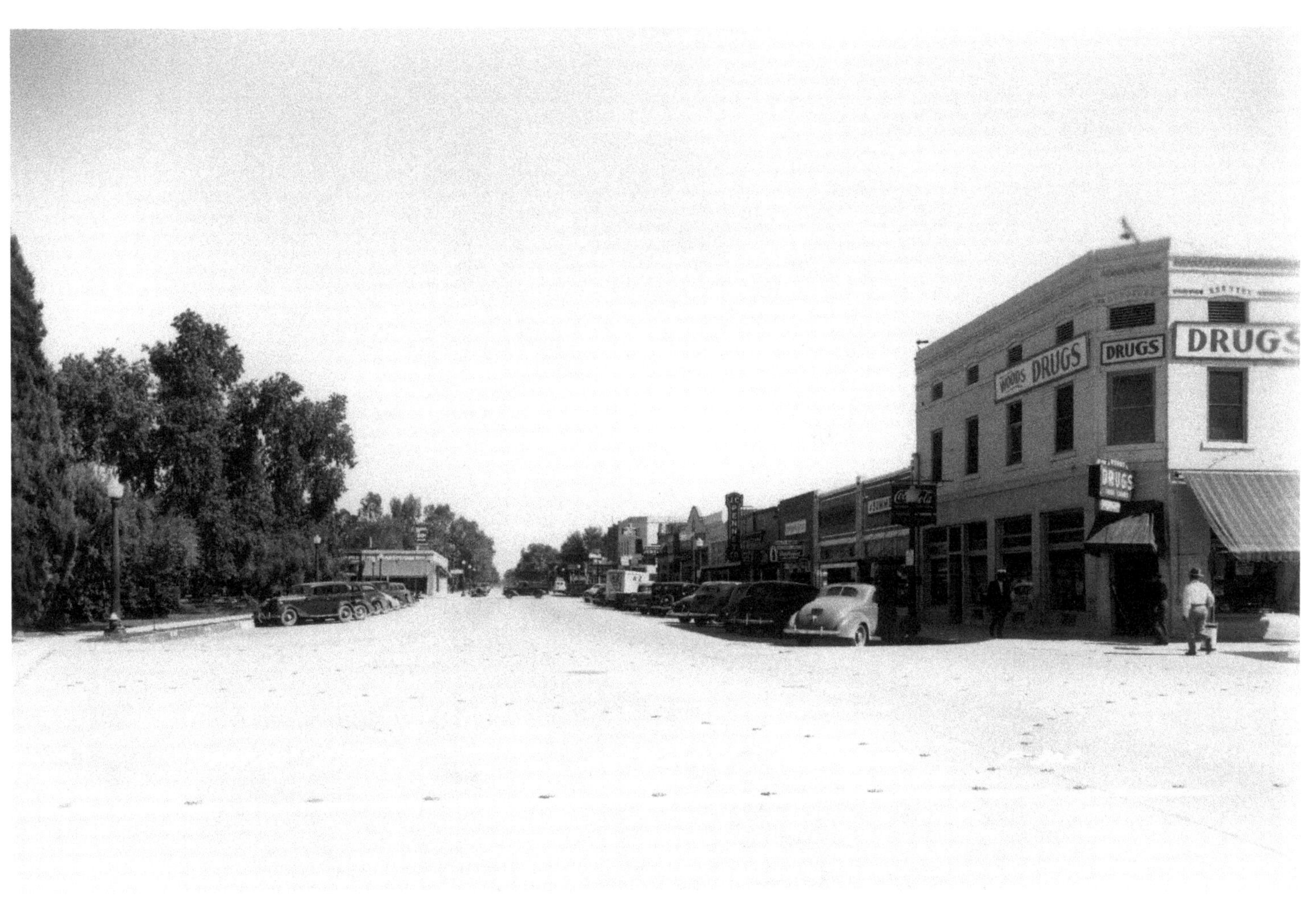

This view of downtown Glendale in the 1940s shows the local J. C. Penney store and Woods Drugs, among various other enterprises.

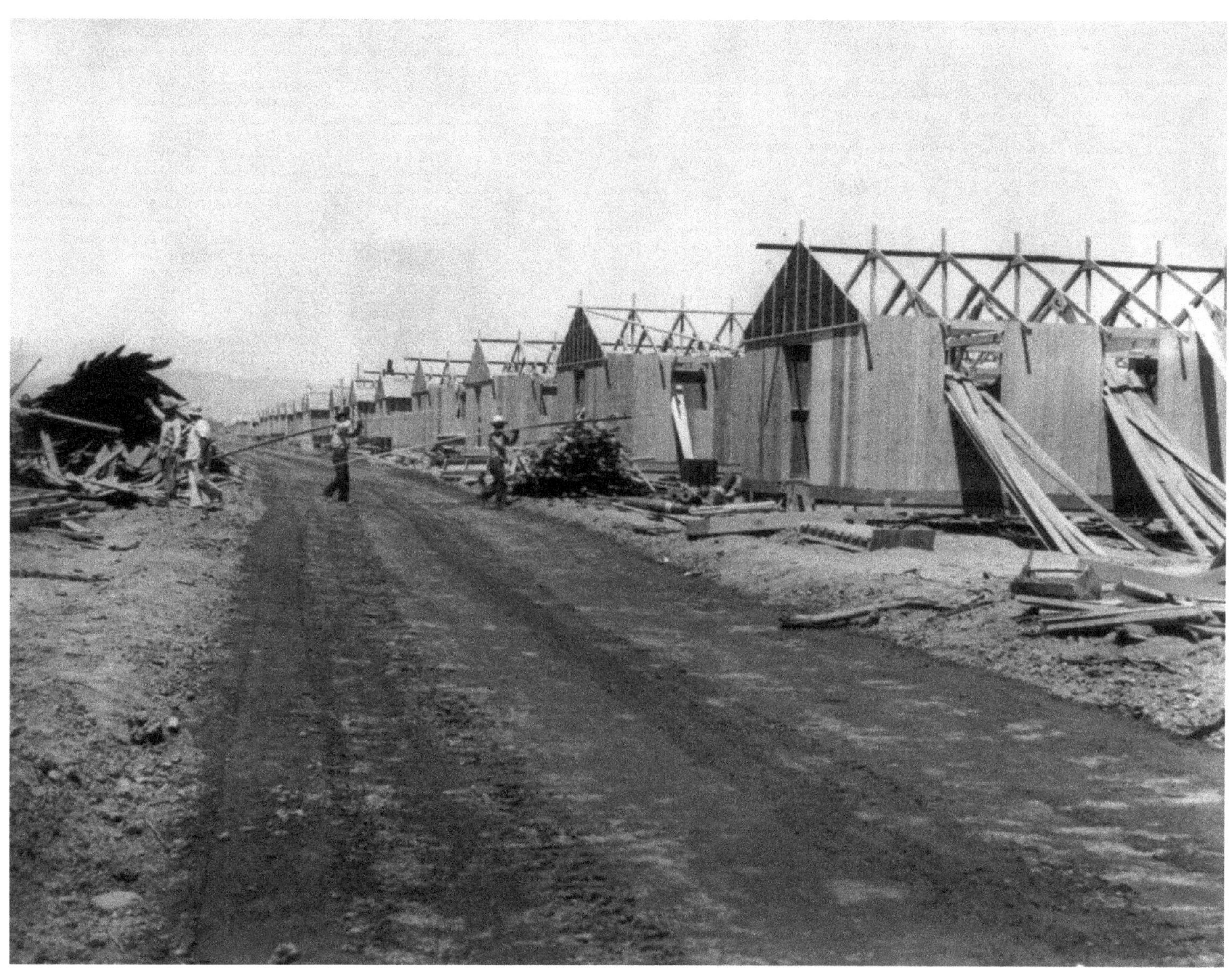

On March 18, 1942, President Franklin D. Roosevelt signed Executive Order 9102, establishing the War Relocation Authority. This action resulted in roughly 120,000 persons of Japanese descent, more than half of them U.S. citizens, being forcibly relocated from their West Coast homes to internment camps. Two of the camps were in Arizona, including one called Poston located along the Colorado River and shown being built in April 1942. The second camp was built along the Gila River on what is today the Gila River Indian Community.

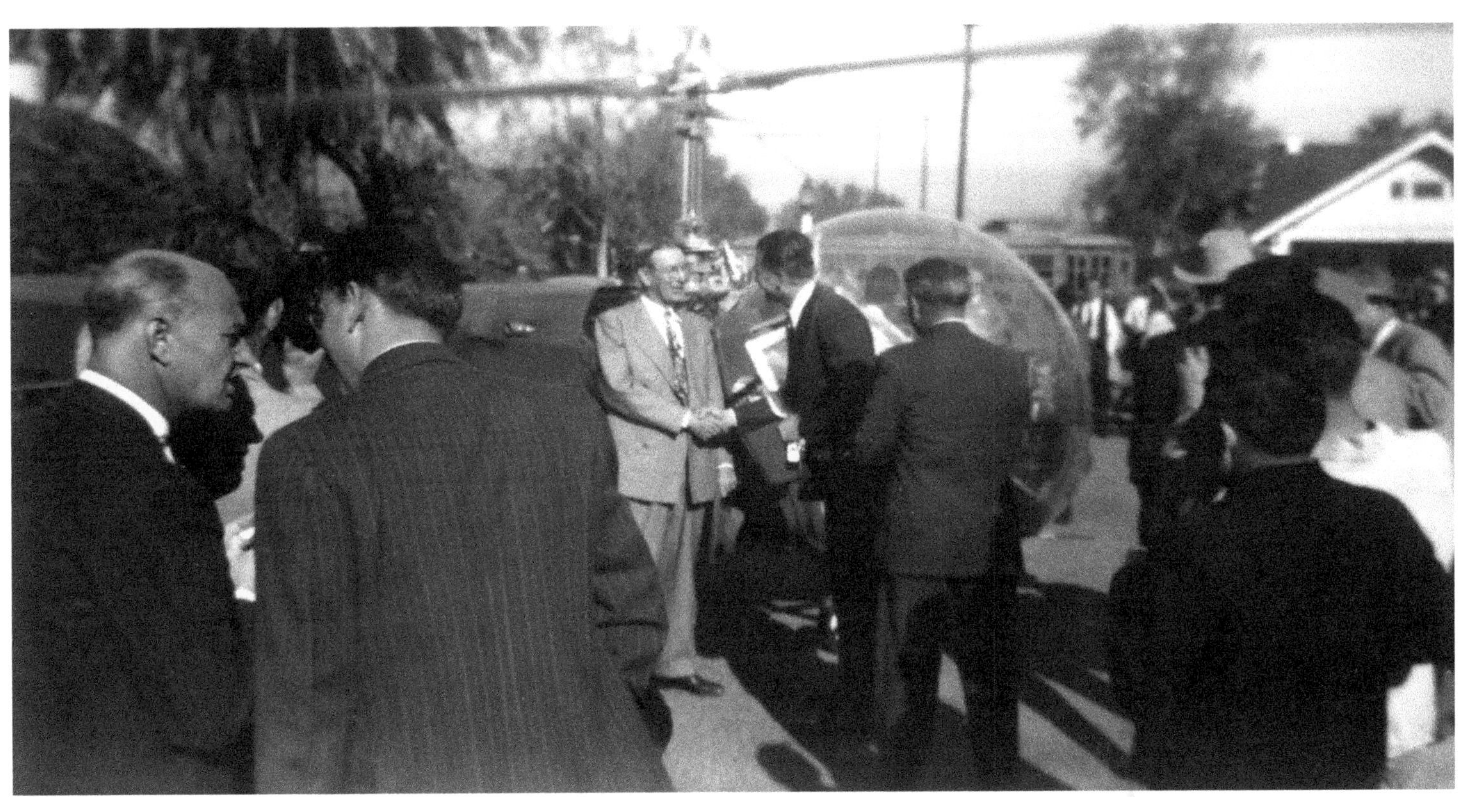

While attending sixth grade, young Sidney Osborn wrote his name in his textbooks as "Sidney P. Osborn, Governor of Arizona." In 1940 his youthful prophecy was fulfilled when he was elected to the first of four consecutive two-year terms as governor. He saw Arizona through the World War II years, and during his tenure he also set a state record for most legislative vetoes. Osborn suffered from amyotrophic lateral sclerosis (ALS), commonly known as "Lou Gehrig's disease," and died while in office on May 25, 1948.

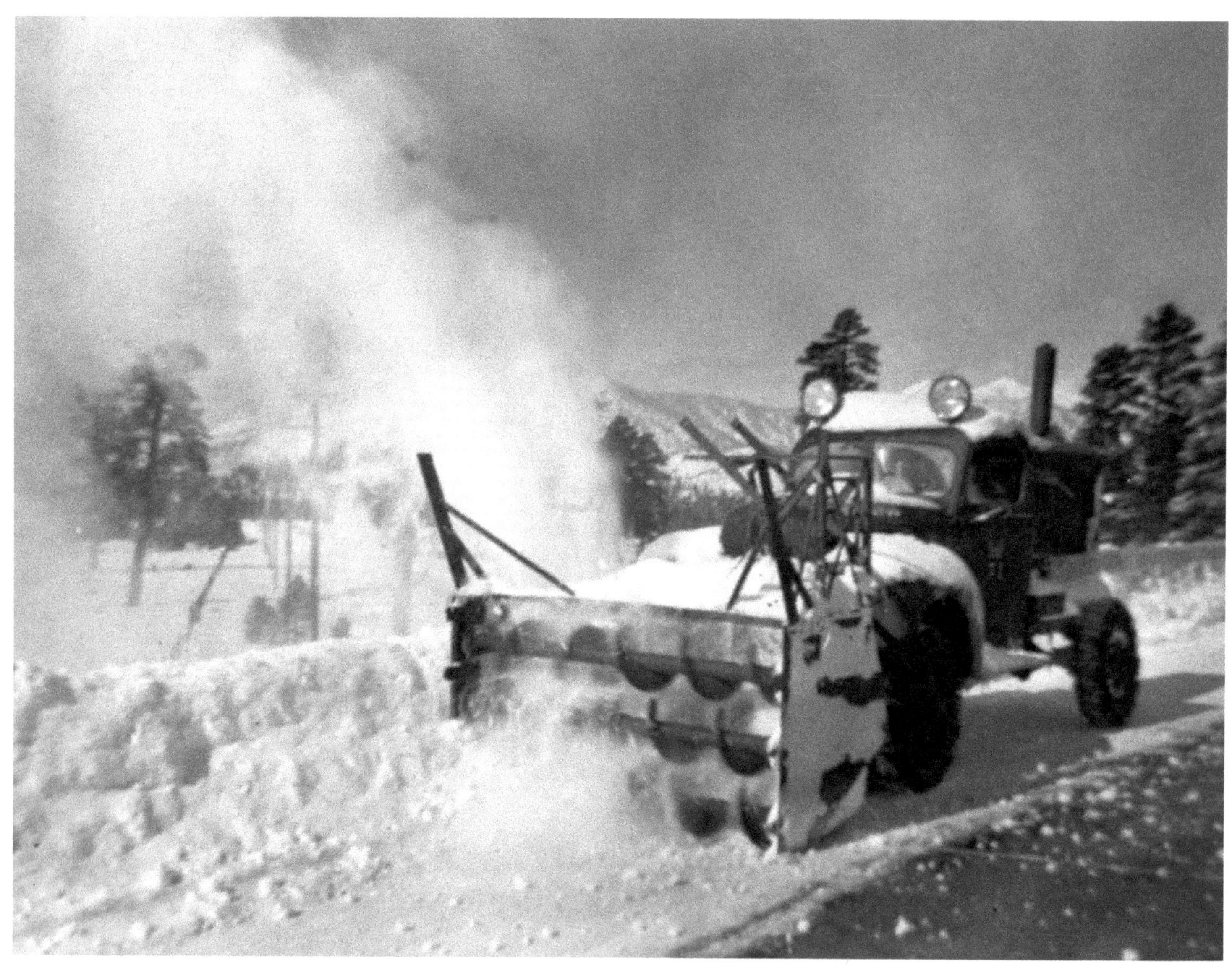

It snows in Arizona! Here a snowplow removes the beautiful white moisture from Route 66 in Flagstaff. In the years since weather records have been kept, the greatest snowfall total in Flagstaff was in 1973, when 210 inches fell on the forest community. The season's earliest snowfall on record was September 19, 1965, and the latest snowfall was June 8, 1907. Today the City of Flagstaff operates 42 snowplows during the winter months.

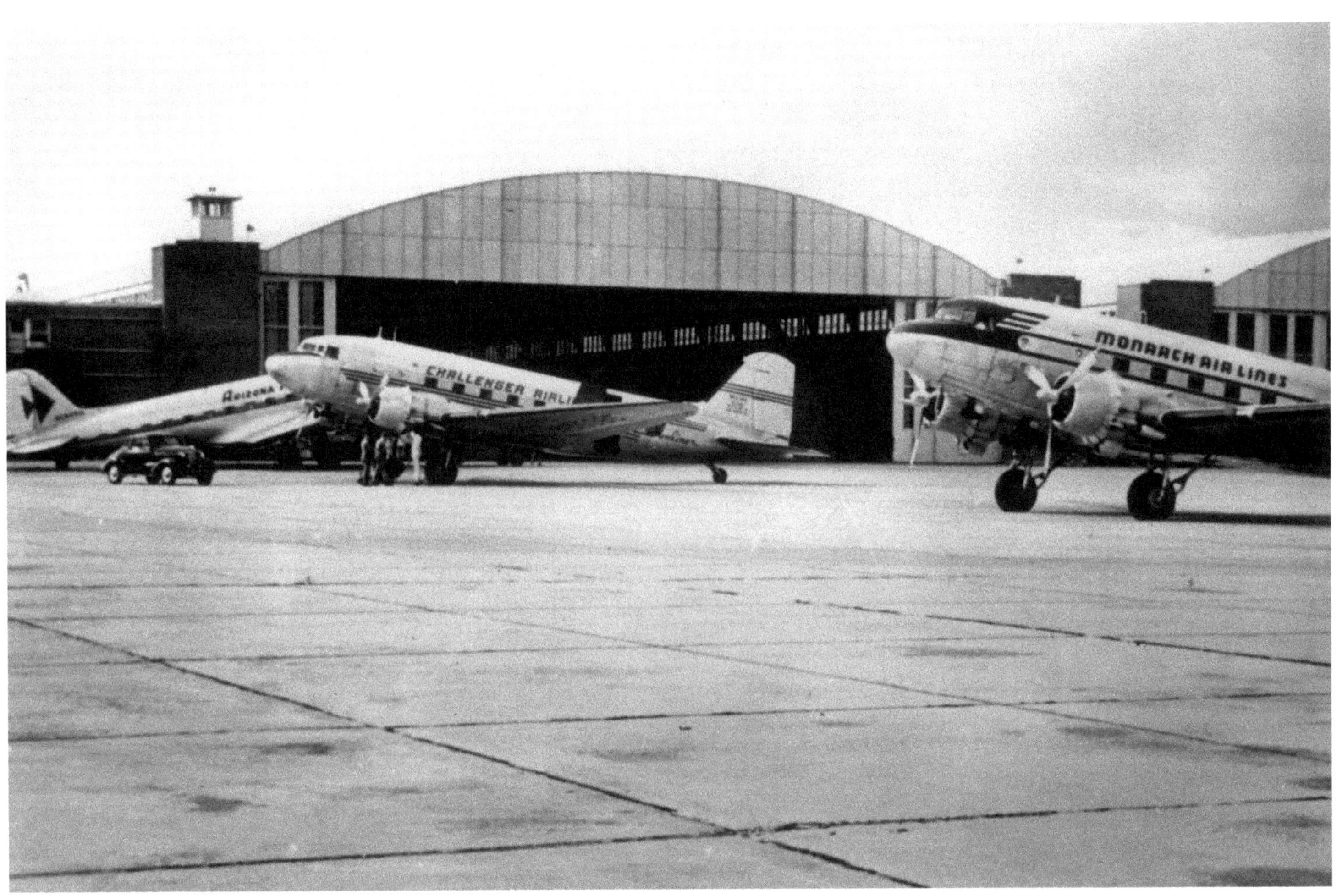

On Labor Day 1929, Sky Harbor Airport was dedicated on the same land where John Y. T. Smith had operated his hay farm in 1865. Phoenix residents called the new airport "the farm," since an airport employee had to chase the cows off the runway each time a plane needed to take off or land. The City of Phoenix bought Sky Harbor in 1935 and still operates the international airport today, as it did when these airplanes were photographed around 1950.

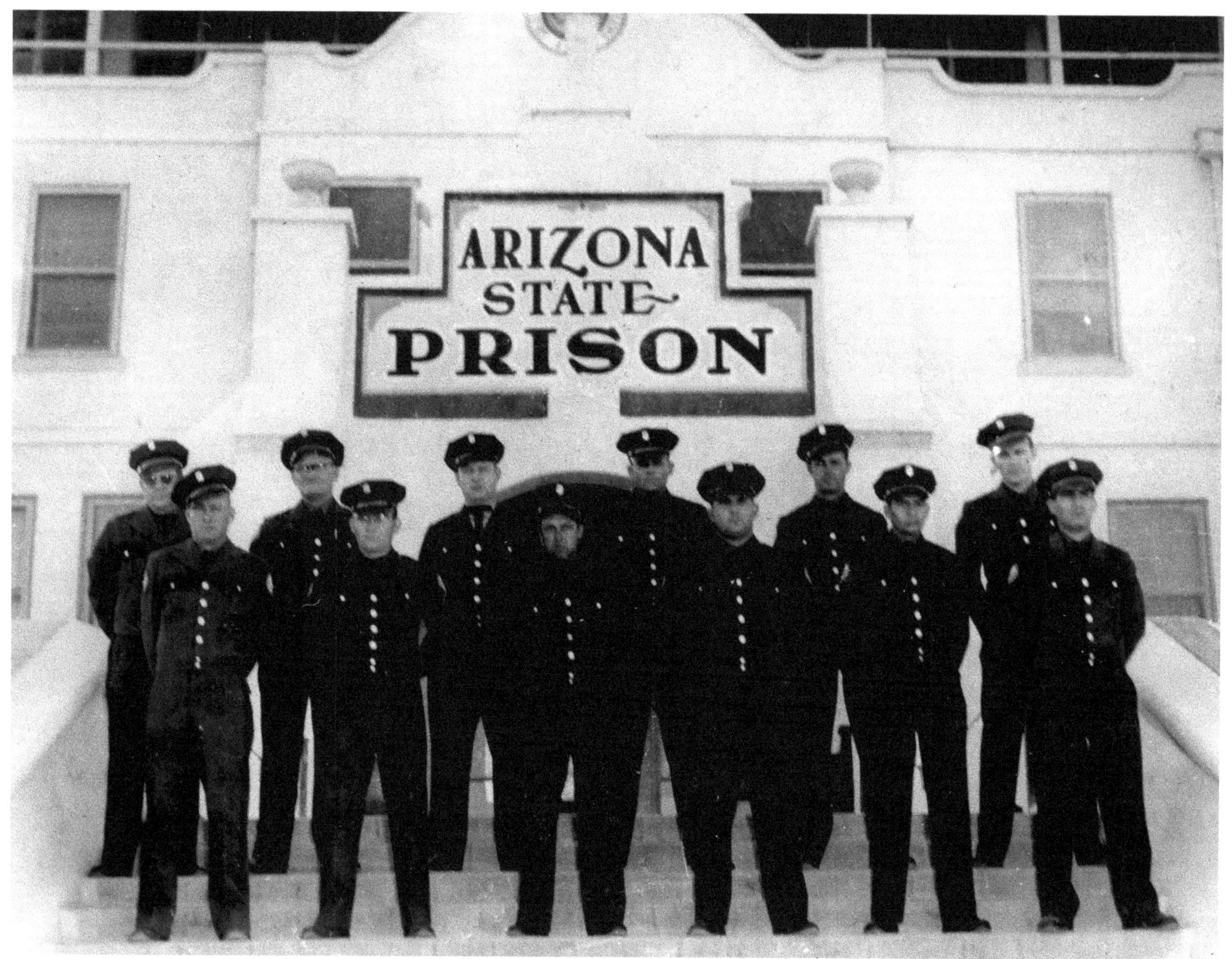

Guarding prisoners has never been an easy job. Here a group of prison guards proudly stand for their picture to be taken at Arizona State Prison in Florence in the 1950s. The state prison moved to Florence in 1909 with the closing of the Yuma Territorial Prison.

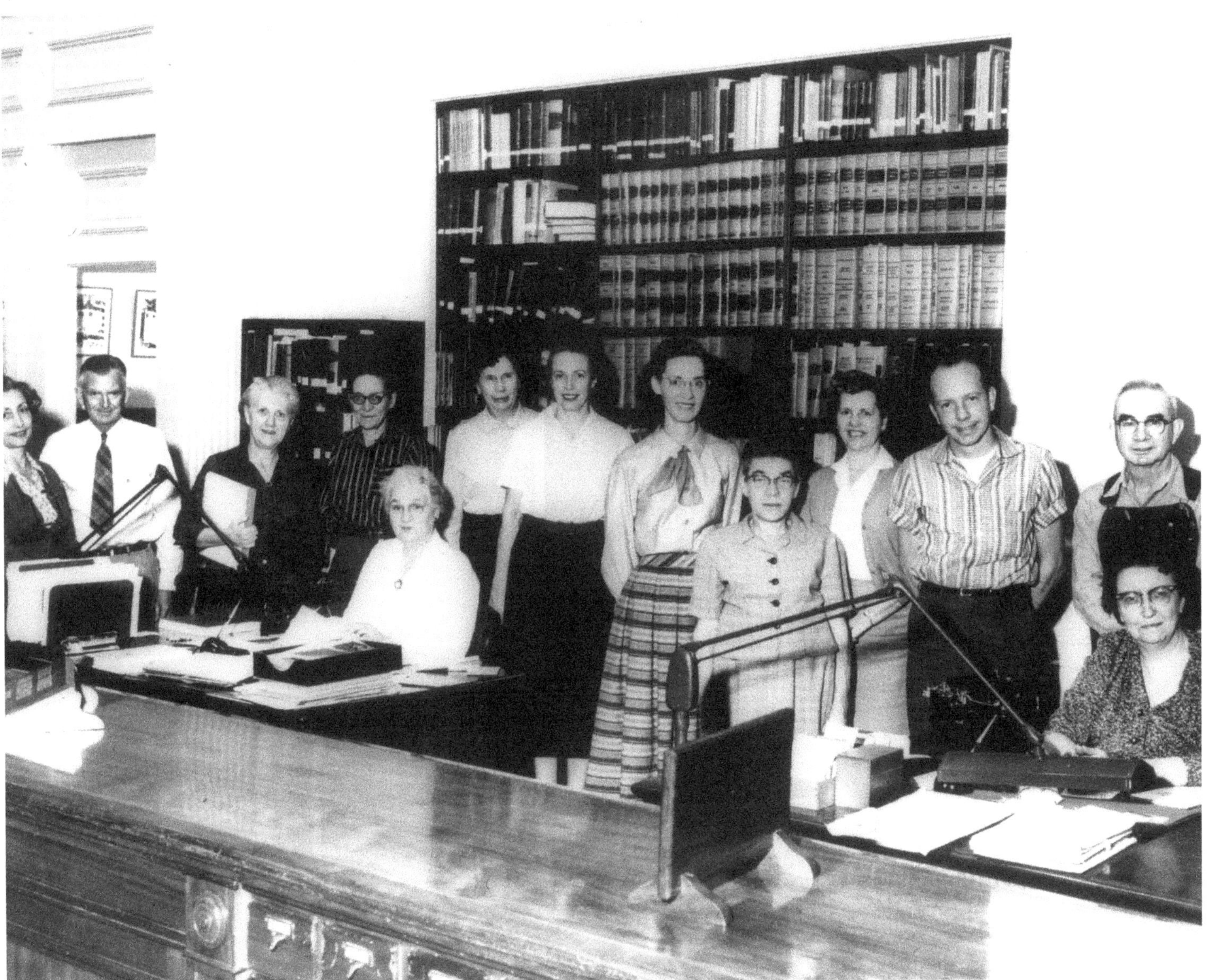

The staff of the Arizona State Library, Archives and Public Records stand ready to serve the citizens of Arizona in their searches of state records. At the time of this 1950s image, the library office was located in the old State Capitol. In 2008 the Arizona State Archives' Special Collection moved to the new Polly Rosenbaum Archives and History Building. Polly Rosenbaum served the citizens of Arizona as a state legislator from 1949 to 1995.

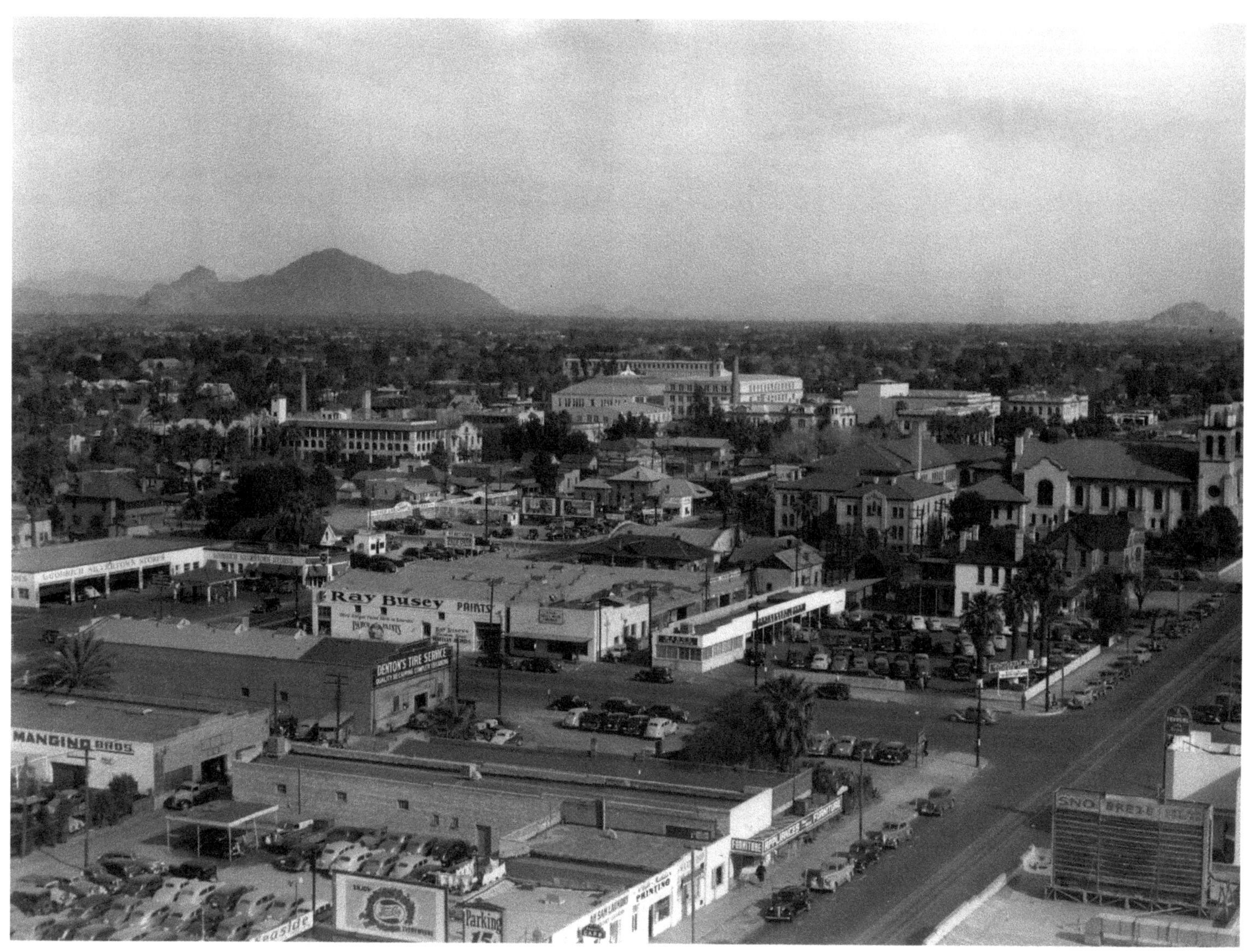

The famous Phoenix landmark Camelback Mountain is seen on the horizon in this view facing northeast from the downtown area. In 1950 Phoenix residents had to travel through mile after mile of citrus groves to reach the popular mountain. Today almost all of the citrus groves are gone, replaced by mile after mile of homes.

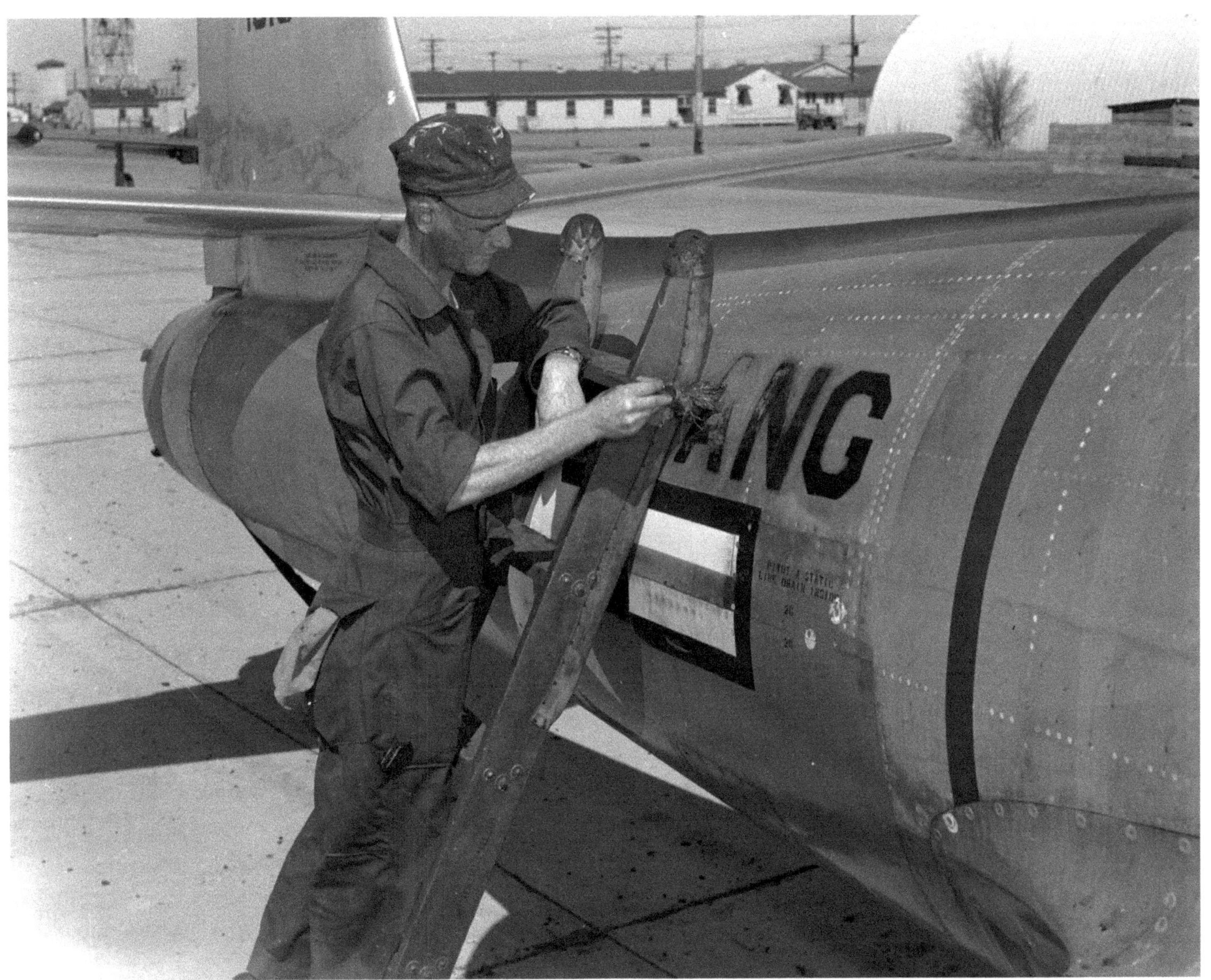

Frank Luke, Jr., graduated in 1917 from Phoenix Union High School. By 1918 he was a fighter pilot for the United States Army Air Service, flying missions over France. In 17 days of combat, young Luke shot down 14 German observation balloons and four enemy airplanes, earning him the nickname "Arizona Balloon Buster." On September 29, 1918, Frank Luke, Jr., was killed in action. Luke Air Force Base in Glendale, shown here in the 1950s, is named in his honor.

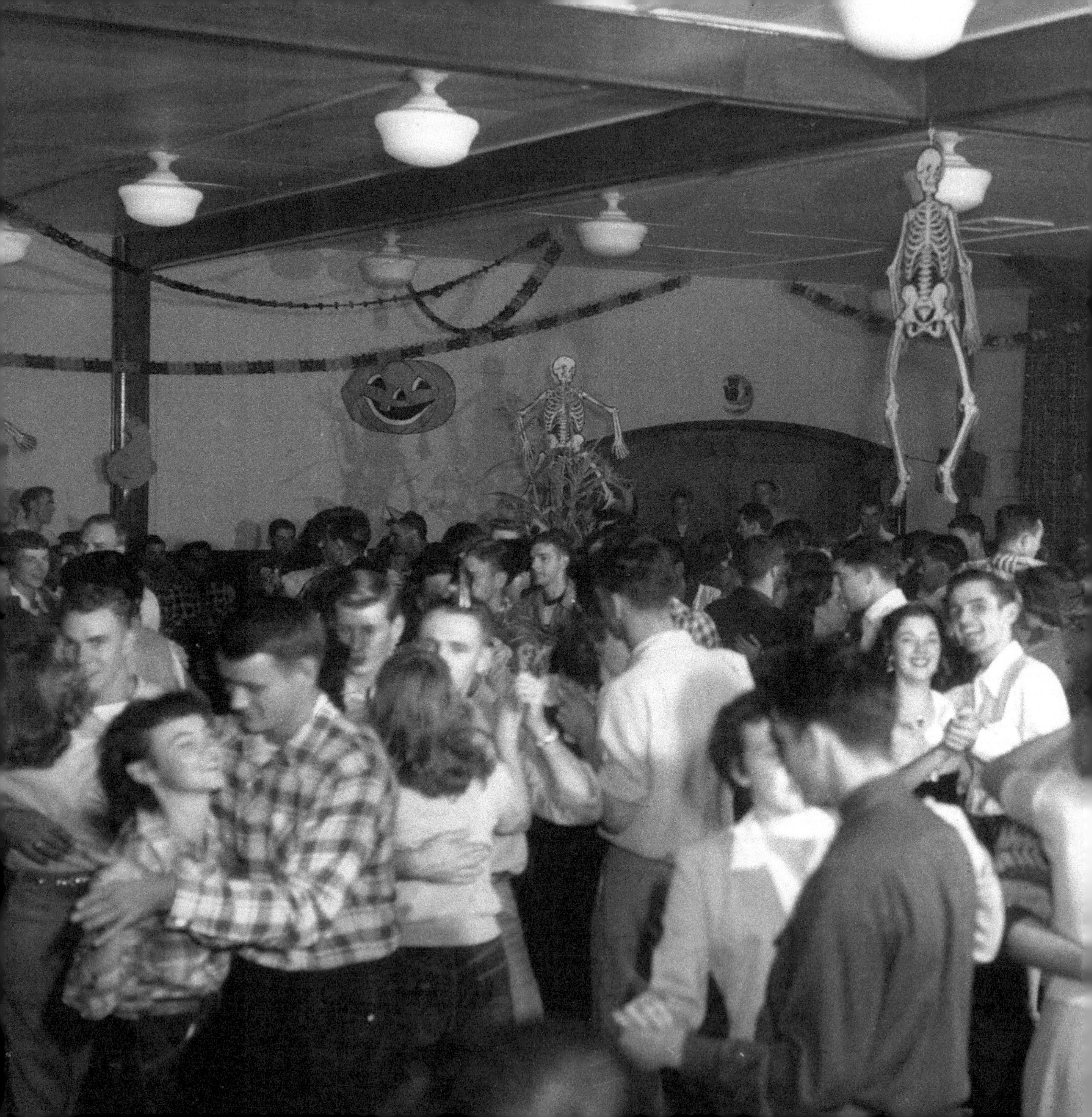

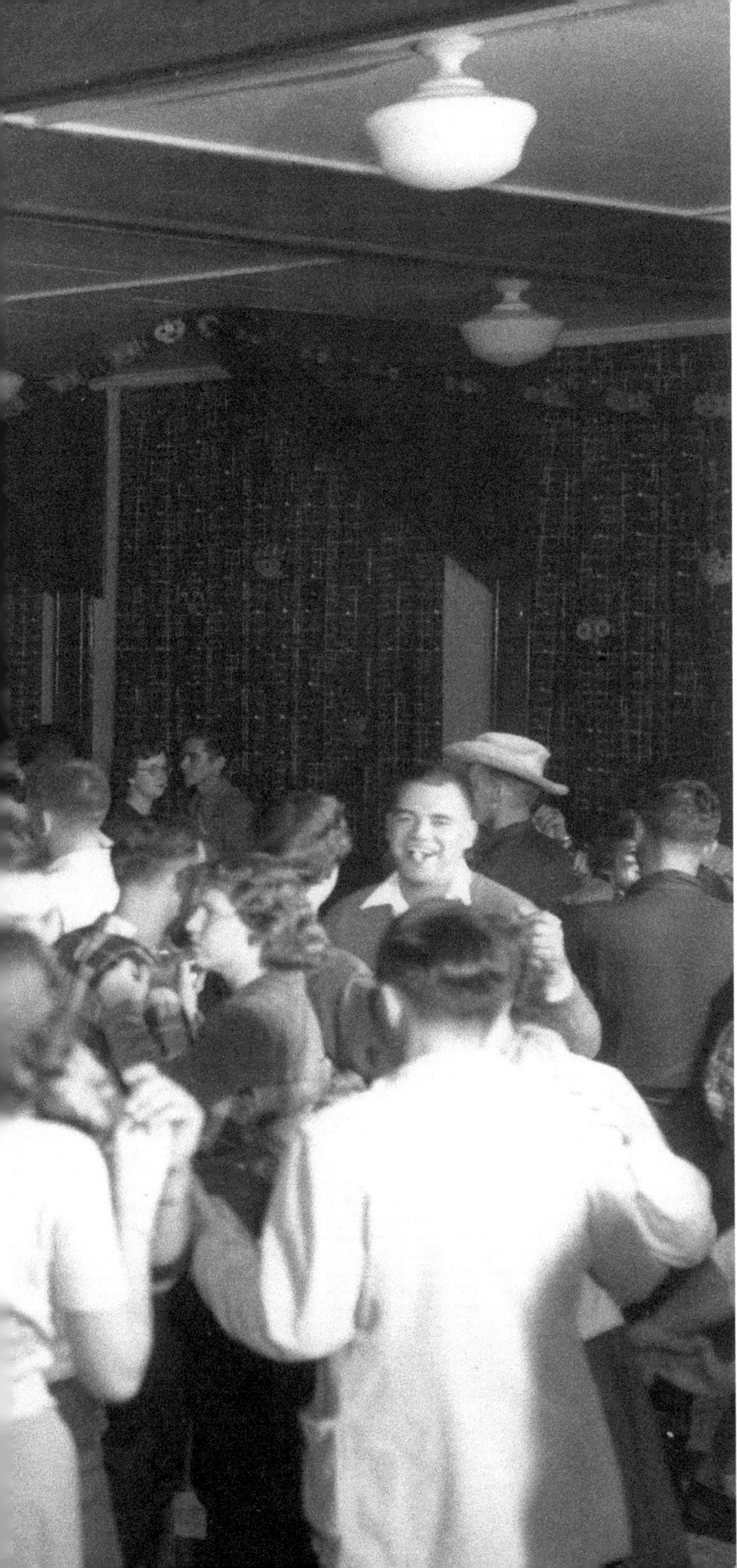

The Del Webb firm began construction at the new Army Air Corps field called Litchfield Park Air Base on March 29, 1941. Arizonans wanted to name the base in honor of Frank Luke, Jr., but a Luke Field already existed at Pearl Harbor. In June 1941 Hawaii released the name, and Arizona was then able to call their new base Luke Field. By the time these flyers and their partners were enjoying a Halloween dance at the base, the Arizona facility had been renamed Luke Air Force Base.

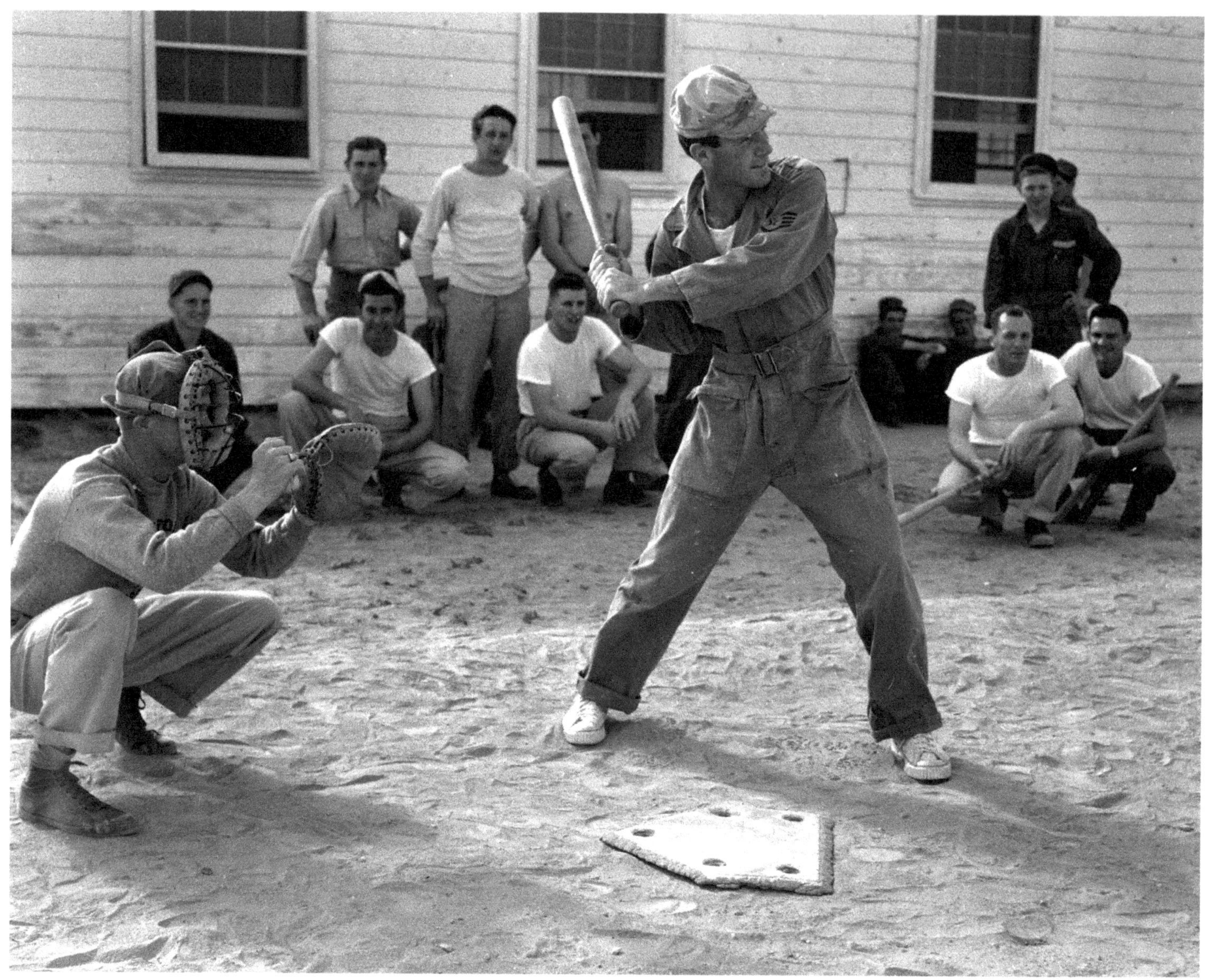

With over 300 days of clear skies annually, Arizona proved an ideal place to train young pilots during World War II. Luke Air Force Base (originally Litchfield Park Air Base) was established in 1941 when the City of Phoenix bought 1,440 acres of land in the far western part of the Valley of the Sun and leased it to the Army Air Corps for $1 a year. Here some Luke airmen enjoy a game of baseball around 1951.

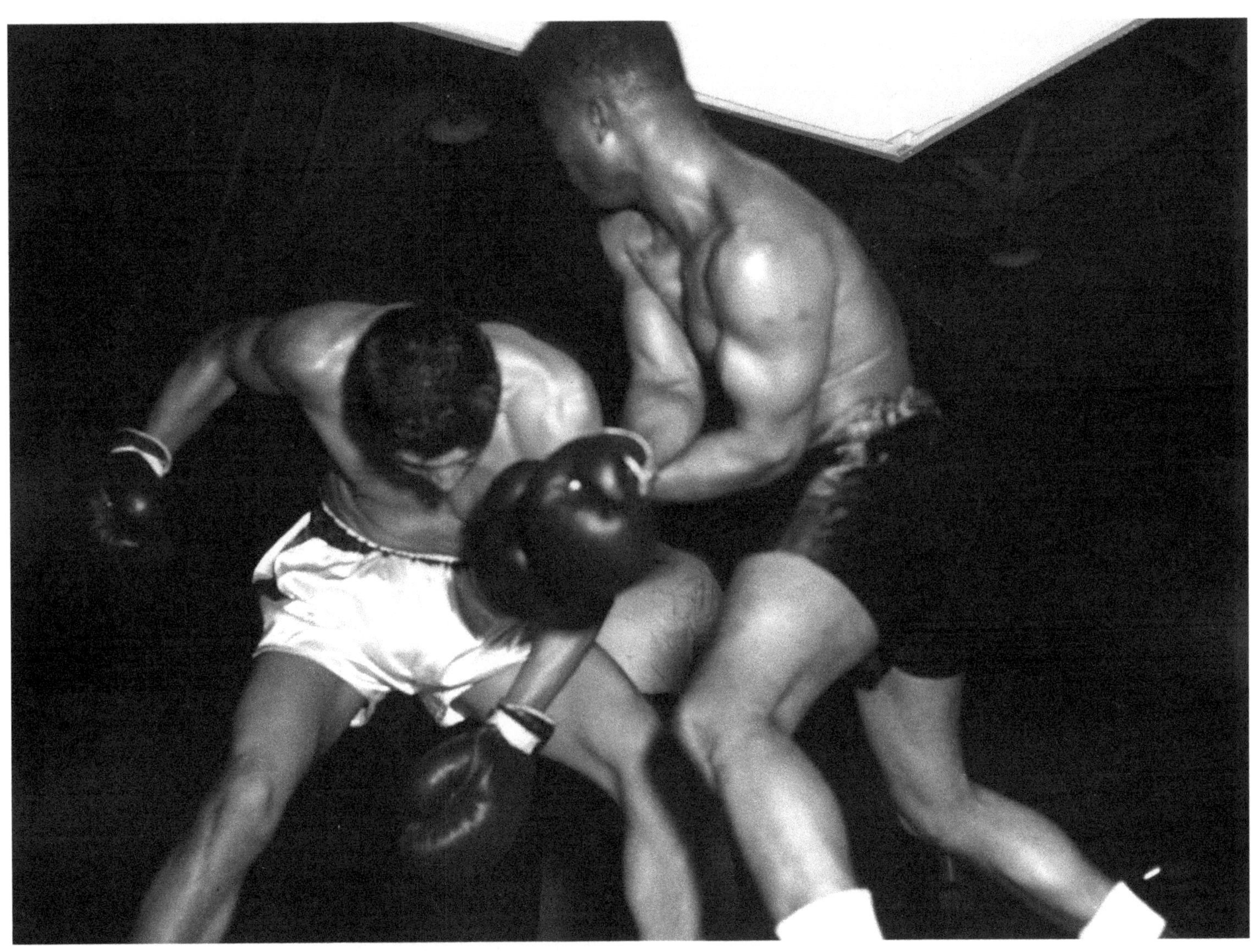

This photo shows two Luke airmen boxing around 1952. The first class of pilots arrived at Luke Field on June 6, 1941, to be trained to fly the AT-6 "Texan." They flew out of Sky Harbor Airport because the runway at Luke Field was not completed. A young captain named Barry Goldwater became the director of ground training at Luke Field in 1942.

After the first Harvey House appeared at a depot on the Atchison, Topeka and Santa Fe Railroad line in 1876, Fred Harvey, dubbed the "civilizer of the West," continued to build the first-class establishments until at the chain's peak there were 84 Harvey Houses. Arizona is fortunate to have two Harvey Houses still in operation—the El Tovar at the Grand Canyon, shown here in 1954, and La Posada in Winslow.

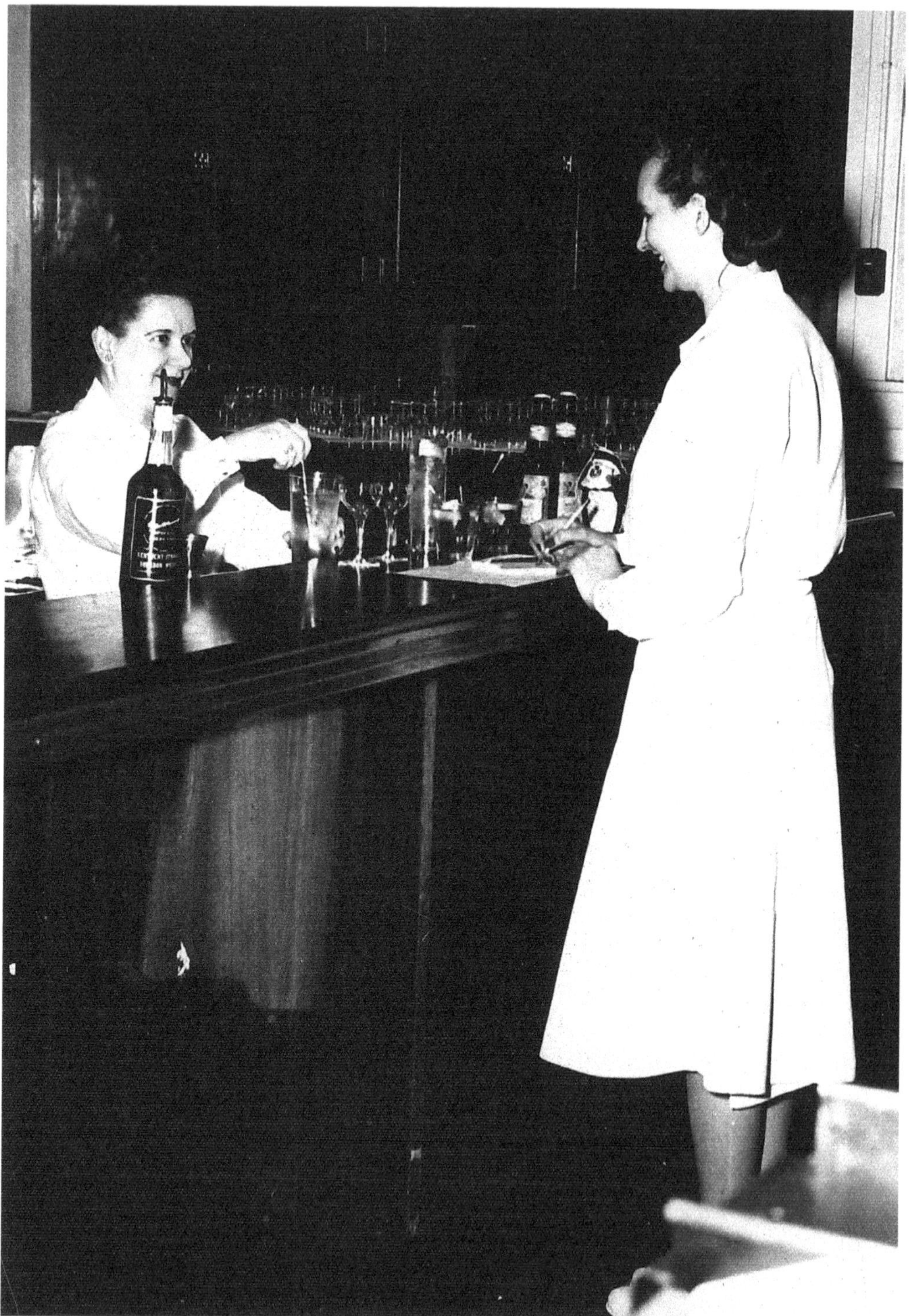

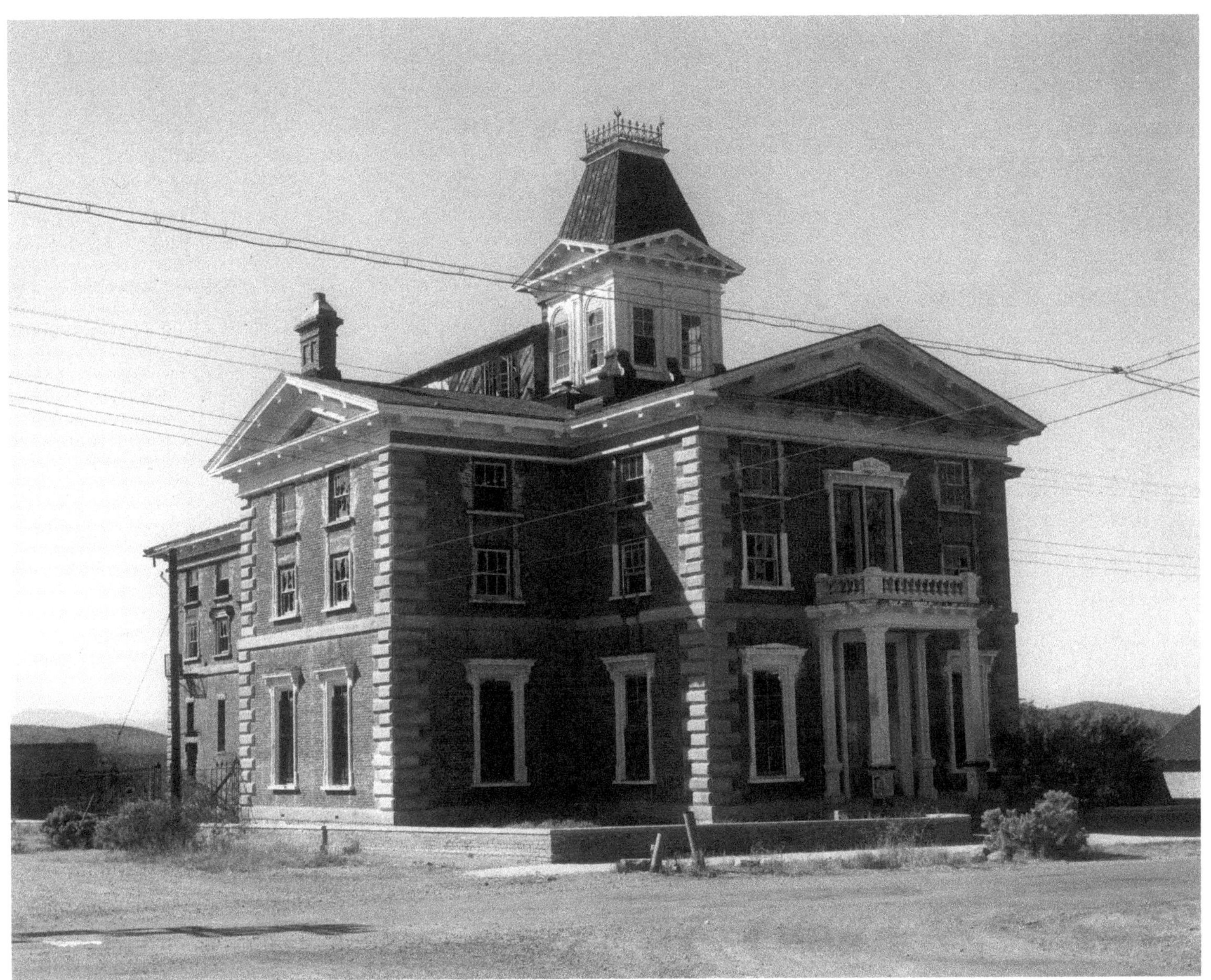

The pride of Tombstone when it was built in 1882, the historic Cochise County Courthouse had fallen into disrepair when this picture was taken in 1955. The Arizona State Parks Department took possession of the old courthouse building in 1959 and restored it to its original beauty. Today the building serves as a museum for visitors seeking to revisit the Wild West and learn the true history of Tombstone.

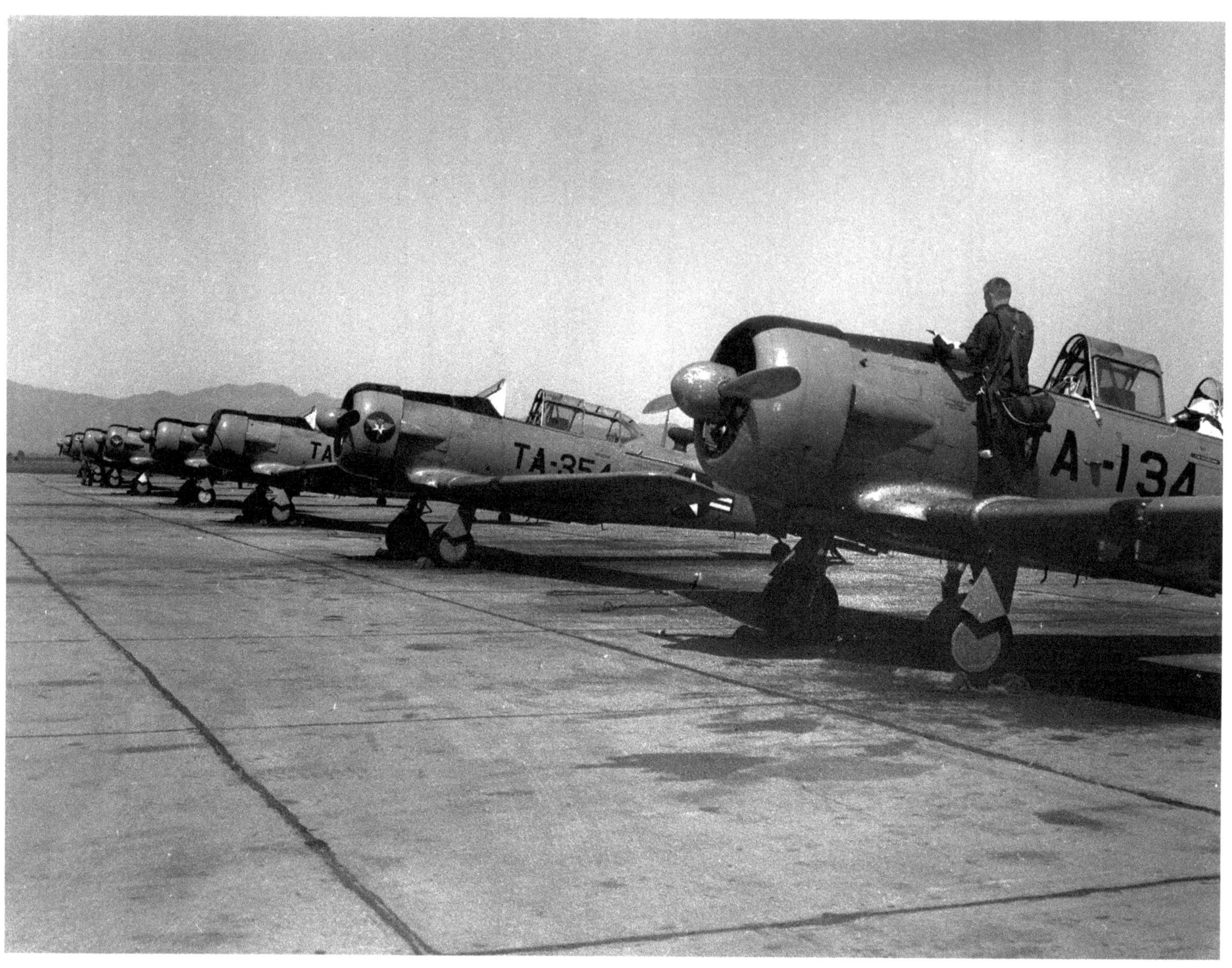

Shown here in 1955, Luke Air Force Base has trained pilots from the United States and other countries around the world for over 65 years. From the days of propeller-driven fighters to the F-16 Falcon, Luke's pilots have served America well. Today Luke Air Force Base is competing to become the primary training base for the U.S. Air Force's new F-35 Lightning fighter jet.

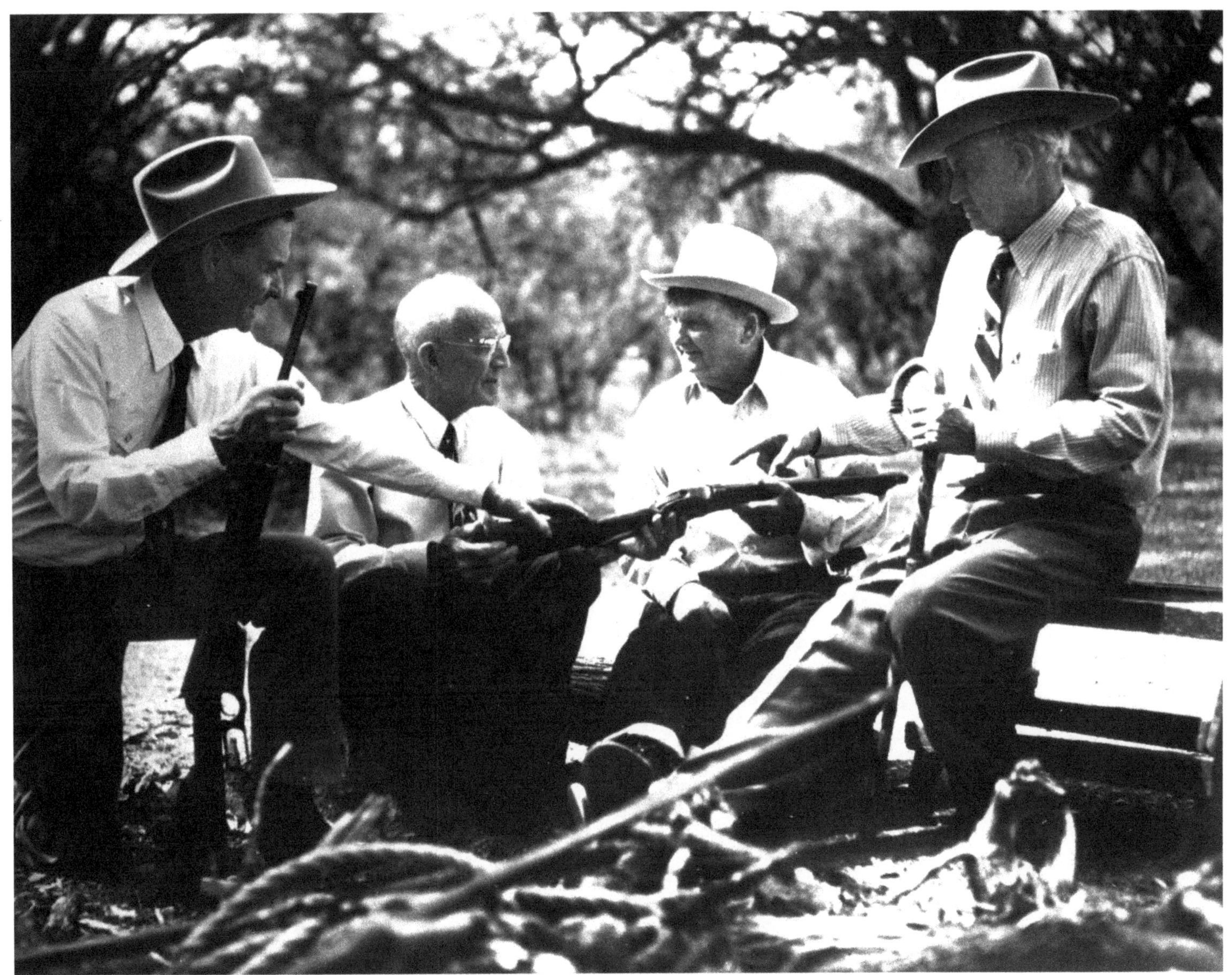

The Arizona Rangers came into being in 1901 to protect the citizens of the Arizona Territory from rustlers and other outlaws and to help prepare the territory for statehood. With a total force never larger than 26 men, the rangers covered the entire territory. They were disbanded in 1909, but the few surviving members reunited in 1957, as shown here, when the Arizona Rangers were reestablished as an all-volunteer group that serves the state even today.

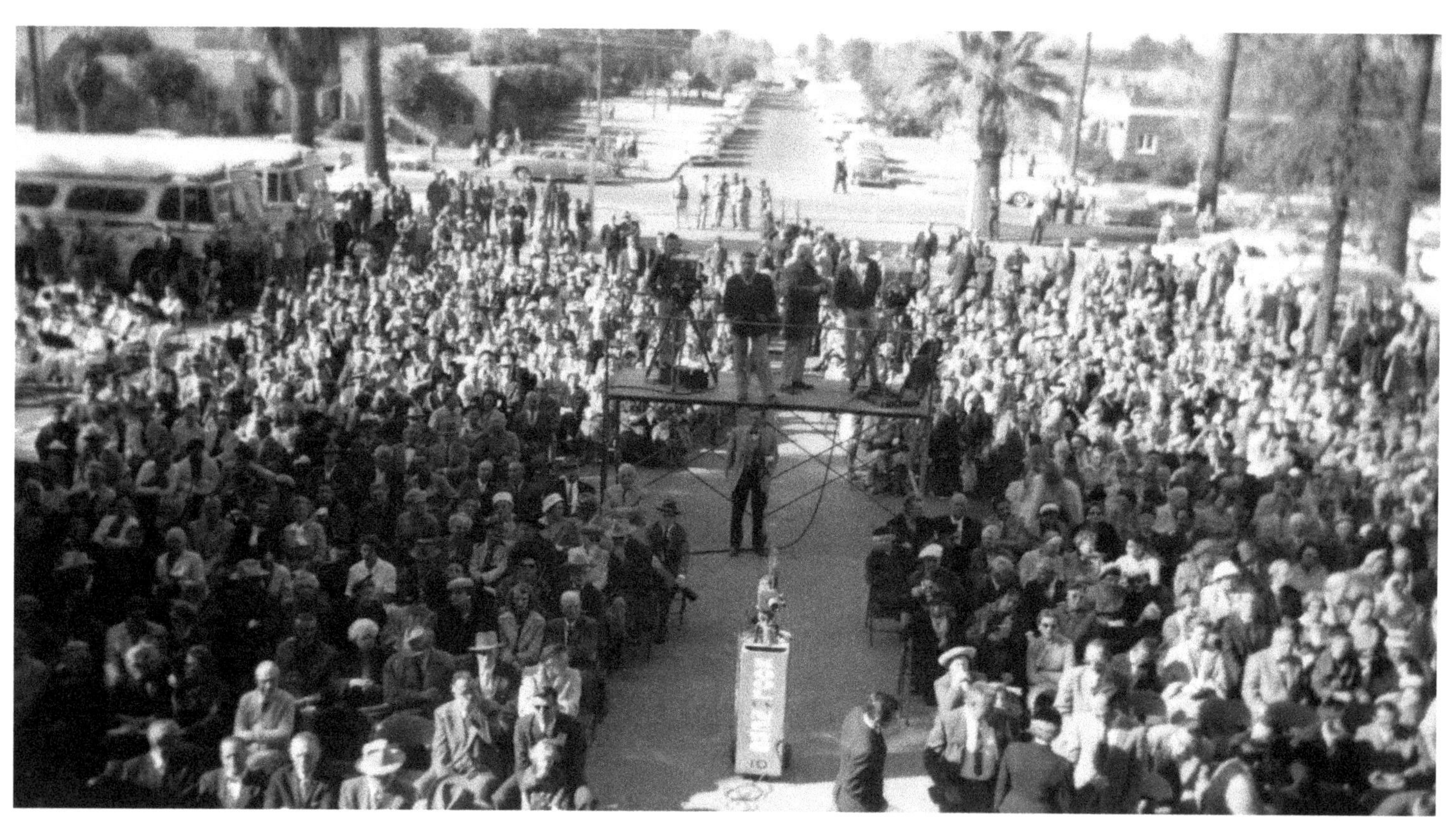

This 1959 photo shows Arizonans in attendance at the inauguration of Paul Fannin, who had been elected the 15th governor of Arizona in 1958. In 1964 Governor Fannin was elected to the United States Senate, when Barry Goldwater chose to run for president of the United States. Fannin served two terms in the United States Senate, retiring from it in 1977.

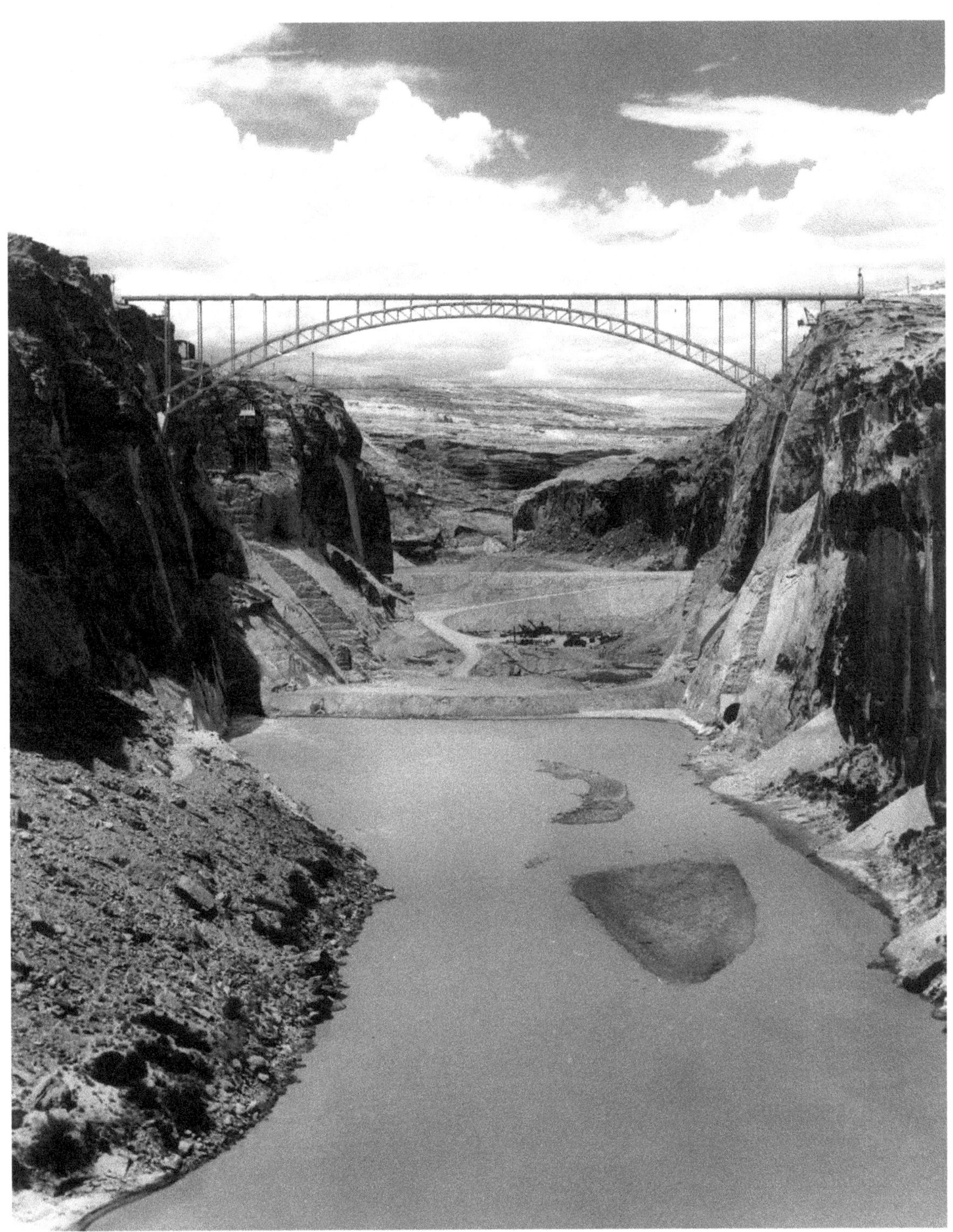

The damming of the Colorado River in northern Arizona's beautiful Glen Canyon was a highly controversial reclamation project. On October 15, 1956, the first dynamite blast shattered this high desert wilderness' calm, and the ten-year construction project had begun. Behind this great dam are held the waters of the hauntingly beautiful Lake Powell.

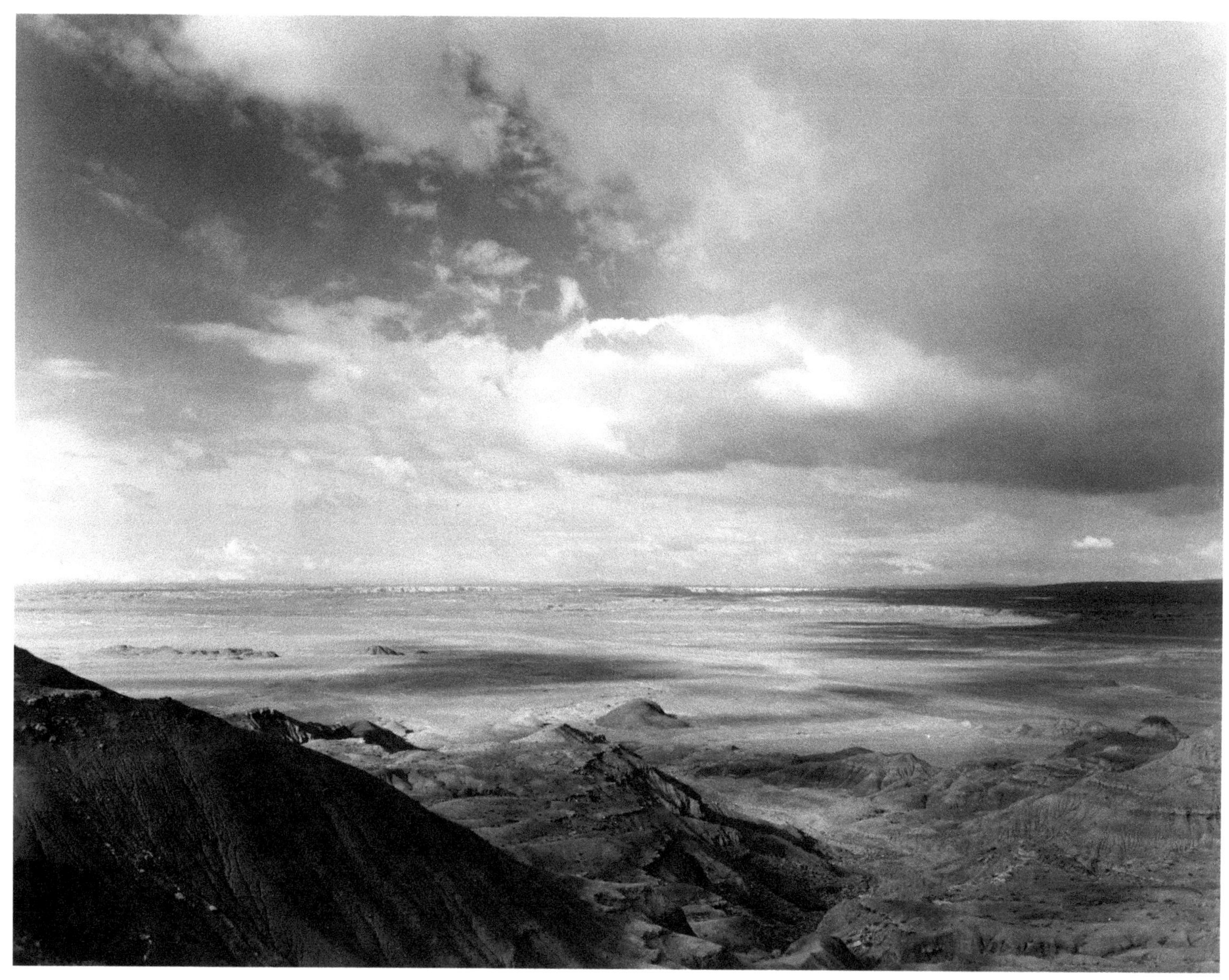

This aerial view around 1960 shows Carson Mesa, which is located on the Navajo Indian Reservation in northeastern Arizona, north of the town of Many Farms. Part of the Chinle Valley, the mesa is in an area of Arizona that contains some of the Southwest's most striking geological formations, including nearby Canyon de Chelley.

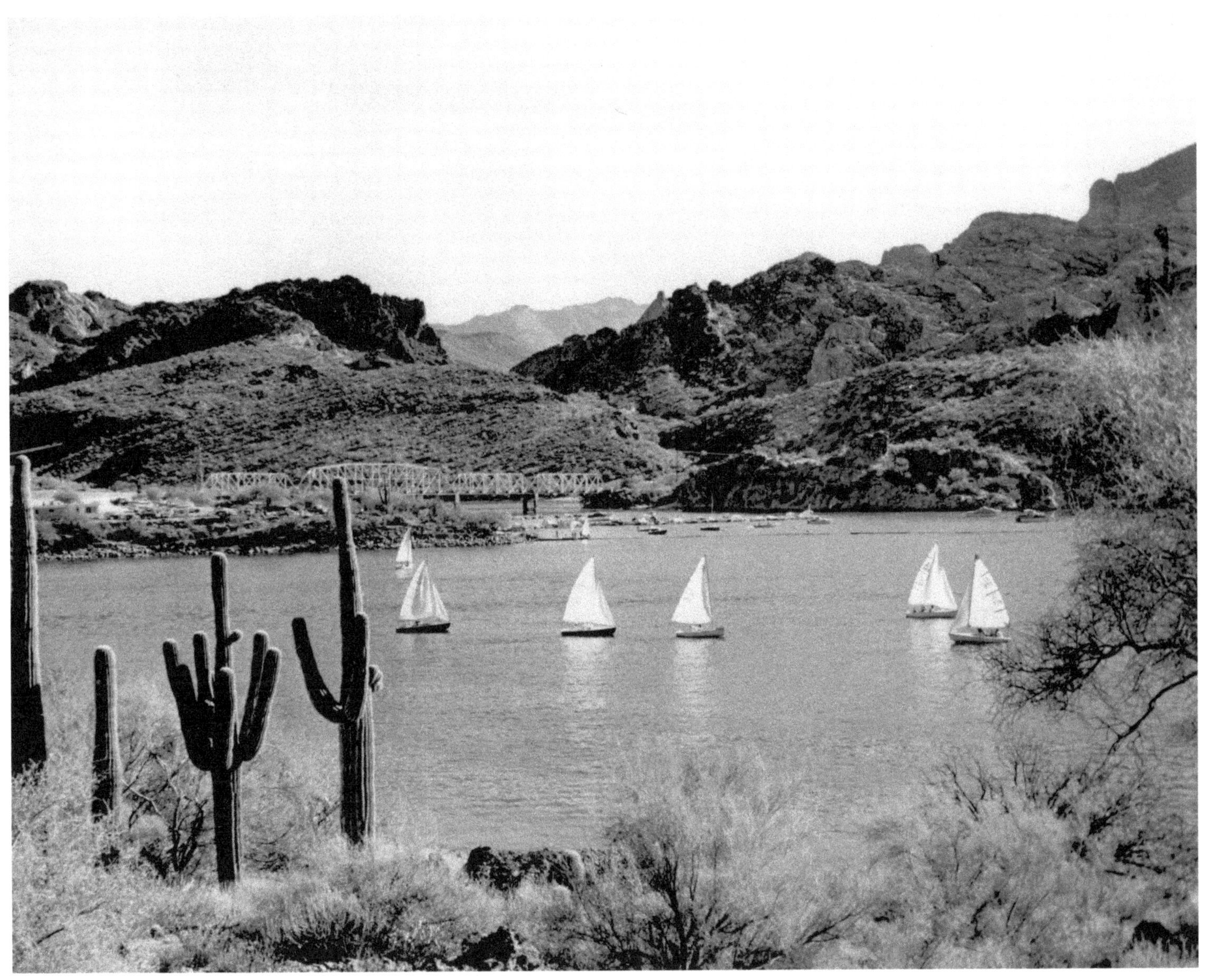

Robert McCulloch, of the McCulloch chainsaw fame, put his dream of building a city on the Colorado River into action when he bought 26 square miles of Arizona desert in 1963 for less than $75 an acre. Continuing to dream, he bought London Bridge and moved it to his new Arizona town, Lake Havasu City, where sailboats and saguaro cacti could be seen side by side.

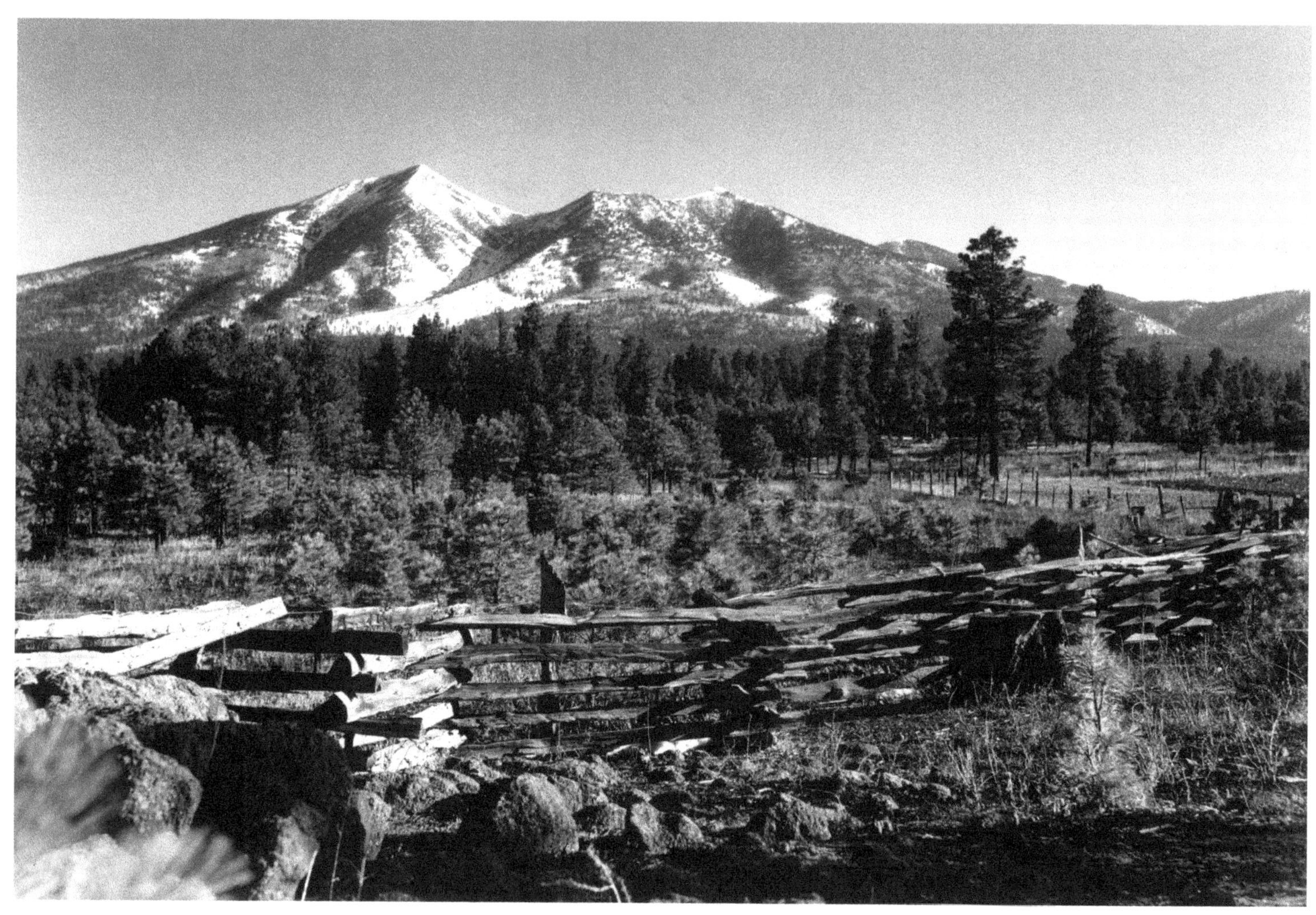

At an elevation of 12,633 feet, Humphrey's Peak is the tallest mountain in Arizona. An extinct volcano, the mountain is part of the San Francisco range located just north of Flagstaff. The 4.8-mile climb to the top, which can only be made in the summer months, allows an adventurous hiker to proclaim, "I have stood on top of Arizona!"

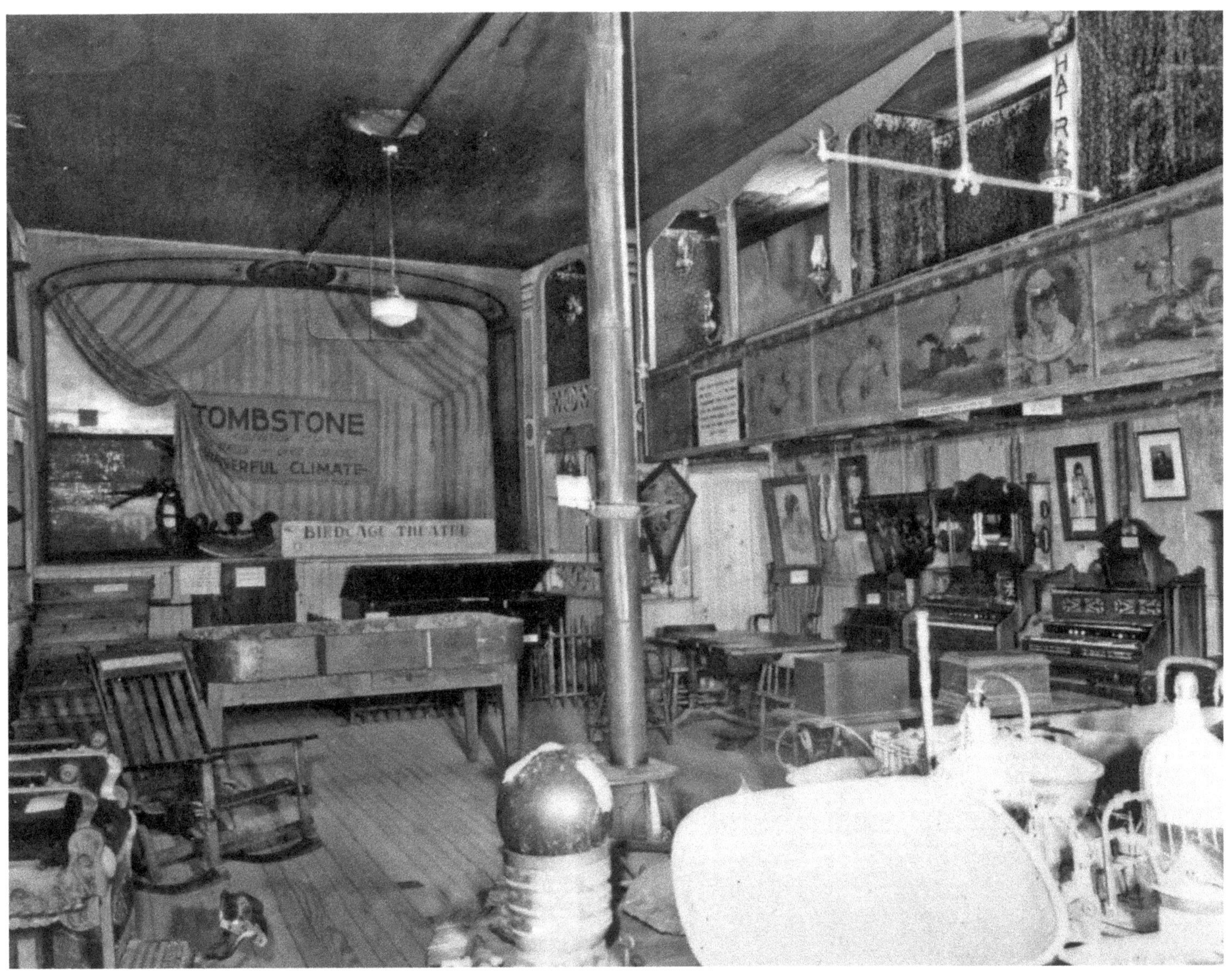

This 1960s view of the interior of the Bird Cage Theatre of Tombstone lore still shows the famous "bird cages" lining the upper-right wall. The cages held the ladies of the night who sold their pleasures 24 hours a day, 7 days a week to the Tombstone miners and cowboys of the 1880s.

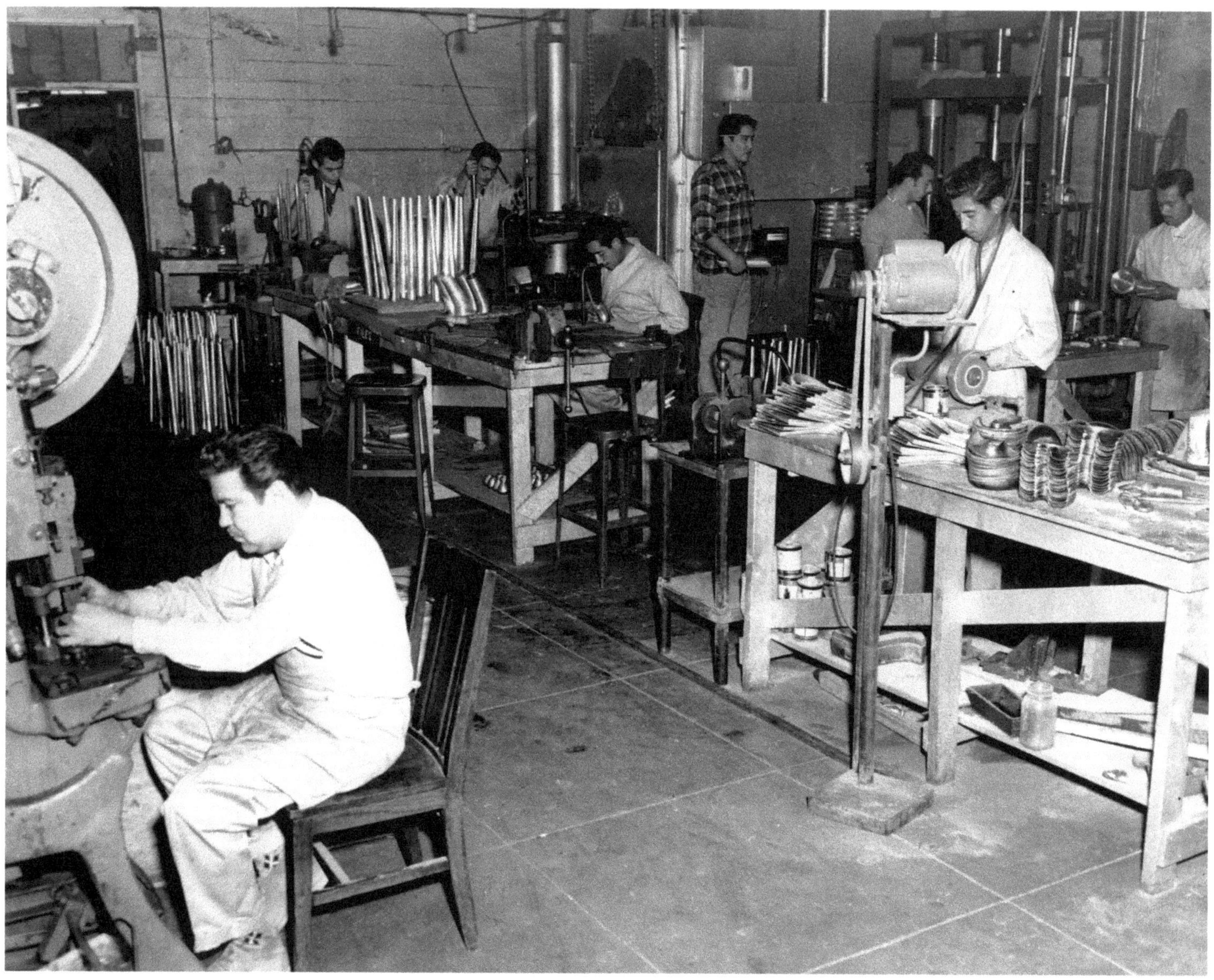

C. G. Conn, a Civil War veteran, was the founder of America's most famous musical instrument manufacturing company, located in Elkhart, Indiana. Elected to the United States Congress in 1892, Conn introduced a bill requiring every army regiment to have its own band, a law that boosted sales of Conn instruments. In 1960 the C. G. Conn firm moved the majority of its saxophone manufacturing business to Nogales, where this photo of the workshop was taken.

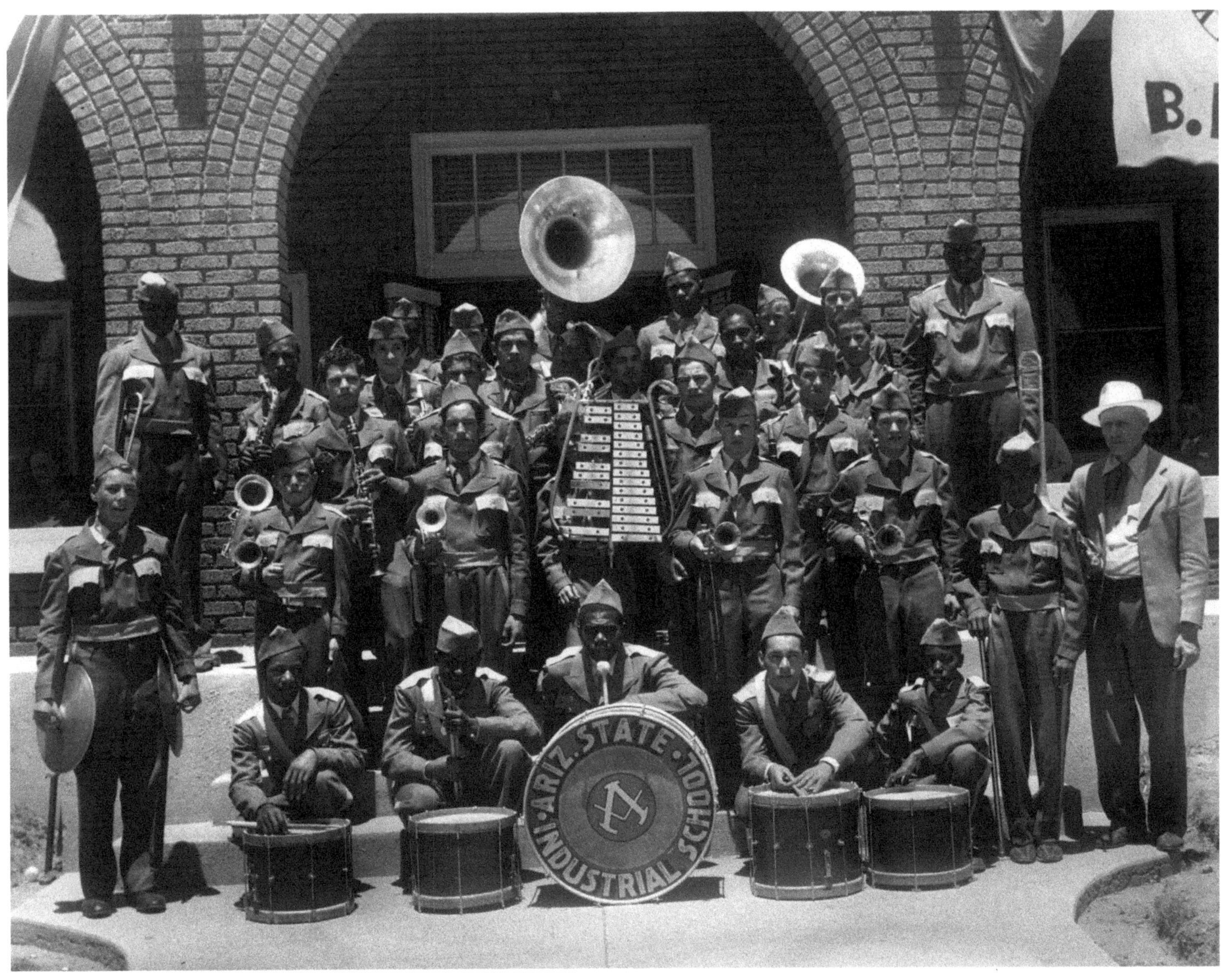

On December 19, 1872, General George Crook ordered the establishment of Fort Grant at the base of Mount Graham in southeastern Arizona. For the 11 companies of United States cavalry and infantry stationed there, the only assignment was to capture the great Apache leader Geronimo. Over the years Fort Grant served many roles, eventually becoming the Arizona State Industrial School, a reform school for boys, where the band was photographed in 1962.

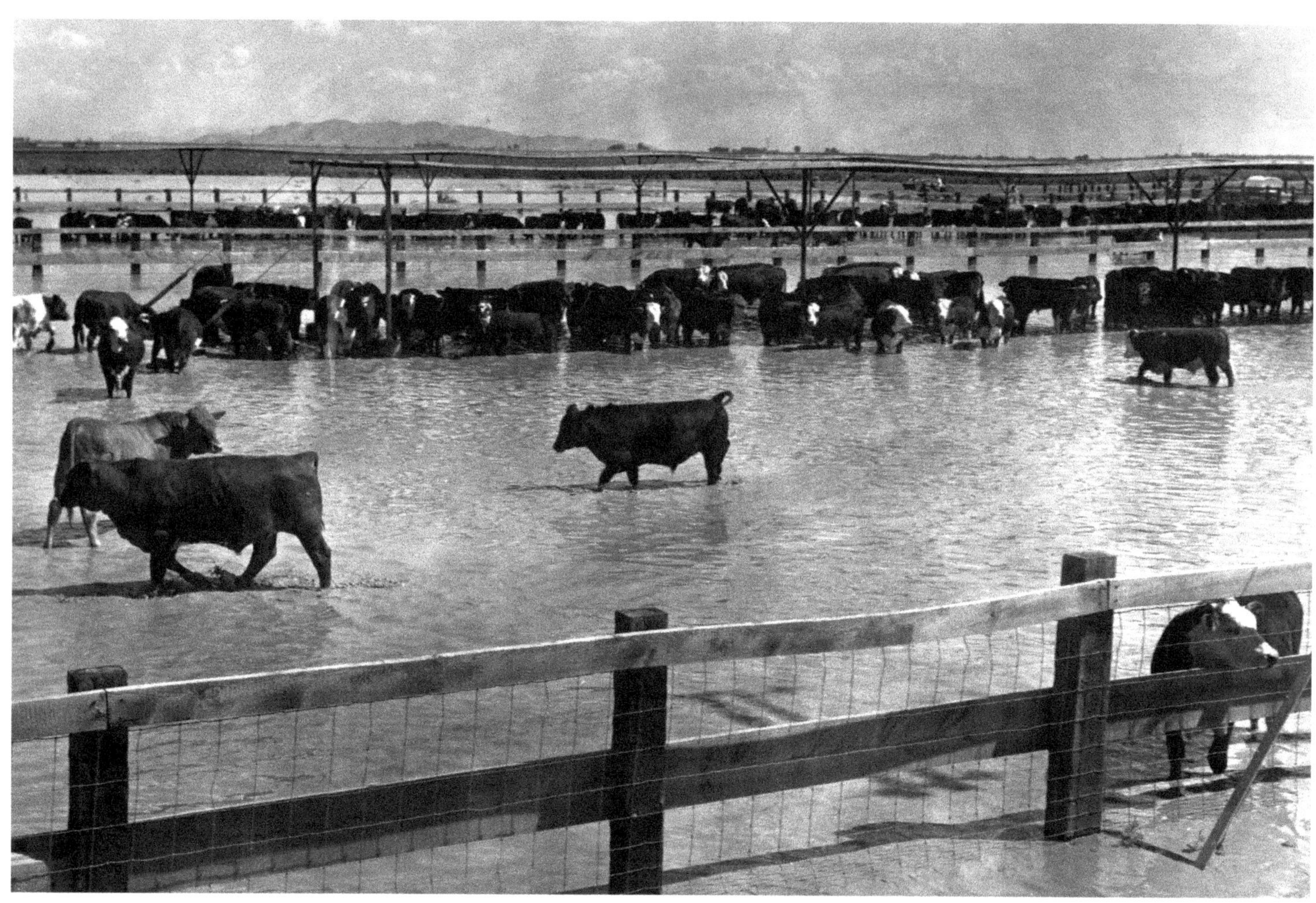

A terrible storm rolled through the Sonoran Desert in late September 1962, sending the Santa Cruz River and Santa Rosa Wash over their banks and flooding large areas of south-central Arizona. The cattle on this ranch near Eloy had to wade through the water and mud even within their feedlots.

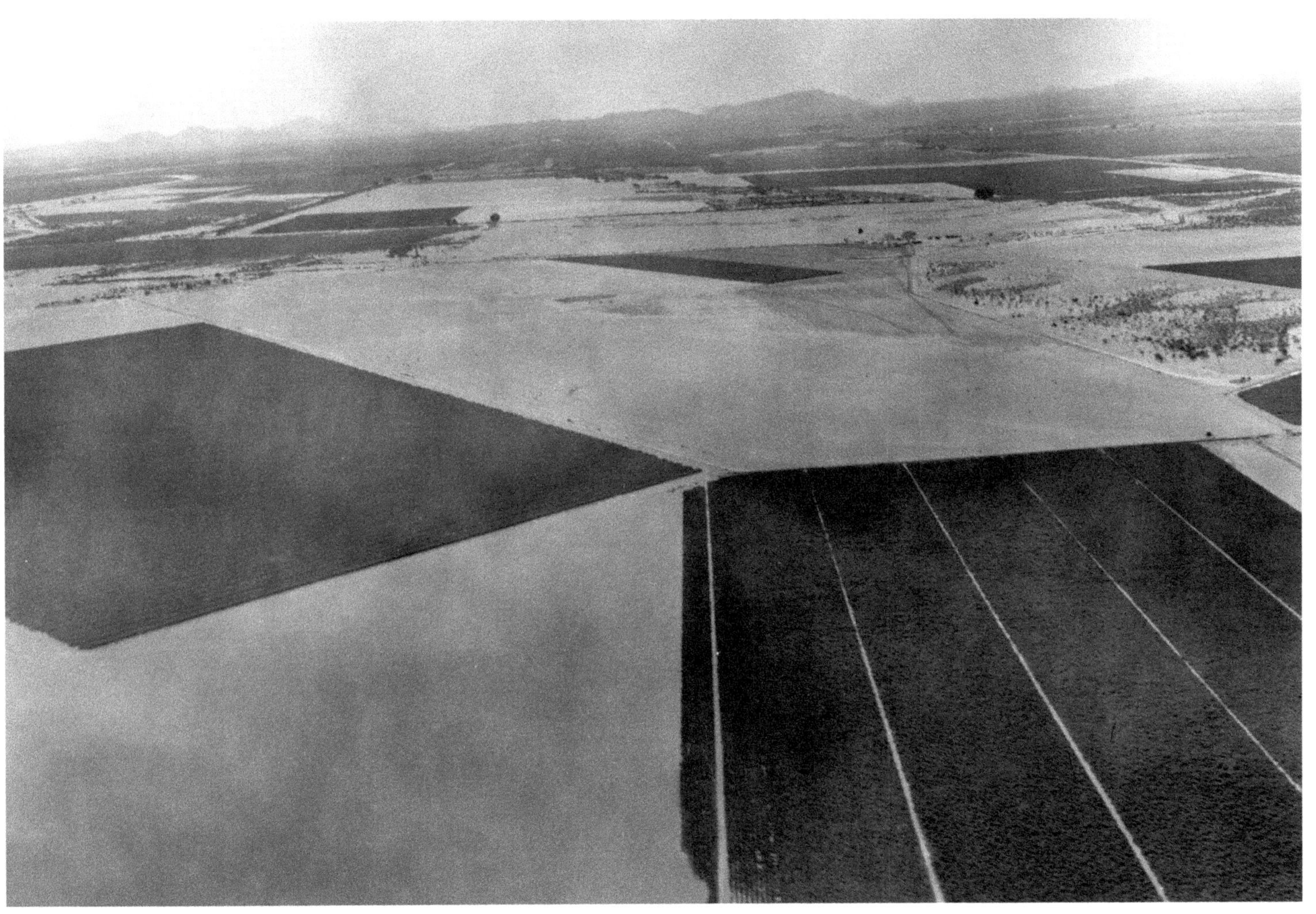

Farmlands near Eloy were inundated when the Santa Cruz River flooded in late September 1962. More than $3 million in damage to the farming communities was caused by this desert river's flooding.

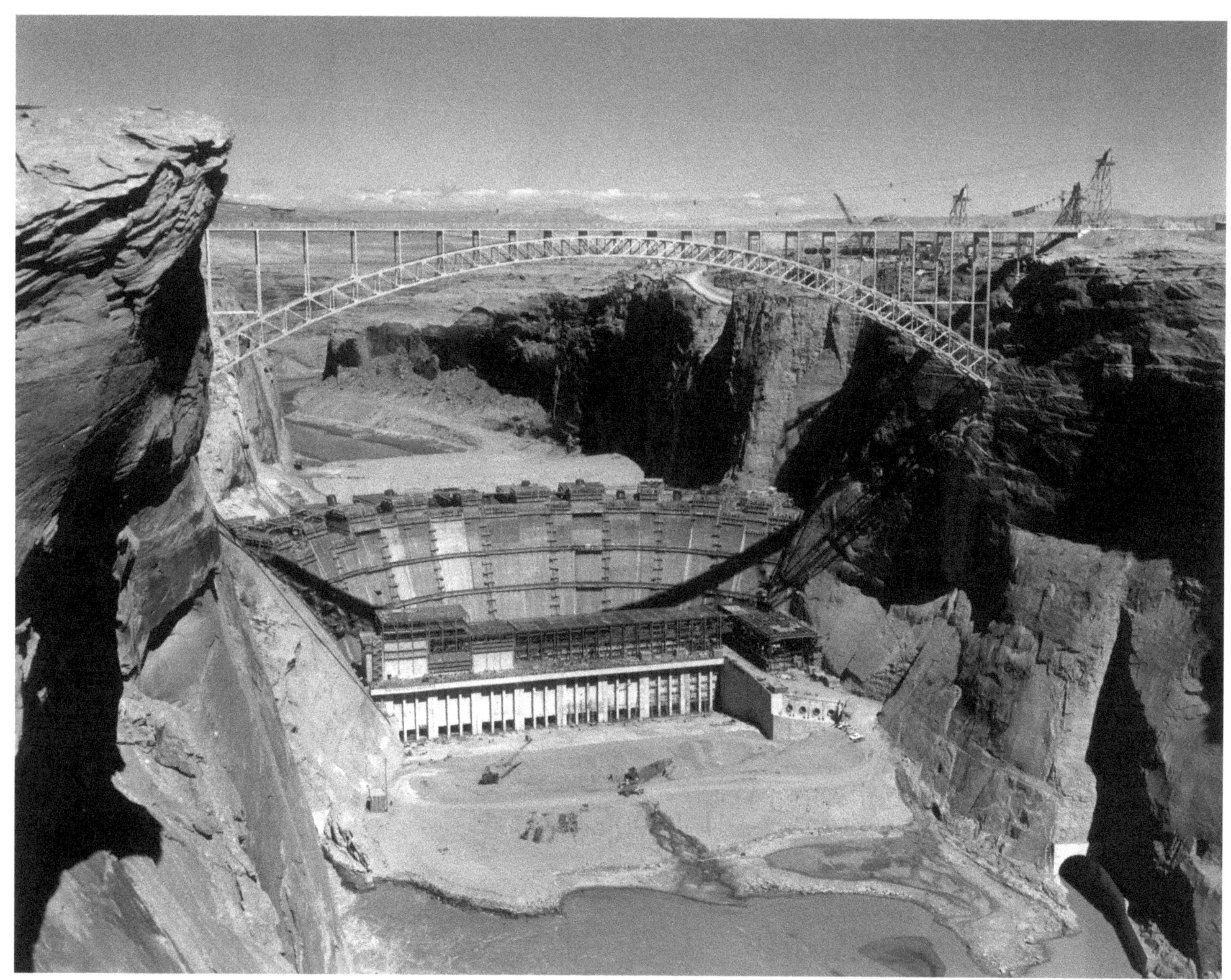

In 1997, one year before his death, Barry Goldwater said that he regretted his support and vote in favor of the construction of Glen Canyon Dam, shown here in 1962. The environmentalist author Edward Abbey spent the last years of his life lobbying for the destruction of the dam. Others argue that without the great dams to store water for the long periods of drought, the modern western cities of Phoenix, Las Vegas, and even Los Angeles would not exist. Today Glen Canyon Dam and Lake Powell remain as examples in the many debates that still rage over the damming of the rivers of the American West.

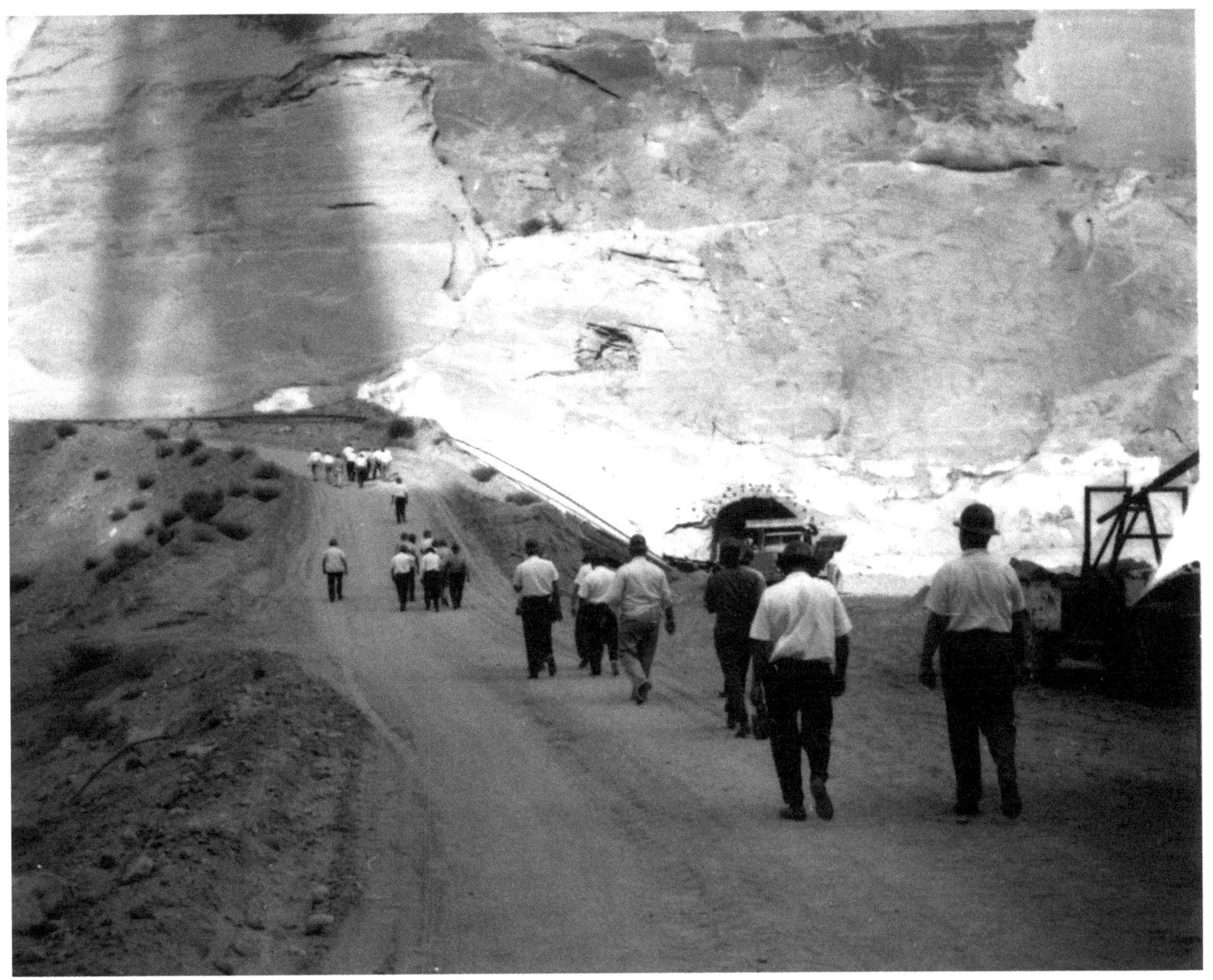

Arizona Highway Department employees are shown at the construction site of Glen Canyon Dam in 1963, the year the dam was deemed sufficiently near completion to begin backing up the waters of the Colorado River, creating Lake Powell.

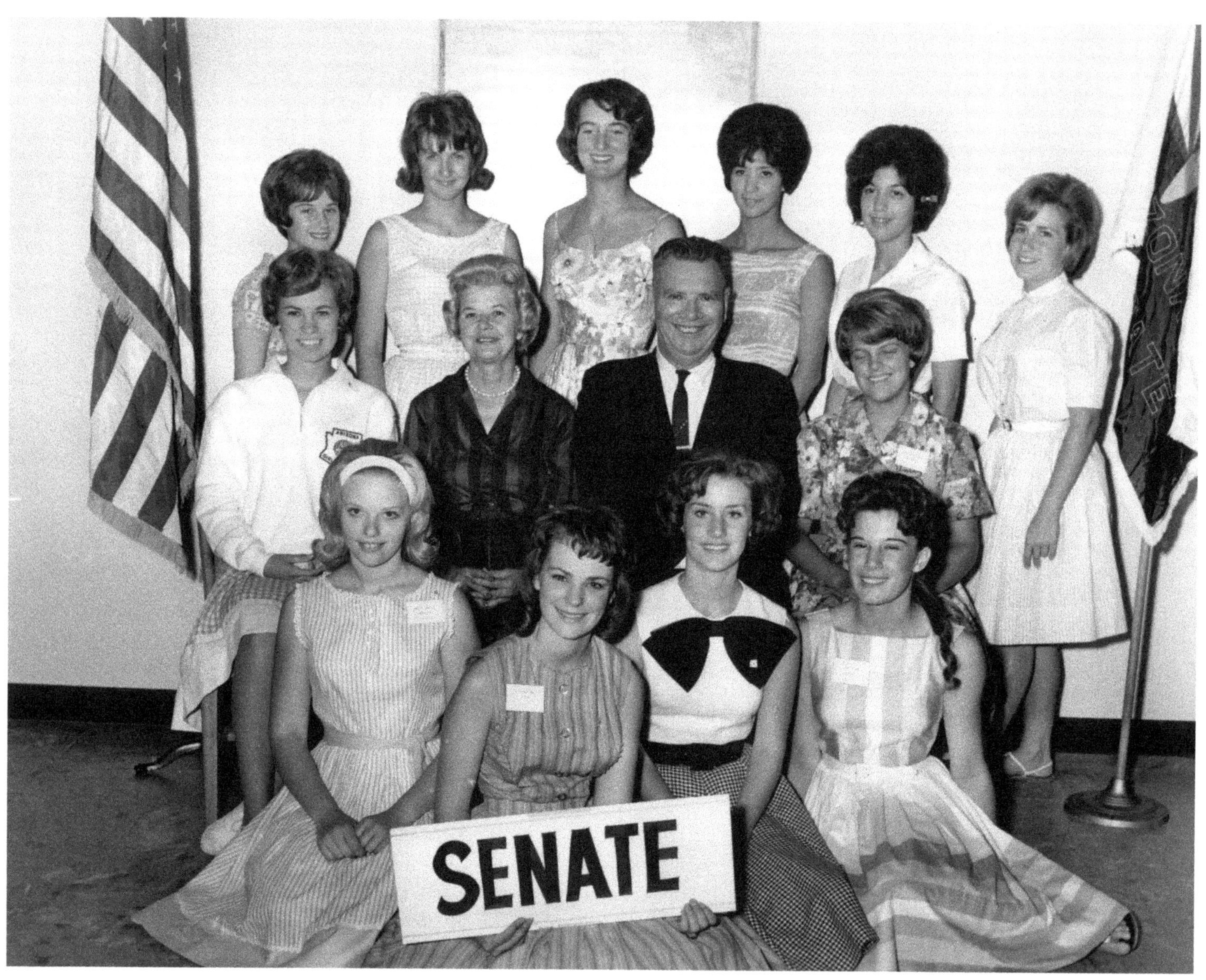

Senator Clarence Carpenter of Miami, Arizona, helps a group of students learn about the legislative process during the 1963 Arizona youth legislature in Phoenix. Miami was a struggling copper mining town in 1963, and Senator Carpenter did much to keep the Gila County towns vital.

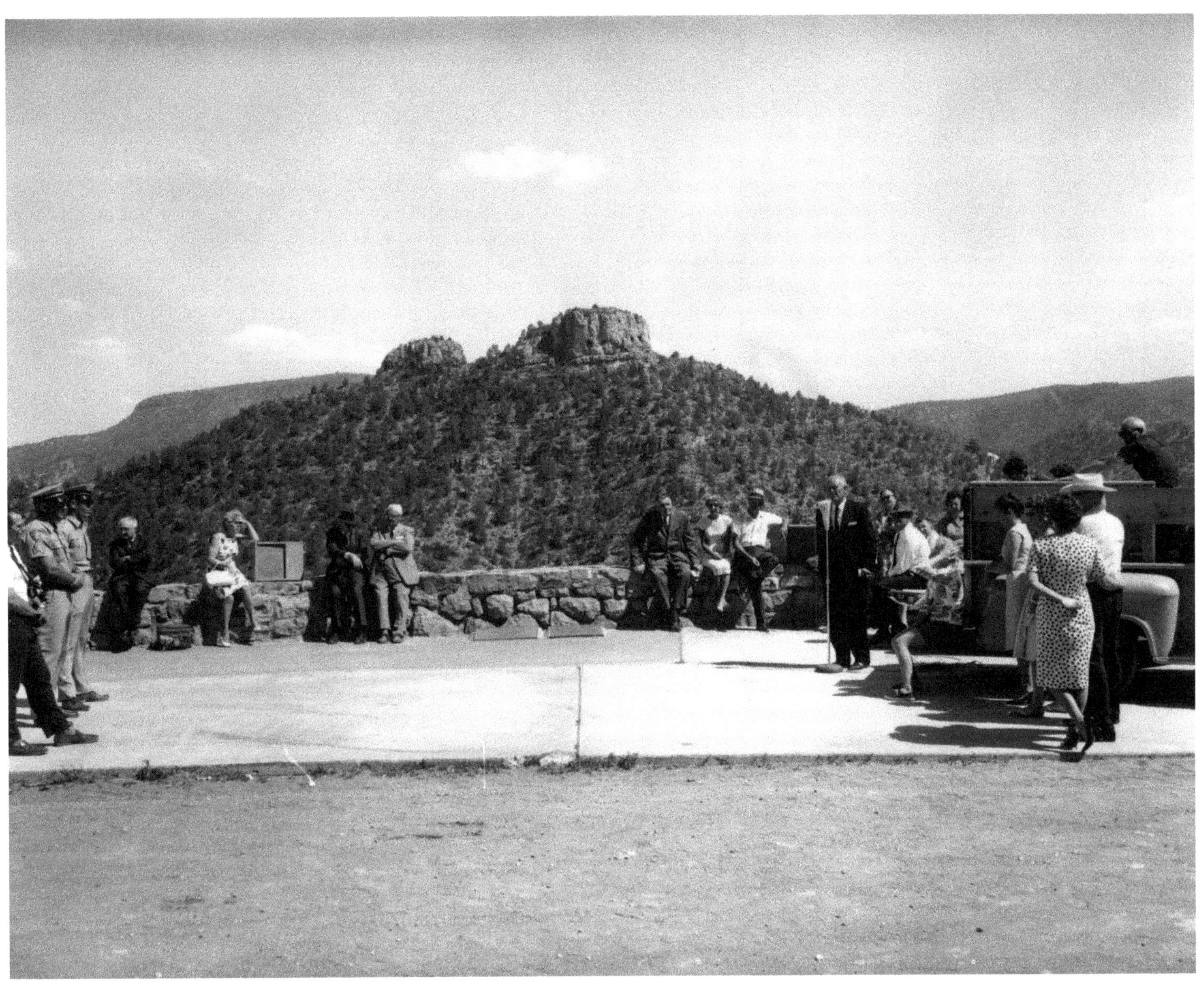

The Salt River Canyon is often called the mini Grand Canyon of Arizona. Located 25 miles north of Globe, the 2,000-foot-deep canyon offers spectacular views from Arizona Highway 77 as it winds its way from the Phoenix area to the recreational areas of the White Mountains. These folks are attending the dedication of Highway 77 in 1964. A modern bridge was constructed across the vast gorge and dedicated in 1977.

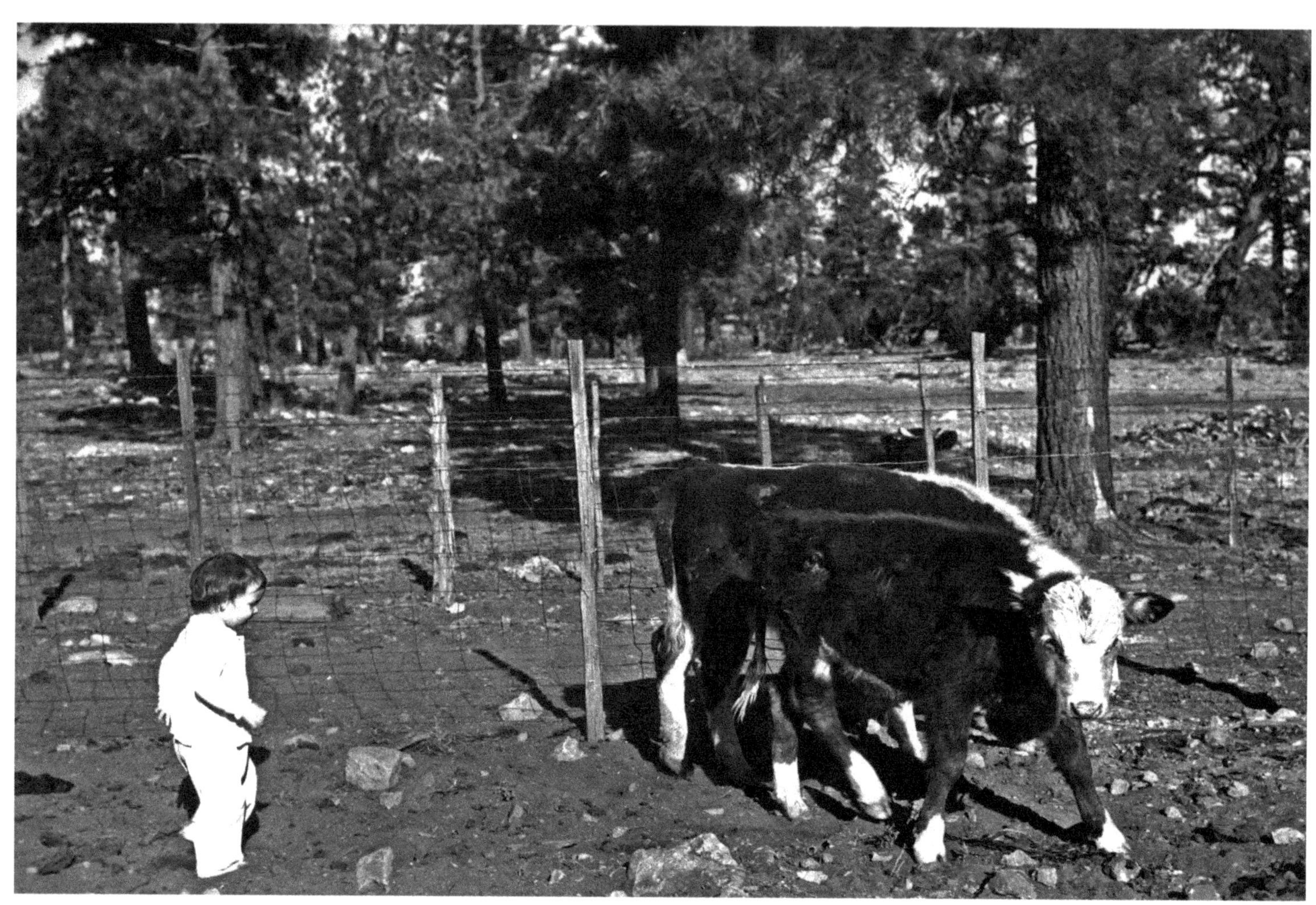

In 1913, when the Tremaine family of Cleveland became interested in ranching in northern Arizona, their agent sought out Boss Chilson to operate their new Bar T Ranch. Over the years, more rangeland was added to the Bar T holdings, including the land that surrounded the famous Meteor Crater. Here the great granddaughter of Boss Chilson frolics on the ranch in the 1960s.

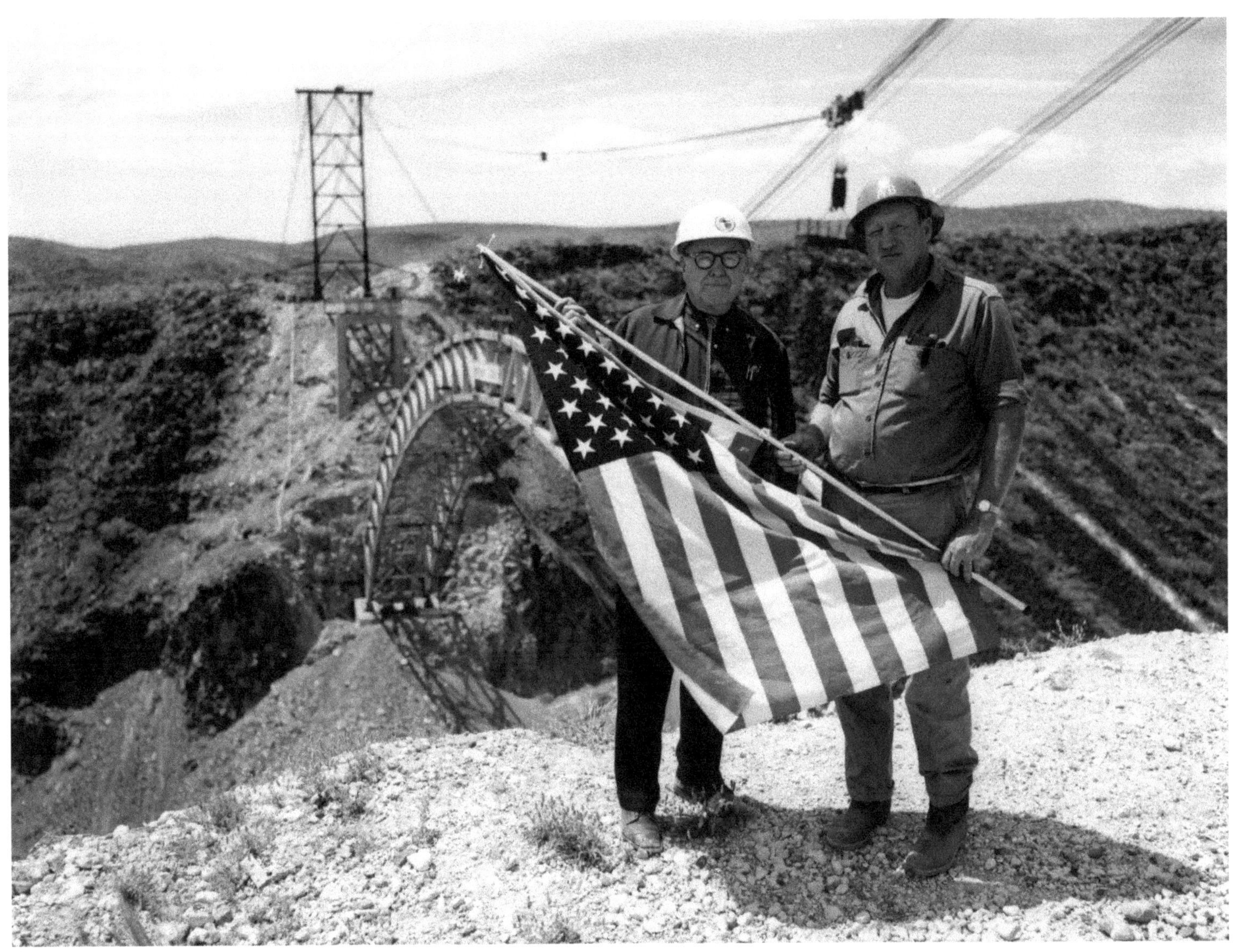

Construction workers unfurl an American flag upon completion of the Burro Creek Bridge in 1965. Burro Creek is located some 15 miles south of Wikieup on U.S. Highway 93, a major highway between Phoenix and Las Vegas.

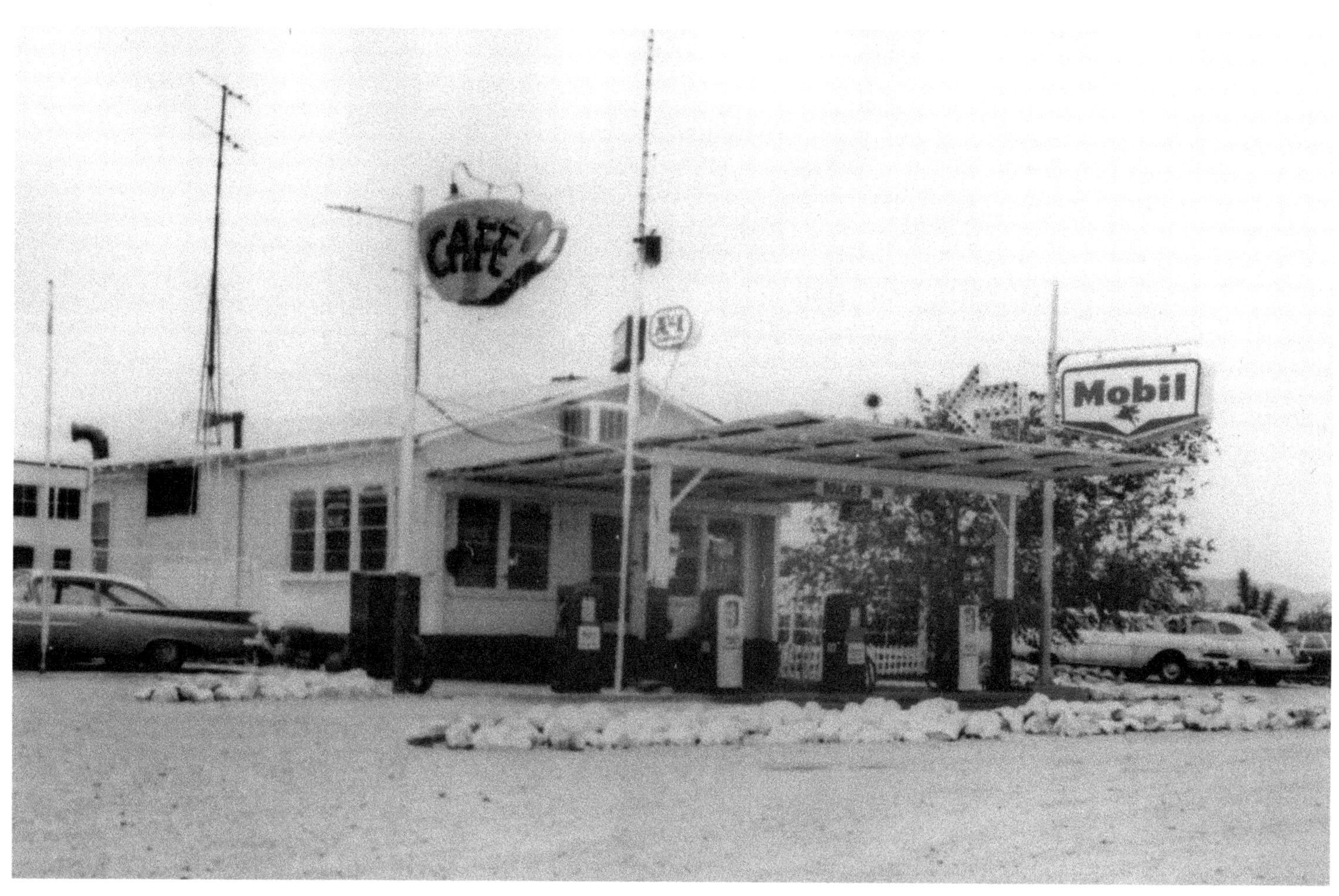

Family-owned service stations were once as much a part of the American story as baseball, apple pie, and ice cream. When a driver pulled into this service station along U.S. 93 near Hoover Dam in 1965, an attendant would pump the gas, check the oil, and put air into the tires while the driver relaxed inside the car. With gas costing only 30¢ a gallon, those just might have been the good ol' days.

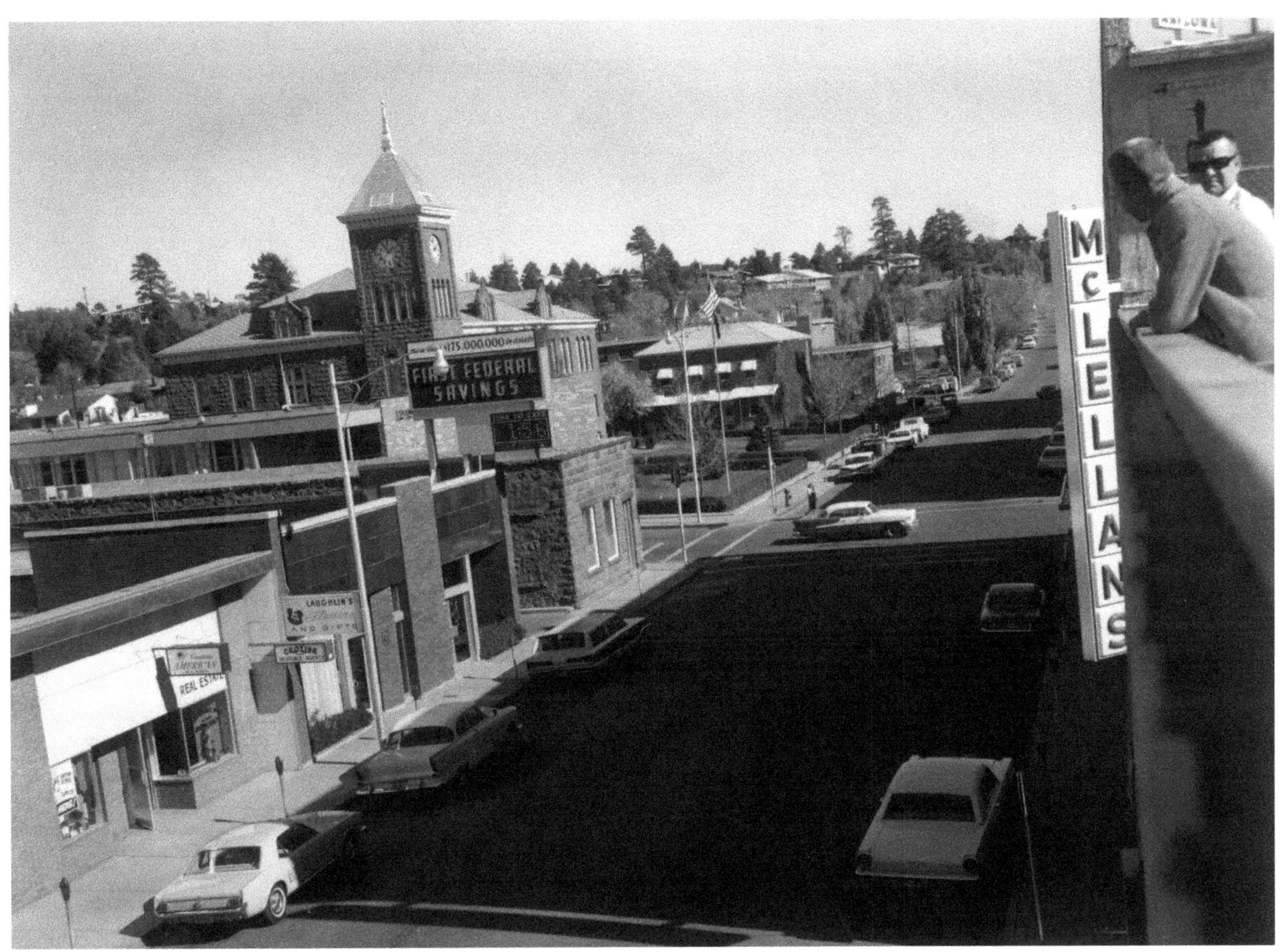

Young men atop a Flagstaff building in 1966 look east down Birch Street toward the old Coconino County Courthouse. Built in 1893, the old courthouse is still used for county offices today.

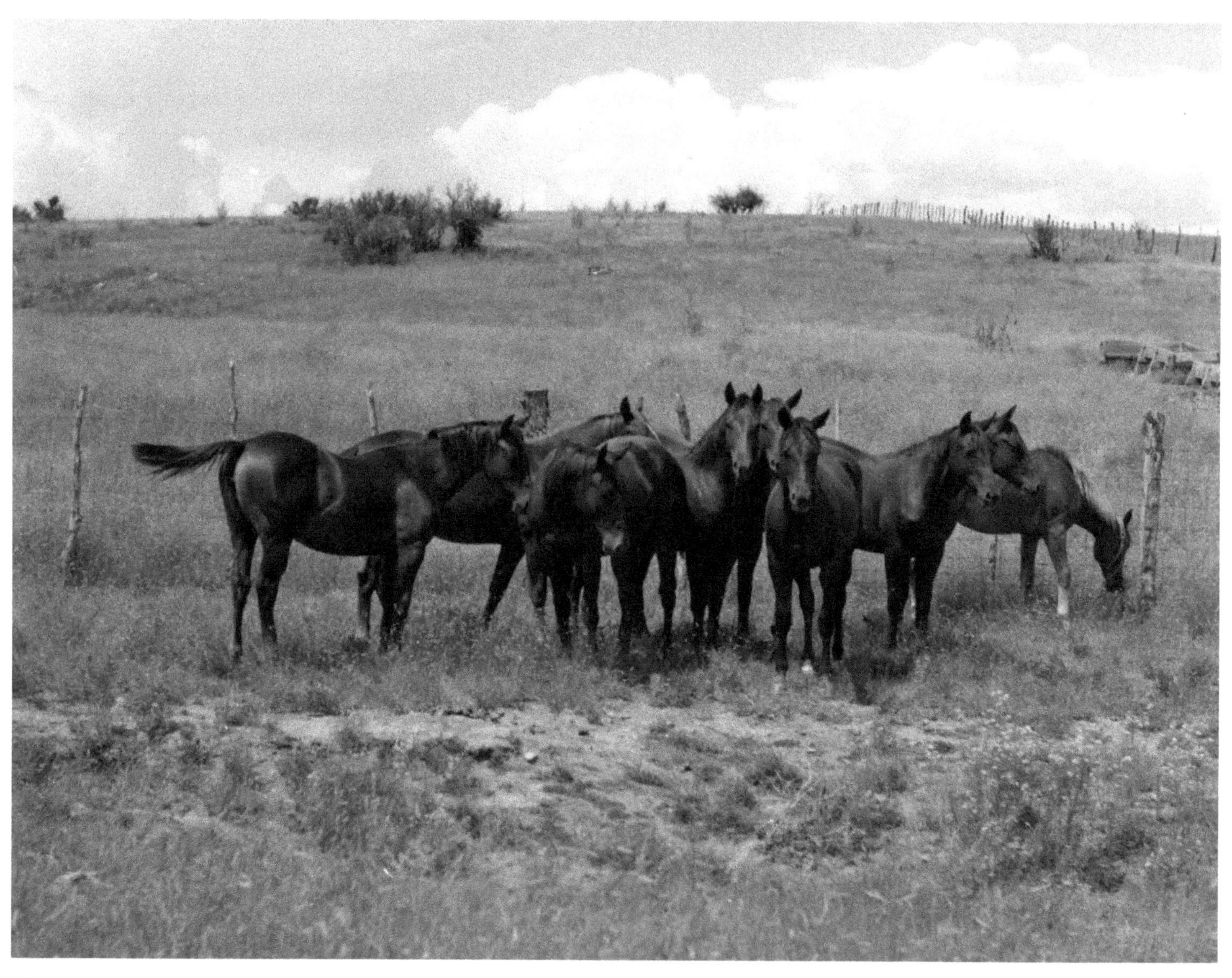

The horse gave freedom to the American cowboy, and together they became symbolic of the Wild West. Since herds of wild horses still run free in parts of Arizona, then surely too does a small bit of that era remain, ready to be discovered by modern dreamers.

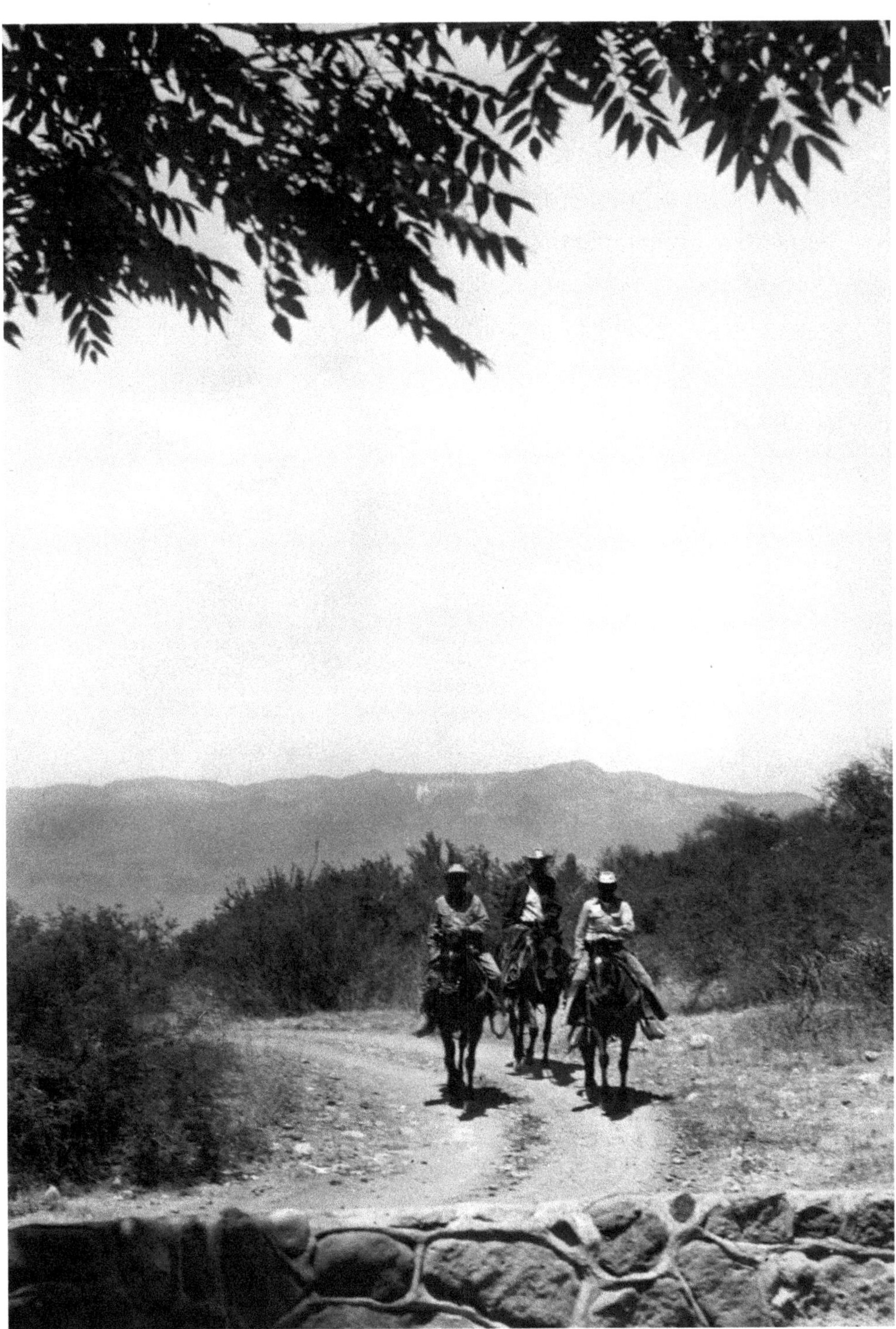

For people whose "heroes have always been cowboys," Arizona is still a place where the beauty and adventure of the American West can be found and enjoyed. Come to Arizona and discover it for yourself!

Notes on the Photographs

These notes, listed by page number, attempt to include all aspects known of the photographs. Each of the photographs is identified by the page number, a title or description, photographer and collection, archive, and call or box number when applicable. Although every attempt was made to collect all data, in some cases complete data may have been unavailable due to the age and condition of some of the photographs and records.

II **Tombstone, 1880s**
Arizona State Library, Archives and Public Records, History and Archives Division, Phoenix
97-0415

VI **Yuma Bridge**
Library of Congress
LC-USZ62-49926

X **Gurley Street**
Library of Congress
LC-USZ6-305

2 **Diamond Fields Route**
Library of Congress
LC-USZC4-5662

3 **Soldiers Battling Apaches**
Library of Congress
LC-USZC4-5663

4 **San Xavier del Bac**
Library of Congress
LC-USZC4-5665

5 **San Xavier del Bac Interior**
Library of Congress
LC-USZC4-5668

6 **Weathered Rock**
Library of Congress
LC-DIG-stereo-1s00270

7 **Apache Family**
Library of Congress
LC-DIG-stereo-1s00342

8 **Surveying Party**
Library of Congress
LC-DIG-stereo-1s00178

9 **Camp Mojave Exploration Party**
Library of Congress
LC-DIG-stereo-1s00145

10 **Prescott Wagons**
Arizona State Library, Archives and Public Records, History and Archives Division, Phoenix
96-3428

11 **Freight Wagon**
Arizona State Library, Archives and Public Records, History and Archives Division, Phoenix
97-0734

12 **Holbrook Sheriff**
Arizona State Library, Archives and Public Records, History and Archives Division, Phoenix
97-9458

13 **Citizens of Yuma**
Arizona State Library, Archives and Public Records, History and Archives Division, Phoenix
97-8216

14 **Stage Station**
Arizona State Library, Archives and Public Records, History and Archives Division, Phoenix
98-9961

15 **Clifton's Main Street**
Arizona State Library, Archives and Public Records, History and Archives Division, Phoenix
96-3170

16 **Clifton Flood Rescue Team**
Arizona State Library, Archives and Public Records, History and Archives Division, Phoenix
96-3173

18 **A. & B. Schuster General Store**
Arizona State Library, Archives and Public Records, History and Archives Division, Phoenix
96-2128

19 **John Heath Lynched**
Library of Congress
LC-USZ62-109782

20 **Fort Verde**
Library of Congress
LC-USZ62-105868

21 **Montezuma Well**
Library of Congress
LC-USZ62-113804

22 **Fort Verde Hunters**
Library of Congress
LC-USZ62-105871

23 **Clear Creek Bivouac**
Library of Congress
LC-USZ62-105873

24 **Buffalo Soldier and Children**
Library of Congress
LC-USZ62-105867

25 Bisbee, 1890s
Arizona State Library, Archives and Public Records, History and Archives Division, Phoenix
96-1742

26 Henry Reed
Arizona State Library, Archives and Public Records, History and Archives Division, Phoenix
96-2123

27 Broad Street
Arizona State Library, Archives and Public Records, History and Archives Division, Phoenix
96-3621

28 Forsee Groceries
Arizona State Library, Archives and Public Records, History and Archives Division, Phoenix
98-0015

29 Tombstone, 1890s
Arizona State Library, Archives and Public Records, History and Archives Division, Phoenix
96-4364

30 Yuma Main Street
Arizona State Library, Archives and Public Records, History and Archives Division, Phoenix
97-2713

31 Pilot Knob Hotel
Arizona State Library, Archives and Public Records, History and Archives Division, Phoenix
97-2914

32 Navajo Weavers
Library of Congress
LC-USZ62-126405

33 Our Lady of Mount Carmel
Arizona State Library, Archives and Public Records, History and Archives Division, Phoenix
97-0585

34 Prescott Fire Fighters
Arizona State Library, Archives and Public Records, History and Archives Division, Phoenix
96-1769

36 Snake Dance at Walpi
Library of Congress
LC-USZ62-101155

37 Freemasons
Library of Congress
LC-USZ62-124538

38 Buckey O'Neill
Arizona State Library, Archives and Public Records, History and Archives Division, Phoenix
96-4391

39 Territorial Legislature
Arizona State Library, Archives and Public Records, History and Archives Division, Phoenix
96-7232

40 Pascoe's Livery Feed Store
Arizona State Library, Archives and Public Records, History and Archives Division, Phoenix
96-3561

41 Jerome High School Football
Arizona State Library, Archives and Public Records, History and Archives Division, Phoenix
96-1880

42 Henry Kemp Hardware
Arizona State Library, Archives and Public Records, History and Archives Division, Phoenix
97-7132

44 Thumb Butte
Arizona State Library, Archives and Public Records, History and Archives Division, Phoenix
97-4474

45 Clifton Locomotive
Arizona State Library, Archives and Public Records, History and Archives Division, Phoenix
97-2866

46 Wagons and Sego
Arizona State Library, Archives and Public Records, History and Archives Division, Phoenix
98-0582

47 Tucson Streetcar
Arizona State Library, Archives and Public Records, History and Archives Division, Phoenix
97-9676

48 Ore Shovel
Arizona State Library, Archives and Public Records, History and Archives Division, Phoenix
96-3295

49 Copper Queen Store
Arizona State Library, Archives and Public Records, History and Archives Division, Phoenix
96-3373

50 McCabe Extension Mercantile Store
Arizona State Library, Archives and Public Records, History and Archives Division, Phoenix
96-3601

51 Train Accident
Arizona State Library, Archives and Public Records, History and Archives Division, Phoenix
96-1535

52 President McKinley
Library of Congress
LC-USZ62-116509

53 Tempe Normal School Football
Arizona State Library, Archives and Public Records, History and Archives Division, Phoenix
95-1950

54 Van Slyck & Meyers Bar
Arizona State Library, Archives and Public Records, History and Archives Division, Phoenix
96-4512

55 Cowboys in Douglas
Arizona State Library, Archives and Public Records, History and Archives Division, Phoenix
96-3123

56 **Kachina Dance**
Library of Congress
LC-USZ62-57182

57 **Painted Desert**
Library of Congress
LC-USZ62-97307

58 **Grand Canyon**
Library of Congress
LC-USZ62-136813

59 **Canyon Diablo Bridge**
Library of Congress
LC-USZ62-61737

60 **Flooding Around the Capitol**
Arizona State Library, Archives and Public Records, History and Archives Division, Phoenix
01-3196

61 **Fort Defiance**
Library of Congress
LC-USZ62-107694

62 **Bisbee Community Parade**
Arizona State Library, Archives and Public Records, History and Archives Division, Phoenix
96-3299

64 **Hopi Women at Walpi**
Library of Congress
LC-USZ62-88309

65 **Grand Canyon's Edge**
Library of Congress
LC-USZ62-124382

66 **Grand Canyon Tourists**
Library of Congress
LC-USZ62-68594

67 **Buffalo Dance**
Library of Congress
LC-USZ62-37346

68 **Tohono O'odham Women**
Library of Congress
LC-USZ62-106258

69 **Petrified Forest**
Library of Congress
pan 6a00845

70 **View of Globe**
Library of Congress
LC-USZ62-112779

71 **Chuck Wagon Dinner**
Library of Congress
LC-USZC4-7971

72 **El Tovar Hotel**
Library of Congress
pan 6a17249

74 **A. L. Boehmer's Drug Store**
Library of Congress
LC-USZ62-105195

75 **Granite Reef Diversion Dam**
Library of Congress
pan 6a17238

76 **Arizona Capitol**
Library of Congress
pan 6a00577

77 **Tepees**
Library of Congress
LC-USZ62-104919

78 **Maricopa Depot**
Library of Congress
LC-USZ62-136283

79 **George W. P. Hunt**
Arizona State Library, Archives and Public Records, History and Archives Division, Phoenix
01-3292

80 **Prescott Football Team**
Arizona State Library, Archives and Public Records, History and Archives Division, Phoenix
97-0335

81 **Working in the Cotton Fields**
Arizona State Library, Archives and Public Records, History and Archives Division, Phoenix
95-2785

82 **Phoenix Post Office**
Arizona State Library, Archives and Public Records, History and Archives Division, Phoenix
97-7070

83 **Pima Woman Weaving a Basket**
Arizona State Library, Archives and Public Records, History and Archives Division, Phoenix
98-6002

84 **Tombstone, 1909**
Library of Congress
pan 6a00647

86 **Flooded Yuma**
Arizona State Library, Archives and Public Records, History and Archives Division, Phoenix
97-2001

87 **Tombstone City Cemetery**
Arizona State Library, Archives and Public Records, History and Archives Division, Phoenix
97-0220

88 **Snowball Fight**
Arizona State Library, Archives and Public Records, History and Archives Division, Phoenix
01-4720

89 **Maypole Dance**
Arizona State Library, Archives and Public Records, History and Archives Division, Phoenix
02-0664

90 **Casa Grande Soda Fountain**
Arizona State Library, Archives and Public Records, History and Archives Division, Phoenix
98-7430

91 **Harvey Girls**
Arizona State Library, Archives and Public Records, History and Archives Division, Phoenix
01-4548

92 **Roosevelt Dam Dedication**
Library of Congress
LC-DIG-hec-03502

93 Glendale Stockyards
Arizona State Library, Archives and Public Records, History and Archives Division, Phoenix
96-4005

94 Arizona State Legislature
Arizona State Library, Archives and Public Records, History and Archives Division, Phoenix
95-2414

95 Jerome, 1915
Arizona State Library, Archives and Public Records, History and Archives Division, Phoenix
96-3759

96 Armed Men with Prisoners
Arizona State Library, Archives and Public Records, History and Archives Division, Phoenix
01-8977

97 Roosevelt Lake
Library of Congress
LC-USZ62-106347

98 Bisbee Deportation
Arizona State Library, Archives and Public Records, History and Archives Division, Phoenix
97-0629

99 Bisbee Deportation 2
Arizona State Library, Archives and Public Records, History and Archives Division, Phoenix
97-0634a

100 Kingman Parade
Arizona State Library, Archives and Public Records, History and Archives Division, Phoenix
96-1936

102 Mountain Empire
Arizona State Library, Archives and Public Records, History and Archives Division, Phoenix
95-2863

103 Bisbee, 1920s
Arizona State Library, Archives and Public Records, History and Archives Division, Phoenix
96-3387

104 Tombstone Speaker
Arizona State Library, Archives and Public Records, History and Archives Division, Phoenix
97-0227

105 Cotton Field
Arizona State Library, Archives and Public Records, History and Archives Division, Phoenix
97-4926

106 Clarkdale Picnic
Arizona State Library, Archives and Public Records, History and Archives Division, Phoenix
01-3884

107 Schoolhouse
Arizona State Library, Archives and Public Records, History and Archives Division, Phoenix
97-1698

108 Horace Mann Junior High
Arizona State Library, Archives and Public Records, History and Archives Division, Phoenix
96-2221

109 Flagstaff Schoolroom
Arizona State Library, Archives and Public Records, History and Archives Division, Phoenix
96-2195

110 School Exercises
Arizona State Library, Archives and Public Records, History and Archives Division, Phoenix
96-2226

111 Church Smelter
Arizona State Library, Archives and Public Records, History and Archives Division, Phoenix
96-3159

112 Man with Horse
Arizona State Library, Archives and Public Records, History and Archives Division, Phoenix
97-1688

113 Hunt and Sells with Tribesmen
Arizona State Library, Archives and Public Records, History and Archives Division, Phoenix
97-6984

114 Glendale Grammar School
Arizona State Library, Archives and Public Records, History and Archives Division, Phoenix
96-1889

115 Prescott Frontier Days
Arizona State Library, Archives and Public Records, History and Archives Division, Phoenix
96-4271

116 Yuma Plank Road
Arizona State Library, Archives and Public Records, History and Archives Division, Phoenix
97-5489

117 Prescott, 1920s
Arizona State Library, Archives and Public Records, History and Archives Division, Phoenix
96-020

118 Posing with an Automobile
Arizona State Library, Archives and Public Records, History and Archives Division, Phoenix
99-9526

119 Cottonwood
Arizona State Library, Archives and Public Records, History and Archives Division, Phoenix
97-1191

120 Hunt at Tempe Normal School
Arizona State Library, Archives and Public Records, History and Archives Division, Phoenix
01-3499

121 Band Parade in Nogales
Arizona State Library, Archives and Public Records, History and Archives Division, Phoenix
01-2863

122 Springerville Barbecue
Arizona State Library, Archives and Public Records, History and Archives Division, Phoenix
01-2191

123 Prison Library
Arizona State Library, Archives and Public Records, History and Archives Division, Phoenix
97-4775

124 Poston Butte
Arizona State Library, Archives and Public Records, History and Archives Division, Phoenix
97-7960

125 San Xavier del Bac, 1926
Arizona State Library, Archives and Public Records, History and Archives Division, Phoenix
01-2374

126 Apache Junction
Arizona State Library, Archives and Public Records, History and Archives Division, Phoenix
96-1799

127 Dome Suspension Bridge
Arizona State Library, Archives and Public Records, History and Archives Division, Phoenix
93-0374

128 Flagstaff Airport Dedication
Arizona State Library, Archives and Public Records, History and Archives Division, Phoenix
01-1481

129 H. C. Day
Arizona State Library, Archives and Public Records, History and Archives Division, Phoenix
01-4618

130 Tombstone, 1930s
Arizona State Library, Archives and Public Records, History and Archives Division, Phoenix
96-4342

131 Rancher with His Cattle
Arizona State Library, Archives and Public Records, History and Archives Division, Phoenix
97-8146

132 President Coolidge in Globe
Arizona State Library, Archives and Public Records, History and Archives Division, Phoenix
96-3550

133 Douglas Border Station
Arizona State Library, Archives and Public Records, History and Archives Division, Phoenix
96-1934

134 Barbed Wire
Arizona State Library, Archives and Public Records, History and Archives Division, Phoenix
97-1697

135 Fort Tuthill
Arizona State Library, Archives and Public Records, History and Archives Division, Phoenix
97-8711

136 Museum Club
Arizona State Library, Archives and Public Records, History and Archives Division, Phoenix
01-3646

137 Franklin D. Roosevelt
Arizona State Library, Archives and Public Records, History and Archives Division, Phoenix
01-4515

138 Apache Junction Museum
Arizona State Library, Archives and Public Records, History and Archives Division, Phoenix
93-0004

139 CWA Workers
Arizona State Library, Archives and Public Records, History and Archives Division, Phoenix
98-3484

140 WPA Well
Arizona State Library, Archives and Public Records, History and Archives Division, Phoenix
96-1680

141 Paving in Mesa
Arizona State Library, Archives and Public Records, History and Archives Division, Phoenix
98-5826

142 Sanatorium Dedication
Arizona State Library, Archives and Public Records, History and Archives Division, Phoenix
98-0516

143 Laird and Dines
Arizona State Library, Archives and Public Records, History and Archives Division, Phoenix
97-0593

144 School Baseball
Arizona State Library, Archives and Public Records, History and Archives Division, Phoenix
96-1902

145 Riding a Bronco
Arizona State Library, Archives and Public Records, History and Archives Division, Phoenix 01-4654

146 Springerville Post Office
Arizona State Library, Archives and Public Records, History and Archives Division, Phoenix 97-0521

147 U.S. Highway 89
Arizona State Library, Archives and Public Records, History and Archives Division, Phoenix 93-1171

148 Bridge at Parker
Arizona State Library, Archives and Public Records, History and Archives Division, Phoenix 98-1579

150 Bird Cage Theatre
Library of Congress HABS ARIZ,2-TOMB,18-1

151 Old Main
Arizona State Library, Archives and Public Records, History and Archives Division, Phoenix 95-9297

152 U.S. Highway 89A
Arizona State Library, Archives and Public Records, History and Archives Division, Phoenix 02-0958

154 Ranch Guests
Arizona State Library, Archives and Public Records, History and Archives Division, Phoenix 95-9802

155 Winslow Street
Arizona State Library, Archives and Public Records, History and Archives Division, Phoenix 99-0490

156 Old Tucson
Arizona State Library, Archives and Public Records, History and Archives Division, Phoenix 95-1030

157 Winslow, 1940s
Arizona State Library, Archives and Public Records, History and Archives Division, Phoenix 99-0501

158 Safford CCC Camp
Arizona State Library, Archives and Public Records, History and Archives Division, Phoenix 96-4312

159 Pinal County Courthouse
Arizona State Library, Archives and Public Records, History and Archives Division, Phoenix 95-3526

160 National Guard at Fort Tuthill
Arizona State Library, Archives and Public Records, History and Archives Division, Phoenix 97-8713

161 Hotel Luhrs
Arizona State Library, Archives and Public Records, History and Archives Division, Phoenix 97-0880

162 Nogales Border Station
Arizona State Library, Archives and Public Records, History and Archives Division, Phoenix 96-3766

163 Glendale Stores
Arizona State Library, Archives and Public Records, History and Archives Division, Phoenix 96-4011

164 Japanese Internment Camp
Library of Congress LC-USZ62-42905

165 Governor Osborn
Arizona State Library, Archives and Public Records, History and Archives Division, Phoenix 97-7767

166 Snowplow
Arizona State Library, Archives and Public Records, History and Archives Division, Phoenix 03-4504

167 Phoenix Airport
Arizona State Library, Archives and Public Records, History and Archives Division, Phoenix 99-0485

168 Prison Guards
Arizona State Library, Archives and Public Records, History and Archives Division, Phoenix 97-4878

169 State Library Staff
Arizona State Library, Archives and Public Records, History and Archives Division, Phoenix 95-3848

170 Camelback
Arizona State Library, Archives and Public Records, History and Archives Division, Phoenix 97-0982

171 Luke Air Force Base
Arizona State Library, Archives and Public Records, History and Archives Division, Phoenix 98-7684

172 Halloween Dance
Arizona State Library, Archives and Public Records, History and Archives Division, Phoenix 98-7885a

174 Baseball at Luke
Arizona State Library, Archives and Public Records, History and Archives Division, Phoenix 98-7690

175 Boxing at Luke
Arizona State Library, Archives and Public Records, History and Archives Division, Phoenix 98-7846a

176 El Tovar
Arizona State Library, Archives and Public Records, History and Archives Division, Phoenix
98-7271

177 Cochise County Courthouse
Arizona State Library, Archives and Public Records, History and Archives Division, Phoenix
96-4371

178 Luke Fighter Planes
Arizona State Library, Archives and Public Records, History and Archives Division, Phoenix
00-0073

179 Rangers Reunion
Arizona State Library, Archives and Public Records, History and Archives Division, Phoenix
96-2381

180 Governor Fannin Inauguration
Arizona State Library, Archives and Public Records, History and Archives Division, Phoenix
97-8196

181 Glen Canyon Dam
Arizona State Library, Archives and Public Records, History and Archives Division, Phoenix
97-6111

182 Carson Mesa
Arizona State Library, Archives and Public Records, History and Archives Division, Phoenix
97-1701

183 Lake Havasu City
Arizona State Library, Archives and Public Records, History and Archives Division, Phoenix
96-3895

184 Humphrey's Peak
Arizona State Library, Archives and Public Records, History and Archives Division, Phoenix
96-3393

185 Bird Cage Interior
Arizona State Library, Archives and Public Records, History and Archives Division, Phoenix
96-4348

186 Conn Workshop
Arizona State Library, Archives and Public Records, History and Archives Division, Phoenix
03-5011a

187 Industrial School Band
Arizona State Library, Archives and Public Records, History and Archives Division, Phoenix
95-2482

188 Cattle Wading
Arizona State Library, Archives and Public Records, History and Archives Division, Phoenix
96-3041

189 Flooded Farmland
Arizona State Library, Archives and Public Records, History and Archives Division, Phoenix
96-3051

190 Glen Canyon, 1962
Arizona State Library, Archives and Public Records, History and Archives Division, Phoenix
97-6109

191 Glen Canyon, 1963
Arizona State Library, Archives and Public Records, History and Archives Division, Phoenix
02-2534

192 Senator and Students
Arizona State Library, Archives and Public Records, History and Archives Division, Phoenix
02-0118

193 Highway 77
Arizona State Library, Archives and Public Records, History and Archives Division, Phoenix
02-1725

194 Child and Cow
Arizona State Library, Archives and Public Records, History and Archives Division, Phoenix
01-4650

195 Unfurling Flag
Arizona State Library, Archives and Public Records, History and Archives Division, Phoenix
93-0609

196 Service Station
Arizona State Library, Archives and Public Records, History and Archives Division, Phoenix
97-1703

197 Looking Down at Flagstaff Street
Arizona State Library, Archives and Public Records, History and Archives Division, Phoenix
98-5325

198 Horses
Arizona State Library, Archives and Public Records, History and Archives Division, Phoenix
01-4117

199 Cowboys
Arizona State Library, Archives and Public Records, History and Archives Division, Phoenix
01-4115

HISTORIC PHOTOS OF ARIZONA

Arizona, the 48th state of the United States of America, is a land of diverse environments and unbelievable natural beauty. It is also a land where many cultures—each with its own food, architecture, music, and art—came together as part of the American story.

Historic Photos of Arizona highlights the unique history of this state as captured in nearly 200 images reproduced in vivid black and white. A photographic journey from the Wild West days of Arizona lore to the modern state Arizona was soon to become, the book showcases landscapes as varied as those of the Sonoran Desert and the state's ponderosa pine forests.

From images of frontier life and copper mining boomtowns, to turn-of-the-century Grand Canyon vistas, to Harvey Houses and Route 66, *Historic Photos of Arizona* presents a fascinating view of a changing land and the people who called it home—a land to which many are still drawn to fulfill their dreams today.

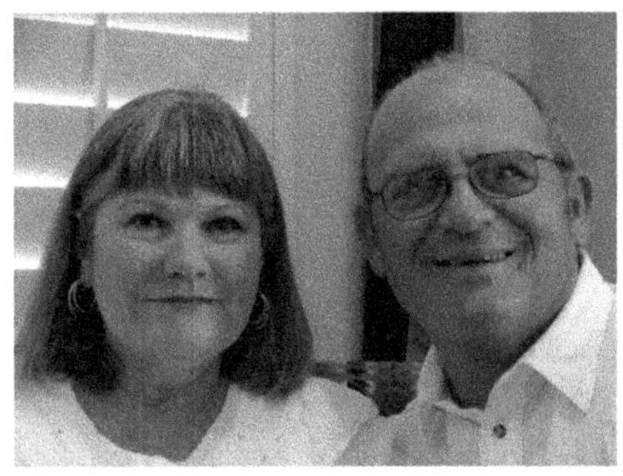

Linda and Dr. Dick Buscher have been writing and teaching on the subject of Arizona for more than 35 years. Linda was in public education for 28 years in the Paradise Valley Unified School District. She is currently a faculty associate for the College of Teacher Training and Leadership of Arizona State University and is an instructor in the Teach for America program. She was the 1985 Arizona PTA Educator of the Year.

Dr. Buscher was a public school teacher and principal for 32 years and is currently a senior lecturer at ASU. He was a 1977 finalist for Arizona Teacher of the Year and was the 1983 Arizona PTA Educator of the Year. Dr. Buscher was also a 1998 recipient of the City of Phoenix's Martin Luther King, Jr., Living the Dream Award.

Together with their friends Teresa and Ken Jackway, the Buschers co-authored *Ali-Shonak: The Story of Arizona.* They currently write about Arizona for the *In & Out of Anthem* magazine.

WWW.TURNERPUBLISHING.COM

www.ingramcontent.com/pod-product-compliance
Lightning Source LLC
LaVergne TN
LVHW060608110826
845154LV00003B/55
9781684420759